Anthea Wilson

Araminta Crace
with Rawdon Wyatt, Alison Bewsher and John Peeb[

D0608485

UPPER INTERMEDIATE

Total English

Teacher's Resource Book

PEARSON
Longman

Contents

Syllabus outline

	UNIT	LESSON 1	LESSON 2	LESSON 3	VOCABULARY	COMMUNICATION
1	**Connect** page 5 Lead-in vocabulary: family members and relationships	**1.1 Good friends** **Grammar:** question tags **Can do:** check information **Skills:** **reading:** read about what makes a good friend **writing:** notes and messages **Lifelong learning:** learning new strategies to improve English	**1.2 Family ties** **Grammar:** *any/every/no/some* **Vocabulary:** making adjectives from nouns **Can do:** express agreement/disagreement **Skills:** **reading:** read about birth order and personality **speaking:** agreeing and disagreeing	**1.3 Mobile connections** **Grammar:** present/future modals of possibility **Vocabulary:** noises **Can do:** make speculations **Skills:** **speaking:** discuss opinions about mobile phones **reading:** read about the increased use of mobile phones and its implications	**Vocabulary:** Phrasal verbs (relationships)	**Can Do:** give detailed descriptions of family relationships
		Film Bank: Good relations (Students' Book page 152 and Teacher's Resource Book page 178) **Photocopiable materials:** Vocabulary, Grammar and Communication (Teacher's Resource Book page 104)				
2	**Work** page 19 Lead-in vocabulary: jobs and related qualities	**2.1 The daily grind** **Grammar:** futures overview **Vocabulary:** verb phrases about work **Can do:** talk about future plans and make predictions **Skills:** **reading:** read about attitudes to work and how work has changed **speaking:** talk about future plans	**2.2 A work of art** **Grammar:** Future Perfect and Future Continuous **Vocabulary:** 'after work' activities **Can do:** do a survey and report the results **Skills:** **listening:** listen to a radio programme about an artist and his work **listening and speaking:** report the results of a survey about work/life balance	**2.3 Ready for business** **Grammar:** *in case* **Can do:** write a formal letter of application **Skills:** **reading:** read extracts from a novel **writing:** write a formal letter of application for a job **Lifelong learning:** usage; ways of improving English	**Vocabulary:** Collocations with prepositions	**Can do:** carry out an effective interview
		Film Bank: Dream career (Students' Book page 153 and Teacher's Resource Book page 179) **Photocopiable materials:** Vocabulary, Grammar and Communication (Teacher's Resource Book page 110)				
3	**Old or new** page 33 Lead-in vocabulary: describing old/new places/people	**3.1 Heroes** **Grammar:** narrative tenses **Vocabulary:** time expressions **Can do:** write a short story **Skills:** **reading:** read the story of the Trojan War and a review of the film *Troy* **writing:** write a short story about a hero or heroine	**3.2 Land of invention** **Grammar:** articles **Vocabulary:** materials **Can do:** talk about materials, possessions and inventions **Skills:** **listening and speaking:** listen to dialogues and discuss objects, clothing and materials **listening:** listen to a radio programme about China in ancient and modern times **speaking:** discuss which are the most important inventions **Lifelong learning:** using technology to help with learning	**3.3 The good old days?** **Grammar:** adjectives and adverbs **Vocabulary:** verb phrases with *take* **Can do:** give a presentation about a place **Skills:** **reading:** read a newspaper article and letters about 'the good old days' **speaking:** make presentations about cities	**Vocabulary:** Making nouns	**Can do:** talk about lessons learned from the past
		Film Bank: Film Heroes (Students' Book page 154 and Teacher's Resource Book page 180) **Photocopiable materials:** Vocabulary, Grammar and Communication (Teacher's Resource Book page 116)				
4	**Risk** page 47 Lead-in vocabulary: risk/achievement	**4.1 Going solo** **Grammar:** *if* structures (1) **Can do:** write a diary entry **Skills:** **reading:** read about Ellen MacArthur's solo sail around the world **writing:** write a diary entry or 'blog' **Lifelong learning:** keep a diary	**4.2 Run free** **Grammar:** expressing obligation **Vocabulary:** physical movements **Can do:** explain how to do something **Skills:** **listening and speaking:** listen to and give instructions about how to do exercises **reading:** read an article about 'free running'	**4.3 Million dollar risk** **Grammar:** emphasis **Vocabulary:** phrasal verbs with *out* **Can do:** compare and contrast photographs **Skills:** **listening:** listen to two people discussing the film *Million Dollar Baby* **speaking:** compare and contrast photos	**Vocabulary:** Distances and dimensions **Skills:** **speaking:** tell a story	**Can do:** exchange information on familiar matters
		Film Bank: Ellen MacArthur (Students' Book page 155 and Teacher's Resource Book page 181) **Photocopiable materials:** Vocabulary, Grammar and Communication (Teacher's Resource Book page 122)				

Syllabus outline

	UNIT	LESSON 1	LESSON 2	LESSON 3	VOCABULARY	COMMUNICATION
5	**The past** page 61 Lead-in vocabulary: memory	**5.1 A lost past** **Grammar:** *used to/get used to/would* **Vocabulary:** appearance **Can do:** describe appearance **Skills:** **reading:** read about a man who has been living at an airport **writing:** write an email describing someone	**5.2 Lasting memories** **Grammar:** expressing ability **Can do:** talk about memories **Skills:** **listening:** listen to people talking about memories **speaking:** talk about photos and memories **listening:** listen to people talking about a photo	**5.3 Memory box** **Grammar:** *although/but/however/nevertheless* **Vocabulary:** feelings **Can do:** talk about books **Skills:** **reading:** read an extract from the novel *The Memory Box* **speaking:** discuss reactions to the novel **Lifelong learning:** read graded readers	**Vocabulary:** Idioms describing people	**Can do:** account for and sustain opinions in informal discussion
	Film Bank: Home Road Movie (Students' Book page 156 and Teacher's Resource Book page 182) **Photocopiable materials:** Vocabulary, Grammar and Communication (Teacher's Resource Book page 128)					
6	**Explore** page 75 Lead-in vocabulary: exploring	**6.1 The jungle bug** **Grammar:** Present Perfect Simple and Continuous **Vocabulary:** adjectives with *-ed* and *-ing* endings **Can do:** write an informal email **Skills:** **reading:** read about a woman who spent four months living in the jungle **pronunciation:** the main stress in adjectives **writing:** write an email describing an experience (Writing bank page 162)	**6.2 A magical kingdom** **Grammar:** questions **Vocabulary:** weather **Can do:** ask and answer questions about unusual places **Skills:** **reading:** read about travel in Bhutan **listening:** listen to people talking about going to Bhutan **speaking:** discuss unusual holidays	**6.3 On the move** **Grammar:** comparatives & superlatives of adjectives and adverbs **Vocabulary:** verb phrases about moving/travelling **Can do:** make comparisons about places and people **Skills:** **reading:** read an article about emigration	**Vocabulary:** Expressions with *go* **Skills:** **speaking:** tell a story	**Can do:** exchange detailed information **Lifelong learning:** learn while travelling
	Film Bank: Bhutan (Students' Book page 157 and Teacher's Resource Book page 183) **Photocopiable materials:** Vocabulary, Grammar and Communication (Teacher's Resource Book page 134)					
7	**Excess** page 89 Lead-in vocabulary: excess	**7.1 Food for thought** **Grammar:** countable and uncountable nouns **Vocabulary:** food and cooking **Can do:** describe how to prepare and cook a dish **Skills:** **reading:** read an article about the film *Super Size me* **pronunciation:** stress; weak forms speaking: talk about how to prepare a dish	**7.2 Buy, buy, buy** **Grammar:** passives **Vocabulary:** verb phrases about money **Can do:** write a formal letter of complaint **Skills:** **listening:** listen to an item of radio news about selling things at auction **speaking:** complain in a shop, restaurant, hotel, etc. **writing:** write a formal letter of complaint (Writing bank page 163)	**7.3 It's a dog's life** **Grammar:** *have/get something done* **Vocabulary:** animal expressions **Can do:** talk about services **Skills:** **reading:** read a text about treating pets as family members and indulging them	**Vocabulary:** Prefixes	**Can do:** use persuasive language to demand satisfaction from a service provider
	Film Bank: Vikings (Students' Book page 158 and Teacher's Resource Book page 184) **Photocopiable materials:** Vocabulary, Grammar and Communication (Teacher's Resource Book page 140)					
8	**Success** page 103 Lead-in vocabulary: success expressions	**8.1 Lead or follow?** **Grammar:** *It's time/I'd rather/I'd better* **Vocabulary:** describing personality **Can do:** describe different types of people **Skills:** **reading:** read a brochure for a leadership training company including what makes a good leader	**8.2 Winners** **Grammar:** reported speech **Vocabulary:** adjectives and intensifiers **Can do:** report and describe what people say to you **Skills:** **listening:** listen to a radio programme about motivation, winners in sport and sports psychologists **speaking:** talk about past successes **Lifelong learning:** the characteristics of a successful language learner	**8.3 Tot.com** **Grammar:** *hard* and *hardly* **Can do:** write a report of survey findings **Skills:** **reading:** read about a school where very young children take exams **speaking:** give opinions about school and education **writing:** write a report of survey findings (Writing bank page 164)	**Vocabulary:** Phrasal verbs with three parts	**Can do:** give and seek personal views and opinions
	Film Bank: The secrets of success (Students' Book page 159 and Teacher's Resource Book page 185) **Photocopiable materials:** Vocabulary, Grammar and Communication (Teacher's Resource Book page 146)					

UNIT		LESSON 1	LESSON 2	LESSON 3	VOCABULARY	COMMUNICATION
9	**Crime** page 117 Lead-in vocabulary: crime and punishment	**9.1 Legal madness** **Grammar:** sequencing devices, e.g. *After + -ing* **Vocabulary:** law and insurance **Can do:** tell a funny story **Skills:** **listening:** listen to a story about a crime **speaking and reading:** read about strange crimes and tell crime stories	**9.2 It's a mystery** **Grammar:** past modals of deduction *must/might/can't have done* **Vocabulary:** compound adjectives **Can do:** speculate about past events **Skills:** **reading:** read about a mysterious crime	**9.3 Sherlock or not?** **Grammar:** relative clauses **Can do:** write an article **Skills:** **reading:** read an article about the character Sherlock Holmes **listening:** listen to an interview with a man named 'Sherlock Holmes' **writing:** write an article about a crime (Writing bank page 164)	**Vocabulary:** Newspaper headlines **Skills:** **speaking:** discuss about newspapers	**Can do:** speculate on the explanation of a problem
		Film Bank: The Bullion Robbery (Students' Book page 160 and Teacher's Resource Book page 186) **Photocopiable materials:** Vocabulary, Grammar and Communication (Teacher's Resource Book page 152)				
UNIT		LESSON 1	LESSON 2	LESSON 3	VOCABULARY	COMMUNICATION
10	**Mind** page 131 Lead-in vocabulary: the power of the mind	**10.1 Look into my eyes** **Grammar:** reflexive pronouns **Can do:** ask about and give your own beliefs and opinions **Skills:** **reading:** read an article about a famous hypnotist and his work **listening:** listen to people giving opinions about hypnotists **speaking:** give and ask for opinions on a variety of topics	**10.2 Persuasion** **Grammar:** gerunds and infinitives **Vocabulary:** advertising **Can do:** write the arguments for and against a point of view **Skills:** **listening:** listen to a radio programme about persuasion tactics in advertising and retail **pronunciation:** main stress **writing:** write an essay	**10.3 Brave New World** **Grammar:** *if* structures (2) **Vocabulary:** ways of speaking **Can do:** talk about your regrets and resolutions **Skills:** **reading:** read an extract from the novel *Brave New World* **speaking:** talk about past regrets and future resolutions	**Vocabulary:** Commonly misspelt words **Lifelong learning:** spelling tips	**Can do:** express personal preferences
		Film Bank: Yes, Prime Minister (Students' Book page 161 and Teacher's Resource Book page 187) **Photocopiable materials:** Vocabulary, Grammar and Communication (Teacher's Resource Book page 158)				

Test A: Unit 1-5 (Teacher's Resource Book page 196)
Test B: Unit 1-5 (Teacher's Resource Book page 202)
Test A: Unit 6-10 (Teacher's Resource Book page 208)
Test B: Unit 6-10 (Teacher's Resource Book page 214)

Teaching and learning are unpredictable experiences. Learners can be dynamic and engaged one lesson and then demotivated, tired or even absent the next. The aim of *Total English* is two-fold: firstly to set new standards in terms of interest level, teachability and range of support materials; and secondly to address the reality of most people's unpredicatable teaching experience as it is, not as we hope it will be.

Research for *Total English* suggested three classroom 'realities' that need to be addressed in a coursebook: 1) learners often lack direction and purpose – they are often not sure about the relevance of what they are learning and where they are going with English; 2) learners need to be genuinely engaged in coursebook content just as they are in the newspapers, TV programmes and films that they see around them; 3) learners often miss lessons and this creates extra work for the teacher to make sure that no-one falls behind.

Finding direction and purpose

Learners need a clear sense of where they are going and how they are going to get there. They need to know what they are learning, why they are learning it and how it can be applied outside the classroom. Clear goals and objectives are crucial. *Total English* contains a clear grammar syllabus and plenty of practice. Each input lesson is organised on a double-page spread and has a grammar and *Can Do* learning objective clearly stated at the start. The *Can Do* objectives give a purpose and reason for learning and mean that students know why they are studying that lesson and how they can use the new language.

The learning objectives in Total English are derived from the *Can Do* statements in the Common European Framework which means teachers can feel confident that *Total English* covers the language areas their students need. The levels of *Total English* correlate to the Common European Framework in the following way:

Elementary	Covers A1 and goes towards A2
Pre-intermediate	Covers A2 and goes towards B1
Intermediate	Covers B1 and goes towards B2
Upper Intermediate	Covers B2
Advanced	Covers C1

Engaging learners' interest

Motivation through engagement is equally important for successful language learning. *Total English* lessons give a new twist to familiar topics – topics that reflect learners' needs and interests. This ensures that learners will always have something to say about the content of the lesson. There are frequent opportunities for learners to exchange ideas and opinions and engage with the material on a personal level. Activities have been designed to be as realistic as possible so that learners can see how the language they're learning can be applied outside the classroom.

In addition to the wide range of topics, texts and activities, each level of the *Total English* Students' Books has a DVD which adds an extra dimension to the course. Containing a range of authentic material from film and TV, the DVDs expose learners to a variety of different English media and give them a feel for how the language is used in real life. Each unit of the Students' Books has a corresponding DVD extract and the Film banks at the back of the Students' Books offer material to use in class or at home while watching the DVD.

Helping learners catch up

One of the most common problems that teachers face is irregular attendance. Learners often have busy lives with work, study or family commitments and attending English classes on a regular basis is not always possible. *Total English* recognises this problem and has been designed to help learners catch up easily if they miss lessons. In addition to the practice exercises in each lesson, there is a Reference page and a Review and practice page at the end of each unit. These provide an accessible summary of the main grammar and vocabulary covered.

The *Total English* Workbooks also have freestanding CD-ROMs that include interactive self-study 'catch-up' material to present and practise language from any lessons learners have missed. With this extensive range of animated presentations, interactive practice exercises and games, *Total English* ensures your students don't get left behind if they miss lessons.

The course package

Total English has five levels and takes learners from Elementary to Advanced. Each level consists of the following:

- **Students' Book**
The *Total English* Students' Books are divided into 10-12 units and contain approximately 80-120 hours of teaching material. Each unit contains a balanced mix of grammar, vocabulary, pronunciation and skills work including writing.

- **DVD**
The 'with DVD' version of the Students' Books has a freestanding DVD which provides additional listening practice linked to the topic areas in the Students' Books.

- **Video**
The DVD material is also available on video (PAL and NTSC).

- **Class Cassettes/CDs**
Total English Class Cassettes/CDs contain all the recorded material from the Students' Books.

- **Workbook**
The *Total English* Workbooks contain further practice of language areas covered in the corresponding units of the Students' Books.

- **Workbook 'Catch-up' CD-ROM**
The *Total English* Workbook CD-ROMs provide extra support for students who miss lessons. In addition to the recorded material from the Workbooks, the Workbook CD-ROMs feature 'catch-up' material related to the key grammar areas covered in the Students' Books.

- **Teacher's Resource Book**
The *Total English* Teacher's Resource Books provide all the support teachers need to get the most out of the course. The Teacher's Resource Books contain teaching notes, photocopiable worksheets, DVD worksheets and tests.

- **Website**
Total English has its own dedicated website. In addition to background information about the course and authors, the website features teaching tips, downloadable worksheets, links to other useful websites as well as special offers and competitions. Join us online at www.longman.com/totalenglish.

The Students' Book

Each unit of the *Total English* Students' Books follows the same structure making the material very easy to use:

- **Lead-in page**
  - acts as a springboard into the topic of the unit and engages students' interest.
  - introduces essential vocabulary related to the topic so that students start with the same basic grounding.

- **Input lessons**
  - three triple-page input lessons, thematically linked, offer interesting angles on the unit topic.
  - each input lesson leads towards a *Can Do* learning objective in line with the Council of Europe's *Can Do* statements.
  - each 90-minute lesson focuses on a specific grammar area and includes vocabulary, pronunciation and skills work.
  - each unit contains at least two reading texts and a substantial listening element.
  - How to ... boxes develop students' competence in using language, in line with the Common European Framework.
  - Lifelong learning boxes offer tips and strategies for developing students' study skills.

- **Vocabulary page**
  - extends students' knowledge on lexical areas such as phrasal verbs, prefixes and suffixes, etc.
  - provides further practice of topic-related language.

- **Communication page**
  - revises language taught in the previous three lessons in a freer, more communicative context.
  - each communication task practises a range of skills and has a measurable goal or outcome.

- **Reference page**
  - summarises the main grammar points covered in each unit and provides a list of key vocabulary.
  - helps learners to catch up if they miss lessons and is an essential revision tool.

- **Review and practice page**
  - provides a range of exercises to consolidate key grammar and vocabulary covered in the unit.
  - can be used to check progress, enabling teachers to identify areas that need further practice.

- **Film bank pages**
  - support the DVD which is attached to the back of the 'with DVD' version of the Students' Books.
  - feature a range of exercises designed to stimulate interest in each DVD extract and make the authentic material contained on the DVD accessible to students.

The Total English Students' Books also feature the following:

- **Do you know?**
  - an optional page to be covered before learners start the course which teaches basic language areas such as the alphabet, numbers and classroom language.

- **Writing bank**
  - provides models and tips on how to write emails, letters and postcards as well as guidance on different writing skills such as punctuation, spelling and paragraph construction.

- **Pronunciation bank**
  - provides a list of English phonemes, guidance on sound-spelling correspondences and weak forms.

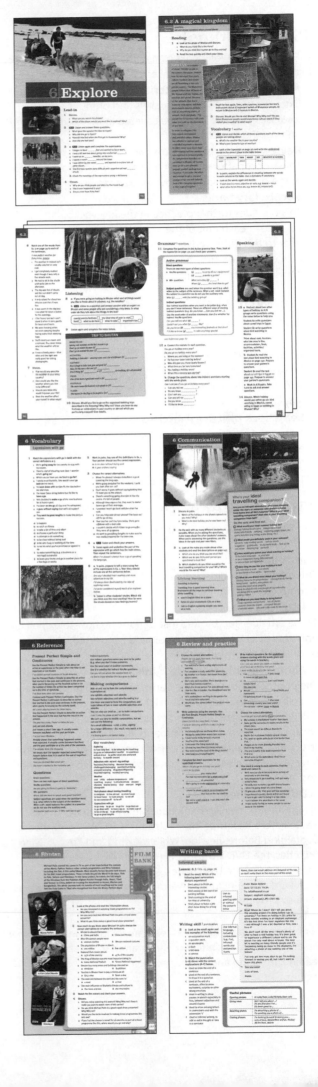

The Workbook

The *Total English* Workbooks contain 10-12 units which correspond to the Students' Book material. Each Workbook contains:

- **Additional practice material**
  Extra grammar, vocabulary, skills and pronunciation exercises practise language covered in the corresponding units of the Students' Books.
- **Review and consolidation sections**
  These occur after each unit and contain additional practice of the grammar and vocabulary covered in the unit.
- **Vocabulary bank**
  This provides further practice in the key vocabulary areas covered in each unit of the Students' Books. Students can refer to this after studying a particular topic and record the new vocabulary they have learned. They can also add new items as they come across them.

The Workbook CD-ROM

In addition to the recorded material from the Workbook, the 'catch-up' section of the CD-ROM contains the following:

- **Grammar presentations**
  Simple, accessible grammar explanations summarise the target language of each unit in a succinct and memorable way.
- **Self-check practice exercises**
  A range of practice exercises (two for each grammar point) enable students to practise the target language.
- **'Can do' game**
  This provides communicative practice of the target language.

The Teacher's Resource Book

The Teacher's Resource Books are divided into the following sections:

- **Introduction**
This explains the aims and rationale of the course and provides a complete description of the course package.
- **Teaching notes**
These provide step by step instructions on how to exploit each unit as well as background notes and suggestions for warm-up, lead-in and extension activities.
- **Photocopiable resource banks**
The photocopiable resource banks contain 60 photocopiable worksheets (6 worksheets for each unit of the Students' Books). The worksheets are designed to practise the grammar and vocabulary covered in the Students' Book units in a freer, less structured and enjoyable context. Detailed instructions on how to use each worksheet are also provided in the Teacher's Resource Book.
- **DVD worksheets**
In addition to the Film bank pages in the Students' Books, the Teacher's Resource Books also have 10 DVD worksheets. Containing Before viewing, While viewing and Post viewing activities, the DVD worksheets provide more detailed exploitation of the DVD material. Instructions on how to use each worksheet including warm-up and extension activities are also provided.
- **Tests**
Four photocopiable progress tests are included in the Teacher's Resource Books. Each test covers grammar, vocabulary, reading, listening and writing skills.

The Test Master CD-ROM

The Teacher's Resource Book includes a Test Master CD-ROM which provides an invaluable testing resource to accompany the course.

Easy to use
- The tests are based strictly on the content of Total English Upper Intermediate, providing a fair measure of students' progress.
- An interactive menu makes it easy to find the tests you are looking for.
- Keys and audio scripts are provided to make marking the tests as straightforward as possible.
- Most tests come in A and B versions. This makes it easier for you to invigilate the test by making it harder for students to copy from each other.
- The audio files for the listening tests are conveniently located on the same CD.

Types of test
The Test Master CD contains five types of test.
- Placement Test/s
- Module Tests
- Progress Tests
- Mid Course Test
- End of Course Test

Flexible
You can print the tests out and use them as they are – or you can adapt them. You can use Microsoft® Word to edit them as you wish to suit your teaching situation, your students or your syllabus. Here are some of the things you may wish to do.
- Delete or add exercises to make the test shorter or longer.
- Delete exercises or items which relate to points which you decided to skip.
- Add in exercises to cover extra content you introduced into the course.
- Edit exercises to make them harder or easier, or to introduce key vocabulary.
- Edit the format of exercises so that they are consistent with other exams that you use.
- Personalise the content of exercises to bring them to life. For example, incorporate the names of students in the class, other teachers in the school, famous people and places from your country …
- Use the audio scripts to create extra listening exercises – for example by removing words to create gap fills, adding options to create multiple choice exercises or introducing deliberate mistakes for the students to correct.
- Add in the name and/or logo of your school at the head of the test, and finally, save your version on your hard drive.

Using this CD
The ideal way to use this CD-ROM is to treat it as a master. Copy the tests to the hard drive of your computer and burn the audio files to CD or copy them on to cassette.
- Test files – The installation wizard will copy the files to your hard drive.
- Audio files – If you don't have a CD burner or if you prefer to teach with cassettes, you can simply put the Test Master CD into the CD drive of an ordinary hi-fi and copy the audio files onto a blank cassette.

Levels
Test Master CDs are available from Starter to Advanced levels of Total English.

Teaching approaches

Grammar

Total English covers all the main language areas you would expect at each level and gives learners a thorough foundation in grammar based on the following principles:

- **Clear presentation/analysis**
  Each triple-page lesson has a clear grammar aim which is stated at the top of the page. New language items are presented in context via reading and/or listening texts and grammar rules are then analysed and explained via the Active grammar boxes which are a key feature of each lesson.

Active grammar

I'm starting the course next month ...
Geoff is working in the US again in March ...

1 Which tense are the sentences?
2 Has Joanna decided to do the course?
3 Has Geoff organised his stay in the States?
4 Are the sentences describing an action in the present or in the future?

Total English takes a 'guided discovery' approach to grammar and learners are actively invited to think about grammar and work out the rules for themselves.

- **Varied, regular practice**
  Once learners have grasped the important rules, all new language is then practised in a variety of different ways so that learners are able to use the grammar with confidence. Practice activities include form-based exercises designed to help learners manipulate the new structures as well as more meaningful, personalised practice. Additional grammar practice exercises can be found in the Review and practice sections at the end of each unit as well as in the Workbooks and on the Workbook CD-ROMs. The Teacher's Resource Books also contain an extensive bank of photocopiable grammar activities which are designed to practise the language in freer, more communicative contexts.
- **Accessible reference material**
  In addition to the explanations contained in the Active Grammar boxes, there is a Reference section at the end of each unit which summarises the rules in greater detail and provides extra information and examples.

Vocabulary

Total English recognises the central role that vocabulary plays in successful communication. The emphasis is on providing learners with high-frequency, useful vocabulary which is regularly practised and revised. New vocabulary is presented and practised in a variety of different ways – via the Lead-in pages which provide a springboard into the topic of each unit enabling teachers to elicit vocabulary that learners already know as well as pre-teach essential vocabulary for the rest of the unit; via the reading and listening texts and related exercises; via special vocabulary sections in the main lessons; via the detailed vocabulary page at the end of the unit. Additional vocabulary practice is provided in the Review and practice sections of the Students' Book, in the practice exercises in the Workbook and special vocabulary worksheets in the Teacher's Resource Book.

Speaking

The key aim for most learners is spoken fluency but low level learners cannot express themselves easily without support. *Total English* develops spoken fluency in a number of ways – by giving learners discussion topics they want to talk about; by setting up situations where they are motivated to communicate in order to complete a specific task; by providing clear models and examples of how to structure discourse and by encouraging them, wherever possible, to express their own ideas and opinions. All lessons feature some speaking practice and there are regular How to … boxes throughout the course which focus on the words and expressions learners need to carry out specific functions.

HOW TO …

order in a fast food restaurant

Ask questions	_____ you have salads?
Say what you want	I'd _____ a cheese sandwich, please.
Ask about prices	How _____ is that?

Communication pages at the end of each unit engage learners in a variety of problem-solving tasks and involve learners in a number of different skills – including speaking. The photocopiable activities in the Teacher's Resource Book are also specifically designed to promote speaking practice.

Listening

Listening is one of the most difficult skills to master and *Total English* pays particular emphasis to developing learners' confidence in this area. Listening texts include short dialogues as well as longer texts (conversations, interviews, stories and songs). There are lots of simple 'Listen and check your answer' exercises as well as more challenging activities where learners have to listen to longer extracts in order to find specific information. The recorded material features a variety of accents including British, American, Australian and some non-native speakers. There is additional listening practice in the Workbooks and the DVDs further enhance learners' confidence in understanding the spoken word.

Pronunciation

Total English pays particular attention to pronunciation which is integrated into all the lessons which present new language. The pronunciation syllabus includes word and sentence stress, weak forms, intonation and difficult sounds. The Pronunciation banks at the back of the Students' Books include a list of English phonemes, guidance on sound-spelling correspondences and weak forms. There is additional pronunciation practice in the Workbooks and on the Workbook CD-ROMs.

Reading

There is a wide variety of reading texts in *Total English* ranging from simple forms and advertisements to short texts from newspapers and magazines. Texts have been chosen for their intrinsic interest as well as for their usefulness in providing a vehicle for the particular grammar and vocabulary points in focus. Many all of the texts have been adapted from authentic, real-life sources (magazines, websites etc.) and related tasks have been carefully selected to develop learners' confidence in dealing with written texts. Activities include comprehension and vocabulary work as well as practice in dealing with different reading sub-skills such as reading for gist. There are a number of jigsaw readings where learners work together and share information. The length and complexity of the texts get more challenging as the course progresses.

Writing

With the growth of email, writing is becoming an increasingly important skill. *Total English* acknowledges this by including regular writing tasks in the Students' Books. These are carefully structured with exercises and examples designed to ensure that learners are actually able to carry out the tasks. Models of different types of writing – emails, postcards, formal and informal letters are provided in the Writing Bank at the back of the Students' Books as well as additional advice and guidance on different writing sub-skills such as punctuation, spelling and paragraph construction.

Revision and testing

There are plenty of opportunities for revision in *Total English* and language is constantly recycled throughout the course. At the end of every unit, there are special Review and practice pages which take the form of mini progress checks enabling learners to identify areas where they might need further practice.

In addition to the Review and practice pages, there are ten Review and consolidation sections in the accompanying Workbook, and a whole range of additional practice material on the 'Catch-up' CD-ROMs. The Teacher's Resource Books include four photocopiable progress tests which cover grammar, vocabulary, reading, listening and writing skills.

Learner training

Total English places a strong emphasis on learner training and good study habits are encouraged and developed via the Lifelong learning boxes which are a featured in many lessons. The Lifelong learning boxes provide useful tips and suggestions on how to continue learning outside the classroom. .

Lifelong learning

Personalise it!
When you want to learn new words, it is useful to write them in a personal sentence.
fridge – *My fridge is very old – it's useless!*
cupboard – *I have a big cupboard in my bedroom.*

Total English and exams

The table below shows how the different levels of Total English relate to the Common European Framework levels and the University of Cambridge ESOL main suite examinations in terms of the language taught and the topics covered;

Elementary	Covers A1 and goes towards A2	Useful for KET
Pre-Intermediate	Covers A2 and goes towards B1	Useful for PET
Intermediate	Covers B1 and goes towards B2	Useful for FCE
Upper Intermediate	Covers B2	
Advanced	Covers C1	Useful for CAE

While *Total English* is not an examination preparation course, a student who has, for example, completed the Upper Intermediate level would have sufficient language to attempt the Cambridge ESOL FCE (First Certificate in English) examination. Many of the exercises in the *Total English* Students' Books, Workbooks and photocopiable tests are similar in format to those found in the Cambridge ESOL main suite examinations but specific training is required for all EFL examinations and we would strongly recommend this.

For further information on the University of Cambridge ESOL examinations, contact:

Cambridge ESOL
1 Hills Road
Cambridge
CB1 2EU

Tel. +44 (0) 1223 553355
Fax. +44 (0) 1223 460278
Email: ESOL@ucles.org.uk
www.CambridgeESOL.org

Total English authors

Total English Elementary

Mark Foley has worked in English language teaching for over 23 years and has extensive experience in teaching (mostly in the UK and Spain), teacher training, examining and materials writing. He is the co-author of a number of publications, including the Longman ELT advanced titles, Distinction and Advanced Learner's Grammar. He is co-author, with Diane Hall, of *Total English* Elementary Students' Book and Workbook.

Diane Hall has worked in English language teaching for over 25 years and has extensive experience in teaching (mostly in the UK and Germany), publishing and materials writing. She is co-author of a number of publications, including the Longman ELT advanced titles, Distinction and Advanced Learners' Grammar. She is co-author, with Mark Foley, of *Total English* Elementary Students' Book and Workbook.

Total English Pre-intermediate and Upper Intermediate

Richard Acklam lives in North London and has been involved in English Language teaching since 1982. He has taught and trained teachers in Egypt, France and the UK and has an M.A. (TEFL) from the University of Reading. His publications include components of the 'Gold 'series and he is co-author, with Araminta Crace, of *Total English* Pre-intermediate and Upper Intermediate Students' Books.

Araminta Crace lives in North London with her two young daughters, Petra and Lola. She has been involved in English Language teaching since 1984 and has taught and trained teachers in Brazil, Egypt, Portugal, Spain and the UK. Her ELT publications include Language to Go and Going for Gold. She is co-author, with Richard Acklam, of *Total English* Pre-intermediate and Upper Intermediate Students' Books.

Total English Intermediate and Advanced

Antonia Clare graduated from University College London in Psychology, and has enjoyed teaching (both adults and younger learners), and teacher training in Europe Asia and South Africa. She is now a full-time writer and freelance teacher trainer based in the UK. Her publications include Language to Go Upper Intermediate and she is co-author, with JJ Wilson, of *Total English* Upper Intermediate and Advanced Students' Books and Workbooks.

JJ Wilson trained at International House London and has taught in Egypt, Lesotho (where he ran a student theatre), Colombia, the UK, Italy and the U.S. His main interests in the field include vocabulary acquisition and the development of innovative methods and materials for the classroom. His short fiction is published by Penguin and Pulp Faction. He is co-author, with Antonia Clare, of *Total English* Upper Intermediate and Advanced Students' Books and Workbooks.

1 Connect

Overview

Summary

Lesson 1: Ss read a text about different people's opinions about the characteristics of a good friend. Then they read, listen to and write some notes and messages. Next, they listen to people talking about friendship and talk about their own ideas about friends and friendship.

Lesson 2: Ss listen to part of a radio programme about the Boehmer family. Then they read an article about 'birth order' and how the position in your family can affect your personality. Ss then discuss their own opinions about 'birth order' and families.

Lesson 3: Ss discuss their opinions about mobile phones and then read an article about the increased use of mobile phones particularly among young people. Ss exchange personal information about each other and get to know each other more.

Vocabulary: Ss focus on a group of phrasal verbs around the topic of relationships.

Communication: Ss listen to a man talking about his family tree. Then they draw their own family tree, describe it to each other and talk about some members of their families.

> **Film bank: Good relations** (3'25")
>
> An extract from the 1947 film version of Nicholas Nickleby which was Charles Dickens' third novel, published in 1839.
>
> In this extract, Nicholas Nickleby, his mother and his sister are all taken into the care of his uncle Ralph, following the death of his father. The uncle arranges for Nicholas to gain a tutoring job at an Academy for boys, where he is shocked by the brutality there.
>
> Possible places to use this short film are:
> ▶ After Lesson 2 to extend the topic of family and friends.
> ▶ At the end of the unit to round up the topic.
>
> For ways to use this short film in class, see Students' Book page 152 and Teacher's Book page 178.

Lead-in

> **OPTIONAL WARMER**
>
> Write two headings on the board: *family relationships* and *non-family relationships* and two words: *colleague* and *cousin*. Ask Ss under which heading each word should go and why. (*cousin = family relationships*; *colleague = non-family relationships*)
>
> Give Ss one minute to brainstorm as many words under each heading as they can in pairs. Get feedback

1▶ Ss look at the photos in pairs and discuss what they think the relationships could be between the various people in them. Get feedback from the class, discussing the reasons for their ideas.

> **Possible answers:** Photo 1: friends or flatmates; Photo 2: a family, inc. a grandfather, mother, daughter, father, son, grandmother; Photo 3: friends; Photo 4: an extended family, inc. aunts, uncles, cousins.

2▶ Ask Ss to work in pairs and discuss the difference in meaning between each pair of words. Encourage Ss to use an English-English dictionary to check the meaning and pronunciation of any of the words they are not sure about. Get feedback from the class.

> **Answers:** 1 step-sister: girl or woman whose father or mother has married her father or mother; half-sister: a sister who is the child of only one of your parents 2 colleague: someone you work with; acquaintance: someone you know, but not very well 3 soulmate: someone you have a very close relationship with because you share or understand the same emotions and interests; close friend: someone you are good friends with 4 partner: someone you are having a serious relationship with; wife: woman that a man is married to

b▶ Ask Ss to read the sentences, focus on the phrases in italics and try to work out what they mean. Ss check ideas in pairs. Get feedback from the class.

> **Answers:** 1 make people think well of you when they first meet you 2 like someone as soon as you meet them for the first time 3 have many similar attitudes or experiences to another person 4 have a similar view about something to somebody else 5 feel you see things in a similar way to someone else

3▶ Ss discuss the questions in small groups. Get feedback from the whole class.

> **EXTEND THE LEAD-IN**
>
> In pairs, Ss write a list of as many things as they can that they have in common. Encourage them to think of interesting/unusual things e.g. same zodiac sign.

1.1 Good friends

In this lesson, Ss read an article about the characteristics of a good friend. They also listen to two friends talking about friendship and give their own ideas about friendship.

Ss also read, listen to and write some notes and messages, thinking about the different situations for writing messages, to whom and what language/abbreviations we use.

After focussing on the use and form of question tags, Ss can get to know each other further by using question tags to check what personal information they know about each other.

> **OPTIONAL WARMER**
>
> Write on the board: *my first friend; my oldest friend; my most recent friend; my most unusual friend*
>
> Ask Ss to think about one or more of these friends and describe them to a partner. E.g. *I've known my oldest friend for over thirty years. We first met because …*
>
> Get Ss to tell the class about their partner's friend.

Reading

▶ Get Ss to look at the photos and to discuss in pairs what kind of friendship they think each group of people has (e.g. close teenage girl friends who share all their secrets).

1a▶ Ask Ss to discuss the question in pairs. Get brief feedback about their ideas.

b▶ Ss quickly read the text and check which of their ideas are mentioned.

2▶ Get Ss to read the text again and write down the name or names of the person or people in the text that correspond to each of the statements. Ss check their answers in pairs. Then get feedback from the whole class.

> **Answers:** 1 Lanza 2 Mick, Haruki 3 Mercedes 4 Debbi 5 Rachel 6 Maciek 7 Stefano 8 Emily

3▶ Ss discuss the questions in pairs or small groups. Ask a few Ss to talk about their opinions to the class.

> **OPTIONAL EXTENSION**
>
> Ask Ss to brainstorm TV programmes, films and songs about friends (e.g. TV drama series: *Friends*; film: *About a boy*; song: *You've got a friend*).
>
> Ss discuss in small groups which are their favourites and why. Encourage them to discuss the type of friendships depicted. Ss give feedback to the class.

Writing

4▶ Get Ss to discuss the question in pairs focusing on the different reasons for writing notes and messages. (e.g. reminding someone to do something, apologising for something). Get class feedback.

5a▶ Read out the five reasons listed. Get Ss to read the notes and messages (A–E) quickly and match each one with one of the reasons. You could ask Ss to underline the part of the notes/messages which tells them the answers.

▶ Ask Ss to check their answers in pairs and then get feedback from the whole class.

> **Answers:** 1 A 2 C 3 E 4 B 5 D

b▶ Ask Ss to read the messages again and decide who might have written each one. Ask them to underline the part of the notes/messages which tells them the answers.

▶ Ask Ss to check their answers in pairs and then give feedback to the whole class.

> **Answers:** A work colleague (sales figures/meeting)
> B wife (xxx – kisses)   C brother (Mum and Dad)
> D flatmate   E friend (Hi! How r u?)

▶ Get Ss to look again at the messages and ask them what the main differences are between how we write a note/message and how we write a letter/email – (In notes/messages we use abbreviations and miss out words).

c▶ Get Ss to work in pairs and work out which words have been left out in messages A–D, wherever the sign * appears. Do the first one as an example. Get feedback by asking individual Ss to read out the complete message.

> **Answers:** A *… **I should be** … . **Do you** fancy lunch? …*
> B *… pick up **your** jacket from **the** dry-cleaner's. **I will** see you at the restaurant **at** about 7p.m.*   C *… **I hope** you …*   D *… **Will you/Please** ring him …*

d▶ Check that Ss know that we often use abbreviations in text messages to save time. Get Ss to decide in pairs what the abbreviations in the message mean. Then get whole class feedback.

> **Answers:** are = r   you = u   Cd=could   b4=before
> Sat.=Saturday   Fri=Friday

> **OPTIONAL EXTENSION**
>
> In small groups, Ss brainstorm other abbreviations used in text messages. (*l8 = late, CUl8r = see you later, LOL = laughing out loud*).

▶ Elicit that we can also get messages in other ways, i.e. answerphone or voicemail messages.

6a▶ Ss listen to three answerphone messages and note down the purpose of each one. Play recording 1.1 then get Ss to check their answers in pairs. Get class feedback.

> **Answers:** 1 to check the evening's arrangements
> 2 to get authorisation for a credit card payment
> 3 to arrange to see a car for sale

b▶ Play recording 1.1 again and get Ss to make notes about the important information. Encourage them not to try to write the whole message, but just the most important bits.

▶ In pairs, Ss then write a brief message to each person using their notes. Remind them to leave out words and use abbreviations. Get class feedback by asking a few Ss to read out each message and briefly compare each one.

Possible answers: 1 Alison – Keith called about tonight. Jackie and Steve can't come. You still want to go to the film? Please call Keith on mobile.   2 James – Please call Tina Jenkins (HSBC Customer Services) – 01303 813 843 a.s.a.p. re. large credit card payment.   3 Brian – Please ring Sarah Shiali – 01273 443 750 to arrange when she can come and see car you're selling.

7 ▶ Ask individual Ss to read out the four statements then get Ss to work in pairs and discuss which of the statements they agree with and why. Encourage them to justify their opinions. Get feedback from the class and establish which of the statements most Ss agree with.

8 ▶ Focus Ss briefly on the photo of two friends, Harry and Fiona. Play recording 1.2 and get Ss to say which of the views in Ex. 7 Harry has. Get feedback from the class.

Answer: New friends will replace old friends.

9 ▶ Play recording 1.2 again and ask Ss to make notes about the people who are mentioned and in what ways they are significant. Get Ss to check their answers in pairs then get feedback from the class.

Answers: Harry talks to **Jamie** about his family; **Paula** about his relationships and love life; **Alex** about work and practical things; **Nigel** is Harry's best friend from school but they have lost touch.

10 ▶ Get Ss to discuss the questions in pairs or small groups. Get feedback from each group and find out if most of the class identifies with Harry's or Fiona's situation.

Lifelong learning

▶ Read the questions with the class. In pairs Ss share strategies that have helped them improve their English.

▶ Then, Ss note down one or two people who are NOT in the class and whose English is better than theirs. For homework, Ss ask these people for advice on improving their English. Ss share these ideas in the next class.

Grammar

OPTIONAL GRAMMAR LEAD-IN

Ask Ss questions around the class using question tags e.g. *You like football, don't you?* Elicit that you are using question tags to check information that you think you know but are not sure about.
Play recording 1.2 again and get Ss to say how many question tags they hear (6).

11a ▶ Focus Ss on the Active grammar box and get them to complete the examples with the missing auxiliary verbs. Get Ss to check their answers in pairs then get whole class feedback.

Active grammar (1)
1 ... **don't** you?   2 ... **didn't** you?   3 ... **isn't** it?   4 ... **can** you?

b ▶ Read Rule A in the Active grammar box to the class. Then ask Ss to work in pairs and match Rule B and Rule C to examples in the box. Get whole class feedback.

Answers: Rule B – 3 and 4;   Rule C – 1 and 2

12a ▶ Get Ss to work in pairs, read the interview and find the three incorrect question tags and correct them.

b ▶ Play recording 1.3 and get Ss to check their answers. Then get whole class feedback.

Answers: Jo: So, Simon, you've been with the company for nearly a year now, **haven't** you?   Jo: Now, you're clear about your targets for this year, **aren't** you?
Jo: ... That hasn't been particular good, **has** it?

13a ▶ Explain that Active grammar box (1) contains the basic rules but that there are some more difficult cases which you will look at in Active grammar box (2).

▶ Get Ss to work in pairs and complete examples 1–6 in the box. Then get whole class feedback.

Active grammar (2)
1 ... **aren't** I?   2 ... **won't** you?   3 ... **shall** we?
4 ... **do** you?   5 ... **did** it?   6 ... **have** they?

b ▶ In pairs, get Ss to refer to examples 1–6 and complete rules A–F in the Active grammar box. Get class feedback.

Active grammar (2)
A **aren't I**   B **won't you**   C **shall we**   D **positive**
E **it**   F **they**

14a ▶ Get Ss to complete the sentences with the correct question tags. They then check their answers in pairs.

b ▶ Play recording 1.4 and ask Ss to check their answers.

Answers: 1 isn't she   2 do they   3 have you   4 can we   5 shall we   6 won't you   7 does it   8 aren't I

c ▶ Explain to Ss that there are also other reasons for using question tags. Elicit or read out the list of reasons. Play recording 1.4 again and get Ss to say which reason applies to each sentence. Get whole class feedback.

Answers: 1 asking for agreement   2 asking for agreement   3 checking information   4 checking information   5 making a suggestion   6 making a suggestion   7 asking for agreement   8 asking for agreement

Person to person

15a ▶ Tell Ss they are going to check how much they know about different Ss in the class. Ask them to write one or two facts they think they know about three other Ss. Encourage them to write some facts they are quite certain about and others they are less certain about, and to use a variety of verbs.

b ▶ Get Ss to check their facts by asking the other Ss using appropriate question tags. Get Ss moving around the class to talk to different Ss.

1.2 Family ties

The Boehmer family is the world's largest family of jugglers and has won a number of awards, performing all over the United States and beyond. They have been performing to audiences with their varied juggling, gymnastics and unicycling skills for over a decade.

In recent years, there has been a lot of research into 'birth order' and how your position in your family and your relationships with your siblings can affect your personality.

In this lesson, Ss listen to part of a radio programme about the Boehmer family and then focus on the grammar connected with the words *any*, *every*, *no* and *some*. They also read an article and discuss their own opinions about 'birth order', position in a family and personality.

OPTIONAL WARMER

Introduce the idea of the circus and circus skills with the class. Ask them these questions.

Q: Have you ever been to a circus? If so, what did you like/dislike about it? Why? If not, would you like to go? Why not?
Q: What different types of circus skills can you name? Which are your favourites to watch? Can you do any of them? (*juggling, tightrope walking, Diablo, acrobatics, trapeze, plate-spinning, clowns, knife-throwing, fire-eating.*)
Q: How do you think circuses have changed over the years? Why? Do you think the changes have been a good thing or not? (The main way most circuses have changed is that many are not allowed to use animals in their acts anymore.)

Listening

▶ Get Ss to look at the photo and tell them that all the people are members of the same family and they all work together as jugglers.

1 ▶ Ask Ss to discuss the questions in pairs or small groups. Encourage them to give reasons for their answers. Get feedback.

2 ▶ Play recording 1.5 and ask Ss to answer the questions. Get them to check their answers in pairs briefly and then get whole class feedback.

Answers: 1 thirteen   2 They are the largest family of jugglers in the world.   3 Performing at the Vatican in Rome

3 ▶ Get Ss to read the questions. Then play recording 1.5 again and tell Ss to answer the questions. Get Ss to check their answers in pairs and then get whole class feedback.

Answers: 1 After his son, Adam, (having seen a circus) asked him what he could do.   2 They saw Larry practising and wanted to join in.   3 In 1989 at an amusement park.   4 Anybody can do it.

4a ▶ Tell Ss that they are going to look at some expressions from the radio programme. In pairs, Ss should look at the tapescript on page 165 and help each other work out what the phrases/expressions mean. Remind them to use the context and the sentences around the expressions to help them. Get whole class feedback.

Answers: 1 to be able to do several things at the same time   2 to find   3 to decide to do something   4 someone who enjoys family life very much   5 to be very happy about something   6 to continually get better   7 to choose

b ▶ Get Ss to work in pairs and to summarise what they heard on the radio programme using the phrases in Ex. 4 as appropriate. Encourage them not to include every detail but just to give a summary of the most important points.

OPTIONAL EXTENSION

Get Ss to write the summary that they discussed in Ex. 4b. Tell them to use their questions/answers in Exs. 2 and 3 to help. Remind Ss not to include every detail and that they should write a maximum of seventy-five words.

OPTIONAL GRAMMAR LEAD-IN

Play a quick game of 'Simon says' with words connected to *any/every/no/some*. Briefly, remind Ss of the rules (You have to do what the teacher says, if he/she starts by saying 'Simon says'. If he/she doesn't say 'Simon says', however, you mustn't do what he/she says and if you do, you're out.) e.g.: *Everyone stand up, someone in the front row turn around, write any letter of the alphabet.*

Grammar

5a ▶ Tell Ss to work in pairs and decide together whether the example sentences in the Active grammar box are correct or not. Get whole class feedback but do not explain the difference in meaning at this stage.

Answers: A Correct B Correct C Correct D Correct E Not correct F Correct G Correct H Not correct

b ▶ Ask Ss to work in pairs and choose the correct alternative for each of the rules 1–5 in the Active grammar box. Get whole class feedback.

Active grammar
1 *Any* 2 *Every* 3 *any* 4 *Nothing* 5 *some*

6 ▶ Get Ss to choose the correct alternative for each sentence. Then they should check their answers in pairs. Then get whole class feedback.

> **Answers:** 1 every 2 Everybody 3 any 4 Nothing 5 every 6 somewhere 7 any 8 any

> **OPTIONAL EXTENSION**
>
> Write some questions on the board for the Ss to discuss, which include words like *anybody, nothing*. Ss could also add questions of their own.
>
> **Q: Do you know anybody who has a special talent?**
> **Q: Do you ever feel that you have nothing to do?**
> **Q: Is there anything you have always wanted to do?**
> **Q: Do you think that anybody can learn to juggle?**

> **OPTIONAL WARMER**
>
> Set up a quick class survey. Write these questions on the board and check Ss know *age gap* and *sibling*. Get Ss to walk around the classroom and ask as many other Ss as possible, noting down the answers.
>
> **Q: How many brothers and sisters have you got?**
> **Q: Are you the first, middle or the last in your family?**
> **Q: What is the age gap between you and your nearest sibling?**
>
> Get Ss to collate their results in pairs and report the most interesting facts back to the class.
>
> *Most people in the class are the first in their family.*

Reading

7 ▶ Get Ss to discuss the questions in pairs. Then ask for two or three opinions as whole class feedback.

8a ▶ Read out the questions to the class. Tell Ss to read the text quickly and answer the questions. Remind them not to worry about all the information at this stage but just to answer the four questions. Ss should then briefly check answers in pairs, before getting whole class feedback.

> **Answers:** Statement 3

b ▶ Get Ss to read the text again and decide if the statements are true or false. Encourage them to underline the part of the text which tells them the answers. Ss check their answers in pairs. Then get class feedback.

> **Answers:** 1 T 2 T 3 F 4 F 5 T 6 F

9 ▶ Get Ss to discuss the question in pairs or small groups. Encourage them to justify their opinions with examples from their own family or a family they know. Ask for three or four opinions from different Ss.

> **OPTIONAL EXTENSION**
>
> Write the following definitions on the board. Ss find the words in the article which correspond to each one.
>
> 1 what you think/hope will happen (paragraph 2) *expectations* 2 wanting to keep someone safe from harm or danger (paragraph 3) *protective* 3 the negative part or disadvantage of something (paragraph 3) *downside* 4 when someone likes someone/thing and thinks they are good (paragraph 4) *approval* 5 when people do things where something bad, unpleasant or dangerous may happen (paragraph 5) *risk-taking* 6 deliberately not obeying people in authority or rules of behaviour (paragraph 6) *rebellious* 7 to be in a very small space between two other things (paragraph 7) *sandwiched*

Vocabulary

▶ Write on the board: *intellect* and *intellectual*. Ask which one is a noun and which is an adjective (*intellect* = noun; *intellectual* = adjective)

10 ▶ Focus Ss on the table and get them to complete the missing words. Encourage them to work in pairs and find the words in the text in Ex. 8 in order to help check their answers. Get whole class feedback.

> **Answers: Noun:** *jealousy loneliness success*
> **Adjective:** *intellectual* artistic *responsible*
> *important skilful frustrated/frustrating*

11 ▶ Get Ss to complete the sentences with the most appropriate word from the table. Ss should check answers briefly in pairs. Then get whole class feedback.

> **Answers:** 1 importance 2 artistic 3 frustrating 4 jealous 5 lonely 6 skill 7 responsibility 8 success

Speaking

12a ▶ Play recording 1.6 and get Ss to say what the two people are talking about.

> **Answers:** The attitude and behaviour of parents towards their children depending whether they are born first, second.

b ▶ Focus Ss on the How to … box and ask them to read through the language. Play recording 1.6 again and get Ss to tick which expressions from the How to … box they hear and to underline which word(s) is/are stressed in each one.

> **Answers:** I <u>totally</u> <u>disagree</u>.   <u>No</u>, that's not true at <u>all</u>. That's <u>probably</u> <u>true</u>.   I think there's <u>some</u> truth in that.

13a ▶ Get Ss to discuss the statements in pairs or small groups. Encourage them to use expressions from the How to … box as appropriate and to refer to their own experience if relevant.

b ▶ Ask each group to report back to the whole class on a few of the most interesting points they discussed.

1.3 Mobile connections

Mobile phones, instant communication and new technology are dominating people's lives more and more. Whilst there are clearly many benefits from these innovations, there are also potential disadvantages, particularly for young people, which we don't yet fully know about or understand.

In this lesson, Ss discuss their opinions about mobile phones and then read an article about the increased use of mobile phones and its implications, particularly for young people. Following this, Ss focus on the grammar of present and future modals of possibility.

Ss also exchange personal information about each other and get to know each other further.

> **OPTIONAL WARMER**
>
> Get Ss to focus on the idea of mobile phones and their enormous growth.
>
> Write on the board:
> *1 1970s/1980s/1990s*
> *2 About 1 million/about 2 million/about 3 million*
> *3 230 million/27 billion/620 billion*
>
> Then ask Ss the following questions and tell them to choose the correct answer for each question from the options on the board.
> **Q: When did mobile phones first start to become available?** *1980s*
> **Q: How many text messages are sent every hour in the UK?** *about 3 million*
> **Q: How many text messages is it estimated will be sent in China in the year 2010?** *620 million*

Speaking

1 ▶ Focus Ss on the photos and get them to describe them in pairs.

2 ▶ Get Ss to discuss the questions in pairs or small groups. Ask for two or three opinions from the whole class.

Reading

3 ▶ Read through the subjects with the class. Ask Ss to read the text and tick the subjects it refers to. Get them to briefly check their answers in pairs. Then get whole class feedback.

> **Answers:** Subjects referred to: 1, 3, 4, 6, 7, 9, 10

4 ▶ Get Ss to read the text again and make brief notes about each of the subjects in Ex. 3 it refers to. You could do the first one with Ss to make sure they understand the level of detail required. Ss should check their answers in pairs. Then get whole class feedback.

> **Answers:** 1 the number of young people who have a mobile phone: *one quarter of 4–15 year olds in Tokyo; half of Japanese high school students* 3 the reasons why young people want a mobile phone: '*lifestyle*', *parents, to keep in touch with friends* 4 how parents feel about their children having a mobile phone: *they think they spend too much time on the phone; makes it difficult to keep a check on who their children are communicating with* 6 the amount of contact teenagers feel they need with their friends: *several times a day* 7 the effect of mobile phones on reading for pleasure: *reducing the amount children read for pleasure* 9 the health risks of mobile phones to children: *children under sixteen should only use mobile phones to make calls in an emergency* 10 some possible educational uses of mobile phones: *to get revision/mock exam questions; for teachers to keep in touch with pupils*

> **OPTIONAL EXTENSION**
>
> You could use this as an opportunity to get Ss to practise the skill of summary writing.
>
> First, get Ss to note down the main points of the article. Tell them to choose 3 - 5 points and remind them that they can look back at the article as well as at their notes in Ex. 4. Get them to discuss which points they have chosen with a partner.
>
> Then tell them to write a paragraph using their points to summarize the article. They could do this in pairs or individually. Remind them to only include the main points and not too much detail. If Ss need further help, you could give them an example for the first sentence: There are a number of worrying issues that have arisen from the increasing use of mobile phones among young people.

5 ▶ Get Ss to discuss the questions in pairs or small groups. Get whole class feedback and find out whether most Ss agree or disagree about these questions.

> **OPTIONAL EXTENSION**
>
> If Ss have access to the Internet, they could do a mini-project to find out more predictions about how mobile phones will change in the next five years. They could report back in the next class.

Vocabulary

> **OPTIONAL WARMER**
>
> Get Ss thinking about the noise that mobile phones make by asking these questions:
> **Q: Do you have a favourite ringtone? What is it?**
> **Q: Do you change the ringtone on your phone much/ever? Why/Why not?**
> **Q: How do you feel about the noise of mobile phones ringing and people talking on phones in public places, e.g. on the train?**

6 ▶ Get Ss to discuss the questions in pairs or small groups. Get whole class feedback and compare which are the most and least popular noises.

7a ▶ Read through the noises in the box but do not explain them at this stage. Play recording 1.7 and ask Ss to match the words they hear with the noises in the box. Get Ss to briefly check answers in pairs. Then get class feedback.

> **Answers:** 1 crash   2 thud   3 snore   4 shout
> 5 bark   6 ring   7 scream   8 bang   9 creak

b ▶ Get Ss to discuss the question in pairs. Then get whole class feedback.

> **Answers:** (There may also be others)
> 1 crash – plate dropping and smashing   2 snore
> – someone sleeping   3 shout – someone attracting
> attention of a friend   4 bark – dog   5 ring – phone,
> doorbell   6 scream – someone in pain, shocked or
> laughing   7 bang – door or window suddenly closing
> 8 creak – old wooden floorboards   9 thud – dropping
> of something heavy

8 ▶ Tell Ss that some of the noises they heard make part of a story. Play recording 1.8 and ask Ss to discuss in pairs how the noises might be linked to make a story. Encourage them to use *may*, *might*, *could*, but do not explain the grammar of these words at this stage. You might want to read the example with the class to get them going.

Get whole class feedback by asking one or two groups to tell their stories.

> **OPTIONAL EXTENSION**
>
> You could get Ss to do some more work on vocabulary of noises.
>
> Divide the class into Students A and Students B. Tell As to look at the words in Group A and Bs to look at the words in Group B. Give them dictionaries and get them to find the meaning, pronunciation and an example sentence for each word.
>
> A: *rattle*, *squeak*, *groan*
>
> B: *whimper*, *scrape*, *howl*
>
> Regroup the Ss into pairs (one A and one B). Tell them to teach each other the words in their group, including meaning, pronunciation and an example sentence.

Grammar

> **OPTIONAL GRAMMAR LEAD-IN**
>
> Remind Ss about the stories they discussed in Ex. 8. Ask them what type of verbs they used (modal verbs – *may*, *might*, *could*) and why (because they were speculating about the story from the noises, but were not sure).

9a ▶ Read through sentences A–E in the Active grammar box with the class. Play recording 1.9 and ask Ss to match each dialogue with the correct sentence. Get Ss to briefly check their answers in pairs. Get class feedback.

> **Active grammar**
>
> 1 D   2 C   3 E   4 A   5 B

b ▶ Get Ss to work in pairs and match sentences A–E with meanings 1–3 in the Active grammar box. They should then decide if each one refers to the present or the future. Get whole class feedback.

> **Active grammar**
>
> A (1) it is possible – present
> B (1) it is possible – present
> C (2) it is not possible – present
> D (3) it is certain – present
> E (1) it is possible – future

c ▶ Get Ss to work in pairs and write other sentences using *may*/*might*/*could*, can't and *must* as appropriate about the dialogues. They should refer to the tapescript on page 165 if necessary. Get whole class feedback by asking different Ss for one more sentence for each dialogue.

10 ▶ Get Ss to complete the second sentence in each pair so that it means the same as the first sentence using *may*/*might*/*could*, *must* or *can't*. Remind Ss to look for clues about how possible or certain the situation is. Ss should check answers in pairs and then get whole class feedback.

> **Answers:** 1 Terry **must be** stuck in traffic. He's never normally late.   2 We **may**/**could**/**might go** and visit my brother in Manchester.   3 Jane **can't want** to go to Morocco this summer. She hates hot weather.   4 Susie **may**/**might**/**could come** to the party tonight.   5 There **must be** better ways of solving this problem.   6 Tarek **may**/**might**/**could change** his mind about lending you his car.

Person to person

11a ▶ Read through the list with the whole class. Tell Ss to choose eight of the pieces of information and write them on a piece of paper. Remind them not to write or say which piece of information is being referred to and not to write them in a particular order (as the idea is for other Ss to guess/speculate as to what they refer to).

b ▶ You could read through the example with Ss or you could do your own example on the board. (Write an answer that applies to you and get Ss to speculate what it refers to).

▶ Get Ss to work in pairs. They should look at their partner's words and say what they think each one refers to, using *might*, *must*, *can't* or *could*.

> **OPTIONAL EXTENSION**
>
> You could get Ss to stand up and walk around the room and show different Ss their words. Ask them to speculate about one piece of information for each student and see how many they get right.

Vocabulary: Phrasal verbs

In this lesson, Ss focus on a group of phrasal verbs around the topic of relationships. They are presented through a listening activity and Ss get a chance to use them.

OPTIONAL WARMER

Write on the board: 1 *I take after my father – we're both really lazy!* 2 *My brother always takes my things out of my room.*

Ask Ss to discuss in pairs what the verbs in each sentence mean and which one is a phrasal verb. (*Take after* is a phrasal verb — to look or behave like someone in your family; *take* is not a phrasal verb.)

1 ▶ Focus Ss on the photo. Play recording 1.10 and get Ss to read the dialogue at the same time. Ask them to decide who the people in the photo are. Ss should check their answers in pairs. Then get whole class feedback.

Answers: Photo shows Tim as a child with his Dad.

2a ▶ Get Ss to work in pairs and ask them to think about the meaning of the phrasal verbs in bold in Ex. 1. Remind them to look at the context around the verbs to help. They should write a short definition of each one.

b ▶ Get Ss to check their definitions using an English dictionary. Then get whole class feedback.

Answers: 1 to look or behave like another member of your family – **to take after** 2 to admire and respect someone – **to look up to** 3 to develop from being a child to being an adult – **to grow up** 4 to try to make people admire you and think you are clever, funny – **to show off** 5 to look after children until they are adults – **to bring up** 6 to have a good relationship with someone – **to get on** 7 to have a romantic relationship with someone – **to go out** 8 to end a marriage or a relationship – **to split up** 9 to have a quarrel – **to fall out** 10 to become friends with someone again after an argument – **to make up**

▶ Remind Ss that a good English-English dictionary helps with: 1 meaning (giving a definition and often an example); 2 grammar (including, in the case of (phrasal) verbs, whether it is transitive [T] or intransitive [I]); 3 pronunciation (stress, sounds and number of syllables).

3 ▶ Get Ss to correct the mistakes in each sentence. Then ask them to check their answers in pairs, before getting whole class feedback.

Answers: 1 going **out**? 2 get on **with** 3 made it **up** 4 bringing **us up** 5 looks up to **you** 6 take **after** 7 **grow** up 8 fallen out **with** 9 show **off** 10 split **up**

4 ▶ Read through the sentences with the class. Ask them to decide which of them are true for themselves and to change the others to make them true. Ss then compare and discuss their sentences in small groups. Get whole class feedback by asking each group to report back about the most interesting sentence discussed

Communication: Your family history

A family tree is a kind of 'map' of the members of a family and how they are connected back through the generations. In recent years, genealogy, or tracing your own family tree, has become a very popular hobby. Websites like www.genesreunited.com have made it more accessible to people.

In this lesson, Ss listen to a man talking about his family tree and describing some of the people in his family. Then they draw their own family tree, describe it to each other and talk about some members of their families.

OPTIONAL WARMER

Focus Ss on the photos. Tell them that the people in the photos are all members of the same family. Ask Ss to work in pairs and describe what they can see in the photos and speculate briefly as to who the people could be. Get brief whole class feedback but do not accept or reject any ideas at this stage.

1 ▶ Tell Ss they are going to listen to a man called Morgan talking about his family tree (some of whom are shown in the photos). Play recording 1.11 and ask Ss to say who the people in the photos are. Get Ss to check their answers in pairs then get whole class feedback.

Answers: Middle photo: Cicely and John around 1925 Left photo 2: Aunt Sue Photos on right 3: Leon

2 ▶ Play recording 1.12 again and get Ss to complete the family tree. Ss should then check their answers in pairs before getting whole class feedback.

Answers: From top down: John, Ben, Julian, Sue, Leon.

3a ▶ Get Ss to draw their own family tree going back to at least their grandparents (or further back if they want to), using the one in Ex. 2 as a model. Tell Ss not to show their family tree to other Ss at this stage.

b ▶ Get Ss to work in pairs and describe their family trees to each other. They still should not show their drawings to each other because the student who is listening should try to draw the family tree being described.

c ▶ When Ss have finished drawing their partner's family tree, they should compare theirs with the 'original' and check how much they have drawn correctly.

d ▶ Tell Ss to choose two people in their family (on their family tree) and tell their partner more details about them. Encourage Ss to ask each other questions.

OPTIONAL EXTENSION

Get Ss to do a project to extend the family tree they have done in this lesson. They could research more information, photographs and other objects to illustrate it and present it to the class at a later date. If your Ss have access to the Internet, refer them to www.genesreunited.com.

Review and practice

1 ▶

Answers: 1 f   2 h   3 g   4 a   5 d   6 e
7 b   8 c

2 ▶

Answers: 1 Not correct: **any** idea.   2 Correct.
3 Correct.   4 Not correct: **Any** help ... .   5 Correct.
6 Not correct: **anywhere** ... .   7 Correct.   8 Correct.
9 Not correct: **Everyone** ... .   10 Not correct: **is**
nothing/isn't **any**thing.

3 ▶

Answers: 1 might   2 must   3 can't   4 may
5 must   6 might   7 could   8 must

4 ▶

Answers: 1 going   2 ex-wife   3 responsibility
4 fiancée   5 barking   6 takes   7 snores
8 colleague

5 ▶

Answers: 1 Her brother's name is Ivan, isn't it?
2 Let's go for a swim this afternoon, shall we?   3 He
never eats meat, does he?   4 Please , make yourself
comfortable, won't you?   5 Nobody told him we were
having a party, did they?   6 I'm in time for the start of
the film, aren't I?   7 Nothing was taken out of her bag,
was it?   8 She can't sing very well, can she?

Notes for using the Common European Framework (CEF)

CEF References

1.1 Can do: check information

CEF B2 descriptor: Can ask follow-up questions to check that he/she has understood what a speaker intended to say, and get clarification of ambiguous points. (CEF page 87)

1.2 Can do: express agreement/disagreement

CEF B2 descriptor: Can keep up with an animated discussion, identifying accurately arguments supporting and opposing points of view. (CEF page 78)

1.3 Can do: make speculations

CEF B2 descriptor: Can outline an issue or a problem clearly, speculating about causes or consequences. (CEF page 79)

CEF quick brief

The Common European Framework is a reference document for teachers. It is about 260 pages long. You can download it for free from www.coe.int. The CEF recommends that Ss use a Portfolio. This is a document that aims to help Ss reflect on, record and demonstrate their language learning. There is a free downloadable Total English Portfolio.

Portfolio task

Download the Total English Portfolio free from www.longman.com/totalenglish.

Objective: help Ss to understand the purpose and value of the Portfolio.

This task can be done in Ss' own language.

Make sure that each student in your class has a copy of the Total English Portfolio.

1 ▶ Ask Ss to complete their personal details on the Portfolio and explain its purpose: to help Ss learn more effectively and demonstrate their language abilities and experiences to others.

2 ▶ Explain that you will ask them to update their Portfolio at regular intervals but you will not 'mark' their Portfolio – it is an aid to learning, not a focus for learning itself.

2 Work

Overview

Summary

Lesson 1: Ss read an article about attitudes to work and how work has changed over the years. They then discuss their own opinions about different ways of working (e.g. working at home), their predictions about working patterns for the future and their own plans for work/study/life in the future.

Lesson 2: Ss listen to a radio journalist talking about Nek Chand, an artist who created the Rock Gardens of Chandigarh in India from recycled materials. This leads into a discussion about recycling and other environmental issues. Ss finish by doing a class survey about work/life balance.

Lesson 3: Ss read three extracts from the novel *The No.1 Ladies' Detective Agency* by Alexander McCall Smith, in which the main character sets up her own business. This leads to analysing and then writing a formal job application letter.

Vocabulary: Ss focus on collocations with prepositions including adjective + preposition and verb + preposition.

Communication: Ss talk about their experiences of job/ university interviews. They then listen to four different interviews and roleplay an interview situation.

Film bank: Dream career (2'35")

An extract from a documentary about a fashion designer, Lindsay Pressdee who started her own business in 1996.

In the film she talks about what her job involves including the hard work and the excitement of showing her clothes at trade fairs and photo shoots.

Possible places to use this short film are:

▶ After Lesson 1 to extend the topic of ways of working.

▶ After Lesson 3 to extend the topic of running your own business.

For ways to use this short film in class, see Students' Book page 153 and Teacher's Book page 179.

Lead-in

OPTIONAL WARMER

Write *jobs* and the categories on the board: *wear a uniform; work mostly outside; work at night; have a long training; work with machines; travel a lot.*

Divide the class into groups and give each group a different category. Tell Ss to write as many different jobs for their category as they can in two minutes. Get class feedback and write the jobs on the board.

1 ▶ Ask Ss to work in pairs to discuss which of the jobs listed is not in the photos. Ss then discuss what they think each job involves. Get class feedback.

Answers: 1 social worker   2 **journalist**: someone who writes news reports for newspapers, magazines, television or radio; **civil engineer**: someone who designs and builds roads, bridges ...; **social worker**: someone who helps people deal with problems such as poor housing ...; **nursery nurse**: someone who looks after young children; **surgeon**: a doctor who does operations

2a ▶ Play recording 2.1 and ask Ss to match each speaker with the correct job in Ex. 1. Ss briefly check answers in pairs before you get whole class feedback.

Answers: 1 journalist   2 nursery nurse   3 surgeon   4 civil engineer   5 social worker

b ▶ Read through the phrases with the class but do not explain them at this stage. Play recording 2.1 again and tell Ss to listen out for the phrases and the context each one is in. After listening, get Ss to discuss in pairs what they think each phrase means. Get whole class feedback.

Answers: a change of career: when someone stops the career that they have been doing and retrains to do something different; **a labour of love**: when someone does a job not for the money but because they really love it; **a career path**: the different steps that someone takes to progress in a certain career; **to take a year out**: to stop working for a year and do something completely different (e.g. travel); **job satisfaction**: the feeling of happiness someone gets from doing their job

3 ▶ Get Ss to work in pairs and think of a job which fits each of the qualities in the box. Get class feedback.

4 ▶ Ss discuss the question in pairs or small groups. Encourage them to give details. Ask two or three Ss to tell the whole class about another student they talked to.

EXTEND THE LEAD-IN

Play a game of 'twenty questions' about jobs. Ss work in small groups and take it in turns to think of a job (but don't say it). The other Ss guess the job by asking a maximum of twenty 'yes/no' questions. Encourage them to ask questions using the phrases in Ex. 3.

2.1 The daily grind

The nature of work has changed radically over the last 1,000 years. Ways of working are very different and more varied now, mostly due to changes to production methods, especially during the Industrial Revolution and more recently due to huge advancements in technology. Despite these changes, however, some things remain constant especially our apparent psychological need to work.

In this lesson, Ss read an article about attitudes to work and how work has changed over the years. They then discuss their own opinions about different ways of working (e.g. working at home, voluntary work).

After listening to four people talking about how they would like to change their working life, Ss look at the grammar for talking about future plans and predictions. They then discuss their predictions about working patterns for the future and their own plans for work/study/life in the future.

> **OPTIONAL WARMER**
>
> Write the following two sentences on the board:
>
> 1 *I work to live.*   2 *I live to work.*
>
> Check Ss understand what they mean (1 = my main reason for work is to earn money to enjoy things in life; 2 = I love my work so much that it is the most important thing in my life).
>
> Ask Ss to discuss in pairs which of the two sentences is closest to their own feelings about work. (If Ss don't have a job at the moment, encourage them to think about a job they would like to do and imagine which of the two sentences would probably be most relevant to them).
>
> Ask for feedback from the whole class and check which of the two sentences is most common in the class.

Reading

1 ▶ Get Ss to discuss the questions in pairs or small groups. Then get feedback but do not accept or reject their ideas at this stage.

2 ▶ Tell Ss to read the text quickly and check their ideas about question 2 in Ex. 1 – in what ways work has changed over the last 1000 years and in what ways it is the same? Ss should briefly check their answers in pairs and then get whole class feedback.

> **Answers:** According to the text, work has changed a lot over the last 1000 years (Pre-industrial age, people worked for goods; after the Industrial Revolution, people worked for money; now, many people work flexible hours often from home).   The overall attitude to work is similar to before – we do it because we have to but we miss it if we don't do it (as implied by the title).

3a ▶ Get Ss to read the text again and decide if the statements are true or false. Encourage Ss to underline the parts of the text which help them with the answers and to say why the false statements are false. Ask Ss to check answers in pairs and then get whole class feedback.

> **Answers:**   1 true   2 false (self-esteem increases if you're paid to work)   3 false (even doing unenjoyable things at work increases self-esteem)   4 true   5 true   6 false (people who don't have work become irritable)   7 true   8 true   9 true   10 false (the writer thinks that working remotely may become more and more common)

b ▶ Ask Ss to summarise the main argument of the text by completing the sentence. Encourage them to be concise and focus only on the main argument. They could compare their sentences with other Ss before getting whole class feedback.

> **Possible answer:**   Although the nature of work has changed over the years, the basic fact that work is good for us remains true.

4 ▶ Get Ss to discuss the questions in pairs or small groups. Encourage them to use examples from their own experience or from people they know to justify their opinions. Get whole class feedback by asking different groups to report on the most interesting part of their discussions.

Vocabulary

5 ▶ Get Ss to work in pairs and help each other to find the difference between the verb phrases in italics in each pair of sentences. Encourage them to use English dictionaries. You may want to remind them that dictionaries can help with pronunciation of new words/ phrases as well as meaning. Get whole class feedback.

> **Answers:**   1a to do voluntary work: to do a job which is not paid   b to work part-time: to do a job for only a few hours or a few days a week but not every day   2a to take early retirement: to decide to stop working completely before the usual age of retirement (in the UK, sixty-five for men and sixty for women)   b to be made redundant: to be told to leave your job because there is no longer enough work   3a to work flexitime: to work a particular number of hours each week or month, but you can change the times at which you start and finish each day   b to do shift work: to have a job in which you work for a particular period of time during the day or night, e.g. in a factory, hospital   4a to be on strike: to deliberately not work for a period of time because of a disagreement about pay, working conditions   b to be on sick leave: to officially spend time away from work because you are sick   5a to be sacked: to be told to leave your job because you have done something wrong   b to resign from your job: to officially tell your employer that you are going to leave your job

6 ▶ Get Ss to complete the sentences using the correct form of the phrases in Ex. 5. Remind them to use each phrase once and that sometimes they may have to change the form of the verb. After Ss have checked their answers in pairs, get whole class feedback.

Answers: 1 do voluntary work   2 work part-time
3 resigned   4 doing shift work   5 taking early
retirement   6 be sacked   7 been on strike   8 being
on sick leave   9 working flexitime   10 made
redundant

7 ▶ Tell Ss to choose six of the questions in Ex. 6 to ask
their partner. In pairs, Ss should discuss their answers.
Get brief whole class feedback by asking two or three Ss
to report back one of their most interesting questions/
answers.

OPTIONAL EXTENSION

Do a 'Find someone who ...' activity with Ss. Give Ss
the following ideas and get them to write 4–6 more
themselves.

Find someone who ...

1 ... works flexi-time

2 ... has had a part-time job in a shop

3 ... would like to work at home but doesn't

4 ... has gone on strike

Ask Ss to walk around the room and ask the questions
to different Ss. Tell them that the aim is to get a
different name for each of the points. Get brief whole
class feedback by asking different Ss to report one of
their points.

Grammar

8 ▶ Read through the questions with the class and
tell Ss they will hear four different people talking (Julia,
Simon, Fran and Patrick). Play recording 2.2 and get Ss
to listen and answer the questions. Ss should check their
answers in pairs before getting whole class feedback.

Answers: a Julia: she's too stressed and fed up/no
definite plans but some ideas.   b Simon: he wants
to retrain/has definite plans but not sure of the
dates yet, probably September.   c Fran: she feels
isolated working from home/has definite plans (job
interview).   d Patrick: he wants to take on more
responsibility/no definite plans.

9a ▶ Tell Ss that examples 1–6 in the Active grammar
box come from the recording they've just heard. Get
them to try to complete the examples from memory.
Then play recording 2.3 and ask Ss to listen and check
their answers. They should check answers in pairs before
getting whole class feedback.

Active grammar

1 ... I**'ll go** ...   2 ... I**'m going to leave** ...   3 I**'m
meeting** ...   4 ... they**'ll offer** ...   5 ... **is going to be** ...
6 He**'s bound to** ...

b ▶ Ask Ss to work in pairs and match the rules A–F in
the Active grammar box with the examples 1–6. Get whole
class feedback.

Answers: 1 E   2 B   3 A   4 D   5 C   6 F

▶ You may want to point out to Ss that the choice of
which future form to use often depends largely on the
attitude of the speaker. For example, if the speaker feels
confident that everything has been arranged, they may
choose to use the Present Continuous. However, other
future forms may also be appropriate and grammatically
correct.

10 ▶ Get Ss to choose the best alternative for each
sentence. Remind them to look for clues in the sentences
as regards the attitude of the speaker (e.g. how sure they
are or if they feel they have any evidence). Ask Ss to check
their answers in pairs and then get whole class feedback.

Answers: 1 going   2 're meeting   3 's bound
to   4 'm going to look for   5 won't go   6 'm playing
7 's bound to

11 ▶ Tell Ss that there are other ways of talking about
future plans apart from the future forms in the Active
grammar box. Get Ss to read through the How to ... box
and to complete sentences 1–5 with the words in the box.
Ss should check their answers in pairs Then get whole
class feedback.

Answers: 1 thinking   2 sure   3 idea   4 depends
5 probably

Person to person

12a ▶ Get Ss to work in pairs and ask them to tell each
other about their work/study/life plans for the future.
Remind them to use the language in the How to ... box as
appropriate and to read the example to get them started.

b ▶ Get whole class feedback on the discussion by
asking various pairs of Ss if any of their plans for the
future are very different and if so, how.

OPTIONAL VARIATION

Instead of getting Ss to discuss their work/study/life
plans for the future, you could give them different,
more specific categories to discuss. They could
discuss the following, and then report back to the
class on the most interesting points they discussed.

Things I want to change this year
What new hobbies I'm interested in starting
My English studies in the next year
My 'three-year-plan'

2.2 A work of art

Nek Chand is India's most visionary artist and creator of the extraordinary Rock Gardens of Chandigarh. He was inspired to collect materials which he recycled and to spend every spare moment creating thousands of sculptures and landscaping his gardens. He worked secretly for eighteen years until finally his work was discovered and became India's second most popular tourist attraction (after the Taj Mahal) with 5000 visitors every day. For more information, go to: www.nekchand.com

In this lesson, Ss listen to a radio programme about Nek Chand and how he created the Rock Gardens. This leads into a discussion about recycling and other environmental issues and a focus on the grammar of the Future Perfect and the Future Continuous.

After listening to the results of a survey about work/life balance, Ss then do their own survey, reporting the results back to the class.

OPTIONAL WARMER

Write these famous parks and gardens on the board.
Parc Guell, Barcelona; *Central Park, New York*; *Kew Gardens, London*; *Shinjuku Gyoen, Tokyo*

Ask Ss to discuss these questions.
Q: What do you know about any of these parks or gardens?
Q: Have you been to any of them? Which would you like to visit?
Q: Can you think of any more parks or gardens in your own country, or in other countries? Tell other Ss about them.

Listening

1a ▶ Focus Ss on the photos and explain that they are the Rock Gardens of Chandigarh in India and that the man's name is Nek Chand. Do not tell Ss any more details at this stage but get them to write two questions they would like to ask about what they can see, in pairs.

b ▶ Read through the three headlines (A, B and C) with the class. Play recording 2.4 and tell Ss to check if their questions are answered and to choose the best headline for the story. Ss should then check their answers in pairs, before getting whole class feedback.

Answers: Best headline: A

2 ▶ Read through the notes with the class. Then play recording 2.4 again and get Ss to complete the notes as they listen. Get Ss to check answers in pairs and then get whole class feedback.

Answers: 1 modest, creative and hard-working
2 farmer   3 Government road inspector 4 the design and construction of his city, Chandigarh
5 building on Government-owned land   6 all kinds of recycled material   7 the Government discovered his gardens   8 the gardens were opened to the public   9 5000   10 happy

3 ▶ Get Ss to discuss the questions in pairs or small groups. Then get whole class feedback, asking each group to report back on one question.

OPTIONAL ALTERNATIVE

Get Ss to discuss question 1 briefly and get feedback. Then, set up questions 2 and 3 for a more lengthy discussion, starting in small groups and then expanding to larger groups. Each small group could discuss one question and then report it back to the class.

Grammar

OPTIONAL GRAMMAR LEAD-IN

Write these sentences (from the Active grammar box) on the board and get Ss to try to complete them using the verbs in brackets.

Tomorrow morning, he'____ the same as he's doing today. (do)

Soon, he ____ half a century working on this garden. (spend)

What ____ in five years' time? (do)

He ____ the garden by the time he retires. (not finish)

Ss should compare their answers in pairs and then look at the Active grammar box on page 24 to check.

4a ▶ Get Ss to match the examples 1–4 in the Active grammar box with the correct tense (A and B in the box). Ss then check in pairs before you get class feedback.

Active grammar

Future Perfect:

2 *Soon, Chand will have spent half a century working on this garden.*

4 *He won't have finished the garden by the time he retires.*

Future Continuous:

1 *Tomorrow morning, he'll be doing the same as he's doing today.*

3 *What will he be doing in five years' time?*

b ▶ Get Ss to complete the rules of form in the box with the correct part of speech. After brief checking in pairs, get whole class feedback.

Answers: Future Perfect: *will/won't + have* + past participle   Future Continuous: *will/won't + be* + present participle

5 ▶ Get Ss to complete the sentences with the Future Perfect or the Future Continuous form of the verb in brackets. Ask Ss to check their answers in pairs and then get whole class feedback. As an extra check you could ask if the action will be *in progress* (Future Continuous) or if it will be *finished* (Future Perfect).

Answers: 1 will have finished   2 will be playing
3 will have gone   4 will be having   5 will have finished
6 will be lying   7 will have spent   8 will be having

OPTIONAL EXTENSION

For intensive pronunciation work, focus on the
auxiliary verbs in these two verb tenses. The auxiliary
verbs are unstressed, weak forms and often run
together (e.g. will have = /wɪləv/; won't have =
/wəʊntəv/; will be = /wɪlbiː/; won't be =
/wəʊntbiː/). Use the sentences in Ex. 5 to get Ss to
listen and repeat.

Person to person

6 ▶ Get Ss to ask and answer the questions in pairs,
reminding them about pronunciation. Then ask for two or
three Ss to feedback to the whole class.

OPTIONAL ALTERNATIVE

Get Ss to stand up and mingle and ask the questions
to as many Ss as they can. They could then report the
most popular answer and the most unusual answer.

Vocabulary

OPTIONAL WARMER

Write *free time* on the board. Then ask Ss to work in
pairs and, in two minutes, write as many words as
they can which use the letters in the words 'free time'.
Each word must have at least two letters and must not
be a name. Get feedback, writing all the words on the
board e.g.: *met, meet, mere, mite, fir, fire, fee, feet,
rim, rite, tire.*

7a ▶ Tell Ss they are going to focus on 'free time' or
'after work' activities. Get them to match words from
column A and column B to make ten verb phrases. Ss
check in pairs. Do not get class feedback yet.

Answers: 1 c 2 d 3 g 4 e 5 h 6 a 7 b 8 f

b ▶ Get Ss to add three more 'after work' activities and
then compare their ideas with a partner. Then get whole
class feedback and write up any new ideas on the board,
checking that all Ss understand them.

8a ▶ Get Ss to complete the sentences with the correct
form of the most appropriate phrase from Ex. 7. Ss then
check in pairs but do not get whole class feedback yet.

Answers: 1 work late at the office 2 visiting chat
rooms 3 do an evening class 4 decorating the living
room 5 studying for a qualification online 6 spend
quality time 7 keep up to date 8 socialising with friends

9 ▶ Ask Ss to discuss the questions in pairs or small
groups. Then ask two or three Ss to feedback to the class.

Listening and speaking

▶ Tell Ss that they are going to listen to someone
reporting the results of a survey about 'work/life balance'.
Check they understand what this means.

10 ▶ Read through the questions with the whole class
and focus students on the two examples. Then get Ss to
work in pairs and discuss what they think the results of
the survey were. Get brief feedback but do not accept or
reject any ideas at this stage.

11a ▶ Play recording 2.6 and Ss listen and see if they
were right. After Ss check in pairs, get class feedback.

Answers: 1 nearly half the group regularly works late
at the office   2 25% of the group had done voluntary
work at some time in their lives   3 The vast majority say
they do at least one evening class, mostly either some
kind of sport or art class   4 Only a few people said they
switched their computer on every evening   5 60% said
they found it easy to switch off after work   6 the vast
majority of people said they would like to change their
work/life balance. Most said they want to work less and
make more time for themselves.

b ▶ Read through the language in the How to ... box with
the class. Play recording 2.7 and get Ss to complete the
How to ... box. Ss check in pairs. Get class feedback.

Answers: 1 out 2 Everyone 3 Nearly 4 any
5 majority 6 minority

12a ▶ Tell Ss that they are going to write their own
survey. To prepare, get Ss to work in pairs and underline
the parts of the questions in Ex. 10 that they can use.

Answers: 1 Do you ever ...?   2 Have you ever ...?
3 How many ...? Which one(s)?   4 Do you usually ...?
5 Do you find it easy to ...?   6 How good do you think ...?

b ▶ Get Ss to work in pairs and choose which of the two
surveys they want to do (the Internet in people's lives or
the Arts in people's lives). They should then write between
six and eight questions for their survey.

OPTIONAL ALTERNATIVE

To give Ss extra help, write these ideas on the board:
The Internet: *working/studying, buying things,
getting information/news, 'chatting', playing games,
downloading music*
The Arts: *going to films/plays/musicals/concerts,
going to art galleries/museums, doing evening
classes, reading/writing, making things*

c ▶ Ss should then ask their questions to as many other
Ss as possible. Remind Ss to make a note of the answers.

13a ▶ Get Ss to work with their partner again and
collect the results of their survey. Remind them to use the
language in the How to ... box as appropriate.

b ▶ Ask each pair to report one result from their survey.

c ▶ Discuss with the whole class which results they
found surprising and why.

2.3 Ready for business

The No. 1 Ladies' Detective Agency by Alexander McCall Smith was published in 1998 and is the first in a series of five books including *Tears of the Giraffe*. It tells the story of the delightfully cunning and enormously engaging Precious Ramotswe, who wants to 'help people with problems in their lives.' Almost as soon as she sets up her detective agency business, she is hired to track down a missing husband, uncover a con man, follow a wayward daughter and find a missing child, who may have been snatched by witchdoctors.

In this lesson, Ss read three extracts from *The No.1 Ladies' Detective Agency*, in which the main character is setting up her own business. This leads to a grammar focus on *in case*. Ss then read and analyse a formal job application letter, finishing by writing one of their own.

OPTIONAL WARMER

Introduce the topic of novels. Discuss these questions with Ss.

Q: Have you read any novels in which the main character is particularly interesting or memorable? Give details.

Q: Have you read any novels which are set in a different country or a particularly interesting place? Give details.

Q: If you were asked to recommend a novel to a friend, which one would you recommend and why?

Reading

1a▶ Focus Ss on the book cover and get them to discuss the questions in pairs. Then get brief whole class feedback but do not accept or reject any ideas yet.

b▶ Get Ss to read extract 1 and check their ideas. Remind them to read quickly to find the answers to these questions but not to worry about other details at this stage. After briefly checking their answers in pairs, get whole class feedback.

> **Answers:** 1 The story is set in Botswana, Africa   2 The main character, Precious Ramotswe, starts her own business – a detective agency

c▶ Read through the lines with the class. Then get Ss to read the text again and explain each of the lines in their own words with a partner. Remind them to look at the context and the surrounding sentences to help them. Get whole class feedback.

> **Possible answers:** 1 People generally think that setting up your own business is easy but then find there are more problems and difficulties than you expected.   2 When she saw how much money she had inherited from her father, she found it was much more than she had expected.   3 She knew that she was going to have to start completely from the beginning with setting up her own business because nothing like this existed already.

2a▶ Read through the questions with the class. Then get Ss to discuss them in pairs. Do brief feedback on their ideas but do not accept or reject any ideas at this stage.

b▶ Get Ss to read extract 2 quickly and check their ideas. Again remind them not to worry about all the details but just focus on answering the two questions. After checking their ideas in pairs, get whole class feedback.

> **Answers:** 1 She finds an office and does it up and decorates it. She buys furniture for the office. She employs a secretary.   2 Not many problems. The office was sorted out quickly because she paid cash and she worked hard herself. She found it easy to find a secretary.

3▶ Get Ss to read extract 2 again and answer the questions. Get Ss to check their answers in pairs, then get whole class feedback.

> **Answers:**   1 curtains, two desks, two chairs and a typewriter   2 a secretary by phoning the local secretarial college   3 No, they weren't busy at first – perhaps because nobody knew about her agency.

4a▶ Get Ss to discuss the questions in pairs and then get brief feedback about their ideas.

b▶ Get Ss to read extract 3 on page 145 and check their ideas. Remind them to read quickly and focus only on answering the two questions. After checking in pairs, get whole class feedback.

> **Answers:** 1 Mma Ramotswe did not feel optimistic about her business. She was convinced there would be no clients and she would close in a month.   2 They did get a client on the first day of business (to their surprise).

c▶ Read the four headings with the class. Ask Ss to read extract 3 again and to write one sentence to summarise each heading. Encourage them to write concisely using one sentence only for each one. Get them to compare their sentences with a partner, then get whole class feedback.

> **Possible answers:** 1 Mma Makutsi seems to be an enthusiastic, well-qualified and professional worker.   2 Mma Ramotswe is hopeful but not very optimistic that her business will succeed.   3 Mma Ramotswe feels quite worried that her employee is too good for the job.   4 When Mma Makutsi 'hurtled through the door', she was excited about the arrival of the client and keen to do a professional job.

5▶ Get Ss to discuss the question in pairs or small groups. Even if Ss haven't started/thought of starting their own business, encourage them to think about the reasons why not; or to think about what specific difficulties they might have if they did. Get brief whole class feedback.

Grammar

OPTIONAL GRAMMAR LEAD-IN

Write the following two sentences on the board and ask Ss to work in pairs and complete them using an appropriate word/phrase (a different one for each sentence). You can help Ss by giving them *in case* and *if* and asking which goes in which sentence?).

1 *She would answer the phone _____ it rang.*

2 *She stayed in the office _____ the phone rang.*

(Answer: 1 *if* 2 *in case*)

6▶ Focus Ss on the examples in the Active grammar box. Then get them to work in pairs and choose the correct alternatives for the rules 1–4. Then get whole class feedback.

Active grammar

1a why somebody did something   2a precautions (things we do in order to be ready for a possible future situation)   3 emphatic   4 at the end

▶ You could clarify the difference between *in case* and *if*:

We use *in case* to say <u>why</u> someone does something. You do something now in case something happens later. *I'll give you my phone number in case you get lost.*

We use *if* to say what will/won't happen if something else (doesn't) happen. *If I get lost, I'll phone you.*

7▶ Get Ss to write sentences using the prompts and *in case*. Focus Ss on the example and remind them that they may need to change the verb tenses and to add words. Get them to check their answers in pairs before getting whole class feedback.

Answers: 1 I always write 'things to do' lists in case I forget something important.   2 I usually leave more time than I need to get to work in case the traffic is bad.   3 I always take a glass of water to bed in case I'm thirsty in the night.   4 I usually take a first aid kit on holiday just in case.   5 I'll give you my phone number in case you get lost.   6 He took his umbrella just in case it rained on the way to the interview.   7 I'll buy extra food in case the children are hungry after the football match.   8 You should write your address on your suitcase in case it gets lost.   9 I won't go out this evening just in case Daniela phones.   10 They wanted me to enter my email address twice in case I'd made a mistake the first time.

Person to person

8a▶ Get Ss to look again at sentences 1–4 in Ex. 7. They should work in pairs and tell each other if they are true for them or not. Get brief class feedback.

b▶ Get Ss to write four more sentences about themselves using *(just) in case*, including three which are true and one which is false. Remind them not to tell their partner which is false.

c▶ Tell Ss to read their sentences to a partner. They should then guess which of their partner's sentences is false. Get brief feedback by asking two or three Ss to report back on their partner's false sentence.

Writing

OPTIONAL WARMER

Tell Ss they are going to read an advert for an assistant manager for a new pizza restaurant. Ask them to work in pairs and make notes about what the advert might ask for (e.g. type of person, experience). Get brief whole class feedback but do not accept or reject any ideas at this stage.

Get Ss to read the advert in Ex. 9 and check their ideas. Get whole class feedback.

9▶ Get Ss to read the job advert (if you didn't do the optional warmer) and the letter of application and answer the questions. Ss should then compare their answers in pairs before getting whole class feedback.

Answers: 1 Experience as a waitress in three different restaurants/cafés and she is very keen, hard-working and sociable.   2 Her aim for the future is to open her own restaurant.   3 It is a good letter of application (appropriate layout, good organisation, formal language and appropriate content – what was asked for in the advert).

10▶ Get Ss to read the letter again and match the descriptions 1–4 with the correct paragraph in the letter. Get whole class feedback.

Answers: Correct order: 4, 2, 3, 1

b▶ Check that Ss understand that this type of formal letter uses more formal language. Read through the informal language in the table with the class. Ask Ss to complete the table with the formal equivalent expressions from the letter. Get Ss to check their answers in pairs. Then get whole class feedback.

Answers: 2 I am writing to apply for the job.   3 I believe that I have gained valuable experience.   4 I feel that I would be suitable for the job.   5 I am particularly interested in this job.   6 I can be contacted on the phone number above.   7 I look forward to hearing from you.   8 Yours sincerely,

Check that Ss understand that when we use formal language,

a) there are some 'set' expressions (e.g. *Yours sincerely*)

b) we don't use contractions (e.g. *I am writing*)

c) we use more formal vocabulary (e.g. *gained, suitable*)

11▶ Get Ss to choose one of the job adverts on page 151. Ask them to write a formal letter of application. Remind them to use the paragraph plan and the language as appropriate in Ex. 10. Set a word limit of 120 words.

Vocabulary: Collocations with prepositions

In this lesson, Ss focus on collocations with prepositions, including both adjective + preposition (e.g. *proud of*) and verb + preposition (e.g. *apply for*).

OPTIONAL WARMER

Write the word *in* on the board and ask Ss what type of word grammatically it is (a preposition). Get Ss to write a list of ten prepositions as fast as they can. They should put their hands up when finished.

Ss compare their lists in pairs. Then get class feedback, writing up all the prepositions (e.g. *from, about, with, at, by, into, onto, over, under, before, after, for, off ... .*)

1 ▶ Tell Ss that some adjectives collocate with particular prepositions. (You may need to explain that collocate means 'go together for no particular reason' and that Ss just have to learn which ones go together). Tell Ss to complete the sentences using the correct preposition which collocates with the adjective in bold. After checking their answers in pairs, get whole class feedback.

> **Answers:** 1 in 2 about 3 of 4 about 5 on
> 6 to 7 from 8 at 9 of 10 about

2 ▶ Tell Ss that some verbs also collocate with particular prepositions. Get them to complete the sentences with the correct preposition from the box which collocates with the verb in bold. Ss check answers in pairs. Get class feedback.

> **Answers:** 1 for 2 from 3 on 4 for 5 in
> 6 about 7 for 8 on 9 in 10 of

3a ▶ Get Ss to match the sentence halves 1–8 with a–h. Tell them that some of them are adjectives and some of them are verbs and that they should try to do it without looking back at Ex. 1 and Ex. 2.

b ▶ Play recording 2.8 and get Ss to check their answers.

> **Answers:** 1 j 2 e 3 d 4 b 5 i 6 a 7 g 8 h 9 c 10 f

4 ▶ Get Ss to complete the questions with the correct preposition. Ss check in pairs. Get class feedback.

> **Answers:** 1 for 2 on 3 about 4 to/from 5 at
> 6 on 7 on 8 for 9 about 10 of

5 ▶ Tell Ss to choose five of the questions in Ex. 4 that they would like to ask their partner. Get Ss asking and answering their questions in pairs. Get brief whole class feedback, asking two or three Ss to report back on their most interesting question/answer.

OPTIONAL EXTENSION

Get Ss to stand up and mingle and ask different questions from Ex. 4 to as many Ss as possible. They then report back briefly to the whole class on their most interesting question/answer.

Communication: The best candidate

In this lesson, Ss talk about their experiences of job and/or university interviews, how they might feel about interviews and how they can prepare properly for them. Ss then listen to parts of four different interviews and finish by roleplaying an interview situation for a job or a place on a course.

OPTIONAL WARMER

Play a quick game of Word Association.

Write the word *interview* on the board and ask Ss to work in pairs and write down any words/phrases that come into their heads associated with *interview.* (They should not think about it too much.)

Get whole class feedback and write the words up on the board. (e.g.: *job, nervous, smart suit, interviewer.*)

1 ▶ Get Ss to discuss the questions in pairs. Then get whole class feedback.

2a ▶ Get Ss to discuss the question in pairs. Then get whole class feedback, encouraging Ss to justify their answers particularly for the more controversial ones.

> **Answers:** The positive ones are: 4, 6, 9, 10

b ▶ Get Ss to discuss the question in pairs or small groups, encouraging them to give details from their own experience. Get class feedback, asking two or three Ss to report back about another student's experience.

3a ▶ Read through the questions with the class. Play recording 2.9 and tell Ss to listen to parts of interviews with four different candidates and answer the questions. Ss check their answers in pairs. Get whole class feedback.

> **Answers: Karen:** job interview/7 – she talked about her previous experience in a negative way
> **Jenny:** university interview/1 – she was late
> **Liz:** university interview/5 – she didn't prepare for the interviewer's questions   **Linda:** job interview/probably 4

b ▶ Tell Ss to try to complete the interviewer's sentences with a partner. Then play recording 2.10 and get Ss to listen and check their answers.

> **Answers:** 1 applying 2 about 3 office
> 4 interviewing 5 reasons 6 plans

4 ▶ Get Ss to work in pairs and choose one of the adverts on page 146. They then prepare for the interview by each following the relevant instructions for the interviewees and the interviewers. They could write notes but should not write out the whole interview. (You could ask two of the 'interviewees' to work together at this stage to help each other. Similarly for the 'interviewers'.)

5a ▶ Get Ss to work in their pairs and roleplay their interview. They may use their notes if necessary.

b ▶ Tell Ss to change roles and prepare and roleplay another interview, following the instructions and making notes.

c ▶ Get whole class feedback by asking Ss the question and encouraging them to justify and explain their reasons.

Review and practice

1▶

> **Answers:** 1 'm going to watch   2 'll have   3 's going to   4 'll go and get   5 'm meeting   6 'll be   7 're going to have   8 'm playing

2▶

> **Answers:**
>
> Sat. 23rd
>
> Hi Antonio,
>
> I can hardly believe it – but by next Friday afternoon, I'll have finished all my exams! Until then, I'm completely up to my eyes in revision. I'll be revising for my exams the whole of this weekend and then every spare minute I get next week. I really can't wait to get them all out of the way.
>
> I'm really excited though, because I've booked a holiday for immediately after. In fact, this time next week, I'll be waiting for my flight to Crete. I'm going with Daniel – we've both been there before and loved it. After this holiday, we'll have been there four times! Anyway, that's why I'm writing really. I just wanted to know if you'll have left your job by then. If you have, why don't you come with us? I know it's short notice, but it would be great if you could come.
>
> Let me know as soon as you can. Either email me or phone anytime. I won't be going to bed early tonight because I've got so much to do. Really hope you can come.
>
> Gianni

3▶

> **Answers:** 1 detail   2 retirement   3 initiative   4 quality   5 surgeon   6 voluntary   7 redundant   8 deadlines

4▶

> **Answers:** 1 complains about   2 worried about   3 succeeded in   4 depends on   5 prepared for   6 modest about

Notes for using the Common European Framework (CEF)

CEF References

2.1 Can do: talk about future plans and make predictions

CEF B2 descriptor: Can give clear, detailed descriptions on a wide range of subjects related to his/her field of interest. (CEF page 59)

2.2 Can do: do a survey and report the results

CEF B2 descriptor: Can synthesise and report information and arguments from a number of sources. (CEF page 81)

2.3 Can do: write a formal letter of application

CEF B2 descriptor: Can express news and views effectively in writing, and relate to those of others. (CEF page 83)

CEF quick brief

The Common European Framework is produced by the Council of Europe. The Council of Europe is concerned with issues like human rights, European identity, education and more. This identity is based on diversity and the Common European Framework gives equal importance to all languages of Council of Europe member nations.

Portfolio task

Download the Total English Portfolio free from www.longman.com/totalenglish.

Objective: help Ss to use the Portfolio to assess their skills.

This task can be done in Ss' own language.

▶ Portfolios are divided into three main sections. The first section is called the 'Passport'. The Passport is designed to summarise relevant language learning experiences and qualifications. This can be shown to others, for example new teachers, employers, etc. Firstly, however, it is helpful for learners to give their own assessment of their abilities in the different skills areas.

1▶ Help Ss to understand the self-assessment grids (there are many translations available as this is a standard document) for levels A1 to B1.

2▶ Ask Ss to assess their own abilities in the different skills areas (listening, reading, spoken interaction, spoken production, and writing). Ss complete the language skills profile by shading in the relevant boxes.

3▶ Explain that Ss can update this profile as they progress and they can fill in profiles for other languages.

3 Old or new

Overview

Summary

Lesson 1: Ss read two texts: the story of the Trojan War and a film review of the recent film *Troy* (based on the story of the Trojan War). Ss then discuss different heroes and write a short story about a hero or heroine.

Lesson 2: Ss listen to a radio programme about China, including facts about life in both ancient and modern times. Ss also focus on inventions and materials, finishing with a discussion about what are the most important inventions.

Lesson 3: Ss read part of a newspaper article and two letters in response to the article about 'the good old days' and how much globalisation and changes in society have affected our lives. Ss then give a presentation about a city they know.

Vocabulary: Ss focus on making nouns, looking at the different suffixes we can use (e.g. *-tion, -ness*).

Communication: Ss listen to someone talking about what he has learned in life and Ss discuss what they have learned in their lives. This leads to a discussion about the importance (or not) of history.

> **Film bank: Film heroes** (6'48")
>
> Extracts from two old adventure films, focussing on the heroes, Sinbad and Ben-Hur.
>
> *The Seventh Voyage of Sinbad*, made in 1958, is most famous for it's monsters and other special effects which are still considered to be spectacular despite the age of the film. *Ben-hur,* made in 1959, stars Charlton Heston and is regarded as a classic, being the first film ever to win eleven Oscars.
>
> Possible places to use this short film are:
> ► After Lesson 1 to extend the topic of heroes/stories/old films or as practice of narrative tenses
> ► At the end of the unit to round up the topic and language
>
> For ways to use this short film in class, see Students' Book page 154 and Teacher's Book page 180.

Lead-in

> **OPTIONAL WARMER**
>
> Introduce the topic of old and new. Ask Ss to think about a place they know well and discuss what they know about: a) one of the oldest buildings and b) one of the newest buildings.
>
> Prompt Ss by asking questions (e.g. *Where is it? When was it built? What's it for? Who built it? Is it open to the public? What do you like about it?*)

1 ► Focus Ss on the photos and get Ss to discuss the questions in pairs. If Ss do not know what/where the places are, you could give them some of the information below. Get whole class feedback.

> **Answers:** A about 3000 BC   B about 1960 AD   C about 440 BC   D about 2000 AD
>
> A **The Parthenon in Athens, Greece** is the most important and characteristic monument of ancient Greek civilization and is dedicated to Athena Parthenos, the patron goddess of Athens.   B **Sydney Opera House in Sydney, Australia** is in Sydney harbour and has become an Australian icon. In the late 1950s, a competition was held for its design. The winner was Danish architect, Jorn Utzon whose evocative design of a ship at full sail creates a dramatic view.   C **The Great Pyramids in Giza, near Cairo, Egypt** are an extraordinary feat of building skill and engineering. The largest one was built as the tomb of Egyptian king, Khufu. It is about 138 metres high (by far the tallest building in the world until very recently) and contains 2,300,000 blocks (the average weight of each is 2.5 tons).   D **The London Eye, in London, England, UK** or the Millennium Wheel, is the first-built and largest 'observation wheel' in the world standing 135 metres high. The wheel carries thirty-two passenger capsules and one revolution takes thirty minutes to complete.

2a ► Explain to Ss that different adjectives collocate with the things in the table. Get Ss to work in pairs to find the three incorrect underlined adjectives in the questions. Remind them to use the table and a dictionary to help. Get whole class feedback.

> **Answers:** 1 antique   4 old   6 ancient

b ► Get Ss to work in pairs and ask and answer the questions together. Get brief class feedback by asking Ss to report back on one of their questions/answers.

> **EXTEND THE LEAD-IN**
>
> Get Ss to give a mini-talk about one of the things in the table in Ex. 2a.
>
> Give them a few ideas of what to talk about (e.g. an elderly relative). Get to make Ss notes to prepare. Then get them to give the mini-talk to a partner.
>
> Finish by asking a few Ss to report back to the class on what their partner told them.

3.1 Heroes

Stories in books and films – old and new – are full of famous heroes and heroines. The Greek poet Homer wrote the story of the Trojan War in his book *The Iliad* (in the 8th century BC). It is a story of love as well as war and the main hero is the legendary warrior, Achilles who while fighting on behalf of King Agamemnon seeks his own glory. The story has been retold throughout the generations, most recently in the form of the film *Troy*, made in 2004 and starring Brad Pitt.

In this lesson, Ss read two texts: the first is the story of the Trojan War and the second is a film review of the film *Troy*. Ss then focus on the grammar of narrative tenses and discuss different heroes from history (Hannibal), fiction (Shakespeare's Romeo and Juliet) and real life (e.g. famous people like Princess Diana and 'ordinary' people like firefighters). Ss finish by writing a short story about a hero or heroine.

> **OPTIONAL WARMER**
>
> Write these words on the board and get Ss to discuss what they think the difference is between them.
>
> *a hero   a celebrity   a champion   an idol*
>
> If you think Ss need more guidance; either, ask them to use dictionaries to look up definitions and then compare them; or, give them these definitions and ask them to match them to the correct word.
>
> *A person who is admired for doing something extremely brave (a hero).*
>
> *A living person who is famous and often in the news (a celebrity).*
>
> *A person who has won a competition especially in sport (a champion).*
>
> *A person who is loved and admired (an idol.)*

Reading

1 ▶ Get Ss to discuss the first question in pairs or small groups. Then get whole class feedback, asking two or three Ss to report back their ideas to the class. Then ask Ss to discuss the second question and get whole class feedback but do not accept or reject any of their ideas at this stage.

2a ▶ Focus Ss on the pictures and read through the questions with the class. Tell Ss to read the text quickly and answer the questions. Then get them to check their answers in pairs before getting whole class feedback.

> **Answers:** 1 King Menelaus of Sparta; Helen (Menelaus's wife); King Agamemnon of Greece (Menelaus's brother); King Priam of Troy; Prince Hector (Priam's eldest son); Paris (Hector's brother); Achilles (Greek warrior fighting for Agamemnon)   2 Achilles (described as 'a hugely skilled and heroic soldier')

b ▶ Tell Ss to read the text again and answer the questions, encouraging them to correct the false statements. Get them to check their answers in pairs. Then get whole class feedback.

> **Answers:** 1 F (it's also about love and passion)   2 F (the purpose was to put their troubles behind them and look forward to a better future together in peace)   3 T   4 T   5 F (Achilles didn't want to help Agamemnon. He only wanted to become famous himself)

3 ▶ Remind Ss that Homer's story was made into a film called *Troy* in 2004 and tell them that they are going to read a review of the film. Tell Ss to read the film review on page 146 and answer the questions. Ss should briefly check answers in pairs. Get class feedback.

> **Answers:** 1 Hector (played by Eric Bana – 'far more heroic than anyone else')   2 generally positive

4 ▶ Ss read the text on page 146 again and complete the notes. They check answers in pairs. Get class feedback.

> **Answers:** 1 the horrors and brutality of war   2 how the events affect the people   3 Achilles and Hector   4 2,000   5 Hector   6 final fight between Hector and Achilles   7 It's not exactly the same as the original story in the Iliad.   8 very good ('an impressive film'/ 'four stars out of five')

5 ▶ Get Ss to discuss the questions in pairs or small groups. Get whole class feedback by asking each group to report back on one point they discussed.

Grammar

> **OPTIONAL GRAMMAR LEAD-IN**
>
> Write these sentences on the board, reminding Ss that they are from the first text on the Trojan War.
>
> *Trade _____ and many cities _____ into ruins.*
>
> *Secretly, while the guests _____ the feast, Paris and Helen _____ the party together.*
>
> Ss work together to complete the sentences without looking back at the text. If the Ss need more help, give them the verbs: *leave, fall, enjoy* and *decline*.
>
> Get whole class feedback and remind Ss that these are all narrative tenses and used for telling stories.
>
> (*had been declining; had fallen; were enjoying; left*)

6a ▶ Get Ss to match the underlined verbs in the Active grammar box to the list of narrative tenses A–D. Get whole class feedback.

> **Answers:**   had been declining – D; had fallen – C; were enjoying – B; left – A

b ▶ Get Ss to complete each explanation in the Active grammar box by writing the name of the correct narrative tense A–D.

> **Active grammar**
>
> 1 Past Simple   2 Past Perfect Simple   3 Past Continuous   4 Past Perfect Continuous

c ▶ Get Ss to look back at the first two paragraphs of the text about the Trojan War in Ex. 2. Tell them to find and underline more examples of narrative tenses with a partner. Then get whole class feedback.

> **Answers:** Past Simple: decided, fell, was, ordered; Past ontinuous: were looking; Past Perfect Simple: had been able; Past Perfect Continuous: had been fighting

7a ▶ Focus Ss briefly on the picture and tell them that the story in this exercise is about Hannibal (a hero from ancient times who used elephants in battle). Tell Ss to choose the best alternative for each verb form. Ss check their answers in pairs. Do not get class feedback yet.

b ▶ Get Ss to listen to the story (recording 3.1), and check their answers. Get whole class feedback.

> **Answers:** 1 had been 2 had been trading 3 had been 4 had taken 5 hadn't managed 6 decided 7 was 8 was marching 9 joined 10 reached 11 had died 12 won

Person to person

> **OPTIONAL WARMER**
>
> Write *Romeo and Juliet* on the board and ask Ss to brainstorm what they know about it.
>
> (One of Shakespeare's most famous plays; a tragedy written in 1594–5. The hero and heroine are lovers who come from families who are 'at war' with each other. The story was most recently made into a film in 1996, directed by Baz Luhrmann and starring Leonardo DiCaprio as Romeo.)

8a ▶ Tell Ss that they are going to tell the story of Romeo and Juliet. Divide the class into Student As and Student Bs. Tell the As to look at page 147 and work together in pairs using the notes to practise telling their part of the story. Bs should do the same on page 148.

b ▶ Organise Ss to work in pairs with one A and one B in each pair. Get them to tell the story of Romeo and Juliet together taking turns as indicated in the notes. Remind them to use narrative tenses as appropriate.

Vocabulary

> **OPTIONAL WARMER**
>
> Write on the board: 1 *While the guests were enjoying themselves, Paris and Helen left the party.* 2 *For the previous few centuries, the two kings had been fighting.*
>
> Ask Ss if the underlined parts of the sentences refer to: A a time before, B a time after, C a specific time, D actions at the same time. (*While* = D; *For the previous few centuries* = A)
>
> Elicit that these are time expressions.

9a ▶ Get Ss to work in pairs and look at the underlined expressions in the box and decide what each one refers to (a, b, c or d). Get whole class feedback.

> **Answers:** a) *For the previous few centuries, Up until that point, Until*   b) *After that, From that point on, Since then*   c) *In the 8th century BC, At that time, In 218 BC*   d) *While, throughout, During*

b ▶ Ss should work in pairs and try to add any other expressions to the box, thinking again about what each one refers to.

10 ▶ Ask Ss to choose the correct alternative in each sentence. Ss should check their answers in pairs. Then get whole class feedback.

> **Answers:** 1 During 2 From that point on 3 For 4 in 5 throughout 6 Up until that point 7 Since then 8 until 9 At that time 10 While

11a ▶ Get Ss to complete the sentences about themselves, encouraging them to write interesting information.

b ▶ Get Ss to compare their sentences with a partner. Tell them to give one or two more details about each sentence. They could also ask each other further questions. Get whole class feedback by asking two or three Ss to report back on one thing their partner said.

Writing

12 ▶ Get Ss to discuss the questions in pairs or small groups, encouraging them to give reasons for their opinions. Get whole class feedback and see if Ss have similar or very different opinions.

13a ▶ Tell Ss that they are going to write a short story about a hero or heroine and ask them to choose one person from the list. You could refer them back to previous discussions to remind them about the different options. Tell them not to tell other Ss which hero or heroine they have chosen (as they will have to guess this later).

b ▶ Get Ss to write brief notes about the events and the characters in the story. Remind them to write notes and not the whole story at this stage.

c ▶ Get Ss to divide their notes into three paragraphs using the paragraph plan.

14a ▶ Tell Ss to write their story using the notes and the paragraph plan. Remind them not to write the name of the hero in their story, but just to use *he/she* and other appropriate nouns, e.g. *the person, the heroine*). Remind them to use narrative tenses and time expressions as appropriate.

b ▶ Get Ss to work with a partner and read his/her story. Ask them if they can guess the name of the hero/heroine their partner has written about. Get brief whole class feedback by asking how many Ss guessed the hero/heroine in their partner's story.

3.2 Land of invention

China is a huge country with an incredibly long and rich history. One of the things ancient China is famous for is being a 'land of invention', credited with inventing many important things, from paper and umbrellas to cast iron and gunpowder. Modern China is a fascinating place too, with 1.3 billion people – a staggering one fifth of the world's population. Agriculture has always been important, but now there are many booming industries too, including production of such things as toys, clothes, cars and electronic goods.
For more information about China, go to: http://www.lonelyplanet.com/worldguide/destinations/asia/china/

In this lesson, Ss listen to a radio programme about China, including facts about life in both ancient and modern times. Ss also focus on possessions, inventions and the materials they are made of, listening to people talking about various possessions. They finish the lesson with a discussion about inventions (such as the TV, the wheel and the light bulb) and decide which are the most important.

> **OPTIONAL WARMER**
>
> Introduce the topic of possessions and objects (which will lead into materials and inventions later).
>
> Ask Ss to work in pairs and ask about three of each other's possessions (e.g. *bag, watch, jacket, hat, pen, iPod*). Tell them they have one minute for each object to find out as much as they can.
>
> You might want to do an example first: Use one student and ask about one of his/her possessions.
>
> *How long have you had that bag? Was it a present? Who gave it to you? Why? Where did you buy it? What do you like about it?*
>
> Get whole class feedback by asking various Ss to report back on one of their partner's objects they asked about.

Vocabulary

1a▶ Get Ss to focus on the pictures. Ss should work in pairs and describe the objects in the pictures using the words in box. Get whole class feedback, checking Ss understand all the words.

b▶ Get Ss to work in pairs and see if they know how to pronounce the words in the box. Then play recording 3.2 and get Ss to check their answers. You could get Ss to repeat the words too.

c▶ Ask Ss to work with a partner and add four more materials to the box. Get whole class feedback, making sure that Ss understand all the new words.

2▶ Get Ss to think of five things they own. Tell them to work in pairs and describe them to each other using the words from Ex. 1. If you did the optional warmer, you could remind Ss to use some of the objects they talked about.

3a▶ Get Ss to match the adjectives with their definitions. After Ss have checked their answers in pairs, get whole class feedback. You could refer back to the objects in the pictures or those that Ss have described for further checks on meaning.

> **Answers:** 1 e 2 f 3 g 4 a 5 b 6 c 7 h 8 d

b▶ Tell Ss to complete the sentences with the most appropriate adjective from the box. Then get Ss to check in pairs but do not get whole class feedback yet.

> **Answers:** 1 slippery 2 smooth 3 furry 4 itchy 5 shiny 6 stretchy 7 rough 8 soft

4▶ Tell Ss to think of an object they have used that day, explaining that they don't have to have the object with them (e.g. *a kettle, money, a bus ticket*). Get Ss to work with a partner and try to guess each other's object by asking *yes/no* questions. Tell them the questions should contain the materials and adjectives in the previous exercises (e.g. *Is it made of leather? Is it stretchy?*). You might want to do an example yourself to start them off.

Listening and speaking

5a▶ Play recording 3.3 and tell Ss to write down which objects and materials are mentioned in each one. After briefly checking answers in pairs, get whole class feedback.

> **Answers:** 1 jumper/jacket/wool/cotton 2 jeans/denim/lycra 3 earrings/silver/gold 4 toy train/computer games/wood/plastic 5 coats/shoes/bags/fur/leather

b▶ Play recording 3.3 again and get Ss to answer the questions for each dialogue. Get Ss to check their answers in pairs and then get whole class feedback.

> **Answers:** 1 Wool makes her skin itchy. 2 They're stretchy and comfortable. 3 She's allergic to her earrings. 4 toys made of wood 5 She doesn't eat or wear any animal products e.g. leather shoes.

6▶ Get Ss to discuss the questions in pairs or small groups. Get whole class feedback by asking each group to report on one of the questions.

Listening

> **OPTIONAL WARMER**
>
> Introduce the topic of China by asking Ss to try to answer these questions in pairs. Encourage them to have a guess even if they don't know.
>
> **Q: What's the population of China?** (1.3 billion)
> **Q: What percentage of the world's population lives in China?** (20%)
> **Q: What's the capital city of China?** (Beijing)
> **Q: What is/are the official language(s) of China?** (Mandarin and Cantonese – also many dialects)
> **Q: What's the most important festival?** (Chinese New Year–usually in February, lasting three days)

7a▶ Get Ss to work in pairs or small groups and discuss what things they associate with modern-day and ancient China. Get whole class feedback and write their ideas on the board.

b ▶ Play recording 3.4 and ask Ss to say if the speakers mention any of the things they talked about. Get whole class feedback, checking with the ideas that you wrote up on the board.

8 ▶ Play recording 3.4 again and get Ss to answer the questions. Tell Ss to check their answers in pairs, encouraging them to correct the ones which are false. Get whole class feedback.

> **Answers:** 1 true   2 false (only in recent years, it's started to flourish economically)   3 false (around 105 AD)   4 true   5 don't know (loads could be carried by one person, but doesn't say who invented it)   6 true   7 true   8 false (15% of the economy is based on agriculture)   9 don't know (these things are produced but we don't know if they are exported)   10 true   11 don't know (it is growing but we don't know by how much)   12 true

9 ▶ Get Ss to discuss the questions in pairs or small groups. Then get whole class feedback by asking two or three Ss to report back to the class.

Grammar

> **OPTIONAL GRAMMAR LEAD-IN**
>
> Write these groups of sentences on the board and ask Ss which one in each group is correct. (Group A–2; Group B–1).
>
> A 1 *China is huge country.* 2 *China is a huge country.* 3 *China is the huge country.*
>
> B 1 *Rice is an important export.* 2 *A rice is an important export.* 3 *The rice is an important export.*
>
> Ask Ss what words they are focussing on in these sentences (Articles). You could also check that Ss know specific terms (*the* = definite article; *a/an* = indefinite article; no article = zero article).

10 ▶ Focus Ss on the Active grammar box. Ask them to complete the box with the underlined words from the tapescript on page 168. Get Ss to check their answers in pairs. Then get whole class feedback.

> **Active grammar**
>
> 1 the gun   2 the Chinese   3 the simplest
> 4 the story   5 a machine   6 China   7 paper

11 ▶ Get Ss to complete the sentences using *the*, *a/an* or the zero article. Ss should check answers in pairs. Then get whole class feedback.

> **Answers:** 1 The/–   2 The/the   3 –/an/the   4 The/the   5 a/the   6 a/a/The   7 The/–   8 a/–

Person to person

12a ▶ Ask Ss to choose one of the topics in the list to talk about. Tell them to think about what they are going to say and make some notes if necessary.

b ▶ Get Ss to work in pairs and take turns to talk about the topics they chose. Remind them to think about appropriate use of articles. You could get brief whole class feedback by asking one person in each group to report back.

Speaking

13a ▶ Tell Ss they are going to listen to two people talking and read the questions through with the class. Play recording 3.5 and get them to answer the questions. After briefly checking answers in pairs, get whole class feedback.

> **Answers:** 1 they have to decide the three most important inventions ever   2 light bulb

b ▶ Focus Ss on the How to … box. Play recording 3.5 again and get Ss to complete the questions in the How to … box. Ask Ss to check their answers in pairs. Then get whole class feedback.

> **Answers:** 1 What do you <u>think</u>?   2 What <u>about</u> you?   3 What <u>else</u> do you think is important?   4 Do you <u>agree</u> that …?   5 How do you <u>feel</u> about …?   6 Isn't it <u>true</u> that …?

14a ▶ Tell Ss to look at the inventions in the box and decide which three are the most important, making brief notes about their reasons.

b ▶ Get Ss to work in pairs or small groups and to try to agree on the three most important inventions. Remind them to use the language in the How to … box as appropriate. You might want to give them a time limit (e.g. three minutes). Get whole class feedback by asking each group to report back on what they agreed on.

> **OPTIONAL EXTENSION**
>
> After the Ss have agreed on the three most important inventions in their pairs, get each pair to join up with another pair. Now tell them to agree in this group of four, again giving them a time limit. You could then get each group of four to join up with another group. Again, tell them to agree in this larger group, giving them a time limit.
>
> Eventually, you might want to have a whole class discussion and get the whole class to agree on the three most important inventions. Remind them to try to communicate interactively, using language from the How to … box at each stage.

Lifelong learning

Focus Ss on the first question in the box. Get them to discuss questions 1 and 2 in pairs or small groups. Get whole class feedback encouraging Ss to give reasons for their opinions.

3.3 The good old days?

Over the last few decades, the phenomenon of globalisation has changed the world. Many people now complain that 'every High Street is the same' with the same shops appearing in High Streets in London, Tokyo, Moscow and Buenos Aires. Some people fear that the individual character and culture of different countries is being eroded and that the world is becoming too uniform. Others view it differently, however, seeing globalisation as a positive thing, with increased choice and diversity available to a much larger number of people.

In this lesson, Ss read part of a newspaper article about globalisation and the so-called 'good old days'. They then do a jigsaw reading of two letters which respond to the article, followed by a discussion of their own opinions about how much these changes have affected our lives. After focussing on the grammar of adjectives and adverbs, Ss give a short presentation about a city they know, including facts about its history, how it has changed and major tourist attractions.

OPTIONAL WARMER

Introduce the topic of the 'old days'. Ask Ss to think about their parents (and/or grandparents) and to discuss these questions. You may want to do an example about your own parents (and/or grandparents) to give them the idea.

Q: What kind of place did they grow up in (e.g. a quiet village, a large city)
Q: What kind of shops and other facilities (e.g. shopping centres, swimming pools) did they have?
Q: What did they do in their spare time (e.g. TV, sports)?
Q: What kind of holidays did they have?

If possible, you could bring in some photos or ask Ss to bring in photos to show different aspects of how their parents' and grandparents' generations lived.

Reading

1 ▶ Get Ss to discuss the question in pairs or small groups. You could give them some more ideas to get them going (e.g. food and restaurants, clothes and fashion, music, sport, languages, travel/holidays, TV programmes and films, technology). And/or, if you did the optional warmer, remind Ss to think about the ideas they discussed then. Do brief whole class feedback and write some of the main ideas on the board.

2 ▶ Tell Ss to read the extract from a newspaper article and say if the writer mentions any of their ideas from the previous discussion. Ss should briefly check their ideas in pairs. Then get whole class feedback.

Answers: Topics mentioned are: food/restaurants, clothes/fashion, music, languages, travel/holidays

3 ▶ Tell Ss that they are going to read two different letters which were written in response to the newspaper article. Read the three summary sentences (A, B and C) through with the class. Divide the class into As and Bs and tell the As to read the text on page 147 and the Bs to read the text on page 148. Student have to choose the correct summary sentence. Tell them to check their answers with another student who read the same text. Then get whole class feedback.

Answers: Text A – sentence C;   Text B – sentence A

4 ▶ Ss should stay in pairs (formed of students who read the same text). Get them to read their text and answer the appropriate questions, checking their answers together. You might need to monitor or help with any difficulties but do not get whole class feedback at this stage.

Answers:
Text A: 1 mostly disagrees   2 'the tyranny of geography' – when people had restricted choice according to where they lived   3 There is a huge amount of choice in his high street.   4 to show that there are shops from many different countries in one high street   5 He says we can now choose much more how we want to be and what we want to do (not defined by our nationality/place we live).

Text B: 1 mostly disagrees   2 She says that different variations of food are being created and that is good.   3 no   4 a type of English which is used for people to communicate with other non-native speakers   5 A single language is when everyone speaks one language e.g. English, and a common language is when people speak their own language but can also speak English, so can communicate with each other.

5 ▶ Regroup the pairs so that Student A is working with Student B. Get Ss to tell each other about the text they read, using their answers from Ex. 4, and to discuss the questions in Ex. 2.

6 ▶ Get Ss to work in different pairs or small groups and discuss the question. Get brief whole class feedback encouraging them to give reasons for their opinions.

Grammar

OPTIONAL GRAMMAR LEAD-IN

Write these two sentences on the board and ask Ss what the difference is between the underlined words and why. (*strong* = an adjective, describing the noun 'opinions'; *strongly* = an adverb describing the verb 'disagree').

I have *strong* opinions about this.

I disagree *strongly* with what he's saying.

Then, write these words on the board and ask Ss to put them into two groups: **adjectives** and **adverbs**. (Answers are in brackets).

differently (**adv.**), *good* (**adj.**), *ugly* (**adj.**), *well* (**adv.**), *different* (**adj.**), *never* (**adv.**), *hard* (**adj./adv.**)

7a ▶ Get Ss to complete rules 1 and 2 in the Active grammar box. If necessary, tell them to find examples in the texts on pages 40, 147 and 148. Ss should briefly check their answers in pairs. Then get whole class feedback.

> **Active grammar**
>
> 1 Adjectives are used to modify **nouns**
>
> 2 Position of adjectives: usually directly **before** the noun

b ▶ Read through rule 3 with the class. You may need to explain/remind Ss that we can use adverbial phrases as well as adverbs (e.g. *in the corner, last year*) and that there are different positions for adverbs (and adverbial phrases) in a sentence. Tell them to look at the underlined adverbs and adverbial phrases in the texts on pages 40, 147 and 148 and to write them in the correct place in the Active grammar box. After checking in pairs, get whole class feedback.

> **Active grammar**
>
> A However B Recently C truly/almost
> D generally E wildly F strongly G with interest
> H throughout the world I all the time

8 ▶ Get Ss to decide if the underlined words are adjectives or adverbs. Refer them back to rules 1 and 3 in the Active grammar box if necessary.

> **Answers:** 1 lovely = adjective; lonely = adjective
> 2 lively = adjective; silly = adjective
> 3 fine = adjective/adverb 4 deadly = adjective
> 5 high = adverb; well = adverb 6 (got up) early =
> adverb; early (train)= adjective 7 friendly = adjective;
> ugly = adjective

9 ▶ Get Ss to write the missing adverb or adverbial phrase in the correct place in the sentences. Remind them that sometimes two different places may be possible and refer them back to rule 4 in the Active grammar box. After checking their answers in pairs, get whole class feedback.

> **Answers:** 1 I **definitely** want to try the local food when I'm in Thailand. 2 I **accidentally** spilt my coffee all over my new jacket. (or: I spilt my coffee all over my new jacket **accidentally**.) 3 I work in a really modern building **on the 19th floor**. 4 I went on a tour of the six capital cities in Europe **last month**. (or: **Last month** I went on a tour of the six capital cities in Europe.) 5 My grandmother has **never** been on an aeroplane in her whole life. 6 The new building is **expertly** designed to be both attractive and practical.

Person to person

10a ▶ Get Ss to complete the pairs of sentences using the correct alternatives. Ss should briefly check in pairs. Then get whole class feedback.

> **Answers:** 1a completely b complete
> 2a definitely b definite 3a late b lately

b ▶ Ask Ss to discuss the questions with a partner. Get brief whole class feedback by asking one student to report back about each question.

Vocabulary

11 ▶ Read through sentences 1–8 with the class. Tell Ss to match the underlined verb phrases with the definitions a–h. If necessary, remind them to do the easier ones first and then go back to the more difficult ones. Get them to check their answers in pairs. Then get whole class feedback.

> **Answers:** 1 f 2 d 3 h 4 e 5 a 6 c 7 g 8 b

12 ▶ Get Ss to complete the sentences with the correct form of the phrases in Ex. 11. After checking in pairs, get whole class feedback.

> **Answers:** 1 take to 2 take it for granted 3 take part in 4 take over 5 take your breath away 6 took off 7 take it in their stride 8 take in

13 ▶ Get Ss to discuss the questions in pairs or small groups. Get whole class feedback by asking each group to report back on the question they enjoyed discussing the most.

Speaking

14a ▶ Tell Ss that they are going to give a short presentation about a city they know (their own city or another). Get them to make notes to prepare for their presentation, using the points listed. Remind them to write just notes (not the whole 'script') and to include adjectives and adverbs where appropriate.

b ▶ Tell Ss that they are going to practise giving their presentation by working with a partner. Tell them to look at the questions, listen to their partner's presentation and give each other feedback. Give Ss some time to make any necessary changes/improvements to their presentations.

15 ▶ Get Ss to give their presentations to the class, using their notes or from memory. To finish, ask the class which of the places they heard about would they most like to visit and why.

> **OPTIONAL EXTENSION**
>
> Ss could write up their presentation in the form of a short essay.

Vocabulary: making nouns

In this lesson, Ss focus on making nouns, using common noun endings. Ss are reminded that this type of word building is a good way of building up their vocabulary.

> **OPTIONAL WARMER**
>
> Write on the board: *neighbourhood, happiness, journalist*. Ask Ss what kind of words they are and how they know (nouns/they have noun endings).
>
> In pairs, Ss write a list of as many noun endings as they can, and an example for each. Get class feedback.

1 ▶ If you did the optional warmer, get Ss to look through the rules and see which ones they thought of and which they did not. Get Ss to work in pairs, read the rules and examples and write more examples. Get class feedback writing the new words on the board.

2 ▶ Get Ss to complete the sentences with the correct noun form by using the word in bold. Get Ss working in pairs and using dictionaries. Get class feedback.

> **Answers:** 1 employer 2 childhood 3 happiness
> 4 supervisor 5 flexibility 6 communication
> 7 violinist 8 reduction 9 development
> 10 membership

3a ▶ Get Ss to find the one incorrect noun and correct it. Ss work in pairs, using dictionaries. Get class feedback or wait for Ss to check answers from the recording in 3b.

> **Answers:** 1 production 2 enjoyment 3 employment
> 4 typist 5 modernity 6 development

b ▶ Play recording 3.6 and get Ss to underline the stress in each word. Ss check their answers as they listen. After Ss check their answers in pairs, get class feedback. Get Ss to repeat the words with correct pronunciation.

> **Answers:** 1 involvement, arrangement, production, replacement 2 friendship, partnership, membership, enjoyment 3 brotherhood, employment, manhood, neighbourhood 4 typewriter, pianist, physicist, scientist 5 forgetfulness, readiness, forgiveness, modernity 6 alteration, donation, development, admission

4a ▶ Get Ss to work in pairs and decide which words have the main stress. Encourage them to say the sentences to each other to listen to where the stress is. Do not get whole class feedback at this stage.

b ▶ Play recording 3.7 and get Ss to check their answers. Get whole class feedback. You could get Ss to repeat the sentences focussing on correct sentence stress.

> **Answers:** The stressed words are: 1 Career development important 2 longest important friendship childhood 3 pollution neighbourhood 4 weaknesses forgetfulness 5 scientists musicians 6 communication essential successful relationship

c ▶ Tell Ss to look again at the sentences and think about how far each sentence is true for them. They could make a few notes to prepare what to say to a partner.

d ▶ Get Ss to work in pairs and compare their reactions to the statements and give reasons for their answers. Get whole class feedback by asking a few Ss to report back on their reactions to one of the statements.

Communication: Lessons from history

In this lesson, Ss discuss various aspects of school subjects. They listen to someone talking about what he has learned in his life and discuss what they have learned in their lives. Ss then discuss what we can learn from history.

> **OPTIONAL WARMER**
>
> Get Ss to compare the education system in England with that in their own country: **Q: At what age: do children start leave/school/take public exams?**
>
> Children in England have to go to school from age five until sixteen, but some stay until eighteen. At sixteen, they take an average of eight public exams known as 'GCSEs' (General Certificate in Secondary Education), in a variety of subjects. Students can stay at school or go to a Sixth Form College to do an average of three 'A-levels' (Advanced level exams).

1 ▶ Get Ss to discuss the questions in pairs or small groups. Then get whole class feedback by asking each group to report back about one of the questions.

2a ▶ Read through the questions with the class. Play recording 3.8 and get Ss to answer the questions. Ss should check in pairs. Then get whole class feedback.

> **Answers:** 1 He hated it and he couldn't do it. 2 He's studying Maths because he needs a Maths qualification in order to be a History teacher. 3 that studying hard and passing exams give you more choice in life

b ▶ Read through the half sentences with the class, checking they understand the phrases. Ss choose one half sentence and complete it to make it true for them.

c ▶ Get Ss to work in pairs and compare and discuss their sentences. Get brief class feedback by asking a few Ss to report back about their partner's sentence.

3 ▶ Read through the three explanations with the class. Then get Ss, in pairs, to read the quotes and match two of the quotes to each explanation. Get class feedback.

> **Answers: A** 'History is a useless ... .' 'History is more or less bunk ... . **B** 'History teaches everything ... .' 'Whoever wishes to foresee ... .' C 'Learning history is easy; ... .' 'To be ignorant ... .'

4 ▶ Get Ss, in pairs, to choose one quote in Ex. 4, discuss if they agree with it or not and give examples and reasons to justify their opinions. Regroup Ss into larger groups to continue the discussion, finishing with a whole class discussion about one or two quotes.

Review and practice

1 ▶

Answers: 1 We had <u>been</u> walking for twenty minutes when it started to rain.   2 <u>Did</u> you remember to bring that book yesterday?   3 When I got to the party, Jack <u>had</u> already gone home.   4 Correct.   5 While Cristina <u>was</u> sitting on the bus, someone stole her wallet.   6 Correct.   7 Someone finally answered the phone after I'd <u>been</u> waiting for ten minutes.

2 ▶

Answers: 1 had been working/wasn't necessary   2 were you doing/was   3 got/had been stolen   4 was doing   5 arrived/had wrapped   6 Had you been learning

3 ▶

Answers: 1 She lives in Alexandra Road. It's not far from <u>the</u> post office.   2 People say that <u>the</u> British are reserved.   3 I'm not sure but I think I'd like to be <u>an</u> architect when I grow up.   4 Don't forget your suncream. <u>The</u> sun is very strong today.   5 Correct.   6 We stayed at <u>a</u> very nice hotel in Barcelona.   7 That was one of <u>the</u> best books I've read for ages.   8 Shall we sit in <u>the</u> garden for a while?

4 ▶

Answers: 1a badly   b bad   2a careful   b carefully   3a perfect   b perfectly

5 ▶

Answers: 1 enormous   2 incredibly   3 quickly   4 completely   5 surprisingly   6 certain

6 ▶

Answers: 1 stretchy ⋯⟩ itchy   2 head ⋯⟩ breath   3 fashion ⋯⟩ trendy / fashionable   4 of ⋯⟩ in   5 while ⋯⟩ during   6 time ⋯⟩ hand   7 on ⋯⟩ in   8 that ⋯⟩ then

Notes for using the Common European Framework (CEF)

CEF References

3.1 Can do: write a short story

CEF B2 descriptor: Can write clear, detailed descriptions of real or imaginary events and experiences, marking the relationship between ideas in clear connected text, and following established conventions of the genre concerned. (CEF page 62)

3.2 Can do: talk about materials, possessions and inventions

CEF B2 descriptor: Can give clear, detailed descriptions on a wide range of subjects related to his/her field of interest. (CEF page 59)

3.3 Can do: give a presentation about a place

CEF B2 descriptor: Can give a clear, systematically developed presentation, with highlighting of significant points, and relevant supporting detail. (CEF page 60)

CEF quick brief

The Common European Framework describes itself as 'a common basis for the elaboration of language syllabuses, curriculum guidelines, examinations, textbooks, etc'. It is not intended to be a definitive description of what to teach but it is designed to offer a 'framework' which the user can build on. In addition it believes that language learning can be measured not by how much grammar or vocabulary a learner knows, but by what a learner can achieve with the language that they know. Grammar and vocabulary are only important in terms of what they empower a learner to do. This is an 'action-oriented' approach to language.

Portfolio task

Download the Total English Portfolio free from www.longman.com/totalenglish.

Objective: help Ss to complete the record of their 'language qualifications' as well as their 'language and cultural experiences' sections of their Passport.

This task can be done in Ss' own language.

1 ▶ Remind Ss that their Passport enables them to demonstrate their relevant experiences and qualifications.

2 ▶ Explain that recording language qualifications and considering language and cultural experiences are important in this. The Total English Portfolio has two separate sections for Ss to give information about these.

3 ▶ Give some examples of your own relevant qualifications and experiences (exams, certificates, exchange trips, holidays, courses, friends with that first language, etc).

4 ▶ Ask Ss to write a list of their own relevant experiences and show a partner.

5 ▶ Ask Ss to complete these sections of their Passport.

6 ▶ Remind Ss that they can update this at any time.

4 Risk

Overview

Summary

Lesson 1: Ss read an article about Ellen MacArthur (the fastest person ever to sail solo round the world) and discuss their reactions to her. After reading short extracts from Ellen's diary, Ss discuss reasons for writing diaries and blogs and write an entry of their own.

Lesson 2: Ss read and listen to instructions about how to do some physical movements and relaxation exercises. They then practise instructing each other. Ss then read an article about 'free running' and discuss their reactions to it.

Lesson 3: Ss listen to two people discussing *Million Dollar Baby* including the theme of risk in the film. Ss also get a chance to practise comparing and contrasting two photos.

Vocabulary: Ss focus on the language of distances and dimensions.

Communication: Ss play a game based on 'Snakes and Ladders', in which they go round a board by responding to questions about the topics and grammar from the unit.

Film bank: Ellen MacArthur (3'10")

An extract from a documentary about Ellen MacArthur and her record-breaking solo voyages around the world in a sailing boat.

The documentary includes footage taken aboard her boat during one of the gruelling trips. There are interviews with Ellen about preparation for the trips, mental attitude, physical endurance, sleep deprivation and food on board.

Possible places to use this short film are:
▶ After Lesson 1 to extend the topic of Ellen MacArthur.

▶ At the end of the unit to round up the topic and language.

For ways to use this short film in class, see Students' Book page 155 and Teacher's Book page 181.

Lead-in

OPTIONAL WARMER

Write the word *risk* on the board. Ask Ss which verb collocates with *risk*. Give them some options (e.g. *make/do/have/take/set?*). (Answer: *take a risk*).

Then play a quick game of word association. Ask Ss to work in pairs and list anything that comes to mind associated with the phrase 'take a risk'.

Get whole class feedback and write the ideas on the board, getting Ss to explain the association to 'take a risk' if necessary.

1 ▶ Focus Ss on the photos and get them to discuss the question. If you did the optional warmer, ask Ss if they had thought of any of the ideas in the photos. Get whole class feedback.

Answers:
A: skydiving is a physical risk (e.g. the parachute might not open or the landing might go wrong).
B: people take risks financially (e.g. in the financial markets by investing money in stocks and shares. Their value could decrease as well as increase).
C: buying a second-hand car could be a risk (e.g. it might not work and be a waste of money).
D: tightrope walking is a physical risk (e.g. you might fall off).

2 ▶ Get Ss to work in pairs and decide which of the alternatives is not possible in each sentence. Give them dictionaries to help if necessary. Get class feedback.

Answers: 1 hazard 2 luck 3 gamble 4 belief 5 vast 6 infatuation 7 hardly

3 ▶ Read through the questions with the class. Play recording 4.1 and get Ss to answer the questions. After briefly checking in pairs, get whole class feedback.

Answers: 1 he went with a friend on a motorbike from 'the top of Africa to the bottom' 2 to go on a sailing expedition to the Galapagos Islands

4 ▶ Get Ss to discuss the questions in pairs or small groups. Get whole class feedback, by asking each group to report back on their most interesting question.

EXTEND THE LEAD-IN

Get Ss to discuss these questions: **Q:** In what ways do you think people can take these risks in their language learning? Do you think it is a good thing to take these risks? Why/Why not? **Q:** How often do you take risks in your language learning? Do you take too many or not enough? Why?

4.1 Going solo

Ellen MacArthur was born in 1976 and grew up in Derbyshire, in the middle of England. Her love of sailing developed from a boating trip with her aunt when she was eight years old and quickly blossomed into an all-consuming passion. In 2001, after several years of dedicated hard work, she finally got the sponsorship she needed. Impressed by her hard work and determination, a European company called Kingfisher backed her with £2 million to enter the world-renowned Vendée Globe – a three-month solo journey around the world. Against the odds, Ellen came second and broke several records: the first female competitor ever to lead the race, the youngest solo sailor to ever finish and the fastest women to circumnavigate the globe. Since then, she has broken several more records and in 2005 she became the fastest person ever to circumnavigate the globe alone, covering over 27,000 miles in seventy-one days, fourteen hours, eighteen minutes and thirty-three seconds. For more information go to: http://www.teamellen.com/

In this lesson, Ss read an article about Ellen MacArthur and discuss their reactions to her. They then focus on the grammar of basic 'if' structures (first, second and third conditionals). After reading short extracts from Ellen's diary, Ss discuss reasons for writing diaries and blogs and write an entry of their own.

> **OPTIONAL WARMER**
>
> Write the following words/phrases on the board:
> A *on your own/by yourself*   B *alone/lonely*
>
> Ask Ss to discuss this question in pairs: **Q: What is the difference, if any, between these pairs of words?**
>
> (Answers: A *on your own/by yourself*: both phrases mean 'alone';   B *alone/lonely*: alone means there is no-one with you; lonely means unhappy because you are alone or do not have anyone to talk to)
>
> Ask Ss to choose two of the words/phrases and write a sentence for each of them about themselves. Ss should then compare and discuss their sentences with other Ss.

Reading

1 ▶ Get Ss to discuss the questions in pairs or small groups. Get brief whole class feedback.

2 ▶ Focus Ss on the photos and tell Ss they are going to read about Ellen MacArthur. Read the topics through with the class. Tell Ss to read the text quickly and tick the topics that are mentioned. Remind Ss not to try to understand everything in the text at this stage. Ss should briefly check their answers in pairs. Then get whole class feedback.

> **Answers:** Topics mentioned: Ellen's achievement; her attitude to her boat; her boat's facilities; the qualities a solo sailor needs; the differences between sailing in 1969 and today.

3 ▶ Read the sentences through with the class and tell them each one comes from the text. Get Ss to read the text again and decide where each sentence should go. Remind Ss to look at the sentences before and after the gaps to help them. After checking answers in pairs, get whole class feedback.

> **Answers:** 1 D 2 E 3 C 4 F 5 B 6 A

4 ▶ Get Ss to discuss the questions in pairs or small groups. Get whole class feedback by asking one or two Ss for their opinions.

> **OPTIONAL EXTENSION**
>
> You could use this as an opportunity to get Ss to practise the skill of summary writing.
>
> First, get Ss to note down the main points of the text. Tell them to choose 3–5 points and remind them that they can look back at the text. Get them to discuss which points they have chosen with a partner.
>
> Then tell them to write a paragraph using their points to summarize the text. They could do this in pairs or individually. Remind them to only include the main points and not too much detail. If Ss need further help, you could give them an example for the first sentence: *Ellen MacArthur is a young British woman who has broken various records for sailing single-handed around the world.*

Grammar

> **OPTIONAL GRAMMAR LEAD-IN**
>
> Write this sentence on the board and ask Ss to complete it in as many different ways as they can, using the verbs *have* and *sail*.
>
> *If I ... enough money, I ... round the world.*
>
> Get Ss to compare their sentences in pairs, encouraging them to explain the difference in meaning between the different sentences.
>
> (Possible sentences:
>
> *If I have enough money, I will sail round the world.*
>
> *If I had enough money, I would sail round the world.*
>
> *If I had had enough money, I would have sailed round the world.*)

5a ▶ Tell Ss to complete examples 1–3 in the Active grammar box using *don't*, *won't*, *would*, *have* and *had*. After checking their answers in pairs, get whole class feedback.

> **Active grammar**
>
> 1 **Would** you be interested in sailing round the world, if you **had** the chance?
>
> 2 If we **had** had all the modern equipment, it would **have** saved us time.
>
> 3 If you **don't** have an extreme mental toughness, you probably **won't** survive.

b ▶ Get Ss to match the rules A–C in the Active grammar box with the examples 1–3. Ss should briefly check answers in pairs. Then get whole class feedback.

> **Active grammar**
>
> A 3   B 1   C 2

6 ▶ Tell Ss to correct the mistake in each sentence. Ss should check answers in pairs. Then get whole class feedback.

> **Answers:** 1 **Will** you phone me if anything goes wrong?   2 What **would** you have done if a nearby boat hadn't picked up your distress call?   3 You **would** feel a lot better about things if you took a risk and left your job.   4 What **would** you like to do if you had some free time and money?   5 If I **hadn't taken** a year off to cycle across Africa, I wouldn't have met my husband.   6 If **you see** John, can you ask him if he's going to come parachuting with us at the weekend?   7 I wouldn't **have suggested** you come if I'd known you were afraid of heights.

Person to person

7a ▶ Get Ss to work in pairs and think of three people they might see or talk to today. Ask them to tell each other what they might say to these people. Get brief whole class feedback.

b ▶ Get Ss to work in pairs and imagine they had more time each week to do the things they enjoy. Ask them to tell each other how they would spend that time. Get brief whole class feedback.

c ▶ Get Ss to work in pairs and to think about major decisions they have made in the past. Ask them to tell each other what they would have done if they had made a different choice. Get brief whole class feedback.

> **OPTIONAL ALTERNATIVE**
>
> You could get Ss to prepare what they are going to say for parts a, b and c at the same time. Then get them to stand up and mingle and tell their sentences to different Ss.

Writing

> **OPTIONAL WARMER**
>
> Tell Ss that Ellen MacArthur writes a diary when she is on her trips. Get Ss to work in pairs and brainstorm the kind of thing they think she writes about in her diary. Get whole class feedback and write some ideas on the board.

8 ▶ Tell Ss to read the extracts from Ellen MacArthur's diary and decide what is the main thing she writes about on Day 1, Day 3 and Day 4. Get Ss to check their answers in pairs. Then get whole class feedback. If you did the optional warmer, you could also ask Ss if any of their ideas were correct.

> **Answers:** Day 1: Her feelings about leaving land and doing the race.   Day 3: The problem with her finger and her boat's speed.   Day 4: The wind and rough seas.

> **OPTIONAL EXTENSION**
>
> You might want to do some vocabulary work on the text. Get Ss to read the extracts again and work with a partner to explain the following phrases. Then get whole class feedback.
>
> Day 1: to sink in 'hadn't really sunk in' (to fully understand information or facts only gradually).
>
> Day 3: to spurt out '*The blood spurted out*' (when a liquid comes out quickly and suddenly).
>
> Day 4: to leap '*leaping over each wave*' (to jump high in the air, often over something).

9 ▶ Get Ss to work in pairs and discuss the questions. Get whole class feedback encouraging Ss to give details and reasons for their opinions.

10a ▶ Tell Ss to read the definition and answer the question with a partner. Get whole class feedback.

b ▶ Read through the questions with the class. Get Ss to read the blog on page 150 and answer the questions. Ss should check their answers in pairs. Then get whole class feedback.

> **Answers:** 1 As a way of keeping in touch with family/ friends and as a way of expressing thoughts

11a ▶ Tell Ss that they are going to write an entry in a diary or a blog. First they should choose what to write about from the ideas in the list or their own ideas. Then they should write some brief notes.

b ▶ Get Ss to write their diary entry or blog. Tell them to write about a hundred words and remind them that the style of a diary or a blog is personal and does not have to be grammatically correct all the time.

Lifelong learning

▶ Read through the lifelong learning box with Ss. Ask Ss if any of them has ever done this. If so, ask those Ss to talk about their experience and share their ideas with the class. Encourage Ss to get a special book and start keeping a diary in English.

4.2 Run free

Free running or 'Parkour' is the fast-growing extreme sport that turns everyday urban landscapes into obstacle courses. It began in 1987 in Paris, where two bored teenagers, Sebastien Foucan and David Belle decided to make life more interesting. They developed a series of moves including climbing up buildings, swinging round lamp posts, leaping over anything. Their hobby grew and grew, becoming a global phenomenon. In 2001, a film was made about free running and the UK-based parkour website gets 10,000 hits a day. For more information go to: www.parkour.com

In this lesson, Ss read and listen to instructions about how to do some physical movements and relaxation exercises. They then practise instructing each other. Ss then read an article about 'free running' and discuss their reactions to it. They finish by focussing on the grammar of obligation in the present and the past.

> **OPTIONAL WARMER**
>
> Introduce the topic of physical movement by playing a quick game of 'Simon says' with parts of the body. Briefly, remind Ss of the rules (You have to do what the teacher says, if he/she starts by saying 'Simon says'. If he/she doesn't say 'Simon says', however, you mustn't do what he/she says and if you do, you're out.) Tell Ss to do things, e.g. touch your shoulder, lift up your left knee, put your hand on your partner's right foot.

Vocabulary

1 ▶ Get Ss to work in pairs and match the drawings to the verbs in the box. You could give them dictionaries to help. Remind them to do the easier ones first and then move on to the more difficult ones. Get whole class feedback.

> **Answers:** a) stretch b) bend c) roll d) swing
> e) lean f) leap g) tuck h) balance i) land
> j) flip

2a ▶ Focus Ss on the drawings and tell them that these moves are part of an extreme sport called 'free running'. Get them to complete the descriptions of the three moves with verbs from Ex. 1. Ss should check their answers in pairs. Then get whole class feedback.

> **Answers:** 1 swing   2 Land   3 Bend   4 Roll
> 5 tuck   6 lean   7 tuck

b ▶ Get Ss to work in pairs and discuss the question. Get brief whole class feedback.

Listening and speaking

3 ▶ Tell Ss that they are going to listen to someone giving instructions on how to do a relaxation exercise. Play recording 4.2 and tell Ss to follow the instructions and do the exercise they hear.

4a ▶ Divide Ss into pairs. Tell Student As to look at the pictures and read the instructions on page 148 and Student Bs to look at the pictures and read the instructions on page 149.

b ▶ Get Ss to work in pairs (one A and one B). Tell them to explain their moves to each other and check that they are doing it correctly. Remind Ss not to show the pictures to each other (until the end) as the idea is to practise giving and understanding instructions.

Reading

> **OPTIONAL WARMER**
>
> Ask Ss to remember the three moves involved in 'free running' that they read about in Ex. 2, without looking back if possible. Get Ss to name the moves and describe them to each other.
>
> Ask Ss to work in pairs and speculate on this question: **Q: What do you need to do to be able to do free running successfully?**
>
> Get brief whole class feedback by asking for some of their ideas.

5 ▶ Get Ss to read the text quickly and answer the question. Remind them not to worry about understanding the whole text at this stage, but just to answer the question. Get Ss to check their answers in pairs. Get whole class feedback. If you did the optional warmer, check if any of their answers were correct.

> **Answers:** To roll, to land and to suppress any last-minute doubts or fears.

6 ▶ Ask Ss to read the article and decide if the statements are true or false. If they are false, encourage Ss to correct them. Get Ss to check their answers in pairs. Then get whole class feedback.

> **Answers:** 1 True   2 True   3 False (a group which later split)   4 False (Foucan is surprised)
> 5 True   6 False   7 False (and couldn't walk for nine weeks)   8 True   9 False (It's scary because ...)

7 ▶ Get Ss to find words in the text which mean each of the definitions. Remind them that the paragraph number is given. Ss should check their answers in pairs. Then get whole class feedback.

> **Answers:** 1 vault   2 opt   3 setback   4 momentum
> 5 cliché   6 rigid

8 ▶ Get Ss to discuss the questions in pairs or small groups. Encourage them to give reasons to justify their opinions. Get whole class feedback by asking two or three Ss to report back about their group's opinions.

Grammar

OPTIONAL GRAMMAR LEAD-IN

Write these sentences about 'free running' on the board and ask Ss to complete them. If you think they need more help, you could give them these options to make it easier *(must, have to, don't have to, should, are supposed)*. Remind Ss that more than one option may be possible. Get Ss to check answers in pairs. Do not get whole class feedback but get Ss to check their answers in the Active grammar box.

You ... know how to land properly.

You ... learn how to roll.

You ... get permission to run across certain buildings.

You ... wear special clothes.

You ... to do it in groups.

9a▶ Get Ss to match each example 1–5 in the Active grammar box with one of the meanings A–E. Ss should check answers in pairs. Then get whole class feedback. Further checking of meaning comes in Ex. 9c.

Active grammar

1 D 2 C 3 E 4 A 5 B

b▶ Get Ss to work in pairs to complete the examples 6–10 in the Active grammar box. Students have to put the sentences in the past. Get whole class feedback.

Active grammar

6 We should **have known** how to land properly.

7 We **had to** learn how to roll.

8 We **had** to get permission to run across certain buildings.

9 We **didn't have** to wear special clothes.

10 We **were supposed** to do it in groups.

c▶ Get Ss to work in pairs and decide if there is any difference in meaning between each pair of sentences, and to explain what they are. Get whole class feedback.

Answers:
1a) is something the speaker feels is necessary to do; b) means that something else is forcing the speaker to stop smoking
2a) means it is not necessary to wear a tie; b) means that it is not a good idea to wear a tie
3a) and b) have a similar meaning
4a) and b) have a similar meaning
5a) means it was not necessary to run for the train (whether or not it was done); b) means that we did run for the train and it was not necessary

OPTIONAL EXTENSION

You might feel that your Ss could benefit from some pronunciation work here. Get Ss to look again at the sentences in the Active grammar box and/or Ex. 9a.

You could ask them to find which parts of the verb forms are weak forms (*to* and *have* are often weak forms).

You could also point out where words run together (*must learn* – we often drop the 't' in natural speech; *supposed to* – the 'd' and 't' run together).

10a▶ Tell Ss that the paragraph is about 'whitewater rafting' and check Ss understand what this is (an extreme sport where people canoe down the fast parts of rivers). Tell Ss that the words in the box are missing from the text and that they should find where each one should go. Ss should check their answers in pairs but do not get whole class feedback at this stage.

b▶ Play recording 4.3 and get Ss to check their answers. Get whole class feedback if necessary as a final check.

Answers:
'One of the best things we did on holiday was to go whitewater rafting. However, I was a bit nervous at first when they told us we **had** to sign something which basically said we wouldn't hold the company responsible if we got injured or died! Anyway, the guy in charge of our boat gave us some instruction before we started off. We **had** to wear lifejackets of course but I was quite surprised that we **didn't** have to wear any kind of crash helmet. We were also **supposed** to wear trainers but I'd forgotten mine so I had **to** wear my sandals. Finally, we got going and the whole thing was fantastic. There were eight of us in a boat and there really was a lot of 'white water'. It was a bit like being on a rollercoaster and I nearly fell in at one point. The one thing I'm sorry about is that I didn't get any photos. I **should** have taken my camera but I was afraid I would drop it in the water.'

Person to person

11▶ Get Ss to look at the list of things and make some notes to prepare what they are going to say. Ss should work in pairs and tell each other one thing for each.

OPTIONAL ALTERNATIVE

Get Ss to prepare what they are going to say and then stand up and mingle and tell different Ss about each thing.

4.3 Million dollar risk

Clint Eastwood was born in Los Angeles in 1930 and is a legend in the world of international movie stars. Some of his most famous films (pictured) are *A Fistful of Dollars* (1964), *Dirty Harry* (1971), *Every Which Way but Loose* (1978), *Bridges of Madison County* (1995) and *Million Dollar Baby* (2004). For more information on Clint Eastwood, go to: http://www.imdb.com/name/nm0000142/

Million Dollar Baby was directed by Clint Eastwood and won several Oscars including Best Picture. Eastwood stars in the film as boxing trainer Frankie Dunn who, because of a painful relationship with his daughter, has been unwilling to let himself get close to anyone for a very long time. Then a determined young woman called Maggie (played by Hilary Swank) walks into his gym and wants him to take her on. The last thing Frankie needs is that kind of responsibility or that kind of risk, but he is won over by Maggie's sheer determination.

In this lesson, Ss listen to two people discussing *Million Dollar Baby*, focussing on the theme of risk that runs through the film. Ss then focus on the grammar of emphasis, including using repetition, adding emphasising words (like *so, such, just, really*), using the structure '*It is … which …*' and adding an appropriate form of 'do'. Ss also get a chance to practise comparing and contrasting two photos.

> **OPTIONAL WARMER**
>
> Introduce Ss to the topic of films.
>
> **Q: Which type of film in each pair would you rather watch and why?**
>
> **1 A cowboy film or a science fiction film?**
>
> **2 A romantic film or an adventure film?**
>
> **3 A comedy drama or a tear-jerker?**
>
> **4 A psychological drama or a horror film?**
>
> You could also ask Ss about recent films they have seen and favourite stars in each of the categories above.

Listening

1a ▶ Focus Ss on the photos and get them to discuss the question in pairs. Get whole class feedback.

> **Answers:** Clint Eastwood was involved in all of them, acting or directing or both. (Names and dates of the films are in the information above).

b ▶ Play recording 4.4 and get Ss to say which of the films in the photos the people are talking about. Briefly check answers in pairs. Then get whole class feedback.

> **Answers:** *Million Dollar Baby*

c ▶ Read the questions through with the class. Play recording 4.4 again and ask Ss to answer the questions. Ss should check answers in pairs, before getting whole class feedback.

> **Answers:** 1 yes 2 risk 3 he doesn't put a promising young boxer up for a big championship fight 4 because she's a woman 5 no 6 he becomes emotional attached to both

2 ▶ Get Ss to work in groups. If Ss know the film *Million Dollar Baby*, they should follow the instructions in part 1. If they don't, they should follow the instructions in part 2.

Grammar

> **OPTIONAL GRAMMAR LEAD-IN**
>
> Write these sentences on the board. Get Ss to work in pairs and decide which sentence in each pair is 'stronger' than the other and why. You do not need to do feedback at this stage (as Ss will look at these sentences in the Active grammar box).
>
> A1: *I like Clint Eastwood.*
> A2: *I do like Clint Eastwood.*
>
> B1: *It was much better than that.*
> B2: *It was much, much better than that.*
>
> C1: *There are so many different themes running through the film.*
> C2: *There are many different themes running through the film.*
>
> D1: *It's the film I've enjoyed the most this year.*
> D2: *I've enjoyed that film the most this year.*

3 ▶ If you did the optional warmer, get Ss to check that the sentences in the Active grammar box are the ones which are 'stronger' or have emphasis. Get Ss to match the examples 1–4 in the Active grammar box with the ways of emphasising A–D. Get whole class feedback.

> **Active grammar**
>
> 1 D 2 A 3 B 4 C

4a ▶ Get Ss to join the two halves of the sentences by adding *do*, *does* or *did* for emphasis. You may need to remind Ss that the form of the verb may change (to the infinitive form). Ss should their answers in pairs, but do not get whole class feedback at this stage.

> **Answers:** 2 I did send you a message this morning. 3 They do like oysters. 4 He did apologise for being so late. 5 You did realise they were married, didn't you? 6 She does need some help with her homework. 7 I do understand how you are feeling.

5a ▶ Play recording 4.5 and tell Ss to listen to the sentences and underline the words/phrases that they hear emphasised. You might want to do the first one as an example to make sure that Ss have got the idea. Ss should check answers in pairs, and then get whole class feedback.

Answers:
1 She had always wanted <u>this job</u>.
2 I went and saw my doctor <u>yesterday</u>.
3 I decided to ask if I could borrow his <u>new Mercedes</u>.
4 She really doesn't like the <u>words</u> to their new song.
5 He wants to study <u>sociology or psychology</u> at university.
6 He broke the <u>kitchen window</u> while he was playing with a ball.

b ▶ Get Ss to rewrite the sentences in Ex. 5a, by beginning each one with *It*, giving special emphasis to the underlined parts of the sentences. Remind Ss to look back at example 4 in the Active grammar box if necessary. Ss should check answers in pairs but do not get whole class feedback at this stage.

c ▶ Play recording 4.6 and get Ss to check their answers.

Answers:
2 It was yesterday that I went and saw my doctor.
3 It was his new Mercedes that I decided to ask if I could borrow.
4 It is the words to their new song that she really doesn't like.
5 It is sociology or psychology that he wants to study at university.
6 It was the kitchen window that he broke while he was playing with a ball.

Person to person

6a ▶ Tell Ss that they are going to talk about one of the things in the list. Ask them to choose one and prepare for their talk by making a few notes about what they want to say. Encourage them to decide what points they particularly want to emphasise and how they are going to do that.

b ▶ Get Ss to work in pairs and tell each other about the thing they have chosen, using their notes. Remind them to pay attention to what they want to emphasise and how.

> **OPTIONAL EXTENSION**
> You could get Ss to write one or two paragraphs about the person/thing they talked about in Ex. 6.

Vocabulary

7 ▶ You may want to tell Ss that phrasal verbs can be learned either grouped by topic (e.g. phrasal verbs about relationships), or by verb (e.g. phrasal verbs with *take*) or, as here, by particle (e.g. phrasal verbs with *out*). Get Ss to match the phrasal verbs in italics in the sentences to the meanings a–h. After checking in pairs, get whole class feedback.

Answers: 1 e 2 c 3 h 4 g 5 b 6 a 7 d 8 f

8a ▶ Get Ss to complete the sentences with one of the verbs from Ex. 7 in the correct form. Ss should check answers in pairs. Then get whole class feedback.

Answers: 1 put 2 find 3 run 4 work 5 turned 6 fallen

b ▶ Get Ss to work in pairs and ask and answer the questions. Encourage them to give details in their answers and to ask follow-up questions where appropriate.

Speaking

> **OPTIONAL WARMER**
> Focus Ss on the two photos. Get them to work in pairs and ask them to describe the two photos briefly and say how they think they would feel about being in each situation and why. Get brief whole class feedback.

9 ▶ Focus Ss on the two photos and tell them they are going to listen to someone comparing and contrasting them. Play recording 4.7 and get Ss to answer the question. After checking answers in pairs, get whole class feedback. If you did the optional warmer, you could compare answers with what Ss talked about.

Answers: She wouldn't like to be in either situation because she hates ironing and she's also scared of heights and climbing.

10a ▶ Get Ss to work in pairs and complete the sentences from the tapescript from memory. Do not get whole class feedback at this stage.

b ▶ Play recording 4.7 again and get Ss to check their answers.

Answers: 1 both 2 can see/kind 3 somehow 4 imagine how 5 much 6 might 7 looking after 8 looks/even 9 also 10 either

11a ▶ Tell Ss that they are going to compare and contrast two different photos. First, read through the language in the How to ... box with the class. Divide the class into pairs. Get Student As to look at the photos on page 149 and prepare to talk about them. Get Student Bs to look at the photos on page 145 and prepare to talk about them.

b ▶ Get Ss to work together in pairs (one A and one B). Tell them to show each other their photos and compare and contrast them. Remind them to use the language in the How to ... box.

Vocabulary: Distances and dimensions

In this lesson, Ss focus on the language of distances and dimensions.

> **OPTIONAL WARMER**
>
> Write these abbreviations on the board: *kg cm l mm g km ml m*.
>
> Ask Ss to say what they mean and put them into the correct category: Distance, Weight, Liquid capacity.
>
> **Answers:** Distance: cm (centimetres), mm (millimetres), km (kilometres), m (metres); Weight: kg (kilograms), g (grams);
> Liquid capacity: l (litres), ml (millilitres))

1a▶ Get Ss to work in pairs and check they know the words in the table. Then ask them to complete the table with the missing parts of speech, using dictionaries if necessary. Do not get class feedback at this stage.

b▶ Play recording 4.8 and tell Ss to check their answers. Get Ss to repeat them with correct pronunciation.

> **Answers:** 1 short   2 widen   3 broaden   4 high
> 5 depth   6 lower

2▶ Ss complete the sentences with a word from the table. After checking in pairs, get class feedback.

> **Answers:** 1 width   2 depth   3 widen   4 lengthening
> 5 shortens   6 low   7 broad

3a▶ Get Ss to work in pairs and discuss the difference between the pairs of phrases. You could give them dictionaries to help. Get whole class feedback by asking different pairs of Ss to explain each pair of phrases.

> **Answers:** 1 there is a small/high chance that things will go wrong   2 a plan that extends a long time into the future/just for a short period into the future.   3 a call to somewhere near your home/in another part of the country or abroad.   4 a quicker, more direct way of going somewhere/a route which takes longer than necessary.   5 someone who is willing to accept behaviour or opinions that are very different from their own/someone who is not.   6 too thin (used in a negative way)/thin in an attractive way (used positively).   7 someone not capable of serious thought/someone who is.

b▶ Read the example through with the class. Get Ss to work in pairs taking turns to describe a situation or a person to illustrate the words/phrases in Ex. 3a. The other student decides which word/phrase is being illustrated.

4▶ In pairs, Ss discuss what they think the expressions mean. Give them dictionaries to check their ideas. Get class feedback.

> **Answers:** 1 to make someone admire you   2 to choose or be made to do a difficult job without having prepared for it   3 to be thinking so hard that you do not notice anything happening around you   4 (informal) to become angry suddenly and violently, usually when there is not good reason   5 a person who is quiet but has strong feelings or a lot of knowledge underneath

> **OPTIONAL EXTENSION**
>
> Get Ss to think of a person or situation to illustrate an expression from Ex. 4 and describe it to a partner. Also get Ss to think about equivalent expressions in their own language and discuss what is the same or different about them.

5▶ In pairs Ss choose the correct alternatives using dictionaries if necessary. Get class feedback.

> **Answers:** 1 expand   2 extended   3 stretches
> 4 distance   5 spreading   6 lengthy   7 contracts
> 8 shrunk

6a▶ Get Ss to work in pairs and prepare a story. The story must involve someone taking a risk and include at least five of the words/phrases from Exs. 1, 3, 4 and 5.

b▶ Get Ss to tell their stories to different Ss in the class. Get whole class feedback by asking Ss which story they think involved the biggest risk.

Communication: Take a risk

In this lesson, Ss play an adaptation of 'Snakes and Ladders.' During the game, players throw a dice and go round the board responding to various questions about the topics and grammar from the unit.

> **OPTIONAL WARMER**
>
> Write these games on the board:
> *Chess   Snakes and ladders   Monopoly*
>
> Ask Ss **Q: 1 What is the connection between these?**
> (They are all board games) **Q: 2 What do you know about them?**
> (Chess: played on a checked board. The idea is to try to trap the other player's King; Snakes and Ladders: players must reach the end of the board first by trying to go up ladders and avoid going down snakes; Monopoly: The idea is to buy as much property as possible and earn the most money.) **Q: 3 Can you add any more?**

1▶ Focus Ss on the game. Get Ss to read the rules of the game. Then check they have understood the rules, by asking questions e.g. How long do you have to speak for? Get Ss to work in groups of 3–5 players and play the game. Monitor and make a note of mistakes you hear. Write them on the board and ask Ss how to correct them in pairs.

Review and practice

1 ▶

> **Answers:** 1 g   2 d   3 b   4 e   5 a   6 f   7 h   8 c

2 ▶

> **Answers:** 1 What will we do if the taxi doesn't come on time?   2 If I had been born a year earlier, I would have done military service.   3 What would you do if you were offered a better job?   4 If I am not home by 11p.m. my dad will be really angry.   5 I wouldn't have hired a car if I had known how expensive it was going to be.   6 If she works really hard between now and the exams, she will probably pass.   7 We would have gone to the cinema if we had been able to find a babysitter.   8 If I were you, I would go on a long holiday.

3 ▶

> **Answers:** 1 You didn't have to wait for me.   2 I am supposed to take some ID.   3 I didn't need to get up early this morning.   4 We've got to be in our seats at the theatre by 7.30pm.   5 You shouldn't have forgotten Janine's birthday.   6 Did you have to do military service when you were eighteen?

4 ▶

> **Answers:** 1 it   2 so   3 just   4 vital   7 does   8 such

5 ▶

> **Answers:** 1 work   2 elbow   3 dream   4 stretch   5 intense   6 heightened   7 shoulders   8 achievement

Notes for using the Common European Framework (CEF)

CEF References

4.1 Can do: write a diary entry

CEF B2 descriptor: Can express news and views effectively in writing, and relate to those of others. (CEF page 83)

4.2 Can do: explain how to do something

CEF B2 descriptor: Can understand and exchange complex information and advice on the full range of matters related to his/her occupational role. (CEF page 81)

4.3 Can do: compare and contrast photographs

CEF B2 descriptor: Can give clear, systematically developed descriptions and presentations, with appropriate highlighting of significant points, and relevant supporting detail. (CEF page 58)

CEF quick brief

Chapters four and five of the Common European Framework set out 'reference levels' as a way to describe someone's ability in language. There are six basic reference levels: A1, A2, B1, B2, C1, C2 which are designed to describe ability in any language, not just English, and are mostly written in the form of 'Can do' statements. Teachers, syllabus designers, writers, etc. can write and add their own statements according to the needs of their users.

Portfolio task

Download the Total English Portfolio free from www.longman.com/totalenglish.

Objective: to introduce students to the Biography section of Portfolio.

This task can be done in Ss' L1.

The second section of the Portfolio is the 'Biography'.

The Biography is for the students to keep a more detailed and personal record of their language learning history, objectives and progress so that they can reflect on successful as well as unsuccessful language learning experiences and hence further develop their language learning skills.

1 ▶ Explain the purpose of the Biography section of the Portfolio and its benefits.

1 ▶ Ask Ss to think about their language learning objectives and to make a list of these. Give examples of your own objectives in a different language to add clarity.

2 ▶ Ask Ss to write details of their English language learning history (12 years at school, etc.) and encourage Ss to reflect critically on what has been successful and what hasn't been successful for them.

3 ▶ Ask Ss compare their notes with a partner before completing the relevant sections of their Biography.

5 Stages

Overview

Lead-in	**Vocabulary:** memory
5.1	**Grammar:** *used to/get used to/would*
	Vocabulary: appearance
	Can do: describe appearance
5.2	**Grammar:** expressing ability
	Can do: talk about memories
5.3	**Grammar:** *although, but, however, nevertheless*
	Vocabulary: feelings
	Can do: talk about books
Vocabulary	Idioms describing people
Com. Focus	Time capsule
Reference	
Practice	

Summary

Lesson 1: Ss read an article about a man who has been living at the international airport in Paris since 1988. Ss also describe people's appearance, and write an email describing someone they met.

Lesson 2: Ss listen to people talking about photographs and their memories, and then talk about their own photos and memories from their childhood.

Lesson 3: Ss read an extract from the novel *The Memory Box* by Margaret Forster, discussing their reactions to the book and how they feel about memory boxes.

Vocabulary: Ss focus on idioms describing people.

Communication: Ss listen to people talking and giving advice about making a time capsule. Ss then discuss their own time capsules, choosing five things to put in.

Film bank: Home Road Movie (4'11")

A short computer-animated film about a father who desperately wanted the family car to make him a better parent.

Made by Robert Bradbrook in 2001, it won some of the most prestigious awards for animation. Bradbrook says the film is 'a true story of my father and our family car'. He reflects on how his dad took them on motoring holidays of a lifetime and how in later years the holidays seemed less perfect and the car gradually became a painful vehicle of his affection. Their dad's struggle to be a loving parent had turned into a battle against rust.

Possible places to use this short film are:
▶ After Lesson 1 to give further practice of used to/get used to/ would.
▶ After Lesson 2 to extend the topic of memories.
▶ At the end of the unit to round up the topic and language.

For ways to use this short film in class, see Students' Book page 156 and Teacher's Book page 182.

Lead-in

OPTIONAL WARMER

Write on the board: 1940s, 1950s, 1960s, 1970s, 1980s, 1990s. In pairs, Ss brainstorm events, famous people, styles of hair/clothes, music, memories associated with each decade (e.g. 1960s – The Beatles).

1 ▶ Focus Ss on the photos and get them to discuss the questions in pairs. Get whole class feedback.

Answers: Main photo: 1960s – style of clothes, glasses, haircuts, that they are sitting on the ground, probably at a music festival.   Photo 1: 1940s – b/w photo, style of clothes, fully clothed on beach, donkey riding on beach.   Photo 2: 1950s – style of décor/furniture/clothes/TV.   Photo 3:1980s – hairstyle, décor.

b ▶ Get Ss to match the sentences with the photos. After briefly checking in pairs, get whole class feedback.

Answers: 1 photo two   2 photo one   3 photo three   4 main photo   5 photo two   6 photo one

2a ▶ Get Ss to work in pairs and to decide if the words in bold in Ex. 1b are verbs, adjectives or nouns and to explain the meanings to each other. Remind them to look at the context and give them dictionaries. Get feedback.

Answers: *nostalgic*: adj. – feel slightly sad when you remember happy events   *remember*: verb – to have in your memory people, places and events   *remind*: verb – to make someone remember something they must do   *memory*: noun – the ability to remember things, places, experiences.   *memorable*: adj.– very good and likely to be remembered   *forgetful*: adj.– often forgetting things   *reminisce*: verb – to talk or think about pleasant events in your past

b ▶ Get Ss to work in pairs and decide how to pronounce the words including where the main stress is. Give Ss dictionaries if necessary. Do not get class feedback yet.

c ▶ Play recording 5.1 and get Ss to check their ideas about pronunciation. Get whole class feedback and get Ss to repeat the words with correct pronunciation.

Answers: no'stalgic   re'member   souve'nir   re'mind   'memory   'memorable   for'getful   remi'nisce

d ▶ Get Ss to write sentences that are true for them using the words in bold in Ex. 2. Ss compare sentences.

3 ▶ Get Ss to discuss the questions in pairs. Get class feedback by asking Ss to report what their partner said.

EXTEND THE LEAD-IN

Get Ss to discuss the following: **Q: What do you/your parents/grandparents reminisce about? Q: Which decade do you think was the most interesting? Why?**

5.1 A lost past

The Terminal (2004) was directed by Steven Spielberg and stars Tom Hanks and Catherine Zeta-Jones. It tells the story of an Iranian-born man who flies to JFK airport in New York only to find he cannot enter the USA but cannot fly home either, due to the outbreak of war. This bureaucratic nightmare means that he ends up totally stranded, living in the airport for over sixteen years.

The whole plot sounds like a fantasy, but the film is based on the true story of Merhan Karimi Nasseri (originally from Tehran) who calls himself 'Sir Alfred'. In 1988, he flew in to Terminal One at Charles de Gaulle International Airport in Paris. But because of a lack of official documents, he was neither allowed to enter, nor was he allowed to leave. So, since then his home has been a bench in a shopping mall of Terminal One. For more information about 'Sir Alfred' go to: http://en.wikipedia.org/wiki/Merhan_Karimi_Nasseri and for more information about *The Terminal* go to: www.theterminal-themovie.com

In this lesson, Ss read an article about 'Sir Alfred' and his life, his 'lost past' and his hopes for the future. They then focus on the grammar of *used to*, *get used* to and *would*, talking about their own pasts. Ss also describe people's appearance, including writing an email describing someone they met.

> **OPTIONAL WARMER**
>
> Get Ss thinking about the topic of waiting (e.g. at airports, train stations) by asking them to discuss these questions. You could tell Ss about your own experience to get them going.
>
> **Q: What do you like doing when you are waiting for a plane or a train?**
> **Q: What is the longest you have ever had to wait for a plane or train? Why did you have to wait so long? What did you do?**
> **Q: What other situations have you been in when you have had to wait a long time? What happened?**
> **Q: Would you describe yourself as a patient person? Why/Why not?**

Reading

1 ▶ Focus Ss on the photos and get Ss to discuss the question in pairs. Get whole class feedback but do not accept or reject any of their ideas at this stage.

2 ▶ Read through the questions with the class. Get Ss to read the text and answer the questions. After checking answers in pairs, get whole class feedback.

> **Answers:** 1 Alfred is actually Merhan Karimi Nasseri. 2 He is self-sufficient. He never sleeps during the day. He keeps himself very clean and well groomed. He always eats a McDonald's egg and bacon croissant for breakfast and a McDonald's fish sandwich for dinner. 3 Alfred hopes that DreamWorks and Steven Spielberg will come and rescue him. 4 The journalist is partly impressed by Alfred and partly feels sorry for him.

3 ▶ Read the sentences through with the class. Tell Ss to read the text again and decide where the sentences belong. Remind them to look at the sentences before and after the gaps to help them. Ss should check in pairs. Then get whole class feedback.

> **Answers:** A 7 B 5 C 2 D 1 E 6 F 4 G 3

4 ▶ Get Ss to discuss the questions in pairs or small groups. Then get whole class feedback.

> **OPTIONAL EXTENSION**
>
> If your Ss have access to the Internet, you could get them to do some further research on the life of 'Sir Alfred' and find out if his situation has changed now. They could then write one or two paragraphs about him and report back to the class.

Grammar

> **OPTIONAL GRAMMAR LEAD-IN**
>
> Write these sentences on the board and ask Ss to work in pairs and decide what each one means. You could get brief whole class feedback but do not accept or reject their ideas at this stage.
>
> *He used to sleep on a bench.*
> *He is getting used to sleeping on a bench.*
> *He is used to sleeping on a bench.*
> *He would sleep on a bench.*

5a ▶ Get Ss to match examples 1–4 in the Active grammar box to the meanings A–D. After briefly checking in pairs, get whole class feedback.

> **Active grammar**
> 1 D 2 B 3 A 4 C

b ▶ Get Ss to decide which of the four sentences is true for Alfred (in the text). Get whole class feedback.

> **Active grammar**
> 3 is true for Alfred.

6a ▶ Get Ss to choose the correct alternative for each sentence. Ss should check in pairs but do not get whole class feedback at this stage.

> **Answers:** 1 didn't use 2 working 3 I'm used to 4 would 5 used to 6 get

7 ▶ Get Ss to work in pairs and explain to each other what each correct sentence in Ex. 6 means in their own words.

8 ▶ Tell Ss that there is one word missing from each of the sentences. Get them to decide what the word is and add it in the correct place. After checking in pairs, get whole class feedback.

Answers:
1 I used to play a lot of volleyball when I was at school. 2 I can't get used to my new boss. She's not very friendly. 3 Did you use to be so close to your brother when you were children? 4 On Christmas Eve we would always go to church. 5 We are slowly getting used to living in the country but sometimes it feels a bit isolated. 6 We didn't use to be vegetarian. It's only something we've started doing in the last couple of months.

Person to person

9 ▶ Get Ss to discuss the questions in pairs or small groups. Get whole class feedback by asking each group to report back on one of the questions they discussed.

OPTIONAL EXTENSION

You could get Ss to do some further work on *used to/ get used to/would*.

Get Ss to choose a famous person they are interested in who is now past his/her 'heyday' and does different things from before. (They could choose one of these people: Madonna, Nelson Mandela, Mick Jagger, Maradona or one of their own ideas.) If your Ss have access to the Internet, you could get them to research the person's life and report back to the class on how life is different for them now.

Lifelong learning

▶ Read through the questions in the box with the class and get Ss to discuss them in pairs or small groups, making notes about any useful ideas. Then ask Ss to stand up and mingle and share their ideas with other Ss.

Vocabulary

OPTIONAL WARMER

Get Ss to think back to 'Sir Alfred', who they read about in Ex. 2, but not to look back at the text. Ask Ss to work in pairs and write down as much as they can remember about his physical appearance. Get whole class feedback and write their ideas on the board.

---

10 ▶ Get Ss to work in pairs and to write the words/ phrases in the box in the appropriate columns in the table. Give Ss dictionaries to help if necessary. You could also encourage them to check pronunciation in the dictionary. Get whole class feedback.

Answers:
HAIR: straight, curly, wavy, dyed, going a bit bald, mousy, spiky
FACE: wrinkles, clean-shaven, round
BUILD: muscular, stocky, a bit overweight, slim, chubby
GENERAL: good-looking, scruffy, elegant, tanned

11 ▶ Get Ss to work in pairs and correct the mistake in each sentence. You might want to do the first one as an example so they get the idea of the type of mistake. Get whole class feedback.

Answers:
1 He's got short, black **hair** and a small moustache. 2 She's lost a lot of weight recently. She's quite a~~a~~ skinny now. 3 I like having a few ~~of~~ wrinkles. I think it gives your face more character. 4 She's got **spiky**, blond hair and striking blue eyes. You can't miss her. 5 Simon's changed in the last few years. He's going a bit **bald** now. 6 She's a~~a~~ terribly elegant and only wears the best designer outfits. 7 His hair used to be very **curly** when he was a baby. 8 He always looks **tanned** and healthy. I think he spends a lot of time in the Caribbean.

12 ▶ Read the example through with the class. Then get Ss to work in small groups. They should take turns to choose one of the categories and describe a famous person. The other Ss should try to guess the person as quickly as possible.

Writing

13 ▶ Get Ss to look at the pictures, read the email and decide which person is being described, underlining the relevant parts of the email. Ss should briefly check in pairs. Then get whole class feedback.

Answer: Third person down

14a ▶ Get Ss to work in pairs and describe the people in the other pictures in as much detail as they can.

b ▶ Tell Ss to imagine that they have met one of the people at a party (not the one described in the email). Get them to write an email to a friend telling them what he/she looks like. Remind them to give as much detail as possible.

OPTIONAL EXTENSION

You could get Ss to write about their own appearance and how it has changed. If possible, tell them to find two photographs of themselves – one recent photo and one from at least 10 years ago. Get them to write a description of what they used to look like in the past, compared with what they look like now.

You may want to do an example using yourself to get them going. You could show Ss two photographs of yourself (one present and one past) and elicit two descriptions.

5.2 Lasting memories

For most people, old photographs often evoke strong memories. In this lesson, Ss listen to a man called Simon talking about two photographs from his childhood. He describes the photos, as well as talking about the memories and feelings they trigger for him.

Ss also focus on the grammar of expressing ability (past, present, future and in general) and then get a chance to talk about some photos, including their own, if they want. They describe the photos and discuss memories from their childhood, including things they could/could not do. Ss also talk about things they can/can't do and things they would like to be able to do in the future.

You may want to get Ss to bring in their own photos in preparation for the speaking in Ex. 5.

> **OPTIONAL WARMER**
>
> Introduce the topic of photographs by asking Ss some or all of the following questions.
> **Q: How often do you take photographs?**
> **Q: What do you generally take photographs of and why?**
> **Q: How good are you at organising the photos that you want to keep? What do you do with them (e.g. put them in albums, frame them, keep them in a disorganised pile)?**
> **Q: Have you got any/many photographs from when you were a child?**

Listening

1 ▶ Focus Ss on the photograph and work in pairs. Tell Ss to read through the sentences, to decide which of them accurately describe the photo and to change the others to make them true. Get whole class feedback.

> **Answers:** 1 True 2 Not true. The woman is looking relaxed and happy. 3 Not true. The cat is to the side and behind the child. 4 Not true. The woman is wearing casual sandals and a floral dress. 5 True 6 True 7 True 8 Not true. She's probably in her 30s or 40s. 9 Not true

2 ▶ Tell Ss that they are going to listen to a man called Simon talking about this photo (which is from his childhood) to his friend Camilla. Play recording 5.2 and get Ss to answer the questions. After briefly checking in pairs, get whole class feedback.

> **Answers:** 1 The woman is the child's nanny. 2 He says he was a model child.

3 ▶ Read through the answers with the class. Play recording 5.2 again and get Ss to write questions that are appropriate for the answers. Ss should check in pairs. Then get whole class feedback.

> **Answers:** 1 How much of the house did they rent? 2 Why did his mother employ Muriel? 3 How long did Muriel stay and look after Simon? 4 What was Muriel like? 5 How old was he when he could say his first few words? 6 How old was he when he could play simple tunes on the piano reasonably well?

4a ▶ Get Ss to look at the tapescript on page 169. Tell them to work in pairs and to discuss what they think the words/phrases might mean. Remind them to look at the context to help try to work it out. Get whole class feedback.

> **Answers:** 1 rambling: having an irregular shape and covering a large area 2 pretty much to ourselves: almost nobody else used it (the garden) 3 haven't changed a bit: am no different 4 mess around: behave in a silly way when you should be paying attention or doing something sensible 5 a model child: a child who is considered to be good because they do everything they should 6 reasonably well: quite well 7 apparently: you have heard something is true but you are not completely sure about it 8 Shame really: you are disappointed about something i.e. It's a pity.

b ▶ Get Ss to describe something in their past (e.g. a friendship, their childhood) to a partner, using three of the words/phrases from Ex. 4a.

Speaking

5 ▶ Get Ss to work in pairs and choose to talk about one of the photos on the page or one of their own favourite photos (which they could bring in to show to other Ss or which they could just refer to and describe). Get Ss to prepare what to say, including details of where it is, who the people are, why it is a favourite and how it makes them feel. Explain that they can make up these details if they are talking about one of the photos on the page.

> **OPTIONAL EXTENSION**
>
> You could get Ss to write one or two paragraphs about the photograph they talked about.

Grammar

> **OPTIONAL GRAMMAR LEAD-IN**
>
> Ask Ss to discuss this question in pairs:
> **Q: What different ways of expressing ability do you know?**
> You might want to start them off by giving *can* and *could* as two ways (e.g. *He can speak Chinese. I could play the piano when I was four.*)

6a ▶ Get Ss to complete each of the example sentences 1–6 and rules A–D in the Active grammar box using *can*, *could*, *able*, *manage(d)* or *succeed(ed)*. After checking answers in pairs, get whole class feedback.

Active grammar

1 able 2 could 3 manage 4 able
5 Can 6 succeeded

A Use **can** to talk about present or 'general' ability.

B Use will be **able** to talk about future ability.

C Use **could** or was/were **able** to talk about past or 'general' ability.

D Use was/were **able**, **manage** to or **succeed** in to talk about ability on a particular occasion.

b ▶ Tell Ss that there other ways of expressing ability. Get them to work in pairs and decide which of the sentences mean approximately the same. If they need more help, tell them that there are four pairs which mean approximately the same and one 'odd one out'. Get whole class feedback.

Answers: 1+4; 2+8; 3+5; 6+9; 7

7 ▶ Tell Ss to find the mistake in each sentence and correct it. After checking their answers in pairs, get whole class feedback.

Answers: 1 I can't ~~to~~ tell you when Mr Fozard will be free if I don't know. 2 I was able **to** drive Sam and Marta to the airport because my uncle lent me his car. 3 Tom and I **managed** to move the piano into the living room this morning. 4 We won't **be** able to play tennis this weekend unfortunately. 5 He said he knew how to **sail** but he's never actually been out on a boat! 6 Very few people have succeeded in **climbing** to the very top of that mountain. 7 We haven't **been** able to find a wedding ring that we both like. 8 I've always been terrible **at** remembering names.

8 ▶ Get Ss to work in pairs and complete the sentences using the words in brackets in the correct form and one of the verbs from the box. Get whole class feedback.

Answers: 1 You **can spend** the night here if you like. The spare room's free. 2 I **couldn't drive** until I was nearly thirty. I just never got round to taking my test. 3 **Did you manage to get** through to someone at your bank and tell them that your credit card had been stolen? 4 I'd like to **be able to swim** but I have problems holding my breath under water. 5 We got lost and so we **couldn't find** the restaurant you told us about but we did end up going to another one which was really good. 6 I was surprised that Chris **was able to beat** Steve at tennis. Steve is a very good player. 7 The sales team have **succeeded in meeting** all their targets this month and so everyone will get a bonus. 8 Fortunately, we **managed to clean** up the house after the party before our parents got home.

9 ▶ Tell Ss that they are going to listen to Camilla (from the previous listening) talking about herself and her brother. Play recording 5.3 and get Ss to write notes about things Camilla and her brother were able to do as children and more recently. Ss should check their answers in pairs. Then get whole class feedback.

Answers:

CAMILLA	HER BROTHER
Was able to swim well by eight	Can swim but doesn't like it
Really good at chess	Never managed to beat Camilla at chess
Recently succeeded in coming down her first black slope without falling over	Great at skiing – a real natural

Person to person

10 ▶ Get Ss to discuss the questions in pairs or small groups. Then get whole class feedback.

OPTIONAL ALTERNATIVE

Get Ss to stand up and mingle and ask and answer the questions with as many different Ss as they can. Encourage them to think hard about question 5 and come up with something, however seemingly insignificant (e.g. *I can wiggle my ears and nobody else can. I can count from one to ten in Chinese.*)

Listening

11 ▶ Remind Ss about Simon and the first photo he talked about in Ex. 1. Read through the list of differences with the class. Play recording 5.4 and get Ss to say which of the differences with the first photo he refers to. Ss should briefly check answers in pairs before getting whole class feedback.

Answers: 2 how he feels about the place; 3 how he feels about the animals

12 ▶ Play recording 5.4 again and then get Ss to read the summary and find three mistakes. Ss should check their answers in pairs. Then get whole class feedback.

Answers: 1 The photo shows him with his parents, his father's older sister Joan and her husband, Jack.
2 The hotel is in the south-west of England.
3 The dogs were not similar to his cat at home. 'His cat was superior and independent ... and he wasn't very interested in kids'

13 ▶ Get Ss to discuss the questions in pairs or small groups. Get brief whole class feedback by asking two or three Ss to report back on one interesting thing they talked about.

5.3 Memory box

The Memory Box by Margaret Forster (published in 2000) is a novel about a young woman who leaves a sealed memory box for her baby daughter before she dies. Years later, as a young woman herself, Catherine finds her mother's box full of strange, unexplained objects, carefully wrapped and numbered, like clues to a puzzle. Finding out what the objects represent is her only chance to find out about the mother she never knew. As she tries to solve the mystery of the box of secrets, she discovers that her mother was far more complex, surprising and dangerous than anyone had ever said. As the story of her mother's past unfolds, Catherine also discovers unexpected truths about herself. Margaret Forster has written a number of other popular novels including *Hidden Lives*, *Precious Lives* and *Shadow Baby*. For more information go to: www.amazon.co.uk

In this lesson, Ss read an extract from the novel *The Memory Box* by Margaret Forster, discussing their reactions to the book and how they might feel about making or being given a memory box. Ss then focus on the grammar of *although, but, however* and *nevertheless* and talk about a book (or film), describing the plot as well as things they liked and didn't like about it.

> **OPTIONAL WARMER**
>
> Introduce Ss to the topic of feelings.
>
> Either, bring some pictures of people with different feelings, or show a feeling on your face and get Ss to guess what the feeling is (e.g. *bored, angry*). Then get Ss to work in pairs and to brainstorm as many adjectives to describe different feelings as they can. Write the words on the board, checking that Ss understand all the words.

Vocabulary

1a ▶ Focus Ss on the picture of the woman and ask them to discuss in pairs how she might be feeling. Get brief whole class feedback encouraging Ss to explain reasons for their decisions but do not say anything about the book at this stage.

b ▶ Read the words in the box through with the class but do not explain the meanings at this stage. Play recording 5.5 and get Ss to match one of the words in the box with each person they hear. Get them to check answers in pairs. Then get whole class feedback checking that Ss understand the meanings of all the words.

> **Answers:** 1 optimistic   2 uninterested   3 confused
> 4 relieved   5 uneasy   6 curious   7 sceptical
> 8 excited   9 annoyed   10 suspicious   11 shocked

2 ▶ Get Ss to work in pairs and complete the sentences with the most appropriate word from Ex. 1. Get whole class feedback.

> **Answers:** 1 relieved   2 excited   3 uneasy
> 4 optimistic   5 annoyed   6 confused   7 sceptical
> 8 curious   9 uninterested   10 suspicious
> 11 shocked

3 ▶ Tell Ss to choose six of the feelings from Ex. 1 and to try to remember the last time they felt each of the feelings. Get Ss to work in pairs and to explain to their partner why they felt like that, giving details. You could get whole class feedback, by asking two or three Ss to report back to the class on one of the feelings they described.

> **OPTIONAL EXTENSION**
>
> You could add a further vocabulary extension activity here. Write the following adjectives on the board and get Ss to work in pairs to match each one with a similar meaning in Ex. 1b. Give them dictionaries to help and encourage them to check the pronunciation as well as the meaning. Remind them that the pairs of adjectives will have similar, but not exactly the same, meanings (e.g. *suspicious – distrustful*).
>
> *apprehensive astonished comforted distrustful doubtful hopeful indifferent inquisitive irritated puzzled thrilled*
>
> (Answers: *confused – puzzled*; *suspicious – distrustful*; *uneasy – apprehensive*; *curious – inquisitive*; *annoyed – irritated*; *excited – thrilled*; *uninterested – indifferent*; *sceptical – doubtful*; *optimistic – hopeful*; *shocked – astonished*; *relieved – comforted*)

Reading

4a ▶ Focus Ss on the cover of the book *The Memory Box* and get Ss to discuss in pairs what they think it might be about. Get whole class feedback but do not accept or reject any ideas at this stage.

b ▶ Get Ss to read the extract quickly and decide who Susannah, Charlotte and Catherine are. Encourage them to read quickly just to answer this question and not to focus on other details at this stage. Get Ss to check their answers in pairs before getting whole class feedback.

> **Answers:** Catherine is the main character ('I' in the book). Susannah is Catherine's real mother (who died when Catherine was a baby). Charlotte is Catherine's stepmother (who died recently when Catherine was grown-up).

5a ▶ Get Ss to read the extract again and answer the questions. Ss should then check answers in pairs before getting whole class feedback. Some of the answers require a subjective response, so get Ss to explain their ideas.

> **Answers:** 1 People often idealise the dead i.e. remember their good points and forget their faults.
> 2 She was sceptical – she didn't believe all the good things that people said about her.   3 He possibly felt uneasy about what it might contain and the effect it might have on Catherine.   4 (various answers possible)   5 (various answers possible)   6 curious, nervous, excited

b ▶ Get Ss to work in pairs and find examples in the text of five of the feelings referred to in Ex. 1. Get them to explain who has the feelings and what causes them. Get whole class feedback.

6 ▶ Get Ss to work in pairs or small groups and discuss the questions. Get whole class feedback.

Grammar

> **OPTIONAL GRAMMAR LEAD-IN**
>
> Write the following words/phrases on the board. Get Ss to divide them into two groups and to justify their groupings. Get whole class feedback.
>
> *and but although besides furthermore*
>
> *however in addition nevertheless*
>
> (Answers:
> To express contrast: *although, but, however, nevertheless*
> To express addition: *and, furthermore, besides, in addition*)

7 ▶ Get Ss to look at the pairs of sentences in the Active grammar box and decide which one is correct, which is not and why. After checking answers in pairs, get whole class feedback.

> **Active grammar**
>
> 1 (b) is correct. *Although* joins two clauses in one sentence. It does not begin a new sentence.
>
> 2 (a) is correct. We do not usually follow *but* with a comma.
>
> 3 (b) is correct. *However* begins a new sentence and comes before the clause which introduces the surprising or unexpected information.
>
> 4 (a) is correct. *Nevertheless* generally begins a new sentence.

8 ▶ Get Ss to choose the correct alternative in each sentence. Ss should check answers in pairs. Then get whole class feedback.

> **Answers:** 1 but 2 Although 3 Nevertheless
> 4 but 5 although 6 However

9a ▶ Get Ss to complete the sentences in a logical way and then compare them with a partner. Get whole class feedback.

> **Possible answers:** 1 The food in the restaurant was extremely good. *However*, it was a lot more expensive than they thought it would be. 2 I like Jane very much *but* she can be very selfish. 3 I realise that you have worked for this company for many years. *Nevertheless*, we have to make some cutbacks. 4 We decided to buy the house *although* all our friends told us we were mad.

b ▶ Get Ss to rewrite their sentences using a different expression of contrast each time. After checking in pairs, get whole class feedback.

Speaking

10a ▶ Get Ss to think about a book or film that they have read/seen recently that they can remember quite well. You might want to get Ss to tell each other about the book/film briefly.

b ▶ Read through the notes about *The Memory Box* with the class. Then get Ss to make some notes about their book/film using the three things in the list. Remind them just to write notes using *The Memory Box* notes as an example.

c ▶ Play recording 5.6 and get Ss to say if the person is generally positive or negative about *The Memory Box*. Ss should check answers briefly in pairs. Then get whole class feedback.

> **Answers:** Generally positive

d ▶ Get Ss to work in pairs or small groups and to tell each other about the book/film they chose. Remind them to talk about the plot, things they liked and any criticisms, using their notes if necessary. They should also use the expressions from Ex. 9 where appropriate. You could get whole class feedback by asking two or three Ss to report back on one of the books/films they heard about in their group.

> **OPTIONAL EXTENSION**
>
> You could get Ss to write a short review of the book or film they talked about. Remind them to divide their writing into four paragraphs: 1 the plot 2 things they liked 3 any criticisms 4 overall opinion/conclusion.

Lifelong learning

▶ Read through the Lifelong learning box with the class. Encourage Ss to go and choose a reader, either by going to the school library, or if your Ss have access to the Internet, you could get them to go to www.penguinreaders.com.

> **OPTIONAL EXTENSION**
>
> When they have chosen and read a book, they could do a short presentation about it for the class (similar to Ex. 10). Ss could recommend books to each other and in this way you could start a kind of 'book club' in the class.

Vocabulary: Idioms describing people

In this lesson, Ss focus on idioms describing people (e.g. a *cold fish*, *a pain in the neck*, *a high-flyer*).

OPTIONAL WARMER

Write these expressions on the board and tell Ss they are all idioms for describing people.

1 *He's a bit of a loner.*
2 *He's a real know-all.*
3 *He's a high-flyer.*
4 *He's a pain in the neck.*
5 *He's an awkward customer.*

Get Ss to work in pairs and to discuss what they think each expression means. Then get them to look at the cartoon pictures in Ex. 1 and match each one to the correct expression.

Picture A:4 Picture B:2 Picture C:5 Picture D:1
Picture E:3

---

1 ▶ Get Ss to match the underlined expressions 1–8 with the correct meanings a–h. If you did the optional warmer, you might want to suggest that Ss do those they discussed first. Ss should check answers in pairs. Then get whole class feedback.

> **Answers:** 1 f) 2 h) 3 b) 4 a) 5 g) 6 c)
> 7 d) 8 e)

2 ▶ Get Ss to complete the sentences. Tell Ss not to look at the expressions in Ex. 1 but to try to remember them. Ss need to write between one and four words in each gap. After checking in pairs, get whole class feedback.

> **Answers:** 1 know-all 2 loner 3 high-flyer 4 in
> the neck 5 awkward customer 6 in the right place
> 7 as nails 8 fish

3a ▶ Get Ss to think about five people they know who they could describe with five of the expressions from Ex. 1. Ss should not tell each other which expressions they have chosen at this stage. They could make notes about how they know the people and what they are like.

b ▶ Get Ss to work in pairs or small groups. Ask them to describe each of their people to the other Ss. They should say how they know the person and what he/she is like, but they should not say the expression. The other Ss should try to decide which expression from Ex. 1 is appropriate for each person. You could get whole class feedback by asking two or three Ss to describe one of their people to the class.

4 ▶ Get Ss to work in pairs or small groups and discuss the questions. Then get whole class feedback.

OPTIONAL EXTENSION

You could get Ss to work in pairs or small groups and to add two or three more idioms for describing people that they know. Then get whole class feedback, making sure that Ss understand all the expressions.

Communication: Time capsule

Time capsules have become more popular in recent years as a way of 'leaving your mark on the future'. People choose items which somehow represent their lives or the world in the present time. These are then put in a special sealed container and buried for future generations to find. Time capsules preserve relevant facts and features of history and can serve as valuable reminders of one generation for another.

In this lesson, Ss listen to people talking about making a time capsule and giving advice about how to do it and what to put in. Ss then discuss their own time capsules, choosing five things to put in.

OPTIONAL WARMER

Get Ss to discuss these questions:
Q: What object have you got that has sentimental value?
Q: If there was a fire in your house and you could only save one thing, what would it be and why?
Q: Which one object of yours would you like your children or grandchildren to keep and why?
Q: In fifty years' time, what everyday objects do you think will be completely different from now?

---

1 ▶ Focus Ss on the photo and advert and get them to discuss the question in pairs. Get class feedback.

> **Answers:** They are putting a time capsule in the ground to help future people know about us. (This photo shows two TV presenters from the children's programme *Blue Peter*, burying a time capsule in 1998 under the Millennium Dome in London. It contains poems, stories and pictures done by children providing a snapshot of their lives as they entered the new millennium.

2 ▶ Tell Ss they are going to listen to someone talking about what she put in a time capsule in 1977. Play recording 5.7 and get Ss to make a note of five general pieces of advice she gives to people who want to prepare a time capsule. After checking in pairs, get class feedback.

> **Answers:** 1 Choose the material your time capsule is made of carefully e.g. aluminium or stainless steel, so that it will last a long time. 2 Make sure that books and papers are printed on the highest quality paper so they don't deteriorate any faster than necessary. 3 Use black and white photographs rather than colour as they are more stable and last longer. 4 Don't use technology which will become redundant. Better to use things that only need eyes or hands. 5 Label the outside of the time capsule clearly with a permanent marker pen.

3a ▶ Get Ss to work in groups and choose five things to put in a time capsule. Encourage Ss to look at the pictures and the examples and to use their own ideas. Remind them to justify their choices by giving reasons.

b ▶ Get each group to explain their choices to the other Ss. Get whole class feedback by asking which group had the best time capsule and why.

Review and practice

1 ▶

> **Answers:** 2 used to be 3 get used to not understanding 4 used to finish 5 get used to having

2 ▶

> **Answers:** 1 The party in the flat upstairs was very noisy. However, I managed to get a few hours' sleep. 2 I would say that Charlotte is my best friend although I've only known her for a few months. 3 I wanted to have a party this weekend but my parents weren't happy about the idea. 4 He is very unreliable. Nevertheless, she seems to be in love with him. 5 Sandra is a very good student. However, she will need to work a bit harder if she wants to pass her exams. 6 Although I had all the necessary qualifications, I didn't get the job. 7 I enjoyed the film but some of the acting was awful.

3 ▶

> **Answers:** 1 Do you think you **will be able** to finish the presentation by Friday? 2 They finally **managed to get** the car out of the mud. 3 I **could draw** quite well as a child. 4 He **wasn't able** to persuade the other employees to go on strike. 5 She **didn't know how to** make his camera work. 6 Did **you manage to** speak to Brian before he went home?

4 ▶

> **Answers:** 1 relieved 2 clean-shaven 3 a bit of a loner 4 muscular 5 pain in the neck 6 confused

Notes for using the Common European Framework (CEF)

CEF References

5.1 Can do: describe appearance

CEF B2 descriptor: Can give clear, detailed descriptions and presentations on a wide range of subjects related to his/her field of interest, expanding and supporting ideas with subsidiary points and relevant examples. (CEF page 58)

5.2 Can do: talk about memories

CEF B2 descriptor: Can convey degrees of emotion and highlight the personal significance of events and experiences. (CEF page 76)

5.3 Can do: talk about books

CEF B2 descriptor: Can give clear, detailed descriptions on a wide range of subjects related to his/her field of interest. (CEF page 59)

CEF quick brief

Though the reference levels in the Common European Framework suggest that students progress 'vertically', from B1 to B2, etc., the Framework itself says that 'learning a language is a matter of horizontal as well as vertical progression'. This means that some learners might like to move from B1 level in a business context to B2 level in a tourist context. The CEF identifies four basic 'domains' that help to understand this horizontal language development: the public domain, the personal domain, the educational domain and the occupational domain.

Portfolio task

Download the Total English Portfolio free from

www.longman.com/totalenglish.

Objective: to help Ss complete the 'important language and cultural experiences' section of their Portfolio Biography.

This task can be done in Ss' own language.

▶ Ss can further improve their language learning skills by reflecting on significant experiences that have helped them to learn another language or about another culture.

1 ▶ Refer Ss back to the section of their Passport where they listed their language and cultural experiences.

2 ▶ Ask Ss to choose the most important experiences that have helped them learn a language or learn about a culture. It can help to give examples of your own.

3 ▶ Ask Ss to compare with each other and explain why they were important.

6 Explore

Overview

Lead-in	**Vocabulary:** exploring
6.1	**Grammar:** Present Perfect Simple and Continuous
	Vocabulary: adjectives with -ed and -ing endings
	Can do: write an informal email
6.2	**Grammar:** questions
	Vocabulary: weather
	Can do: ask and answer questions about unusual places
6.3	**Grammar:** making comparisons
	Vocabulary: verb phrases about moving/travelling
	Can do: make comparisons about places and people
Vocabulary	Expressions with *go*
Com. Focus	Travelling companions
Reference	
Practice	

Summary

Lesson 1: Ss read an article about Charlotte Uhlenbroek, who spent over four months living in the jungle and talk about how they would feel about doing the same. Ss also write an email describing an interesting experience.

Lesson 2: Ss listen to people talking about going to the remote Himalayan country of Bhutan and then answer questions and discuss two other unusual holidays.

Lesson 3: Ss read an article about emigration. They then discuss their opinions about emigration and compare different places and people.

Vocabulary: Ss focus on expressions with *go*.

Communication: Ss talk about types of holidays they like and do a quiz to find a good travelling companion.

Film bank: Bhutan (4'32")

An extract from a BBC documentary about Bhutan from the series *Himalaya* with Michael Palin who is well-known for his BBC travel programmes. The whole series involved six months of hard travelling and took Palin through India, Nepal, Tibet and Yunnan to China, before recrossing the Himalayas to Bhutan.

Possible places to use this short film are:
▶ After Lesson 2 to extend the topic of Bhutan.

▶ At the end of the unit to round up the topic and language.

For ways to use this short film in class, see Students' Book page 157 and Teacher's Book page 183.

Lead-in

OPTIONAL WARMER:

Write on the board: *Methods of transport.*

Get Ss to work in pairs and write down as many different methods of transport as they can in two minutes including more unusual ones.
e.g. *glider, rickshaw, camel.*

Get whole class feedback, writing them on the board, and making sure that Ss understand all the words.

1▶ Get Ss to discuss the questions in pairs or small groups. Get whole class feedback.

2▶ Read through the questions with the class. Play recording 6.1 and get Ss to answer the questions. Ss check answers in pairs. Then get class feedback.

Answers: 1 She saw her friend's holiday photos. 2 To learn Spanish and get used to being away from home. 3 She found it hard because she experienced culture shock, everything was very different, lots of things went wrong and she was homesick. 4 She loved it.

3a▶ Get Ss to read the sentences before they listen. Play recording 6.2 and Ss complete the expressions. After checking in pairs, get whole class feedback.

Answers: 1 itchy 2 territory 3 independent 4 wandering 5 bug 6 culture

---

b▶ Get Ss to work in pairs and check the meanings of the expressions in Ex. 3a. Give them dictionaries to help. Get whole class feedback.

Answers: 1 to have itchy feet: to want to go somewhere new or do something different 2 to go into uncharted territory: to go to a place which is quite unexplored, where there are few, if any, maps 3 to go as an independent traveller: to travel on your own not as part of an organised group or tour 4 to wander around: to walk slowly around an area, usually without clear direction or purpose 5 to be bitten by the travel bug: to have a sudden strong urge to travel more 6 to experience culture shock: to feel confused or anxious when you visit a place that is very different from the one you are used to

---

4▶ Get Ss to discuss the questions in pairs or small groups. Get whole class feedback.

EXTEND THE LEAD-IN

In small groups Ss discuss the following, based on the methods of transport from the optional warmer.
Q: Which of these methods of transport have you tried? What was the situation? Did you enjoy it? Would you do it again? Why/Why not? Q: Which of these methods of transport would you most/least like to try? Why?

6.1 The jungle bug

Dr Charlotte Uhlenbroek was born in England but grew up mostly in Ghana in Africa and Kathmandu in Nepal. After doing a PhD in Zoology, she went to Tanzania to study chimpanzees with the world-famous Jane Goodall. Since then, she has been part of several programmes for the BBC, including *Cousins* (about chimps), *Talking with Animals* (about animal communication) and *Jungle* in which she explored the rainforests of South-East Asia, the Amazon and Africa. For more information, go to: www.bbc.co.uk/nature/programmes/who/charlotte_uhlenbroek.shtml

In this lesson, Ss read an article about Charlotte Uhlenbroek and her experiences exploring the jungles of the Congo, the Amazon and Borneo when filming for the TV series *Jungle*. Ss focus on the grammar of the Present Perfect Simple and Continuous and talk about some of their experiences. They finish by writing an email to a friend describing an interesting experience.

> **OPTIONAL WARMER**
>
> Play a quick game of word association.
>
> Write the word *jungle* on the board. Get Ss to work in pairs and to write down as many words/phrases associated with the jungle as they can. You could give them an example or two to get them going (e.g. *snakes, Amazon rainforest, sweat*). Get whole class feedback, making sure that Ss understand all the words/phrases.

Reading

1 ▶ Focus Ss on the photos and tell them that the woman in the picture is Charlotte Uhlenbroek and that she spent over four months in the jungle. Get Ss to discuss the questions in pairs. Get whole class feedback about their ideas.

2 ▶ Get Ss to read the text and answer the two questions in Ex. 1 about Charlotte. Ss should check answers in pairs. Then get whole class feedback.

> **Answers:** 1 things she found difficult: being bitten by insects   2 things she wanted to do: have long, hot showers, see her family and enjoy her favourite meal

3 ▶ Tell Ss to read the text again and decide if the statements are true, false or we don't know. Encourage them to correct the false statements and give an explanation for the ones we don't know. Get them to check answers in pairs. Then get whole class feedback.

> **Answers:** 1 false (she fits in in both places)   2 false (she was worried the ropes would break)   3 false (the sand flies were the itchiest)   4 don't know (it mentions 'tears' but we don't know if she cried)   5 don't know (they might have done, but they also wanted to film the leeches)   6 true   7 don't know (there wasn't much water, but we don't know if it was dirty or not)   8 don't know (she enjoys eating with her family, but the text doesn't mention cooking)

4 ▶ Get Ss to discuss the question in pairs or small groups. Encourage them to give reasons. Get whole class feedback by asking a few Ss to report back to the class.

Grammar

> **OPTIONAL GRAMMAR LEAD-IN**
>
> Write the following on the board: *She's worked in the jungle _____. She worked in the jungle _____.*
>
> Ask Ss to choose which of these phrases best completes them: *last year/since last month* and to say why. (Answers: *She's worked in the jungle since last month. She worked in the jungle last year.*)
>
> Then, write the following on the board: *She's worked _____. She's been working _____.*
>
> Ask Ss to choose which of these phrases best completes them: *in three different jungles/in the jungle for four months* and to say why. (Answers: *She's worked in three different jungles./She's been working in the jungle for four months.*)
>
> You may not want to get whole class feedback on why each sentence is correct at this stage, but to wait until Ss look at the Active grammar box.

5 ▶ Get Ss to match the examples 1–4 with the correct rules A–D in the Active grammar box. Ss should check their answers in pairs. Then get whole class feedback.

> **Active grammar**
> 1 D   2 A   3 B   4 C

6 ▶ Read through the rules in the Active grammar box about *just, yet* and *already* with the class. Get Ss to correct the mistake in each sentence. (Questions 1–6 relate to *just/already/yet*, question 7 relates to *since/for* and question 8 relates to state verbs.) After checking in pairs, get whole class feedback.

> **Answers:** 1 I **went** to the Brazilian rainforest in 2003.   2 She's **already bought** her plane tickets.   3 I've **visited** friends in Italy three times this year.   4 What **have** you been doing since I last spoke to you?   5 Have you seen that film, *Sahara* **yet**?   6 He **has just** spoken to the tour guide about it.   7 I've been learning Spanish **for** two months.   8 Have you **known** each other long?

7 ▶ Get Ss to complete the questions by using the prompts in brackets. Remind them to use one of the four verb tenses from the Active grammar box. Ss should check answers in pairs. Then get whole class feedback.

> **Answers:** 1 **Have you ever been** to a jungle?   2 **Have you decided** where to go for your next holiday?   3 How long **have you been studying** English?   4 What do you want to do today that **you haven't done yet**?   5 Where **did you go** for your last holiday?   6 How much coffee **have you had already** today?   7 **Have you ever had** a bad insect bite?   8 Where **have you been living** for the last year?

Person to Person

8a ▶ Get Ss to work in pairs and ask and answer the questions in Ex. 7.

b ▶ Tell Ss to choose one of the questions they asked and ask their partner more details about it. You could get whole class feedback by asking two or three Ss to report back to the class about their partner's answers.

> **OPTIONAL EXTENSION**
>
> You could get Ss to write one or two paragraphs about either their own experience or their partner's experience that they discussed in detail in Ex. 8b.

Vocabulary

9a ▶ Get Ss to work in pairs. Tell them to find the adjectives in the text on page 76 and discuss what they think they mean. Discourage them from using dictionaries for this exercise and remind them to use the context around the words to help work out the meaning. Get whole class feedback, making sure that Ss understand all the words.

> **Answers:** 1 fascinating = extremely interesting
> 2 daunting = frightening in a way that makes you feel less confident   3 challenging = difficult in an interesting or enjoyable way   4 petrified = extremely frightened, especially so that you cannot move or think
> 5 annoying = making you feel slightly angry
> 6 disgusting = extremely unpleasant and making you feel sick   7 inspiring = giving people a feeling of excitement and a desire to do something great
> 8 worried = unhappy because you keep thinking about a problem or that something bad might happen

b ▶ Get Ss to look at the words in context again and to choose the correct alternatives for the two rules. Get whole class feedback.

> **Answers:** 1 -ed   2 -ing

c ▶ Get Ss to write sentences using the adjectives from Ex. 9a. Ss should compare their sentences in pairs. Then get whole class feedback.

Pronunciation

10 ▶ Play recording 6.3 and get Ss to mark the stress for each adjective. You might want to do the first one as an example. After checking in pairs, get whole class feedback. Then get Ss to repeat the words.

> **Answers:** 1 <u>fasci</u>nated, <u>fasci</u>nating   2 <u>daun</u>ted, <u>daun</u>ting   3 <u>chall</u>enged, <u>chall</u>enging   4 <u>petri</u>fied, <u>petri</u>fying   5 a<u>nnoy</u>ed, a<u>nnoy</u>ing   6 dis<u>gus</u>ted, dis<u>gus</u>ting   7 in<u>spir</u>ed, in<u>spir</u>ing   8 <u>wo</u>rried, <u>wo</u>rrying

11a ▶ Tell Ss to read each mini-dialogue (A/B) first and then to complete it with the most appropriate adjective from Ex. 10. Ss should check their answers in pairs, but do not get whole class feedback at this stage.

b ▶ Play recording 6.4 and get Ss to check their answers. Then get whole class feedback.

> **Answers:** 1 petrified   2 daunting   3 worried
> 4 inspiring   5 annoyed   6 disgusting   7 fascinating
> 8 challenging

12a ▶ Get Ss to work in groups and to ask and answer the questions (A) in Ex. 11a with other Ss. Tell them to use the adjectives in Ex. 10a and to try to give true answers.

b ▶ Get whole class feedback by asking Ss to say who has the most similar feelings to them. Encourage them to give details.

> **OPTIONAL ALTERNATIVE**
>
> If possible, you could get Ss to stand up and mingle while they ask the questions in Ex. 12a. Tell them to ask as many Ss as possible and remind them to make notes about the answers.

Writing

13 ▶ Refer Ss to the Writing Bank on page 162. Read through the four summary sentences with the class. Tell them to read the email and to say which of the sentences best summarises the email. After briefly checking in pairs, get whole class feedback.

> **Answer:**   Sentence 2

▶ Read through the Useful Phrases box with the class. Remind Ss that this language can be used but it is an informal email to a friend so there are no fixed rules about language to include.

14 ▶ Tell Ss that they are going to write an email to a friend about an experience they had. Get them to choose one of the situations in Ex. 11a to write about and read through the paragraph plan with the class. Tell them to write an email using the paragraph plan, Maisie's email and the language in the Useful Phrases box on page 162. You could also encourage them to use some adjectives from Ex. 10 as appropriate.

> **OPTIONAL EXTENSION**
>
> You could get Ss to read each other's emails and do some peer correction. Get them to check:
> • if the paragraphs are appropriately divided,
> • if the language from the Useful Phrases box is correct and appropriate,
> • if any adjectives are correct and appropriate.
> Encourage Ss to give each other constructive feedback and then to rewrite their email incorporating any comments. Then get them to reread each other's new versions.

6.2 A magical kingdom

Bhutan is a country of about 750,000 people in the eastern Himalayas, between India and China. It is a very private country where culture, tradition and nature are all flourishing. The Bhutanese people believe that all forms of life, human and non-human, are precious and sacred. People live in harmony with each other and with nature, creating a clean country, with a huge variety of plant and animal life and virtually no discrimination at all. In order to safeguard this rich natural environment and peaceful culture, Bhutan has adopted a cautious and controlled approach to tourism. In 2003, there were fewer than 6000 tourists and this number is not expected to increase greatly. No independent travellers are permitted in Bhutan; all tourists must go on a pre-planned, prepaid, guided, package tour.

In this lesson, Ss read a short text about Bhutan and then listen to people asking for more information about the culture, the weather and what you can do there. Ss focus on the grammar of direct and indirect questions, and then ask and answer questions about other unusual holidays. They finish by discussing which one they would like to go on and why.

> **OPTIONAL WARMER**
>
> Write these words on the board: *Africa, Colombia, Europe, Austria, Asia, Australasia, New Zealand, Tanzania, South America, China.*
>
> Ask Ss to work together and answer these questions:
> **Q: Divide them into two groups: Continents and Countries.   Q: Which country is in which continent? Q: Add two more countries to each continent group.**
>
> Get whole class feedback. (**Answers:** Tanzania is in **Africa**; Austria is in **Europe**; China is in **Asia**; New Zealand is in **Australasia**; Colombia is in **South America**)

Reading

1a ▶ Focus Ss on the photo and map of Bhutan and get them to discuss the questions in pairs. Get whole class feedback but do not accept or reject any ideas yet.

b ▶ Get Ss to read the text and check their ideas. Ss check their answers in pairs. Then get class feedback.

> **Answers:** 1 The environment is very clean, nature is flourishing and there is peace amongst the people with no discrimination.   2 Few tourists go because tourism is strictly controlled by the government in order to preserve the peaceful, clean state of the country.

2 ▶ Read through with the class the three things (a, b and c) that the Ss have to summarise. Tell Ss to read the text again and then work with a partner to summarise each of the things. Get whole class feedback by asking Ss for their summaries.

> **Possible answers:** a One of the main beliefs of the Bhutanese people is that you shouldn't harm any kind of living thing, human or non-human.   b The natural environment in Bhutan is incredibly clean and contains a huge variety of different animals and plants.   c The few tourists that Bhutan allows have to come on organised trips, not as independent travellers.

3 ▶ Get Ss to discuss the questions in pairs or small groups. If necessary, remind them what 'experience culture shock' means. Do brief whole class feedback.

Vocabulary

> **OPTIONAL WARMER**
>
> You could ask Ss to speculate about the weather in Bhutan. Get them to look again at the photo and the map and discuss their ideas. Do not accept or reject any of their ideas at this stage but encourage them to explain any reasons for their ideas.
>
> You may want to tell Ss that they will come back to the topic of Bhutan (and its weather, amongst other things) later in the unit.

4 ▶ Read the two questions through with the class. Play recording 6.5 and tell Ss to decide which of the questions each of the three people is talking about. After checking in pairs, get whole class feedback.

> **Answers:**   1 A   2 B   3 A

5a ▶ Get Ss to work in pairs and look at the tapescript on page 171. Tell them to write the underlined words in the correct place in the table. Get whole class feedback to confirm which column each word goes in but do not explain the meanings at this stage.

> **Answers:** (including answers for 5c)
> **Cold:** cool (a), chilly (a), subzero temperatures (a+n)
> **Warm/Hot:** mild (a), humid (a), humidity (n), scorching (a)
> **Rain:** pours (v), showery (a), shower (n), drizzle (n+v)
> **Windy:** breeze(n), breezy (a)
> **Sky:** clear (a), bright (a), overcast (a)
> **Weather in general:** changeable (a)
> (a = adjective, n = noun, v = verb)

b ▶ Tell Ss to work together and explain the difference in meaning between the words in each column in the table. Give them dictionaries if necessary. Get class feedback.

> **Answers:** cool = low in temperature but not cold, often in a way that feels pleasant   chilly = cold enough to make you feel uncomfortable   subzero temperatures = below zero or freezing   mild = fairly warm   humid = if the weather is humid, you feel uncomfortable because the air is wet and it is usually hot   scorching = extremely hot   to pour = to rain very hard   showery = when the weather has short periods of rain   drizzle = light rain   breeze = gentle wind   clear = no clouds   bright = sunny and light   overcast = when the sky is dark with clouds   changeable = when the weather is likely to change, or changes often

c ▶ Get Ss to work in pairs and decide if each word in the table is a noun, adjective or verb, and what other forms there are. Get whole class feedback.

Answers: See 5a above

6▶ Get Ss to match one of the words from Ex. 5 with each of the sentences. Ss should check answers in pairs. Then get whole class feedback.

Answers: 1 mild   2 pour   3 scorching   4 overcast   5 showery   6 chilly   7 drizzle   8 subzero temperatures   9 changeable   10 bright

7▶ Get Ss to work in pairs or small groups and discuss the questions. Get whole class feedback by asking two or three Ss for their opinions.

Listening

OPTIONAL WARMER

Get Ss to write a list of everything they can remember about Bhutan and compare the list with other Ss. Get whole class feedback and write the list on the board.

8a▶ Ask Ss to discuss the question in pairs. Get brief whole class feedback.

b▶ Tell Ss that they are going to listen to a question and answer session with an expert on Bhutan and some people who are considering a trip there. Read through the things in the box with the class. Play recording 6.6 and get Ss to answer the question. Ss should check answers in pairs and then get whole class feedback.

Answers:
Order: 1 the ideal time of year to visit 2 what to do there   3 what to take   4 organised trips   5 food   6 special events/festivals

9▶ Ask Ss to read through the notes quickly. Play recording 6.6 again and get Ss to complete the notes. Ss check their answers in pairs. Get class feedback.

Answers: 1 it's cold and snow makes travelling difficult   2 it's very hot and often wet   3 plants   4 walking boots   5 sunglasses   6 food   7 camping equipment   8 chilli   9 offer thanks to their gods   10 communicate with the heavens

10▶ Get Ss to discuss the questions in pairs or small groups. Get whole class feedback.

OPTIONAL EXTENSION

You could get Ss to write a paragraph about the festival or celebration that they talked about in Ex. 10.

If they are interested in the topic, they could do a longer piece of writing and perhaps bring some photos to illustrate it. They could then do a short presentation to the class.

Grammar

OPTIONAL GRAMMAR LEAD-IN

Ask Ss to think back to the listening in Ex. 8. Tell them to work in pairs and try to remember as many of the questions as they can that the Bhutan expert was asked.

Get whole class feedback and write on the board one direct question and one indirect that Ss can remember. Ask them what the difference is between them.

11▶ Get Ss to work in pairs and complete the questions in the Active grammar box. Then tell them to look at the tapescript on page 171 and check their answers. Get whole class feedback if necessary. Check that Ss understand the difference between object and subject questions and between direct and indirect questions.

Active grammar

1 **Would we need ...** ?   2 **Do you ...** ?   3 ... **do you recommend**?   4 ... **is ...** ?   5 ... **goes ...** ?   6 ... **they are**?   7 ... **the food is ...** ?   8 ... **if there are ...** ?   9 ... **whether we need ...** .

12a▶ Get Ss to correct the mistake in each question. (They are all direct questions). Ss should check answers in pairs and then get whole class feedback.

Answers: 1 Where **are you** living at the moment?   2 **Has he** ever been trekking before?   3 Who **gave** you those lovely flowers?   4 What time **will** you be here tomorrow?   5 **Are** you having a holiday soon?   6 When **was this company** started?

b▶ Tell Ss to change the direct questions in Ex. 12a into indirect questions starting with the words given. Remind them to think about word order. Get Ss to check their answers in pairs. Then get whole class feedback.

Answers: 1 ... where you are living at the moment?   2 ... if/whether he has ever been trekking before?   3 ... who gave you those lovely flowers?   4 ... what time you will be here tomorrow?   5 ... if/whether you will be having a holiday soon?   6 ... when this company was started.

Speaking

13a▶ Divide Ss into groups (A and B) and tell them that they are going to find out about two other types of holiday. Get Student As to write questions about camel trips in Egypt and Student Bs to write about bird watching in Mexico. Tell them to look at the list of ideas to help and encourage them to use indirect as well as direct questions.

b▶ Tell Ss that they are going to prepare answers to their partner's questions. Get Student As to read the text about bird watching in Mexico on page 150 and prepare answers. Get Student Bs to read the text about camel trips in Egypt on page 145 and prepare answers.

c▶ Get Ss to work in pairs (one A and one B) and to take turns to ask and answer questions.

14▶ Get Ss to work in pairs or small groups and discuss the questions. Encourage them to give reasons to justify their opinions. Get brief whole class feedback.

6.3 On the move

Emigration is certainly not only a modern phenomenon. Over the last few centuries, many thousands of people from many different countries have gone to find a better life abroad. Emigration by British people to North America started as long ago as 1585 and the first successful settlement there was in Jamestown in 1607. Since then, British people have principally emigrated to places such as the USA, Canada, Australia and New Zealand and more recently to Spain. Their reasons are many and varied: some were sent to work, some were sent as convicts (mainly to Australia), some were escaping hardship, famine and persecution and some were just seeking a better life. The trend to move abroad continues today, with over 400,000 people from Britain alone leaving every year.

In this lesson, Ss read an article about emigration, including facts about what kinds of people emigrate and their reasons. They then discuss their reactions to the text and their opinions about emigration. Ss focus on the grammar of making comparisons, including comparatives and superlatives of both adjectives and adverbs. They then make comparisons about different places and people.

> **OPTIONAL WARMER**
>
> Write the word *emigrate* on the board and check Ss understand what it means (to leave your country and go to live in another one).
>
> Get Ss to work in pairs and write a list of all the words you can make using the letters of the word *emigrate*. Tell them that each word must contain at least two letters and must not be a name. Give them a time limit of two minutes.
>
> Ask how many words each pair wrote down. Get whole class feedback and write the words on the board. (Some possible words: *ate, gate, mate, grate, eat, meat, great, rim, time, grime, rat, rate, mat, rig, gem, ram, gram, tea, team, tar.*)

Vocabulary

1 ▶ Get Ss to work in pairs. Tell them to match the underlined verb phrases with the correct definitions a–h. Give them dictionaries to help if necessary. Get whole class feedback.

> **Answers:** 1 c   2 a   3 b   4 g   5 d   6 f   7 h   8 e

2 ▶ Get Ss to complete the questions with the correct form of a phrase from Ex. 1. Ss should check their answers in pairs. Then get whole class feedback.

> **Answers:** 1 leave home   2 see you off   3 set off   4 abroad   5 emigrated   6 moved house   7 are you off   8 roamed around

3a ▶ Tell Ss to look again at the questions in Ex. 2 and to make a note about what they think their partner's answers will be.

b ▶ Then get Ss to work with their partner and to ask and answer the questions. Get whole class feedback and see how many of their predictions each pair got right.

> **OPTIONAL EXTENSION**
>
> You could do some further work on vocabulary here, especially to extend Ss knowledge of phrasal verbs.
>
> Divide the class into group A and group B. Group A should look at list A and Group B should look at list B.
>
> A: *put someone up*; *set something aside*
>
> B: *put someone off*; *set something up*
>
> Get Ss to learn the meaning of the phrasal verbs in their list, making sure that they write an example sentence for each one. You could give out dictionaries for this.
>
> Reorganise the Ss into pairs (one A and one B). Get them to teach each other their phrasal verbs. Encourage them to write their own example sentences for the verbs they learn from their partner.

Reading

4a ▶ Read the statements (A–C) through with the class. Get them to discuss in pairs if they think the statements are true or false. Get brief whole class feedback but do not accept or reject any of the ideas at this stage.

b ▶ Get Ss to read the text quickly and check their answers. Encourage them to correct the ones that are false. Remind them to read only to check their answers and not to worry about other details at this stage. After briefly checking answers in pairs, get whole class feedback.

> **Answers:** 1 false (over 400,000 British people emigrate every year)   2 true   3 false (after three years)

5 ▶ Read through the summary sentences with the class. Tell Ss to read the text again and to match each paragraph with the most appropriate summary A–G. Tell them that three of the summary sentences cannot be used. Get Ss to check their answers in pairs. Then get whole class feedback.

> **Answers:** 1 D   2 G   3 A   4 C (not used: B, E and F)

6 ▶ Get Ss to discuss the questions in pairs or small groups. Encourage Ss to give as much detail as they can and to ask further questions to keep the discussion going. Get whole class feedback by asking each group to report on one interesting aspect of their discussion.

> **Possible answers:** 1 independent, determined, brave, sociable, good at fitting in, good at languages, flexible in terms of work

OPTIONAL EXTENSION

You could do some further intensive work on vocabulary from the text here.

Write the following words/phrases on the board:

prestigious (para. 2); *funding* (para. 2); *recognition* (para. 2); *appealing* (para. 3); *fed up of* (para. 3); *romanticise about* (para. 4); *take for granted* (para. 4)

Ask Ss to find them in the text. Get Ss to work in pairs and answer these questions for each word/phrase. You could give them dictionaries to help if necessary, but also encourage them to use the context of the text to help.

1 What part of speech is it (noun, adjective or verb)?

2 What does it mean?

3 How do you pronounce it?

4 Can you make a sentence using it that is relevant to you?

You could also ask Ss to find one or two more words/ phrases which they would like to remember and answer the questions about them too.

OPTIONAL EXTENSION

You might want to do some work on writing summaries as an extension to the reading.

Tell them to write the four or five main points from the text in note form. They should then compare their ideas with a partner. Next tell them to write a paragraph including only these points. Again, get Ss to compare their summaries with a partner.

Grammar

OPTIONAL GRAMMAR LEAD-IN

Write these adjectives and adverbs on the board:

cheap, fast, hot, nice, popular, carefully, sunny, well, badly

Get Ss to work in pairs and to write the comparative and superlative forms for each one. Get whole class feedback.

(Answers:

cheaper/the cheapest; faster/the fastest; hotter/the hottest; nicer/the nicest; more popular/the most popular; more carefully/the most carefully; sunnier/ the sunniest; better/the best; worse/the worst)

7 ▶ Get Ss to complete the rules in the Active grammar box. Ss should check answers in pairs. Then get whole class feedback.

Active grammar

1A adding -er and -est   1B doubling the consonant and adding -er and -est   1C adding -r and -st

2A using *more and most*   2B changing the *y* to *i* and adding -er and -est

3A different   3B the same

4A the best   4B worse

5A small   5B large

8 ▶ Tell Ss to complete the second sentence so that it means the same as the first. Get Ss to read the example and remind them to use between two and four words (including the word in bold). Ss should check their answers in pairs. Then get whole class feedback.

> **Answers:** 1 My sister learns foreign languages **much more easily** than me.   2 I'd prefer to live somewhere that **isn't as wet as** this.   3 Ten years ago I was **slightly less adventurous than** I am now.   4 My life abroad is **much simpler** than it was at home.   5 I think I should've planned my time on holiday **more carefully**.   6 My lifestyle here in Canada is **as good as** it was in England.

Person to person

9a ▶ Tell Ss to write six sentences about themselves using comparatives and superlatives. They should write four true sentences and two false sentences. Encourage them to use different forms, including (*not*) *as … as* and modifiers where appropriate. Remind them to use the sentences in Ex. 8 to help with ideas.

b ▶ Get Ss to say their sentences to a partner and tell them to try to guess which sentences are true and which are false.

OPTIONAL EXTENSION

You might want to extend the topic of living in another place and/or doing something different and to provide extra practice of comparatives and superlatives.

Get Ss to choose one of the following: (a) somewhere you might consider moving to (either in your country or in another country), or (b) something you might consider studying that you've never studied before.

Then get them to (a) write notes about the positive and negative things about moving there, or (b) write notes about the positive and negative things about doing it.

Then, tell Ss to work in pairs or small groups and to use their notes to discuss the relevant questions below with each other.

a

Q: Where is the place you might consider moving to?
Q: How similar to/different from where you live now is it?
Q: What are the positive things about moving there?
Q: What are the negative things about moving there?

b

Q: What is the thing you might consider studying?
Q: Have you ever done anything similar?
Q: What are the positive things about doing it?
Q: What are the negative things about doing it?

Vocabulary: Expressions with *go*

In this lesson, Ss focus on expressions with *go*, including *to have a go*, *to go back on* and *to be on the go*.

OPTIONAL WARMER

Get Ss to brainstorm expressions and phrasal verbs with *go*. Tell Ss to work in pairs and write down three expressions or phrasal verbs with *go* that they know. Get them to share their ideas with other Ss and explain meanings to each other if possible.

Get whole class feedback and make sure Ss understand all the expressions.

1 ▶ If you did the optional warmer, start by asking Ss to look at the expressions in bold, and check if they had thought of any of them. Get Ss to match the expressions with *go* in bold with the correct definitions a–j. After checking answers in pairs, get whole class feedback.

Answers: 1 j 2 a 3 d 4 h 5 b 6 e
7 i 8 g 9 f 10 c

2 ▶ Get Ss to test each other in pairs. Explain that they should take turns to say a definition in Ex. 1 and that their partner should say the correct expression. Get Ss to read the example to get them going.

3 ▶ Get Ss to choose the correct alternatives. Encourage them not to look at Ex. 1 while they are doing it. Tell Ss to check answers in pairs but do not get whole class feedback at this stage.

4a ▶ Play recording 6.7 and get Ss to check their answers. Get whole class feedback if necessary.

Answers: 1 have 2 away 3 saying 4 on
5 make 6 on 7 on 8 down 9 for 10 great

b ▶ Play recording 6.7 again and get Ss to underline the part of the expression that has the main stress. Read through the example with the class before they listen. Ss check their answers in pairs. After getting class feedback, get Ss to repeat the sentences in pairs.

Answers: Main stress: 1 go 2 away 3 saying
4 on 5 go 6 back 7 go 8 down 9 go
10 lengths

5a ▶ Read through the three sentences with the class. Tell Ss that they are going to tell a story including one of the sentences and five of the expressions in Ex. 1. Get Ss to prepare their story, making brief notes if necessary.

b ▶ Get Ss to tell each other their stories in small groups. Get class feedback by asking Ss the two questions.

OPTIONAL EXTENSION

Get Ss to write the story they told in Ex. 5. Remind them to include the sentence and the five expressions they chose and to organise their story into paragraphs.

Communication: Travelling companions

In this lesson, Ss talk about types of holidays they like. Then they do a quiz to find a good travelling companion who likes/dislikes the same things as them on holiday.

OPTIONAL WARMER

Write the following words/phrases on the board (and/or any other words/phrases from the quiz that you think Ss might need to check).

a package holiday scuba diving a sleeping bag a penknife a romantic novel a tent an open-ended holiday mosquitoes a souvenir a tropical disease

Get Ss to work in pairs or small groups and to explain the meanings of the words/phrases. Give them dictionaries to help if necessary.

1 ▶ Get Ss to look at the photos and to discuss the questions. Get whole class feedback.

2 ▶ Tell Ss that they are going to try to find someone in the class who would make a good travelling companion. Read through the introduction paragraph of the quiz with the class. You may also want to pre-teach the word *dread* in question 5. (*To dread* = to feel anxious or worried about something that is going to happen or may happen).

Tell Ss to do the quiz with as many different Ss as they can. Remind them that when they are asking the questions, they should make notes about the other Ss' answers. And that when they're answering the questions, they should use the ideas in the quiz as well as their own ideas.

3a ▶ Get Ss to read the four descriptions on page 147 and to answer the questions.

b ▶ Get Ss to work in pairs and discuss the questions. Get whole class feedback, encouraging Ss to give reasons for their decisions.

Lifelong learning

▶ Read through the Lifelong learning box with the class. Get Ss to work in pairs or small groups and brainstorm some more ways to continue learning while travelling.

OPTIONAL EXTENSION

Get Ss to work in pairs or small groups with other Ss who they found would make the best travelling companions. Tell them to plan their ideal holiday, including details of where, when, who with, how long, activities, accommodation.

You could remind them about the places they have learned about in this unit (e.g. the jungle, Bhutan, Egypt, Mexico) or encourage them to think of their own ideas too.

You could either get whole class feedback and ask Ss to report their ideas to the class, or you could get Ss to write a paragraph or two about their ideal holiday.

Review and practice

1 ▶

> **Answers:** 1 I've been writing 2 saw 3 for 4 been
> 5 ever 6 I've lived 7 's been working 8 just

2 ▶

> **Answers:** 1 He's already phoned me three times
> today. 2 We went to India for three weeks
> last summer. 3 I've just seen a really fantastic
> musical. 4 Have you heard the news yet? 5 I've
> been decorating the living room all day. 6 I've known
> my best friend since primary school. 7 Have you ever
> read the *Lord of the Rings* books? 8 How long have
> you been studying English?

3 ▶

> **Answers:** 1 How long have you had your
> motorbike? 2 What's she going to study at
> university? 3 How tall are you? 4 Can you reach
> that box on the top shelf for me?

4 ▶

> **Answers:** 1 Can you tell me what time this shop
> closes? (Or: Can I ask you ...?) 2 I'd like to know if
> I can buy theatre tickets here. 3 Would you tell me
> what time you'll finish your homework? 4 Can you
> tell me what the most interesting country you've ever
> visited is?

5 ▶

> **Answers:** 1 much 2 worst 3 as 4 most 5 quite
> 6 friendly 7 a 8 best

6 ▶

> **Answers:** 1 putting ⟶ setting 2 scratchy ⟶ itchy
> 3 make ⟶ have 4 of ⟶ with
> 5 speaking ⟶ saying 6 country ⟶ culture
> 7 to ⟶ on 8 away ⟶ off

Notes for using the Common European Framework (CEF)

CEF References

6.1 Can do: write an informal email

CEF B2 descriptor: Can write letters conveying degrees of emotion and highlighting the personal significance of events and experiences and commenting on the correspondent's news and views. (CEF page 83)

6.2 Can do: ask and answer questions about unusual places

CEF B2 descriptor: Can engage in extended conversation on most general topics in a clearly participatory fashion, even in a noisy environment. (CEF page 76)

6.3 Can do: make comparisons about places and people

CEF B2 descriptor: Can take an active part in informal discussion in familiar contexts, commenting, putting point of view clearly, evaluating alternative proposals and making and responding to hypotheses. (CEF page 77)

CEF quick brief

The reference levels in the Common European Framework (A1–C2) allow a correlation with common international exams as well as exams within a country or institution. This means that employers can have a more accurate idea of what a student with a particular qualification can actually do. For more information see the introduction at the start of this Teacher's Book.

Portfolio task

Download the Total English Portfolio free from www.longman.com/totalenglish.

Objective: to help Ss start using the Portfolio to assess their progress and priorities in English.

This task can be done in Ss' own language.

▶ The Biography section of the Portfolio contains the Can do statements from each lesson in the book. Ss can use this section to review and keep track of their progress. It is helpful to remind students to complete the tick boxes in this section at a regular intervals, perhaps at the end of every unit or at the end of semester.

1 ▶ Ask Ss to look at the Can do statements in the Biography section of their Portfolio. Show how the statements relate to the work they have completed in their coursebooks.

2 ▶ Ask Ss to look through the statements at B1 level and complete the tick boxes.

3 ▶ Explain that as they progress through the course, they will be able to achieve more Can do goals at B1 and will also start to complete goals at B2 level.

Overview

Lead-in	**Vocabulary:** excess
7.1	**Grammar:** countable and uncountable nouns
	Vocabulary: food and cooking
	Can do: describe how to prepare and cook a dish
7.2	**Grammar:** passives
	Vocabulary: verb phrases about money
	Can do: write a formal letter of complaint
7.3	**Grammar:** *have/get something done*
	Vocabulary: animal expressions
	Can do: talk about services
Vocabulary	Prefixes
Com. Focus	Can I help you?
Reference	
Practice	

Summary

Lesson 1: Ss read an article about the film *Super Size Me* and discuss their opinions about the film and junk food in general. They also listen to someone talking about how to make traditional British Christmas dinner and then talk about how to prepare a dish of their choice.

Lesson 2: Ss listen to an item of radio news about selling things at auction. They then do a roleplay as customers complaining in various situations and finish by writing a formal letter of complaint.

Lesson 3: Ss read an article about how some people treat their pets as family members, indulging them with things like proper beds, salon haircuts, jewellery and clothes. Ss also talk about their own attitudes to animals.

Vocabulary: Ss focus on prefixes including *over-*, *under-*, *mono-*, *multi-*, *bi-*.

Communication: Ss listen to dialogues in a restaurant, a shop and a hairdresser and then roleplay their own.

Film bank: Vikings (5'28")

An extract from a documentary about a Viking Re-enactment Society.

Many people in Europe and the USA who are fascinated by the Vikings and their whole way of life are members of 'Re-enactment Societies' and spend their spare time living exactly as the Vikings did. There are many other Re-enactment Societies too for different periods in history. This extract shows what the members of these societies do to be as accurate as they can about every detail including clothes, food and battles.

Possible places to use this short film are:
▶ After Lesson 1 to extend the topic of excessive lifestyles.

▶ At the end of the unit to round up the topic and language.

For ways to use this short film in class, see Students' Book page 158 and Teacher's Book page 184.

Lead-in

OPTIONAL WARMER

Introduce Ss to the topic of 'excess' by getting them to discuss these questions, encouraging them to give details.

Q: What's the most unusual hairstyle you've ever had or seen?
Q: What's the biggest meal you've ever eaten?
Q: What's the longest you've ever gone without sleeping?
Q: What's the most over-the-top exercise/training programme you've ever heard about or done?
Q: What the most unusual person you know or have ever heard about?

1 ▶ Get Ss to discuss the questions in pairs or small groups. Get whole class feedback.

2 ▶ Play recording 7.1 and get Ss to discuss the questions in pairs. Get whole class feedback, encouraging Ss to give reasons to justify their opinions.

3a ▶ Read the questions through with the class. Then get Ss to work in pairs and to discuss the meaning of the words in bold. Give them dictionaries to help if necessary. Get whole class feedback.

Answers: 1 extravagant = spending or costing a lot of money, especially more than is necessary or more than you can afford 2 excessive = much more than is reasonable or necessary 3 luxury = something expensive that you do not need but you buy for pleasure and enjoyment 4 extra-large = very large 5 spoilt = when someone (usually a child) is rude and behaves badly because they have always been given what they want and been allowed to do what they want 6 overpriced = when something is more expensive than it should be 7 far-fetched = extremely unlikely to be true or to happen 8 spending spree = a short period of time when you do a lot of spending

b ▶ Get Ss to ask and answer the questions with a partner. Get whole class feedback by asking Ss to report back on how many/which of their answers were similar to their partner's.

EXTEND THE LEAD-IN

You could get Ss to write a paragraph about either, one of the questions they discussed in Ex. 3a, or, if you did the optional warmer, one of the questions they discussed then.

7.1 Food for thought

Super Size Me, made in 2003, is a film which documents Morgan Spurlock's one-month existence on fast food and its disastrous consequences. In the film, Spurlock eats three McDonald's meals a day, every day, for a month. He only eats food from McDonald's and every time an employee asks if he would like to 'super size' the meal, he agrees. Spurlock knew the experiment was extremely unhealthy but his intention was to show people what this kind of diet can do to you. The film could represent your life: in thirty days you see what could happen to you over twenty or thirty years of over consumption.

In this lesson, Ss read an article about the film *Super Size Me*. They discuss their opinions about the film and junk food in general. Ss then go on to focus on the grammar of countable and uncountable nouns. They also listen to someone talking about how to make traditional British Christmas dinner and then talk about how to prepare a dish of their choice.

> **OPTIONAL WARMER**
>
> Get Ss to discuss these questions: **Q: What have you eaten in the last twenty-four hours? (Give details.) Where did you eat it, who cooked it, and did you enjoy it? Q: Is this a fairly typical twenty-four hours of eating ? If not, what is?**

Reading

1 ▶ Focus Ss on the photo and get them to discuss the questions in pairs. Get brief whole class feedback.

2a ▶ Get Ss to read the text quickly and answer the question. Remind them to focus only on answering the question and not to worry about understanding everything at this stage. Ss check in pairs. Get class feedback.

> **Answers:** You should eat healthy food because eating a lot of junk is seriously bad for your health.

b ▶ Get Ss to read the text again and to work in pairs to explain what each of the phrases means. Remind them to look at the phrases in context and use any clues they can to work out the meaning. Get whole class feedback.

> **Answers: 1** People might be excited about eating a lot of McDonald's food, but it was actually a really bad experience. **2** To increase the size of every part of the meal for very little extra cost. **3** Spurlock knew that eating so much McDonald's was not a sensible healthy thing to do but did it anyway. **4** Doctors knew this diet would have negative effects on his body, but didn't realise it would have such a huge negative impact. **5** All three doctors advised him to stop because it was affecting his body so badly. **6** Eating so much junk food in a month showed what can happen if you do it over a longer time as part of your life. **7** Spurlock thinks that customers have a right to correct information about what is in the food and what effects it has. **8** Spurlock says that McDonald's want to create a happy positive link between playing and eating their food. **9** Although the ideas in the film are depressing, Spurlock himself is funny and the film is well made. **10** Spurlock wants families to have proper meals together so they can talk to each other.

3 ▶ Get Ss to discuss the questions in small groups. Get class feedback by asking a few Ss to report back to the class about the main points of their group's discussion.

Grammar

> **OPTIONAL GRAMMAR LEAD-IN**
>
> Write these sentences on the board:
> 1 I had a delicious *food/meal* yesterday.
> 2 I had some delicious *food/meal* yesterday.
>
> Get Ss to work in pairs and to decide which of the alternatives in each sentence is correct and why. Get whole class feedback. (Answers: 1 *meal*: it is countable and therefore we use *a*; 2 *food*: it is uncountable and therefore we use *some*).

4a ▶ Get Ss to look at the underlined words in the examples in the Active grammar box and decide if each one is countable or uncountable. Ss should check in pairs. Then get whole class feedback, checking that Ss understand that some words (e.g. coffee) can be both countable and uncountable, depending on the context.

> **Active grammar**
>
> 1 *meals* = countable   2 *food* = uncountable
> 3 *(a black) coffee* = countable   4 *coffee* = uncountable

b ▶ Get Ss to work in pairs and divide the words in the box into three groups: countable, uncountable and those which can be both. Get whole class feedback.

> **Answers: 1** raw **2** stir **3** salty **4** chop **5** sweet **6** boil **7** dish **8** cooker **9** roast **10** cabbage

> **Active grammar**
>
> **Countable:** meal, diet, burger, trip
>
> **Uncountable:** food, meat, sugar, salt, bread, fruit, weather, luggage, travel, equipment, advice, furniture, information, news
>
> **Both:** coffee, chicken, chocolate, cake, paper, iron business, hair

c ▶ Remind Ss that for the words that can be both countable and uncountable, the meaning is slightly different in each case. Read through the example with the class. Then get Ss to work in pairs and to discuss the difference in meaning for the words that can be both. Get whole class feedback.

> **Answers:** For all these words, when we use them in the countable way, we are talking about a single one (e.g. a chocolate), a whole one (e.g. a chicken), a cup of something (e.g. a coffee). When we use them in the uncountable way, we are not saying exactly how much, but just *some*.

3 ▶ Remind Ss that we can use other modifiers with countable and uncountable nouns (not just *some*). Read through the sentences with the class. Then get Ss to discuss the question in pairs. Get class feedback.

> **Answers:** *few* and *little* (without a) are used to talk about negative ideas   *a few* and *a little* are used to talk about more positive ideas

6 ▶ Get Ss to complete the sentences with the correct word/phrase from the box. After checking in pairs, get whole class feedback.

> **Answers:** 1 many   2 a little   3 much   4 piece
> 5 some   6 lots   7 a great deal of   8 slice
> 9 a few   10 lot

7 ▶ Get Ss to find the mistakes in eight of the sentences and correct them. Ss check in pairs. Get class feedback.

> **Answers:** 1 Do you spend **a lot of** time doing exercise?
> 2 Have you given anyone **some** good advice recently?
> 3 How **much** sugar do you have in your coffee?
> 4 When was the last time you had **a piece** of cake?
> 5 correct   6 How **much fruit** do you usually eat every day?   7 Do you like **very hot** weather?
> 8 correct   9 When did you last go on an interesting **trip**?   10 When did you last buy some new **furniture**?

Person to person

8 ▶ Get Ss to ask and answer the questions in Ex. 7, in pairs. Get whole class feedback by asking a few Ss to report back about one thing their partner talked about.

Vocabulary

> **OPTIONAL WARMER**
>
> If you did the optional warmer at the beginning of this lesson, get Ss to try to remember what they talked about. If you did not do it, get Ss to work in pairs and to write down all the different food they have eaten in the last twenty-four hours, categorising it by type of food: e.g. fruit, vegetables, meat, drink. Get class feedback and write the words on the board.

9a ▶ Get Ss to work in pairs and put the words in the box in the correct place in the mind map. Give them dictionaries to help if necessary. Get whole class feedback, checking that Ss understand all the words.

> **Answers: Food:** beef, a peach, cabbage, parsley; **Ways of cooking:** to bake, to scramble, to fry, to roast, to boil, to grill; **Kitchen equipment:** a saucepan, an oven, a cooker, a frying pan, a wooden spoon, a plate; **Taste:** sweet, bitter, salty, sour, savoury

b ▶ Get Ss to work with a partner and to discuss the difference between the pairs of words. Again, give them dictionaries to help if necessary. Get whole class feedback by asking different pairs of Ss to explain each one.

> **Answers:** 1 *A cook:* a person who cooks. *A cooker:* the machine you use for cooking. 2 *A vegetable:* a food like carrot, potato. *A vegetarian:* a person who does not eat meat. 3 *A recipe:* instructions about how to cook something. *A dish:* the thing you make e.g. beef stroganoff. 4 *Rare:* cooked only a little (usually for meat, especially steak). *Raw:* not cooked at all
> 5 *To stir:* to mix slowly. *To beat:* to mix quickly.
> 6 *To slice:* to cut into thin pieces. *To chop:* to cut into small squares. *To grate:* to use a grater to make very small pieces of food e.g. cheese or carrots.

c ▶ Get Ss to work in pairs and to add at least two more words to each group of words in the mind map. Get whole class feedback, making sure Ss understand all the words.

10a ▶ Get Ss to choose the correct alternatives. Ss check answers in pairs. Do not get class feedback yet.

> **Answers:** 1 raw   2 stir   3 salty   4 chop   5 sweet
> 6 boil   7 dish   8 cooker   9 roast   10 cabbage

Pronunciation

11a ▶ Look at the example with the class. Get Ss to work in pairs and to decide together which syllable in each word has the main stress. Then play recording 7.2 and get Ss to check their answers. Get whole class feedback.

> **Answers (for 11a and b):** Underlined part is the main stress and part in bold is weak form /ə/ (schwa):
> 1 <u>sauce</u>**pan**   2 <u>ov</u>**en**   3 <u>veg</u>e**table**   4 veg**e**<u>tar</u>**ian**
> 5 <u>bit</u>**ter**   6 <u>sa</u>**vou**ry   7 <u>car</u>**rot**   8 <u>su</u>**gar**

b ▶ Remind them that the syllable(s) which is/are not stressed is/are often a weak form or 'schwa' /ə/. Look again at the example *cooker* with the class and elicit/tell them that the second syllable is a weak form. Get them to work in pairs and to decide which of the syllable(s) in the words are weak forms. Then play recording 7.2 again and get them to check their answers. Get whole class feedback. (Answers above).

Speaking

12 ▶ Focus Ss on the photo and tell Ss that they are going to listen to someone talking about a traditional British Christmas dinner. Play recording 7.3 and get Ss to answer the question. Get whole class feedback, encouraging Ss to justify their answers.

13a ▶ Read the list of things through with the class. Ask Ss to choose one of the things and to think about how it is prepared and cooked. Encourage them to make notes and to use the vocabulary from Ex. 9.

b ▶ Get Ss to work in pairs or small groups and to tell other Ss what their dish is and how to prepare/cook it.

c ▶ Get whole class feedback by asking Ss which of the dishes they would like to eat most and why.

> **OPTIONAL EXTENSION**
>
> Ask Ss to write a recipe of the dish they talked about, including a list of ingredients and instructions. Ss collect their recipes together and make a 'Class Recipe Book'.

7.2 Buy, buy, buy

Two of the most famous auction houses operating internationally are Sotheby's (established in London in 1744) and Christie's (also established in London in 1766). People go to look, to bid and perhaps to buy a range of different items, especially collectable art, furniture and jewellery.

Nowadays, however, traditional auctions also need to compete with online auctions like eBay. eBay was founded by Frenchman Pierre Omidyar in 1995. It started small, and has now become a massive success with some 125 million users, buying and selling an endless array of different products. Buyers and sellers are brought together quickly and easily: sellers can list items for sale, buyers can bid for items of interest and all eBay users can browse through listed items in a fully automated way.

In this lesson, Ss listen to an item of radio news about selling things at auction (both traditional and online). They hear about and discuss their reactions to the extraordinary things people buy and the incredibly high prices people pay. After focussing on the grammar of passives, Ss do a roleplay as customers complaining in various situations and finish by writing a formal letter of complaint.

OPTIONAL WARMER

Introduce Ss to the topic of shopping by asking them to discuss some or all of these questions.
Q: What is the best adjective to describe how you feel about clothes shopping? Why? Q: Do you prefer shopping alone or with other people? Why (and who)? Q: What do you think about online shopping? What experience have you got of it? Q: When was the last time you bought something that you regretted? What was it and why? Q: What is one of your favourite shops? Why do you like it?

Listening

1 ▶ Focus Ss on the photos and get them to discuss the questions. Get whole class feedback on their ideas but do not accept or reject any of their ideas at this stage.

2 ▶ Tell Ss that they are going to listen to part of the radio news. Play recording 7.4 and get them to check their ideas about the question in Ex. 1. After checking their ideas in pairs, get whole class feedback.

Answers: Each of the things/people in the pictures was sold or sold something at auction (either traditional or on eBay).

3 ▶ Read through the statements with the class. Play recording 7.4 again and get Ss to decide if the statements are true or false or we don't know. Encourage Ss to correct the ones which are false. Get Ss to check their answers in pairs. Then get whole class feedback.

Answers: 1 F (she found it herself in her own attic) 2 DK 3 F (someone bought it for $61,000) 4 F (only one of the original six) 5 T 6 F (it was sold on eBay) 7 F (there was no proof) 8 DK 9 F (he sold them on eBay) 10 T

4 ▶ Get Ss to discuss the questions in pairs or small groups. Get whole class feedback.

OPTIONAL EXTENSION

Either: If your Ss have access to the Internet, you could get them to do some research for a mini-project about someone who collects interesting or unusual things. They could write a short essay about it, or prepare a short presentation to give to the class.

Or: If any Ss in your class have an interesting collection of anything, ask them to prepare a short presentation to give to the class. They could bring some items from their collection to show.

Vocabulary

5 ▶ Get Ss to work in pairs and to discuss the difference in meaning between the verb phrases in italics in each pair of sentences. Encourage them to look at the context and try to work out the meaning. You could also give them dictionaries to help. Get whole class feedback, making sure that Ss understand all the meanings.

Answers: 1a *to bid for something* = to offer to pay for something at an auction   b *to haggle for something* = to offer to pay less than the price (especially in a market)   2a *to get a bargain* = to pay a low price for something good   b *to get a discount* = to pay less than the original price because the seller lowers the price   3a *to get a refund* = to take something back to a shop and get your money back   b *to get a receipt* = to get a piece of paper from the shop to prove you bought something   4a *to be able to afford something* = to have enough money to pay for something   b *to be worth it* = for something to be the value of what you paid for it

6a ▶ Get Ss to read the sentences and decide which verb phrase you could use for each. After checking in pairs, get whole class feedback.

Answers: 1 to bid   2 a bargain   3 a discount   4 can't afford   5 a refund   6 to haggle   7 not worth it   8 a receipt

b ▶ Get Ss to rewrite the sentences using the correct form of the verb phrase they decided on in Ex. 6a. Ss should check answers in pairs but do not get whole class feedback at this stage.

c ▶ Play recording 7.5 and get Ss to check their answers. Get whole class feedback if necessary.

Answers: 1 One man bid £5000 for a small antique chair. 2 Ten CDs for only £50 – that's a bargain! 3 I asked for a discount, but the shop assistant said no. 4 I'd like to buy a motorbike but I can't afford it. 5 This DVD player broke after only a week. I'd like a refund please. 6 I always try and haggle with market traders. 7 The rent on that tiny flat isn't worth it. 8 Don't forget to keep the receipt.

Grammar

> **OPTIONAL GRAMMAR LEAD-IN**
>
> Write the following sentences on the board and get Ss to complete them with the most appropriate verb.
>
> 1 Someone _____ the bikini for $61,000.
>
> 2 The bikini _____ for $61,000.
>
> Get Ss to check their answers in pairs. Then get whole class feedback. (**Answers:** 1 *bought* 2 *was bought*). Get Ss to discuss in pairs what the difference between the verbs is. (**Answer:** 1 active 2 passive).

7a ▶ Get Ss to look at the example sentences in the Active grammar box and answer the questions in pairs. Get whole class feedback on question 1 but not on question 2 at this stage.

> **Active grammar**
>
> 1 *was bought* = passive; *bought* = active

b ▶ Get Ss to check their answers to question 2 by reading the rules of meaning A and B in the box. Then get whole class feedback.

> **Active grammar**
>
> 2 You would choose passive because in sentence 1, the action is more important than who causes the action and in sentence 2, the longer expression is put at the end of the sentence

c ▶ Get Ss to read the rule of form in the box and complete the sentences. Remind them to use the correct passive form of the verb in brackets for each sentence. Ss check answers in pairs. Then get class feedback.

> **Answers:** 1 is being cleaned   2 was found   3 was being displayed   4 have been bought   5 had been spat   6 will be paid   7 is going to be opened   8 can be bought

The email in Ex. 8 is about a jukebox. Jukeboxes originated in the USA in the 1930s and production continued on a large scale until the 1960s. A limited number are still produced today. They were found in many bars and pubs in USA, the UK and elsewhere – people put money in and chose the record they wanted to hear. Jukeboxes are now highly collectable items with people paying anything from $100 to $30,000 depending on the type and how rare they are.

8 ▶ Get Ss to complete the email with an appropriate form of the verbs in brackets. Remind Ss that the verbs may be both active and passive. Ss should check their answers in pairs. Then get whole class feedback.

> **Answers:** 1 was persuaded   2 were given   3 had   4 bought   5 is going to be delivered/is being delivered   6 couldn't be sent   7 gave   8 will arrange   9 will be asked   10 has been sorted

Speaking

9 ▶ Read through the four situations with the class. Get Ss to discuss with a partner what they would do in each situation and why. Get whole class feedback and see how many Ss feel similarly to each other. Encourage them to give reasons for their opinions.

10a ▶ Read through the questions with the class. Play recording 7.6 and tell Ss to answer the questions. After briefly checking in pairs, get whole class feedback.

> **Answers:** 1 situation 4   2 frustrated and irritated but resigned   3 to make an appointment for an engineer to come on Friday

b ▶ Get Ss to read through the How to ... box. Play recording 7.6 again and tell them to complete the language in the How to ... box. Ss should check their answers in pairs. Then get whole class feedback.

> **Answers:** 1 manager   2 assistance   3 seems   4 apologise   5 replacement.

c ▶ Ask Ss to add one more sentence to each section of the How to ... box. Get whole class feedback and write the sentences on the board.

11 ▶ Get Ss to work with a partner and to choose one of the situations in Ex. 9 for a roleplay in which the customer complains about the situation. Remind Ss to use the language in the How to ... box. You may want Ss to change roles and do the roleplay again, or to choose a different situation for the second roleplay.

Writing

12 ▶ Refer Ss to the Writing Bank on page 163. Get Ss to read the letter and answer the questions. After checking answers in pairs, get whole class feedback.

> **Answers:** 1 Three problems: the late arrival of the DVDs, the fact that one of them was broken and the way she was treated by the staff on the phone.   2 She wants a replacement DVD or a refund.

▶ In the writing skill section, get Ss to look again at the letter and answer the question. Get whole class feedback.

> **Answer:** Formal language

▶ Tell Ss to read the sentences and mark whether each one is formal (F) or informal (I). After checking in pairs, get whole class feedback.

> **Answers:** Formal: 2, 3, 6, 7, 10, 11; Informal: 1, 4, 5, 8, 9, 12

13 ▶ Tell Ss that they are going to write a formal letter of complaint. Get them to choose one of the situations in Ex. 9 (or use their own idea). Tell Ss to look again at the model in the Writing Bank on page 163 and to write their letter. Remind them to use language from the Useful Phrases box on page 163 and to use the paragraph plan in Ex. 13 to organise their writing.

7.3 It's a dog's life

In some parts of Europe and the USA, many pet owners see their cat or dog as a member of the family. In the UK, owners spend an amazing €4 billion annually on keeping their pets fit, well and entertained. In one survey, it was found that up to 40% of owners said they bought gifts for their pets, including Christmas and birthday presents. Owners happily pamper their pets with increasingly lavish lifestyles, including toys, furniture, accessories and 'gourmet' food. There are also pet psychologists for those with problems, pet passports for those who want to travel and a whole range of services on offer. There are hundreds of retail outlets offering owners a vast array of products.

In this lesson, Ss read a magazine article about how some people overindulge their pets and they discuss their own reactions and attitudes to animals. After focussing on the grammar of *have/get something done*, Ss talk about services they have done. Ss finish by looking at different animals and animal expressions.

> **OPTIONAL WARMER**
>
> Introduce Ss to the topic of animals. The following activity is a bit of 'pop psychology' – a fun way to find out more about yourself, which should not be taken too seriously.
>
> Get Ss to write down their favourite animal and one adjective to describe it. Next, ask Ss to write down their second favourite animal and one adjective to describe it. Finally, get them to write down their third favourite animal and one adjective to describe it. Then write on the board: 1 *how you see yourself* 2 *how others see you* 3 *how you would really like to be.*
>
> Get Ss to work in pairs and tell each other about themselves using the animals and adjectives they chose and the interpretation on the board. Remind them that it is a bit of fun and not to be taken too seriously!

Reading

1 ▶ Focus Ss on the photos and get them to discuss the questions in pairs or small groups. Get brief whole class feedback.

2 ▶ Get Ss to read the text quickly and answer the question. Remind them not to try to understand everything at this stage but just to focus on the one question. After briefly checking in pairs, get whole class feedback.

> **Answers:** The dog in the bed and the dog with the necklace are mentioned but the dog in the coat is not.

3a ▶ Read the four statements through with the class. Get Ss to read the first paragraph (the whole first column) again and to decide if the statements are true, false or we don't know. Remind them to correct the false statements. Ss should check in pairs. Then get whole class feedback.

> **Answers:** 1 T 2 F (40%) 3 DK 4 T

b ▶ Tell Ss to read the rest of the text and to decide which of the descriptions apply to which pet or pets or none of them. Encourage Ss to underline the part of the text which tells them the answers. Get Ss to check their answers in pairs. Then get whole class feedback.

> **Answers:** 1 Pixie 2 Beauty/Mignon 3 Pixie
> 4 none 5 Pixie/Beauty 6 Mignon 7 none
> 8 Beauty

4 ▶ Get Ss to discuss the questions in pairs or small groups. Get whole class feedback by asking each group to report back about their opinions.

Grammar

> **OPTIONAL GRAMMAR LEAD-IN**
>
> Write these sentences on the board:
>
> 1 *I cut my hair.*
>
> 2 *I had my hair cut.*
>
> 3 *I got my hair cut.*
>
> Ask Ss to discuss this question in pairs: What is the difference in meaning (if any) between them? (**Answers:** Sentence 1 – I cut my hair myself; Sentences 2 and 3 – I arranged for my hair to be cut by someone else).

5a ▶ Get Ss to complete the examples A–C in the Active grammar box using had, have and gets. Then tell them to look again at the text in Ex. 2 and check their answers. Get whole class feedback.

> **Active grammar**
>
> 1 I take her to the beauty parlour to **have** her fur done.
>
> 2 On her last birthday, Mignon **had** the fur from the top of the head pulled back and tied as a ponytail.
>
> 3 She **gets** the dog anaesthetised so that she stands still at the hairdresser.

b ▶ Get Ss to complete the rule of form in the box with the correct part of speech. Ss should check in pairs. Then get whole class feedback.

> **Active grammar**
>
> Form: *have* (or *get*) + object + **past participle**

c ▶ Tell Ss to work in pairs and to look at rule 1 in the box and answer the question. Get whole class feedback.

> **Answers:** b – arranging for something to be done by somebody else

d▶ Tell Ss to work in pairs again and to look at rules 2 and 3 in the box. Get them to match each rule (2 and 3) with the correct example D–F. Get whole class feedback.

> **Answers:** Rule 2 – D and E; Rule 3 – F

6▶ Get Ss to find the mistakes in six of the sentences and correct them. After checking answers in pairs, get whole class feedback.

> **Answers:** 1 I've never had my hair **dyed.**
> 2 correct   3 **never have my house decorated** – I
> do it myself.   4 I haven't had my eyes **tested** for
> ages.   5 I've got a lot of things to get **done** by this
> weekend.   6 I have **some of my clothes dry-cleaned**
> every month.   7 correct   8 I'd like to get my photo
> **taken** by a professional photographer.

Person to person

7▶ Read through the questions and the examples with the class. Then get Ss to work in pairs and discuss the questions. You could get brief whole class feedback by asking two or three Ss to report back one interesting fact about their partner.

Vocabulary

8a▶ Get Ss to work with a partner and to divide the animals in the box into six groups. Read through the example with the class to get them going. Get whole class feedback.

> **Answers:**
> Possible groups (there may also be other way of
> grouping them)
> **Domestic animals:** dog, cat
> **Farm animals:** bull, horse
> **Wild animals:** bear, bat
> **Sea animals:** fish, whale
> **Birds:** duck, eagle
> **Insects:** fly, spider

b▶ Get Ss to work in pairs again and to add at least three more words to each of the groups. Get whole class feedback and write the animals on the board, making sure that Ss understand all the words.

9a▶ Tell Ss to label the parts of the animals in the pictures using the words in the box. Then play recording 7.7 and get Ss to check their answers. Get whole class feedback if necessary.

> **Answers:** A feathers   B wings   C beak   D claws
> E fur   F tail   G paws   H whiskers   I horns
> J hooves   K fins

b▶ Get Ss to look at the words in the box in Ex. 9a again. Tell them to work with a partner and to decide which of the underlined vowel sounds have the same sounds as each other. Then play recording 7.7 again and tell them to check their answers. Get whole class feedback and get Ss to repeat the words.

> **Answers:** Same sound /ɪ/ – wings, whiskers,
> fins   Same sound /ɔː/ – paws, claws, horns

c▶ Read through the example with the class. Then get Ss to work in pairs and take turns to describe an animal using the words in the box. Their partner should try to guess which animal it is.

> **OPTIONAL EXTENSION**
> Either: If you did not do the optional warmer for this lesson, you could do it here.
> Or: You could ask Ss to discuss some or all of these questions.
> **Q: How many famous animals do you know from films or TV? (e.g.** *Lassie, Free Willy, Shiloh, Babe*).
> **Q: Which is your favourite? Why?**
> **Q: Do you like films about animals? Why/Why not?**
> If your Ss have access to the Internet, you could get them to research animals in films and prepare a short presentation for the class about either animals in films in general, or one particular animal in a film.

10a▶ Tell Ss to complete the expressions in italics by writing the name of an animal. Get Ss to check their answers in pairs but do not get whole class feedback at this stage.

b▶ Play recording 7.8 and get Ss to check their answers. Get whole class feedback if necessary.

> **Answers:** 1 straight from the **horse's** mouth   2 take
> the **bull** by the horns   3 (to be) as blind as a
> **bat**   4 (to be) like a **bear** with a sore head

11a▶ Get Ss to work in pairs and discuss what they think each expression means. Remind them to read the descriptions again and make a guess using the context to help. Do not get whole class feedback at this stage.

b▶ Get Ss to match each expression (1–4) in Ex. 10a with the correct definition a–d. Ss should briefly check answers in pairs. Then get whole class feedback.

> **Answers:** 1 c   2 d   3 a   4 b

c▶ Get Ss to choose two of the expressions and to tell other Ss about a person or situation using them. Get brief whole class feedback by asking two or three Ss to report back on their stories to the class.

d▶ Get Ss to work in pairs or small groups and to discuss the question. Get whole class feedback.

Vocabulary: Prefixes

In this lesson, Ss focus on prefixes such as *over-*, *mono-*, *bi-*.

> **OPTIONAL WARMER**
>
> Write the items A-D from Ex. 1 on the board. Ask Ss, in pairs, to think of one example for each situation (e.g. A= someone talking loudly on a mobile on a bus).

1a ▶ If you did not do the optional warmer, read the list (A-D) with the class. Play recording 7.9 and get Ss to match the people speaking with the correct item A–D. One item cannot be used. Ss check in pairs. Get feedback.

> **Answers:** 1 D 2 C 3 A

b ▶ Play recording 7.9 again and tell Ss to make brief notes about each story.

c ▶ Get Ss to work in pairs and to retell each story together using their notes.

2a ▶ Get Ss to work with a partner and to look at the tapescript on page 172. Tell them to find a word to match each definition. Get whole class feedback.

> **Answers:** 1 oversleep (overslept) 2 underestimate(d)
> 3 ex-boss 4 retrain 5 bilingual 6 multinational
> 7 unusual 8 extra-large 9 monotonous

b ▶ Tell Ss to look at the words from Ex. 2a again and to write the appropriate prefixes in the table. Get them to check answers in pairs. Then get whole class feedback.

> **Answers:** 1 mono 2 bi 3 multi 4 over 5 under
> 6 ex 7 re 8 extra 9 un

c ▶ Read the rule about hyphens through with the class. Ss, in pairs, write one more example for each prefix. Get class feedback and write the words on the board.

> **Possible answers:** 1 monocycle/monopoly
> 2 bimonthly/bilateral 3 multicoloured/multimedia
> 4 overspend/overripe 5 underage/underperform
> 6 ex-wife/ex-employer 7 redo/reboot 8 extra-sensitive/extra-light 9 undecided/unfair

3a ▶ Get Ss to complete the sentences with a word from the box. Not all the words can be used. Ss check their answers in pairs. Do not get whole class feedback yet.

b ▶ Play recording 7.10 and Ss check their answers.

> **Answers:** 1 biannual 2 multipurpose 3 extra-strong 4 undercooked 5 overworked
> 6 monolingual 7 rewrite 8 ex-girlfriend

4a ▶ In pairs, Ss choose an item in Ex. 1a to tell a story about. Get them to prepare the story together using as many words in Exs. 2a and 3a as they can.

b ▶ Ss tell their stories to other Ss. Remind them not to say which item the story is about. Ss listening to the stories should say which item the story is about.

Communication: Can I help you?

In this lesson, Ss listen to dialogues in a restaurant, a shop and a hairdresser and then roleplay their own.

> **OPTIONAL WARMER**
>
> Get Ss to discuss these questions in pairs. Then get class feedback: **Q: When did you last go to a restaurant/clothes or shoe shop? Who did you go with? Why/where did you go? What did you eat/buy? Was it overpriced or not/Did you get a bargain? Did you enjoy it? Why/Why not?**
> **Q: When did you last go to the hairdresser? What did you have done? What did you do while you were waiting/having your hair done? Did you get value for money? Did you enjoy it? Why/Why not?**

1a ▶ Focus Ss on the photos and get them to work in pairs. Tell them to complete the mind maps, including as many words as possible related to each place.

b ▶ Get Ss to compare their mind maps with other Ss. Then get whole class feedback and write the new words on the board, making sure that Ss understand them all.

2a ▶ Get Ss to work in pairs, to look at the sentences and answer the question. Get whole class feedback.

> **Answers:** Restaurant – 2, 5, 7, 11; Shoe shop – 1, 4, 8;
> Hairdresser – 3, 6, 9, 10

b ▶ Tell Ss they are going to listen to three dialogues. Play recording 7.11 and get them to number the sentences in Ex. 2a in the order they hear them. After checking in pairs, get whole class feedback.

> **Answers:** Correct order: 11, 7, 5, 2, 1, 4, 8, 9, 3, 6, 10

3a ▶ Get Ss to work in pairs and choose one of the situations from the listening. Tell them to look at the tapescript on page 172 and to underline any important phrases (e.g. *Good evening. Have you got a reservation?*).

b ▶ Tell Ss to roleplay the situation they chose. Remind them to use ideas from the listening and their own ideas.

4a ▶ Read the table through with the class. Get Ss to work with a partner and to add some ideas to the table. Get class feedback and write their ideas on the board.

> **Possible answers: Restaurant:** *food is too salty/cold, there's a hair in the food, waiter is rude, the bill is wrong, the table wasn' t available at the right time*
> **Shoe/clothes shop:** *the clothes are torn/stained, the zip/buckle is broken* **Hairdresser:** *hairdresser ignored customer's wishes, had to wait a long time, water too cold, hair wash too quick, hair washer got water/shampoo in your eyes*

b ▶ Get Ss, in pairs, to choose a different place. They should decide on a few things to complain about and then roleplay the situation. Get some pairs to act out their situations in front of the class. Get Ss to practise their roleplays so that they do not have to use their notes.

Review and practice

1 ▶

> **Answers:** 1 some   2 luggage   3 much   4 is
> 5 some   6 a few   7 a   8 some

2 ▶

> **Answers:** 1 is included   2 was sent   3 will be
> delivered / are going to be delivered   4 is being
> repaired   5 has been opened   6 will be caught
> 7 were charged 8 had been employed

3 ▶

> **Answers:** 1 She had new tyres fitted to her car
> yesterday.   2 She had a new cooker delivered
> yesterday.   3 She had her hair cut and had highlights
> done this morning.   4 She's having a carpet fitted in
> the living room at the moment.   5 She's going to have
> her watch repaired this afternoon.   6 She's going to
> have her eyes tested tomorrow.   7 She's going to have
> her windows cleaned tomorrow.   8 She's going to
> have her coat dry-cleaned tomorrow.

4 ▶

> **Answers:** 1 raw   2 for   3 worth   4 horse's   5 paw
> 6 refund   7 boil   8 bear

5 ▶

> **Answers:** 1 over   2 under   3 mono   4 re   5 bi
> 6 multi   7 re   8 un

Notes for using the Common European Framework (CEF)

CEF References

7.1 Can do: describe how to prepare and cook a dish

CEF B2 descriptor: Can give a clear, detailed description of how to carry out a procedure. (CEF page 81)

7.2 Can do: write a formal letter of complaint

CEF B2 descriptor: Can explain a problem which has arisen and make it clear that the provider of the service/customer must make a concession. (CEF page 80)

7.3 Can do: talk about services

CEF B2 descriptor: Can understand and exchange complex information and advice on the full range of matters related to his/her occupational role. (CEF page 81)

CEF quick brief

One of the key ideas within the Common European Framework is that learning a language is a lifelong task; it requires 'lifelong learning' skills. Like all skills, we can improve how we learn and one of the teacher's responsibilities is to show Ss how to do this. The Lifelong learning boxes in Total English offer help in this task and showing Ss how to use their Portfolio is another way that teachers can help.

Portfolio task

Download the Total English Portfolio free from www.longman.com/totalenglish.

Objective: to introduce Ss to the Dossier section of their Portfolio.

This task can be done in Ss' own language.

The Dossier section of the Portfolio allows Ss to record and store examples of good work in English to show other people. It can include anything from stories to recorded interviews to videos.

1 ▶ Explain the purpose of the Dossier section of the Portfolio to Ss.

2 ▶ Ask Ss to look back at their work over the last few months and choose one or two pieces of work which they feel proud of.

3 ▶ Ask Ss to compare the work in groups and explain why they feel proud.

4 ▶ Ask Ss to record details of the work relevant section of their Dossier and store the work separately in a Dossier folder. If necessary, learners might like to redo the work, correcting mistakes from the original version.

Overview

Lead-in	**Vocabulary:** success expressions
8.1	**Grammar:** *It's time/I'd rather/I'd better*
	Vocabulary: describing personality
	Can do: describe different types of people
8.2	**Grammar:** reported speech
	Vocabulary: adjectives and intensifiers
	Can do: report and describe what people say to you
8.3	**Grammar:** *hard* and *hardly*
	Can do: write a report of survey findings
Vocabulary	Phrasal verbs with three parts
Com. Focus	Radio phone-in
Reference	
Practice	

Summary

Lesson 1: Ss read part of a brochure for a Leadership Training company and discuss their ideas about the qualities of a successful leader. Ss also talk about if they are good leaders, describing different sides of their own personalities.

Lesson 2: Ss listen to part of a radio programme about motivation, winners in sport and the use of sports psychologists. They also talk about their own successes and people who helped them to succeed.

Lesson 3: Ss read an article about Ryde College, a school which pushes children as young as two to use computers and to take exams early. Ss then do a survey about attitudes to school and education. They finish by writing a report of their survey findings.

Vocabulary: Ss focus on phrasal verbs with three parts, including *catch up with*, *cut down on* and *make up for*.

Communication: Ss listen to extracts from a radio phone-in in which the callers talk about their problems and get advice. Ss then get a chance to roleplay a similar radio phone-in.

Film bank: The secrets of success (3'38")

A series of inteviews where seven people talk about their work and their secrets of success.

The seven people talk about what they do, how/when they got started and their tips for success, including: 1 Stay passionate 2 Get some help 3 Be your own boss 4 Have a good idea 5 Choose your partner 6 Know your customer 7 Don't give up.

Possible places to use this short film are:
▸ After Lesson 2 to extend the topic of success.
▸ At the end of the unit to round up the topic and language.

For ways to use this short film in class, see Students' Book page 159 and Teacher's Book page 185.

Lead-in

OPTIONAL WARMER

Write these seven verbs on the board and ask Ss to say which is the odd one out and why: *succeed   triumph   flourish   thrive   fail   achieve   accomplish*

(**Answer:** All the verbs have a similar meaning to succeed except fail which means the opposite).

Then ask Ss to work in pairs. Tell half the class (Students A) to look at the verbs *succeed, flourish and thrive*, and the other half (Students B) to look at *achieve, accomplish and triumph*. Give them dictionaries and get them to write a definition and an example sentence for each of their three verbs. Reorganise Ss into A/B pairs and get them to tell each other the definitions and examples for the verbs they looked at.
Possible example sentences:
*Doctors **succeeded in** curing her cancer.*
*The economy is booming and small businesses are **flourishing.***
*The tourist industry **thrives** in good weather.*
*She **achieved** her goal of becoming a surgeon.*
*The charity **accomplished** a great deal in its first year.*
*It was a long and difficult race but in the end he **triumphed** and won gold!*

1 ▸ Focus Ss on the photos and get them to discuss the questions in pairs. Get brief whole class feedback.

2a ▸ Get Ss to work with a partner and to complete the sentences with the words/phrases in the box. Give them dictionaries and remind them to use the context of the sentence to help. Do not get whole class yet.

b ▸ Play recording 8.1 and get Ss to check their answers. Get whole class feedback if necessary.

Answers: 1 go under   2 best-seller   3 give up
4 have had their day   5 succeed   6 up to scratch
7 have a go

---

3 ▸ Get Ss to work in pairs or small groups and tell each other about the last time they achieved something special. Encourage them to think about smaller achievements as well as big things. Get whole class feedback by asking each group to report back about one of the things they talked about.

EXTEND THE LEAD-IN

Continue the discussion about success/achievement. Get Ss to complete these sentences about themselves.

1 Recently I managed to ... 2 I'm quite proud of myself for ... 3 The last time I won something was when ... 4 One of my main ambitions in life is to ... 5 My definition of *success* is ...

Then ask them to compare and discuss them with other Ss. Finally get whole class feedback and see how far the sentences are the same or different.

8.1 Lead or follow?

Leadership training and management training is an important part of most companies nowadays. People generally now accept that almost anyone can be a successful leader or manager as long as they get the appropriate training and support. For two examples of courses in Leadership training, go to: www.ashridge.org.uk/leadership_training.htm and www.leadersinstitute.com/high-impact-leaders/

In this lesson, Ss read part of a brochure for a (fictional) Leadership Training company and discuss their ideas about the qualities of a successful leader. They listen to part of a work appraisal interview and focus on the grammar of *It's time*, *I'd rather* and *I'd better*. Ss discuss if they think they are (or could be) good leaders, describing different sides of their own personalities.

OPTIONAL WARMER

Introduce Ss to the topic of leaders/leadership. Get them to discuss the following questions.

Q: Which of the following jobs do you think require good leadership skills? Why? *teacher, politician architect, manager, social worker, football coach*

Q: Can you think of anyone (famous or not) who you would consider to be a good leader? What do you think makes him/her a good leader?

Reading

1 ▶ Get Ss to discuss the questions in pairs or small groups. Get whole class feedback.

2 ▶ Get Ss to read the text quickly and to match the questions in Ex. 1 with the correct paragraphs. Remind Ss not to try to understand every detail of the text at this stage but just to match the questions with the paragraphs. After briefly checking answers in pairs, get whole class feedback.

> **Answers:** A 3   B 4   C 1   D 2

3 ▶ Get Ss to read the text again and decide if the statements are true, false or we don't know. Remind Ss to underline the relevant parts of the text and to correct the false statements. Ss should check answers in pairs. Then get whole class feedback.

> **Answers:** 1 true   2 false (all kinds of groups, including social groups, need leaders)   3 true   4 we don't know (he says that true leaders are born but he doesn't specifically include himself)   5 false (leaders should overcome their fears)   6 false (leaders should allow all group members to contribute)

4 ▶ Read the quotes through with the class. Get Ss to work in pairs or small groups and to discuss whether they agree with the quotes or not and why. Get whole class feedback.

(Tony Blair is the Prime Minister of Britain leading the Labour Party to victory in 1997.

Teddy Roosevelt was President of the USA keeping the Republicans in power from 1901 to 1909.

George S. Patton was a leading USA Army General during World War II.)

Grammar

5 ▶ Tell Ss that they are going to listen to part of a work appraisal interview. Make sure they understand what a work appraisal interview is (a formal discussion between an employee and his/her boss to assess positive and negative aspects of the employee's work and specific goals for their future work).

▶ Read through the three summary sentences with the class. Play recording 8.2 and tell Ss to decide which of the sentences best summarises the main points. After briefly checking in pairs, get whole class feedback.

> **Answer:** Sentence 3

6a ▶ Get Ss to work with a partner and to try to complete sentences 1–4 in the Active grammar box. Play recording 8.3 and get Ss to check their answers. Get whole class feedback.

Active grammar

1 I feel that it's **time** I moved on now.

2 I think **I'd rather** you did the first course.

3 **I'd rather** not wait for two months.

4 **I'd better** get your name on the list immediately.

---

b ▶ Get Ss to complete the rules of form in the Active grammar box by writing *past tense* or *infinitive*.

Active grammar

A *It's time* + subject + **past tense**

B subject + *would rather* + object + **past tense** (+ than)

C subject + *would rather* + **infinitive** (+ than ...)

D subject + *had better* + **infinitive**

---

c ▶ Tell Ss to look at sentences 1–4 in the Active grammar box again and to explain to a partner what each one means. Remind them to read the rules about meaning (in the box) to help them.

7a ▶ Get Ss to complete the dialogue using *It's time*, *'d rather* or *'d better* and the correct form of the verb in brackets. Ss should check answers in pairs but do not get whole class feedback at this stage.

b ▶ Play recording 8.4 and get Ss to check their answers. Get whole class feedback.

> **Answers:** 1 it's time I had   2 I'd rather stay   3 I'd rather you were   4 I'd better go

Person to person

8a ▶ Tell Ss to write three sentences about themselves starting with *It's time …* . Read the examples through with the class to get them started and remind Ss that their sentences can be about small, more trivial things or larger, more important things.

b ▶ Get Ss to work in pairs and to compare their sentences. Encourage them to include details in their answers and to use *I'd better* and *I'd rather* where appropriate.

Vocabulary

> **OPTIONAL WARMER**
>
> Ask Ss if they can remember any of the adjectives used to describe successful leaders (in the text they read in Ex. 2). Get them to look back at the text (especially paragraph 4) to check their ideas.
>
> Get Ss to discuss these questions:
>
> **Q: Which of the adjectives from paragraph 4 of the text do you think are the most important to be a successful leader?**
> **Q: Can you add two more adjectives to describe a successful leader?**
>
> Get whole class feedback and compare Ss opinions. (There is a discussion about describing successful leaders in Ex. 11c, so you may want to keep it fairly brief here).

9a ▶ Divide the class into Students A and Students B. Give them dictionaries and get them to look at the relevant part of the table to find the meanings and pronunciation of their five words.

b ▶ Get Ss to work in pairs (A and B) and to tell each other about the meaning and pronunciation of the five words in their group.

> **Answers:** *outgoing* = someone who likes meeting and talking to new people   *open* = honest and not wanting to hide things from people   *proactive* = someone who makes things happen or change, doesn't just react to events   *opinionated* = someone who expresses very strong opinions about things in a way that annoys people   *single-minded* = having one aim and working hard to achieve it   *easy-going* = not easily upset or worried   *selfish* = caring only about yourself rather than other people   *witty* = using words in a funny, interesting and intelligent way   *manipulative* = good at secretly controlling or tricking people to get what you want   *headstrong* – very determined to do what you want

▶ Then get Ss to work with their partner and to add some adjectives which have opposite meanings and similar meanings to the ones in the box.

c ▶ Tell Ss to compare the adjectives they have added with other Ss. Get whole class feedback and make sure that Ss understand all the words.

> **Possible answers:** (These are not absolute synonyms or antonyms).   outgoing = extrovert ┈┈> introvert   open = sociable ┈┈> reserved   proactive ┈┈> enthusiastic ┈┈> lazy   opinionated = arrogant ┈┈> modest   single-minded = determined ┈┈> undecided   easy-going = relaxed ┈┈> uptight   selfish = egotistic ┈┈> generous   witty = amusing ┈┈> dull   manipulative = controlling ┈┈> upfront   headstrong = determined ┈┈> irresolute

10 ▶ Play recording 8.5 and get Ss to write one adjective from the table in Ex. 9 which best describes each person. Ss check answers in pairs. Then get whole class feedback.

> **Answers:** 2 single-minded 3 headstrong 4 witty 5 outgoing 6 open 7 opinionated 8 selfish 9 proactive 10 manipulative

11a ▶ Tell Ss to think of three people they know who they could describe using some of the adjectives in Ex. 9.

b ▶ Get Ss to work with a partner and to describe the people they thought of. Encourage them to give examples of the ways in which each person behaves and to use some of the adjectives they thought of (as well as the ones in the table in Ex. 9a).

c ▶ Get Ss to discuss the question about successful leaders with a partner. If you did the optional warmer, remind Ss to think back to the adjectives they thought of then, and to add to their list from those they looked at in Ex. 9. Get brief whole class feedback about their ideas.

12a ▶ Get Ss to work in pairs and to match the expressions in the box with the correct pictures. Tell them to decide together what they think each one means. Get whole class feedback.

> **Answers:** 1 to be a complete doormat = to be someone who lets other people treat them badly and never complains   2 to be the centre of attention = to be the person who everyone is interested in, listens to.   3 to be down-to-earth = to be practical and direct in a sensible, honest way   4 to be really high maintenance = to be someone who demands or expects people to look after them a great deal   5 to be a party animal = to be someone who enjoys going to parties and drinks a lot of alcohol and behaves in a loud and often rude way

b ▶ Ask Ss to discuss the question in pairs. Then get whole class feedback.

13a ▶ Tell/elicit from Ss that we all have different sides to our personality and that we behave differently in different situations. Read through the situations in the box with the class. Ask Ss to think about how they behave in different situations using the ideas in the box and their own ideas.

b ▶ Read through the example with the class. Then get Ss to work in pairs and tell each other about the different sides of their personality in different situations. Remind them to use the adjectives and expressions from Exs. 9 and 12 as appropriate. Get whole class feedback by asking two or three Ss to report back about their partner.

8.2 Winners

Sports psychology is a huge industry. Most athletes use a psychologist to help with motivation and mental preparation. The radio programme in this lesson talks about some famous sportspeople who are naturally focussed on winning and don't seem to need any help with motivation including boxer Mohamed Ali. It also talks about runner Kelly Holmes who struggled with injury and a negative mental attitude. She used a sports psychologist to help her go on to win two gold medals at the Athens Olympics in 2004. Also mentioned are the New Zealand All Blacks rugby team who prepare and start every game by doing their famous Haka war dance. This is a traditional Maori chant with hand gestures and foot stamping originally performed by warriors before battle to show their strength and to intimidate the opposition.

In this lesson, Ss listen to a radio programme about winners in sport and the use of sports psychologists. Ss focus on the grammar of reported speech and then talk about their own successes and people who helped them to succeed.

> **OPTIONAL WARMER**
>
> Also Ss to discuss these questions:
>
> **Q: What sports do you enjoy playing/watching? Why? How does it make you feel? Q: Are you are competitive person? Why/Why not? Q: Are there any sportspeople that you particularly admire? Why? Q: What kind of people do you think make successful athletes?**

Listening

1 ▶ Focus Ss on the photos and read the three feelings in the box through with the class. Get them to work with a partner, match the photos with the most appropriate feeling and discuss question 1. Get whole class feedback. (More information about photos 1 and 3 will come in the listening so do not give any detail about them yet).

> **Answers:** 1 completely ecstatic (Kelly Holmes winning the 1500m race at the Athens Olympics in 2004   2 absolutely devastated (Ryan Giggs playing for Manchester United against Bayer Leverkus in UEFA Champions league 2002)   3 totally single-minded (The New Zealand All Blacks rugby team doing the Haka war dance before a game)

▶ Then get Ss to discuss question 2 in pairs or small groups. Get whole class feedback.

2 ▶ Read the questions through with the class and tell Ss they are going to listen to part of a radio programme. Play recording 8.6 and get Ss to answer the questions. After checking answers in pairs, get whole class feedback.

> **Answers:** 1 'almost all' sportspeople   2 to focus themselves on winning and intimidate the other team

3 ▶ Play recording 8.6 again and get Ss to write one sentence summarising the speaker's main points about each thing in the list. Ask Ss to compare their sentences in pairs. Then get whole class feedback.

> **Possible answers:** 1 There are some famous athletes like Mohamed Ali and Michael Schumacher who have succeeded because they have complete self-belief in their ability to win.   2 Sports psychologists can work with sportspeople to help change their negative thoughts about failing into positive ones about winning.   3 Some athletes and teams have specific routines that they do in order to focus themselves on the goal or to bring the players together as a team.

4 ▶ Get Ss to discuss the question in pairs or small groups. Get whole class feedback by asking each group to report back about one thing they talked about.

> **OPTIONAL EXTENSION**
>
> If your Ss have access to the Internet, get them to research and prepare a mini-project/presentation on one of the following: Superstitions in sport. Sports psychology. Un/lucky numbers. The New Zealand All Blacks. Kelly Holmes. Another sportsperson.

Vocabulary

5a ▶ Get Ss to look at the underlined adjectives in the table and discuss the question in pairs. Get class feedback.

> **Answers:** Gradable adjectives: the meaning is relative (e.g. can be *extremely big, very big, quite big*). Non-gradable adjectives: the meaning is extreme.

b ▶ Get Ss to work in pairs and match the gradable adjectives 1–4 with the correct non-gradable adjectives a–d. Get whole class feedback.

> **Answers:** 1b   2d   3a   4c

> **OPTIONAL EXTENSION**
>
> Write the following adjectives on the board and get Ss to make pairs as in Ex. 5b, saying which is the gradable and which is the non-gradable adjective.
>
> *hot, boiling, clean, filthy, fascinating, freezing, small, spotless, dirty, tiny, cold, interesting*
>
> Answers: non-gradable adjectives are in brackets – hot (boiling); cold (freezing); small (tiny); dirty (filthy); clean (spotless); interesting (fascinating)

6a ▶ Read the rules A and B through with the class. Get Ss to look at the sentences and decide if one or both of the intensifiers is correct. Ss should check answers in pairs but do not get whole class feedback at this stage.

b ▶ Play recording 8.7 and get Ss to check their answers. Get whole class feedback.

> **Answers:** 1 really/absolutely   2 extremely/very   3 really   4 really/absolutely   5 absolutely   6 really

7 ▶ Read the three phrases in Ex. 1 with the class. Tell Ss to think of a true story about themselves relating to one of the phrases and to tell their story to a partner.

Grammar

┌───┐
OPTIONAL GRAMMAR LEAD-IN

Get Ss to think back to Ex. 7 and try to remember the story that their partner told them. Ask them to write down two sentences from their partner's story.

Then ask them to rewrite the two sentences in reported speech. (e.g. '*I worked hard for my exams.*' *He said that he had worked hard for his exams.*) Get feedback by asking Ss to report to the class on what their partner said, using reported speech.
└───┘

8a ▶ Play recording 8.8 and tell Ss to complete the sentences and questions. Ss check in pairs. Get feedback.

> **Answers:** 1 I want   2 I won   3 I'm not going/today
> 4 You can   5 are you feeling   6 Will you/me tomorrow?

b ▶ Get Ss to look at the reported speech in the Active grammar box and to compare it with the direct speech in Ex. 8a. Get Ss to find examples of changes/differences between the direct and reported speech and to write them in the box (1–6). Ss check in pairs. Get class feedback.

> **Active grammar**
>
> 1 *won ⟶ had won; am not going to ⟶ wasn't going to*
>
> 2 *will ⟶ would*
>
> 3 *I ⟶ she*
>
> 4 *you ⟶ him; me ⟶ her*
>
> 5 *today ⟶ that day; tomorrow ⟶ the following day*
>
> 6 *are you feeling ⟶ he was feeling*

9 ▶ Tell Ss to read rules A–F in the Active grammar box. Then get them to decide if the sentences are correct or not, correcting the ones which are wrong. Get Ss to check answers in pairs. Then get whole class feedback.

> **Answers:** 1 Correct   2 ...**that** evening. (Change in time reference.)   3 Correct – The 'back-stepping' rule is ignored here because the situation is still true.   4 She **told** him ... (No object after said.)
> 5 Correct   6 I asked her **if** she wanted ... (You need *if* in reported yes/no questions.)   7 Correct   8 Correct – The 'back-stepping' rule is ignored here because the situation is still true.

10a ▶ Read the sentences with the class. Get Ss in pairs, to check they understand the meanings of the verbs in bold. Give Ss dictionaries. Get feedback.

> **Answers:** *remind*: make someone remember something *admit*: to agree (usually unwillingly) that something is true or that someone else is right *explain*: to tell someone about something in a way that is clear and easy to understand *promise*: to tell someone that you will definitely do something or something will definitely happen *suggest*: to tell someone your ideas about what should happen *warn*: to tell someone that something bad or dangerous might happen so they can avoid or prevent it *decide*: to make a choice or judgement about something

b ▶ Explain to Ss that these verbs are followed by particular verb constructions. Get them to write the verbs in bold from Ex. 10a in the correct place in the table. Remind them to look at the verb patterns which follow the verbs in bold. Get whole class feedback.

> **Answers:**
>
> | Verbs | Constructions |
> |---|---|
> | *say, explain* | verb + (*that*) |
> | *tell, warn* | verb + object + (*that*) |
> | *ask, remind* | verb + object + infinitive |
> | *promise, decide* | verb + infinitive |
> | *admit, suggest* | verb + gerund |

11 ▶ Get Ss to rewrite the statements in reported speech starting with the words given. Remind them to change all necessary parts of the sentences (including pronouns, time references) After checking answers in pairs, get whole class feedback.

> **Answers:** 1 He admitted breaking the window the previous day when he kicked a ball through it by mistake.   2 He suggested trying the new Italian restaurant when they went out that Friday.   3 She decided to stay in that night because she was completely exhausted.   4 He told me he was going to buy his girlfriend some flowers as a way of saying sorry.   5 She asked me if I was going to book tickets for the cinema or if I was going to just turn up.   6 She warned me not to be late for my interview that afternoon.   7 The teacher reminded us to bring our homework to her by 9.00 the following Monday morning.   8 He promised to pay me back all the money he owed me by the next day.

Person to person

12 ▶ Tell Ss to choose option A or B. Then get them to follow the instructions for the one they have chosen, writing notes and then telling their partner.

Speaking

13a ▶ Focus Ss on the photos and get them to discuss in pairs what they think is happening in each one. Get whole class feedback about their ideas.

b ▶ Get Ss to think about someone who has helped them to succeed in something. Tell them to make notes using the questions to help.

14 ▶ Get Ss to work in small groups and tell each other about the person who helped them to succeed (using their notes if necessary). Tell them to make notes about other Ss' experiences as they are listening to each other.

b ▶ Ask Ss to report back to the class about the most interesting story they heard. Remind them to use reported speech where appropriate.

Lifelong learning

▶ Read through the bullet points with the class. Then get Ss to discuss the questions in pairs. Get Ss to add more points to the list. Get class feedback.

8.3 Tot.com

Ryde Teaching Services (based in South-east England and formerly known as *Ryde College*) run a number of courses for students of all ages. The courses range from ICT and computing to Maths, English and French. What makes them different is their belief that children should be allowed to progress according to their ability rather than their age. This philosophy means that they have children as young as two taking their courses and students taking GCSE exams at the age of six or seven. (GCSEs or 'General Certificate in Secondary Education' are public exams in Britain and are usually taken at the age of sixteen). Some people feel it is wrong to push children to study so hard so young but Ryde believes that 'children have an amazing ability to learn' and want to offer 'courses that will help your child excel in many subjects and help boost their confidence in learning.' For more information go to: www.rydeteaching.co.uk

In this lesson, Ss read an article about Ryde College and the perceived advantages of pushing children to study intensively at a very young age. Ss discuss their own reactions to the text and then focus on the grammar of *hard* and *hardly*. Ss then do a survey about attitudes to school and education. They finish by writing a report of their survey findings.

OPTIONAL WARMER

Write the word *computer* on the board.

Get Ss to work in pairs and give them a time limit of two minutes. Tell them to write down as many words as they can using the letters in the word *computer*. Words must have at least three letters and must not be names. At the end of two minutes, ask each pair how many words they have. Get whole class feedback and write all the words on the board, checking Ss understand the meanings.

(Some answers – not a complete list: *come mop put mute term cut cute cuter mope pure cure core met pet cup top cop cot port pot crept more pour poet compute comet court true tour route rope our out*.)

Reading

1 ▶ Focus Ss on the photo and get them to discuss the questions in pairs. Get whole class feedback.

2 ▶ Read the question through with the class. Tell Ss to read the text quickly and to answer the question. Remind Ss to look for the answer to the question only, and not to try to understand all the details at this stage. After checking their answer in pairs, get whole class feedback.

Answers: He feels that children avoid wasting time as they do in the first years of secondary school.

3a ▶ Get Ss to read the article and decide where each of the sentences 1–6 should go. Encourage them to look at the context of the sentences before and after each gap to help them.

b ▶ Tell Ss to read the text through again from beginning to end, to check their answers. Then get whole class feedback.

Answers: 1 D 2 C 3 E 4 A 5 F 6 B

4 ▶ Read the list of words through with the class. Get Ss to work in pairs and find the words in the article. Tell them to write a short definition for each one, reminding them to decide on the part of speech and to look at the context around the word. Get whole class feedback.

Answers: 1 nappies – noun: a piece of cloth or paper that you put between a baby's legs and fasten around its waist 2 former – adjective: happening, existing or true in the past but not now 3 spread – verb: to be communicated 4 cope – verb: to deal with something successfully 5 head start – noun: an advantage that helps you to be successful 6 qualms – noun: worries or doubts about whether what you are doing is right 7 mood – noun: the way that someone feels at a particular time 8 hothouse – noun: a heated glass building, used for growing tropical plants

5 ▶ Get Ss to discuss the question in pairs or small groups, encouraging them to give reasons to justify their opinions. Get whole class feedback.

OPTIONAL EXTENSION

You could do some work on vocabulary on the topic of computers here.

Write the following two headings on the board:
1 *Parts of a computer*
2 *Verbs associated with computers*

Ask Ss to work in pairs and to write as many words/ phrases for each heading as they can. Give them a time limit of two or three minutes. Get whole class feedback and write the words on the board.

(Possible answers:
1 Parts of a computer: *mouse, keyboard, printer, hard drive, software, monitor, modem*;
2 Verbs associated with computers: *download/upload, log on/log off, copy, cut, paste, print, drag, click*)

Grammar

OPTIONAL GRAMMAR LEAD-IN

Write these sentences on the board and get Ss to complete each one with one word. (If they need more help, tell them to use either *hard* or *hardly*).

1 *Studying every weekend for my exams was _____ work.*

2 *The children are encouraged to work _____ for their exams.*

3 *The pupils in the college are _____ out of nappies.*

4 *I'm very tired this morning. I _____ slept last night.*

5 *I have _____ any money. I must go to the bank.*

6 *She _____ ever comes to visit us. Just once or twice a year.*

(Answers: 1 *hard* 2 *hard* 3 *hardly* 4 *hardly* 5 *hardly* 6 *hardly*)

6a ▶ Get Ss to look at examples 1–3 in the Active grammar box and decide if the words in bold are adjectives or adverbs. After checking in pairs, get whole class feedback. (Check that Ss know that *hard* can be both an adjective and an adverb, and that *hardly* is always an adverb).

> **Active grammar**
>
> 1 *Studying every weekend for my exams was **hard** work.* Adjective
>
> 2 *The children are encouraged to work **hard** for their exams.* Adverb
>
> 3 *The pupils in the college are **hardly** out of nappies.* Adverb

b ▶ Tell Ss to look at examples 4–6 in the box. Get them to work in pairs and explain the meaning of each one in other words (not using hardly). Get whole class feedback.

> **Active grammar**
>
> Possible answers: 4 This person had almost no sleep last night.   5 This person has almost no money.
> 6 This person rarely visits us.

7 ▶ Get Ss to complete the sentences using hardly and a verb from the box in the correct form. Ss should check answers in pairs. Then get whole class feedback.

> **Answers:** 1 hardly have   2 hardly said   3 hardly changed   4 hardly know   5 hardly walk
> 6 hardly believe

8 ▶ Tell Ss to decide if each sentence is correct or not and to correct those which are wrong. After checking in pairs, get whole class feedback.

> **Answers:** 1 Correct   2 Correct   3 Not correct. (He's hardly eaten anything all day.)   4 Correct   5 Correct
> 6 Not correct. (We've got hardly any milk left.)

Person to person

9 ▶ Get Ss to complete the sentences so that they are true for them. Then get them to compare their sentences with a partner. You could get whole class feedback by asking two or three Ss to report back about what their partner said.

> **OPTIONAL EXTENSION**
>
> In order to give Ss further speaking practice using *hard* and *hardly*, you could get them to look again at the three sentences in Ex. 9.
>
> Tell them to choose one of the sentences and prepare to talk about it for about one minute. Tell them that they can make a few notes to help them before they start. Then get Ss to work in pairs or small groups and to take turns to speak about their sentence for one minute. Tell them that the emphasis is on fluency at this point, encouraging them to continue speaking and not to worry about mistakes they may make.

Speaking

10 ▶ Get Ss to read the questions and make a note of their answers. Do not get them to discuss the questions with other Ss at this stage.

11a ▶ Read the language in the How to ... box through with the class. Get them to add one more way of giving opinions and one more way of justifying opinions.

b ▶ Get Ss to ask and answer the questions in Ex. 10 with as many other Ss as possible. Remind them to make notes about the responses when asking, and to use the language in the How to ... box when answering.

c ▶ Tell Ss to make notes about the main findings of their survey. Encourage them just to write notes at this stage (as they will be writing them up as a more formal report in the section that follows).

Writing

12 ▶ Refer Ss to the Writing bank on page 164. Tell Ss to read the report and answer the question. Ss should check answers in pairs. Then get whole class feedback.

> **Answer:** Topic 3 _ What are the most important qualities of a good teacher?

▶ In the Writing Skills section. Get Ss to discuss the questions with a partner. Then get whole class feedback.

> **Answers:** 1 Introducing the topic of the report
> 2 Reporting on the main results of the survey
> 3 Stating the main conclusion based on the survey
>
> 1 Introduction   2 Survey results   3 Conclusion

13 ▶ Get Ss to work in small groups and to find words or phrases in the report which might be useful in other similar reports. Get whole class feedback.

14 ▶ Tell Ss to choose a topic in Ex. 10 to write a report about. Tell them to write their report in 120–140 words. Remind them to use the paragraph plan and their notes from Ex. 11. Encourage also to look again at the model and the Useful Phrases box in the Writing bank on page 164.

> **OPTIONAL EXTENSION**
>
> You could use this as an opportunity for Ss to look critically but supportively at each other's writing.
>
> Tell Ss that they are going to read each other's reports and to comment constructively on them using the questions below to help.
>
> 1 Is the report divided into appropriate paragraphs?
>
> 2 Is the language used, appropriately formal?
>
> 3 Are personal opinions given only in the conclusion?
>
> Get Ss to work in pairs and to give each other their written report to read. They should then give feedback to each other using the questions as guidelines. Remind them to be positive and constructive in their criticism.

Vocabulary: Phrasal verbs with three parts

In this lesson, Ss focus on phrasal verbs with three parts, including *catch up with*, *cut down on* and *make up for*.

OPTIONAL WARMER

Get Ss to look back at the text Tot.com on page 110 and to find two phrasal verbs with three parts (in the third and last paragraph). (Answers: *put in for*, *make up for*).

Ask Ss to work in pairs and discuss the meanings of the two verbs. Remind them to use the context around each one to help.

1 ▶ Get Ss to match the phrasal verb in italics with the correct meanings a–j. After checking answers in pairs, get whole class feedback.

Answers: 1 h   2 j   3 c   4 d   5 a   6 f   7 g
8 b   9 e   10 i

2a ▶ Get Ss to complete the sentences with one of the phrasal verbs from Ex. 1 in the correct form. Ss check in pairs, but do not get whole class feedback at this stage.

b ▶ Play recording 8.9 and get Ss to check their answers. Get whole class feedback if necessary.

Answers: 1 cut down on   2 get away with   3 looking forward to   4 put up with   5 keeping up with
6 put in for   7 come up with   8 made up for   9 look up to   10 catch up with

c ▶ Play recording 8.9 again and get Ss to decide which part of the phrasal verb is stressed. After checking in pairs, get whole class feedback.

Answer: The second part of each phrasal verb is stressed.

3a ▶ Read the sentences through with the class. Then get Ss to discuss the question in pairs. Get whole class feedback.

Answers: 1 and 6 are correct

b ▶ Get Ss to discuss the question in pairs. Then get whole class feedback.

Answer: The three parts of three-part phrasal verbs are inseparable.

4 ▶ Get Ss to discuss the questions in small groups.

OPTIONAL EXTENSION

Get Ss to work in pairs and give them a dictionary. Tell them to find two more phrasal verbs with three parts and to write down the meaning and an example sentence. Then get Ss to tell other Ss their verbs with the meanings and example sentences. Get whole class feedback and write the new verbs on the board.

Communication: Radio phone-in

A 'phone-in' is a radio or television programme in which you hear ordinary people expressing opinions or asking questions about various topics over the telephone.

In this lesson, Ss listen to extracts from a radio phone-in in which the callers talk about their problems and get advice. Ss then get a chance to roleplay a similar radio phone-in.

OPTIONAL WARMER

Introduce Ss to the idea of problems and advice. Ask them to discuss these questions:
Q: **What is a 'Problem page' in a magazine?**
Q: **What kinds of problems do they typically have?**
Q: **Do you ever read them? Why/Why not?**
Q: **Do you think they are good thing or not? Why?**

1 ▶ Focus Ss on the photo and get Ss to discuss the questions. Get whole class feedback.

2a ▶ Tell Ss they are going to listen to extracts from a radio phone-in. Play recording 8.10 and get Ss to answer the question. After checking in pairs, get whole class feedback. (You could also get Ss to match the problems with the illustrations).

Answers: 1 She doesn't understand why a man at work has started avoiding her.   2 A marathon runner has lost her confidence.   3 He doesn't understand why he hasn't been promoted at work.

b ▶ Play recording 8.10 again and get Ss to decide what advice they would give each caller and why. Ss should discuss their answers in pairs. Then get class feedback.

3 ▶ Get Ss to work in pairs or small groups and discuss the questions. Get whole class feedback.

4a ▶ Divide the class into Student As and Student Bs. Get them to decide on some interesting problems for a radio phone-in. Encourage Ss to be imaginative and not take it too seriously.

b ▶ Get Ss to work in pairs (one A and one B) and to take turns to roleplay phoning a radio phone-in programme and asking for advice. You could get one or two pairs to act out their roleplays in front of the class at the end.

OPTIONAL EXTENSION

If you did the optional warmer, remind Ss about problem pages in magazines. If you didn't, you could have a short discussion about them now.

Then get Ss to choose one of the problems they heard in Ex. 2 or talked about in Ex. 4 and to write a short letter to a problem page about their problem. They then give their letter to another student.

Ss read the letter they have been given and write a reply, as if they are the 'agony aunt' at the magazine. Finally get them to give the reply to the relevant student who reads the letter and discusses how they feel about the advice they have been given.

Review and practice

1 ▶

> **Answers:** 1 I'd better **go** to the shops now before they close.   2 **Would** you rather I didn't say anything to your boss?   3 Correct.   4 I'd rather not **work** this weekend if at all possible.   5 **Had** you better take a raincoat in case it rains?   6 Correct.   7 What's that smell? I think it's time you **got** the cake out of the oven.   8 I'd rather **take** just hand luggage on the plane than a large suitcase.

2 ▶

> **Answers:** 1 Tony asked me if I would like to play tennis this/that weekend.   2 They told me the best time to visit Egypt was in January or February.   3 Helen said she didn't know what time the firework display started.   4 He asked me when I wanted to go and see the London Eye.   5 My boss told me I had to make a presentation at the Sales conference next March.   6 The newspaper said one of our athletes had failed a drugs test.

3 ▶

> **Answers:** 1 to do   2 to me   3 to sell   4 taking   5 us   6 to go   7 being

4 ▶

> **Answers:** 1 hard   2 hardly   3 hardly   4 hard   5 Hardly   6 hard

5 ▶

> **Answers:** 1 attention   2 opinionated   3 ecstatic   4 succeeded   5 forward   6 outgoing   7 scratch   8 headstrong

Notes for using the Common European Framework (CEF)

CEF References

8.1 Can do: describe different types of people

CEF B2 descriptor: Can give clear, detailed descriptions on a wide range of subjects related to his/her field of interest. (CEF page 59)

8.2 Can do: report and describe what people say to you

CEF B2 descriptor: Can plan what is to be said and the means to say it, considering the effect on the recipient(s). (CEF page 64)

8.3 Can do: write a report of survey findings

CEF B2 descriptor: Can synthesise information and arguments from a number of sources. (CEF page 62)

CEF quick brief

The Common European Framework suggests that learners need more than language knowledge to communicate successfully in a language. They also need 'communicative competences' which empower the learner to actually use their knowledge. The How to boxes in Total English are designed to develop communicative competences.

Portfolio task

Download the Total English Portfolio free from www.longman.com/totalenglish.

Objective: to reinforce student autonomy in updating the Portfolio.

This task can be done in Ss' L1.

1 ▶ For homework, ask Ss to update the Passport section of their Portfolio. They might like to reassess their abilities in the different skills areas or add to their list of language learning and intercultural experiences.

2 ▶ Ask Ss to bring their Passport sections in and show them to other Ss.

Overview

Lead-in	**Vocabulary:** crime and punishment
9.1	**Grammar:** sequencing devices e.g. *After + -ing*
	Vocabulary: law and insurance
	Can do: tell a funny story
9.2	**Grammar:** past modals of deductions (*must/ might/can't have done*)
	Vocabulary: compound adjectives
	Can do: speculate about past events
9.3	**Grammar:** relative clauses
	Can do: write an article
Vocabulary	Newspaper headlines
Com. Focus Reference Practice	Mind benders

Summary

Lesson 1: Ss listen to a story about a crime involving cigars. They also read some stories about strange crimes and tell stories to each other using pictures.

Lesson 2: Ss read/hear about two mysterious crimes and speculate about what might have happened.

Lesson 3: Ss read an article about the character Sherlock Holmes and how he was created by Sir Arthur Conan Doyle. They listen to an interview with an American man whose parents named him Sherlock Holmes after the famous detective. Ss also write an article.

Vocabulary: Ss focus on the language used in newspaper headlines including *quit, blast, riddle* and *plea*.

Communication: Ss read and try to solve six lateral thinking puzzles by discussing their ideas with other Ss.

Film bank: The Bullion Robbery (3'20")

An extract from the classic comedy film *The Lavender Hill Mob*, made in the UK in 1951. Mr Holland, (played by Alec Guinness) dreams of being rich. For twenty years, he has worked faithfully for a bank delivering gold bullion. One day he befriends Pendlebury, and they hatch a plan to smuggle gold from England to France by forging it into harmless-looking toy Eiffel Towers. They convince professional criminals Lackery and Shorty to join them and together they plot their crime, leading to unexpected twists and turns.

Possible places to use this short film are:
▶ After Lesson 1 to extend the topic of strange crimes.

▶ At the end of the unit to round up the topic and language.

For ways to use this short film in class, see Students' Book page 160 and Teacher's Book page 186.

Lead-in

Vocabulary: crime and punishment

OPTIONAL WARMER

Introduce Ss to the topic of crime by asking them to discuss the following questions.
Q: How many TV programmes about crime can you name?
Q: Do you like crime dramas on TV or films about crimes? Why/Why not? Which are your favourites?
Q: Why do you think crime dramas and films are so popular?

1a ▶ Focus Ss on the photos and get them to discuss the question in pairs. Get brief whole class feedback.

b ▶ Read through the columns and example words with the class, making sure Ss understand all the words. Get them to work in pairs and think of more words and expressions connected with crime and the law. Get whole class feedback and write the new words on the board.

2 ▶ Read through the headlines with the class. Get Ss to work in pairs and to explain the headlines to each other. Give them dictionaries if necessary. You may want to remind them that newspaper headlines are written in a particular way (we miss out words and use slightly different vocabulary sometimes). The vocabulary page will focus further on the language used in newspaper headlines. Get whole class feedback.

Answers: 1 A Member of Parliament for the area of the newspaper has been stopped by police for driving above the speed limit. 2 Crime connected to the Internet has increased by 50%. 3 A report has strongly criticised prisons for holding too many prisoners. 4 Witnesses in a case of someone accused of fraud have been threatened. This has led to confusion over the future of the trial. 5 A teacher was involved in an angry exchange with another car driver. He/She has been given a sentence which he/she will have to do if he commits another crime. 6 An enthusiastic police officer has given out more fines than any other police officer.

---

3 ▶ Get Ss to discuss the questions in pairs or small groups. Get whole class feedback about their ideas.

EXTEND THE LEAD-IN

You could continue the discussion about crime by asking Ss to discuss these questions:

Q: What are some different ways of punishing people who commit crimes?
Q: How do you think society can prevent people from committing crimes?
Q: What do you think should be done to improve the crime situation in your area?
Q: Do you think society in general is becoming more violent? Why do you think this is?

9.1 Legal madness

Ss listen to a true story about a crime involving cigars. The story is based on legal 'loopholes'. A loophole is a small mistake in the law that makes it possible to avoid doing something that the law is supposed to make you do. In this story, actions which could be classed as crimes are legally viewed as innocent and seemingly innocent actions are legally viewed as crimes. The result is an absurdly comical story totally based on the truth.

After focussing on the grammar of sequencing devices (*Having + -ed* and *After + -ing*), Ss tell each other stories based on picture stories about crimes which went wrong.

> **OPTIONAL WARMER**
>
> Write these words on the board. (All the words are from the vocabulary in Ex. 1).
>
> *insurance   premium   fraud   to file a claim*
> *to sue someone   to guarantee   an appeal   arson*
> *to convict someone of   to sentence someone to*

▶ Get Ss to work in pairs and tell each other the meanings of any of the words/phrases that they know. Do not give them dictionaries at this stage. Get whole class feedback about their ideas but do not accept or reject any of their ideas at this stage.

1 ▶ Get Ss to match the words/phrases 1–10 with the appropriate definitions a–j. If you did the optional warmer, get Ss to check which ones they got correct. Get whole class feedback.

> **Answers:** 1 c 2 b 3 i 4 g 5 f 6 h 7 j
> 8 e 9 a 10 d

2a ▶ Get Ss to complete the sentences with the words/phrases from Ex. 1 in the correct form. Ss should check in pairs, but do not get whole class feedback at this stage.

b ▶ Play recording 9.1 and get Ss to check their answers. Get whole class feedback if necessary.

> **Answers:** 1 sue 2 sentenced 3 appeal
> 4 premium 5 convicted 6 insurance
> 7 guarantee 8 arson 9 filed 10 fraud

3 ▶ Get Ss to discuss the questions in small groups. Get whole class feedback about their ideas.

> **OPTIONAL EXTENSION**
>
> You could extend the discussion (in Ex. 3) by asking Ss to discuss some or all of the questions below in pairs or small groups.
>
> **Q: When was the last time you saw a film or television drama about crime? What was it about?**
> **Q: Choose one film or television drama about crime that you've seen and describe what happens. Use some of the vocabulary from Ex. 1 and from the Lead-in page.**

Listening

4a ▶ Focus Ss on the picture of a man smoking cigars. Tell them that they are going to listen to a story about a crime involving cigars. Get Ss to work with a partner and suggest what the story might be using as many of the words in Ex. 1 as possible. Get whole class feedback about their ideas but do not accept or reject any of their ideas at this stage.

b ▶ Play recording 9.2 and get Ss to compare their ideas with the actual story. Ss should check in pairs what the actual story was and how similar/different it was from theirs. Get whole class feedback.

5 ▶ Get Ss to read the sentences quickly to themselves. Then play recording 9.2 again and get Ss to put the sentences in the correct order. After checking in pairs, get whole class feedback.

> **Answers:** 9 A lawyer buys some rare cigars. 7 He insures the cigars against fire. 5 He smokes the cigars. 3 He makes a claim against the insurance company. 2 The insurance company refuses to pay. 8 The lawyer sues the insurance company. 6 The insurance company pays the lawyer. 1 The lawyer is arrested. 4 The lawyer is sentenced to jail.

6a ▶ Read the expressions through with the class. Play recording 9.2 again and get Ss to say which of the expressions they hear. Get whole class feedback.

> **Answers:** Go on; The way it goes is that; Fair enough; What on earth for?; You're kidding!; Cross my heart

b ▶ Tell Ss to find the expressions in the tapescript on page 174 and get them to work in small groups and discuss the meanings of each one. Remind them to use the context around the expression to help with the meaning. Get whole class feedback.

> **Answers:** *Go on.* = Continue with the story/what you were saying. *The way it goes is that ...* = This is how the story goes ... *Fair enough.* = That sounds reasonable and fair to me. *What on earth for?* = I can't understand that! What for?! *You're kidding!* = You're joking./You must be joking. *Cross my heart.* = I promise.

> **OPTIONAL EXTENSION**
>
> You could get Ss to do some more work with the expressions in Ex. 6.
>
> First play recording 9.2 again and get Ss to repeat the expressions focussing on the pronunciation. Then get them to work in pairs and choose three of the expressions. Get them to tell a story to each other (it could be true or made up) using the three expressions. You could then get them to change pairs and tell their story to other Ss.

OPTIONAL EXTENSION

You might want to extend the topic of strange laws and loopholes in the law. If you have access to the Internet, you could get Ss to do some research either individually or in pairs. They could choose one of the following topics and then report back to the class.

1 Strange laws in my country.

2 Strange laws from throughout the world.

3 Strange laws about clothes.

4 Strange laws about food.

You could tell them the examples of strange laws below to get them started:

• You may not have an ice cream cone in your back pocket at any time. (USA)

• Clothes may not be hung to dry on Sunday. (Switzerland)

• Hitting a vending machine that stole your money is illegal. (USA)

• A man may be arrested for wearing a skirt. (Italy)

• Only licensed electricians may change a light bulb. (Australia)

Grammar

OPTIONAL GRAMMAR LEAD-IN

Get Ss to complete this sentence from the listening, from memory if possible. (If not, get them to find it in the tapescript).

_____ the cheque, the lawyer was arrested. (Answer: *After cashing* ...)

Then, get Ss to complete this sentence so that it means the same as the sentence above.

Having _____ the cheque, the lawyer was arrested. (Answer: ... *cashed*...)

Tell Ss that they are both sequencing devices (ways of showing the order of events.)

7a ▶ Tell Ss to look at the sentences in the Active grammar box. (They are the same sentences used in the optional grammar lead-in). Get Ss to complete the structures A and B in the box by writing the correct part of speech for each one. Ss should check in pairs. Then get whole class feedback.

Active grammar

A: *Having* + past participle   B: *After* + gerund

b ▶ Get Ss to discuss the question in pairs, reminding them that both these constructions are sequencing devices (ways of showing the order of events.) Get whole class feedback.

Answers: Clause 1 comes first in the order of events.

8 ▶ Get Ss to complete the sentences by writing the correct form of a verb from the box. After checking in pairs, get whole class feedback.

Answers: 1 going   2 promised   3 doing   4 read   5 won   6 staying

9a ▶ Tell Ss to think about three things that happened to them last week and what they did after each one. You might want to read the example in Ex. 9b through with the class at this stage.

b ▶ Get Ss to work in pairs and tell each other the first of the things they did. Their partner should try to guess what they did next. Remind them to tell each other if they were correct or not.

Speaking and reading

OPTIONAL WARMER

Tell Ss that they are going to look at stories about stupid criminals and crimes that went wrong. Get them to work in pairs or small groups and brainstorm different ways in which different crimes could go wrong for the criminal. You may want to give them a time limit (e.g. two minutes). Get Ss to report back their ideas to the class.

10 ▶ Get Ss to work in pairs and tell them that they are going to look at two picture stories about stupid criminals and crimes that went wrong. Tell Student As to look at the pictures for story 1 on page 120 and Student Bs to look at the pictures for story 2 on page 151. Tell them that the pictures make a story (in the correct order) and they should work out the story with their partner.

11 ▶ Tell Ss to read the story which goes with their picture story to check if their ideas were correct or not. Student As should read the story on page 149 and Student Bs should read the story on page 120.

12a ▶ Tell Ss to prepare to tell their story to another student. Get them to use the language in the How to ... box to help, but remind them to adapt the language for their particular story.

b ▶ Get Ss to work in pairs with one A and one B. Tell them to show each other their picture stories and to tell their stories. Remind them to include the structures with *Having* + past participle and *After* + present participle as appropriate.

OPTIONAL EXTENSION

You could get Ss to write one of the stories in their own words without looking at the text. They could then compare their version with the text and check how much is similar and if they have missed anything out.

9.2 It's a mystery!

In this lesson, Ss hear/read about two crimes. The first is a crime which happened near Cambridge, UK in 2005. A computer software engineer caught a burglar red-handed when he set up a webcam and turned his own PC into a sophisticated surveillance system. He even worked out how to obtain the pictures if, as it turned out was the case, the thief stole the webcam and computer itself. The second crime is the mysterious case of D.B. Cooper on a flight to Seattle, USA in 1971. He hijacked the plane and demanded $200,000 and four parachutes. Then, after apparently parachuting out of the plane, was never seen again. No trace has ever been found of him or the money and he has now entered history books as an authentic American legend. For more information about the D.B. Cooper mystery, go to: www.crimelibrary.com/criminal_mind/scams/DB_Cooper

Ss listen to the story of the 'webcam burglar' and focus on the grammar of past modals of deduction (*must/might/can't have done*), speculating about what could have happened. Ss then read about the crime and mystery surrounding D.B. Cooper and discuss their reactions to the story, again speculating about the various mysterious elements in the story.

OPTIONAL WARMER

Introduce Ss to the topic of home security.

Tell Ss to look at these words: *guard dog, security camera, caretaker,* and say what they have in common (Answer: they are related to the theme of home security – all ways of protecting your home/property). Check Ss understand all the words.

Then ask them to work in pairs and continue the list, adding more ways of protecting your home against burglars and intruders. You could ask which ones Ss have personal experience of.

(Possible answers: *burglar alarms, remote-controlled gates, combination locks, padlocks, deadlocks, window locks, door chains, window bars and grilles, shutters, peepholes, CCTV/video surveillance*)

Grammar

There is no optional grammar lead-in here because the grammar comes directly from the photos and the listening in Exs. 1 and 2.

1 ▶ Focus Ss on the photos and ask them to discuss the question. Get whole class feedback about their ideas but do not accept or reject any of their ideas at this stage.

2 ▶ Play recording 9.3 and tell Ss to answer the question. Ss should check answers in pairs. Then get whole class feedback.

Answers: Someone is stealing computer equipment from someone's house.

3 ▶ Get Ss to read the examples 1–3 in the Active grammar box and complete rules A–C. Ss should check in pairs. Then get whole class feedback.

Active grammar

A Use *might have* + past participle to say that you think something is possible in the past.

B Use *can't have* + past participle to say that you think something is not possible in the past.

C Use *must have* + past participle to say that you are certain about something in the past.

4 ▶ Get Ss to choose the correct alternative in each sentence. After checking answers in pairs, get whole class feedback.

Answers: 1 can't 2 might 3 must 4 can't 5 might 6 must 7 must 8 can't

5a ▶ Tell Ss to complete the sentences using *must/might/can't have* and an appropriate word from the box. Ss should check their answers in pairs but do not get whole class feedback at this stage.

b ▶ Play recording 9.4 and get Ss to check their answers. Tell Ss to pay attention to the pronunciation of *must/might/can't have* while they are listening and answer the question. Get whole class feedback.

Answers: 1 might have been 2 can't have forgotten 3 might have gone 4 must have told 5 can't have spent 6 must have left 7 can't have finished 8 might have dropped *have* is pronounced as a weak form /əv/

6 ▶ Tell Ss to think back to the story in the photos in Ex. 1. Briefly, get them to discuss how they think the police found the photos. Then play recording 9.5 and get Ss to check their ideas. Get whole class feedback.

Answers: Duncan Grisby (the homeowner) had set up a webcam which started recording when it detected movement and then sent the pictures automatically to a private email address.

Vocabulary

OPTIONAL VOCABULARY LEAD-IN

Write these words on the board randomly: *minute single last minded*

Ask Ss to make two new adjectives by combining them. (Answers: *single-minded; last-minute*). Check that Ss understand the meanings (Answers: *single-minded* = focussed and determined; *last-minute* = the latest possible time before something happens). Elicit/tell Ss that they are called compound adjectives (made up of two parts).

7 ▶ Get Ss to combine a word from column A with a word from column B to make compound adjectives. Give them dictionaries to help if necessary and get them to check answers in pairs. Then get whole class feedback.

> **Answers:** 1 single-minded   2 one-way   3 middle-aged   4 left-handed   5 home-made   6 last-minute   7 part-time   8 so-called   9 time-consuming   10 brand-new

8a ► Get Ss to complete the sentences with the compound adjectives from Ex. 7. Ss should check answers in pairs but do not get whole class feedback at this stage.

> **Answers:** 1 brand-new   2 middle-aged   3 single-minded   4 one-way   5 time-consuming   6 last-minute   7 left-handed   8 so-called   9 part-time   10 home-made

9 ► Get Ss to discuss the questions in small groups. Get whole class feedback by asking each group to report back about the most interesting point they discussed.

OPTIONAL EXTENSION

You could get Ss to find and learn some more compound adjectives. Divide the class into Groups A and B. Group A should look at list A below and Group B should look at list B. Get them to use dictionaries to find the compound adjectives given, checking the meaning and pronunciation. Tell them to write an example sentence for each too.

A: *big-headed*; *two-faced*; *well-off*; *sugar-free*

B: *self-centred*; *absent-minded*; *hard-up*; *off-peak*

Then regroup Ss into pairs (one A and one B). Tell them to teach each other their adjectives, focussing on meaning and pronunciation and giving their partner an example sentence.

Reading

OPTIONAL WARMER

You could get Ss to speculate about the story of D.B. Cooper before they read it. Tell them the story is a mystery about a man called D.B. Cooper who stole $200,000 and who was never caught. Tell them the story includes the words: *briefcase*, *flight attendant*, *parachutes*, *waterlogged bag*, *submarine*.

Get Ss to work in pairs or small groups and to discuss what they think the story might be. Get whole class feedback but do not accept or reject any ideas at this stage.

10 ► Tell Ss to work in pairs and to discuss the question. Check that they can say the amount of money correctly ($200,000 = two hundred thousand dollars). Get whole class feedback about their ideas.

11 ► Get Ss to read the article quickly and tell them to briefly summarise how D.B. Cooper managed to steal $200,000. Remind them not to worry about understanding all the details at this stage. Ss should check their answers in pairs. Then get whole class feedback.

> **Answers:** He got on a plane and persuaded a flight attendant he was carrying a bomb. He demanded money and parachutes and then jumped out of the plane.

12 ► Tell Ss to read the article again and answer the questions. After checking answers in pairs, get whole class feedback.

> **Answers:**
> 1 A briefcase.   2 $200,000 and four parachutes by 5p.m.   3 Because of his single-minded behaviour.   4 A few minutes after 7.30pm.   5 At 8.12pm.   6 Because they flew too fast.   7 Federal agents and Army troops.   8 A waterlogged bag containing 294 mouldy $20 notes.   9 It was the first 'skyjacking' for money. No one was hurt and the skyjacker just disappeared under the noses of the FBI.   10 There have been three books, a play, a film, a song and thousands of D.B. Cooper bars and restaurants. There is also an annual 'DB Cooper Days festival' including a D.B. Cooper look-alike contest and half-a-dozen parachutists make a jump.

13 ► Tell Ss to find three compound adjectives in the text. (They are all from Ex. 7). Get whole class feedback.

> **Answers:** middle-aged;   one-way;   single-minded

14 ► Get Ss to discuss the questions in pairs or small groups. Get whole class feedback about their ideas.

OPTIONAL EXTENSION

You could use the text to do some further work on numbers.

Get Ss to find and underline all the different numbers in the text (times, amounts of money, flight numbers). Get whole class feedback and write them on the board. (Answers below). Then ask Ss to work in pairs and check with each other how to say each of the numbers. Get whole class feedback.

(Answers:
2pm = two p m; *24th November 1971* = the twenty fourth of November nineteen seventy one; *a $20 note* = a twenty dollar note

Flight 305 = three oh five; *$200,000* = two hundred thousand dollars; *10,000 feet* = ten thousand feet; *7.30pm* = seven thirty p m; *8.12pm* = eight twelve pm; *F–106 fighter planes* = one o six

Boeing 727 = seven two seven; *1980* = nineteen eighty; *294* = two hundred and ninety four; *$20 notes* = twenty dollar notes)

Ss could then practise saying more numbers by writing a list of a variety of types of numbers and asking another student to say them correctly.

9.3 Sherlock or not?

Sir Arthur Conan Doyle published the first Sherlock Holmes story in 1887. The popularity of the character grew rapidly as he appeared in an ongoing series of self-contained stories. Soon people loved Holmes so much that they refused to believe he wasn't a real person; letters addressed to 'Sherlock Holmes, Consulting Detective' arrived daily at 221b Baker Street, each begging him to take on a real case. Although Holmes is, of course, a fictional character he was largely based on a real person. Dr Joseph Bell, the man who inspired the character of Sherlock Holmes shared many qualities with the famous detective. Conan Doyle met Dr Bell in 1877 at the University of Edinburgh Medical School. For more information go to www.sherlock-holmes.co.uk

In America, there is a man whose parents were so keen on Sherlock Holmes as a character and a phenomenon, that they named their son after him. 'Sherlock Holmes', who likes to be called Holmes, is also a huge fan of the books and collects all sorts of 'Sherlockiana'. He says he gets many different reactions to his name: from general surprise to people who are totally convinced he is the real detective.

In this lesson, Ss read an article about the character Sherlock Holmes and how he was created by Sir Arthur Conan Doyle after being inspired by his professor Dr Joseph Bell. Ss then focus on the grammar of relative clauses (both defining and non-defining). Ss also listen to an interview with the American man whose parents named him Sherlock Holmes after the famous detective. They finish by writing an article.

OPTIONAL WARMER

Introduce Ss to the topic of detective stories. Write the word 'Whodunit' on the board and ask Ss to discuss what it is. (Answer: Whodunit = 'who done it' and is another way of describing a detective story or a murder mystery book.)

Ask Ss to discuss these questions:
Q: Do you like reading 'whodunits'? Why/Why not?
Q: Can you name any authors or characters of famous detective books? (Most famous ones are: Sherlock Holmes/Sir Arthur Conan Doyle; Agatha Christie; Hercule Poirot.) Which is your favourite? Why?
Q: Why do you think murder mystery books are so popular?

Reading

1a ▶ Focus Ss on the photo and get Ss to discuss the questions in pairs. Get whole class feedback but do not accept or reject their ideas at this stage.

b ▶ Tell Ss to read the text quickly and check their answers. Ss should check their answers in pairs. Then, get whole class feedback.

Answers: 2 No, he is a fictional character (but he was inspired by a real person) 3 He is famous for being a fictional detective in the stories by Arthur Conan Doyle, starting with the first book in 1887 and continuing today.

2 ▶ Get Ss to read the text again and complete the notes. Ss should check answers in pairs. Then get whole class feedback.

Answers: 1 Professor – student
2 University of Edinburgh Medical School
3 1877 4 playing sport 5 bird-watching
6 tattoos 7 hands 8 1887 9 Baker Street and Scotland Yard

3 ▶ Tell Ss to work together and read the text again to find words that mean each of the definitions given. Remind them that the paragraph numbers are given and they should look at the context of the sentence to check their ideas. Get whole class feedback.

Answers: 1 to inspire 2 brilliant 3 a ward
4 an innovation 5 to beg

4 ▶ Get Ss to discuss the questions in pairs or small groups. Get whole class feedback about their ideas.

OPTIONAL EXTENSION

You could get your Ss to read a Sherlock Holmes story and then write a short review or give a short presentation to the class about it. There are several Sherlock Holmes stories in the Penguin Readers series. The most appropriate for this level are: *Sherlock Holmes short stories* (level 5 – Upper Intermediate) and *Three adventures of Sherlock Holmes* (level 4 – Intermediate).

Grammar

OPTIONAL GRAMMAR LEAD-IN

Write these two sentences on the board and ask Ss to discuss with a partner the difference in meaning between them.

1 *The book which I read yesterday was fantastic.*

2 *The book, which I read yesterday, was fantastic.*

(Answer: Sentence 1 is referring to a specific book which I read yesterday. The information 'which I read yesterday' is crucial to defining which book we are talking about.

Sentence 2 is referring to a book which we both already know about and the fact that I read it yesterday is additional but not essential information about it.)

You could elicit/tell Ss what these types of clauses are called. (Answers: 1 = a defining relative clause; 2 = a non-defining relative clause)

5 ▶ Tell Ss to read the information in the Active grammar box and decide which of the examples 1–5 contain 'defining relative clauses' and which contain 'non-defining relative clauses'. Ss should check answers in pairs. Then, get whole class feedback.

Active grammar

1 Defining 2 Non-defining 3 Defining
4 Non-defining 5 Non-defining

6 ▶ Get Ss to join the pairs of sentences to make one sentence. Remind them to think about the use of commas and read the example through with the class to get them going. After checking in pairs, get whole class feedback.

Answers: 1 John, who has been my best friend since school, is helping me to start a new business. 2 My current flat, which I've been in for a couple of years, needs redecorating. 3 Tamsin, whose parents emigrated to Australia last year, is going there for the winter. 4 My neighbour, who I've always liked, has given me his old computer. 5 The family at the end of the road, whose dog barks constantly, are thinking of moving. 6 Tina's car, which she's had for years, is up for sale.

7 ▶ Ask Ss to complete the sentences in a way that makes sense. Tell them that there is no one right answer and ask them to compare their sentences with another student. Get whole class feedback.

Possible answers: 1 Where are the jeans which you wanted me to mend? 2 That's the pop star who said we should increase aid to Africa. 3 She's the little girl whose bike was stolen. 4 I'd like to find a place where I can get a good cup of coffee. 5 I think that's the couple whose car is blocking my drive. 6 We went to a shop where they had some amazing jewellery. 7 Wasn't it your father who was on the TV news last night? 8 She bought the mobile phone which was on sale because it was last year's model.

Person to person

8 ▶ Read the example and the three starter sentences through with the class. Get Ss to tell each other three interesting things about themselves starting with the words given. Get whole class feedback by asking three or four Ss to report back about their partner.

Listening

9a ▶ Tell Ss that they are going to listen to an interview with an ordinary American man whose name is 'Sherlock Holmes'. First, get them to discuss the questions in pairs. Get whole class feedback about their ideas but do not accept or reject their ideas at this stage.

b ▶ Play recording 9.6 and get Ss to check their ideas. After discussing in pairs, get whole class feedback.

Answers: 1 Because his parents were great fans of the original Conan Doyle stories. 2 People don't forget you. People make funny comments. People think you can solve mysteries.

10 ▶ Play recording 9.6 again and get Ss to explain the significance of the things in the list. Ss should check their answers in pairs. Then, get whole class feedback.

Answers: 1 This is what the American Sherlock Holmes likes to be called. 2 His parents were great fans of these. 3 Sherlock Holmes was his parents' favourite literary figure. 4 This is what people sometimes ask him when they're trying to be funny. 5 People think he can explain what TV magicians do. 6 This is someone who asked him to help find her son. 7 This is how much the son had taken from his work to help him start his new life. 8 This is what he used to look for clues in the house of his friend's son.

11 ▶ Get Ss to discuss the questions in pairs or small groups. If possible, get Ss to move around and talk to as many other Ss as they can. Get whole class feedback, comparing different opinions in the class.

Writing

12 ▶ Refer Ss to the Writing Bank on page 164. Tell Ss to read the article which is based on the interview with Sherlock Holmes in Ex. 9. and find five differences between the article and the interview. Ss should check their answers in pairs. Then get whole class feedback.

Answers: 1 He prefers to be called 'Holmes' not 'Sherlock'. 2 They didn't always know they were going to give him this name. They discussed a number of possible first names. 3 He didn't get angry about people's reactions to his name early on. 4 He's never been interested in magic. 5 The police didn't call him – it was the mother of an old family friend.

▶ In the Writing Skill section: Get Ss to work with a partner. Tell them to look at the underlined words in the text and say what each one refers to. Get whole class feedback.

Answers: 1 'in the heart of the USA' 2 his parents 3 the name 'Sherlock Holmes' 4 his name 5 a shop assistant 6 the police

▶ Ask Ss to discuss the question in Ex. 2b in pairs. Then get whole class feedback.

Answer: Referencing words improve a text by making it flow cohesively without the need for so much repetition.

13 ▶ Tell Ss that they are going to write an article about a famous crime. Focus Ss on the photos and tell them they are going to listen to a description of how Nick Leeson (the man in the photos) broke the Barings Investment Bank. Play recording 9.7 and get Ss to make notes about the story. Get Ss to follow the instructions and write their article.

> **OPTIONAL ALTERNATIVE**
>
> Ss do not need to write the article about Nick Leeson and Barings Bank if they know enough information about another famous crime to write about.

Vocabulary: Newspaper headlines

In this lesson, Ss focus on the language used in newspaper headlines which are usually made short to fit them on the page and to create more impact. To achieve this, headlines often miss out words (e.g. articles, pronouns) and use slightly different vocabulary such as *quit* and *plea*.

> **OPTIONAL WARMER**
>
> Write *headline* on the board. Make sure Ss understand what it means. Get Ss, in pairs, to write a list of as many words starting with, the word 'head' as they can in two minutes. Get class feedback. Write the words on the board and make sure Ss understand them. (E.g.: *heading, headache, headlong, headquarters, headstrong, headdress, headfirst, headhunt, headset, headmaster, headphones, headstand, headscarf*)

1 ▶ Get Ss to discuss the questions in pairs. Get brief whole class feedback about their opinions.

2 ▶ Explain that headlines often use slightly different vocabulary, especially shorter words for more impact. Get Ss, in pairs, to match the words 1–12 (from headlines) with the meanings a–l using dictionaries if necessary.

> **Answers:** 1 k 2 f 3 j 4 h 5 c 6 l 7 d 8 g 9 i 10 b 11 e 12 a

b ▶ Ask Ss to discuss, in pairs, what they think the two headlines at the top of the page mean. Get class feedback.

> **Answers:** 1 A well-known Hollywood actor has been involved in a tense situation in a bank, maybe a robbery. 2 The Prime Minister's diaries have disappeared and no one knows why.

3 ▶ Get Ss to choose the most likely alternative in each headline. After checking in pairs, get class feedback.

> **Answers:** 1 Key 2 axes 3 blaze 4 back 5 drama 6 clash 7 bids 8 quits

4 ▶ Get Ss to look at the headlines and discuss the questions in pairs. Remind them to justify their opinions. Get class feedback by asking each pair which headlines they would most/least be interested in reading and why.

> **Answers:** 1 Exported goods have increased as the result of a cut in interest rates. 2 A prince and a fashion model are going to get married. 3 Someone who works for a top bank is taking them to court because of sex discrimination. 4 Manchester United football team have lost heavily in a tournament. 5 An MP has been involved with a spy in some way. 6 There is a mystery surrounding a 2nd painting by Van Gogh. 7 Someone who worked as a butler for Buckingham Palace has resigned. 8 Cape Town is attempting to be the host for the next Olympic Games. 9 A bomb has exploded in northern India. 10 There has been a problem with recording the votes in an election in California. Some may have been stolen or changed.

5 ▶ Ask Ss to discuss the questions in small groups. Then get whole class feedback.

> **OPTIONAL EXTENSION**
>
> Get Ss to look at an English newspaper (in a library, online or buy one) and to choose some headlines and/or an article which caught their eye and to explain to the class what they found interesting about them. (They could prepare a short summary of what the article is about.)

Communication: Mind benders

Lateral thinking puzzles are stories in which you have some basic clues to a realistic scenario, but the clues don't tell the full story. You need to work out the full story using problem-solving that involves looking at the situation from unexpected angles. You need to think 'outside the box'. For more lateral thinking puzzles, go to: eluzions.com

In this lesson, Ss work on trying to solve six lateral thinking puzzles by discussing their ideas with other Ss. They get the chance to read the actual answers to each puzzle.

> **OPTIONAL WARMER**
>
> Write these different types of puzzles on the board and ask Ss to explain to each other what they are. *crossword, sudoku, wordsearch, lateral thinking puzzle, jigsaw puzzle, anagram*
>
> Ask Ss to discuss the following questions:
> **Q: Can you add any more types of puzzle to the list?**
> **Q: Which are your favourite types of puzzle? Why?**

1 ▶ Tell Ss that they are going to try to solve six lateral thinking puzzles. Get them to follow instructions 1–3. You could then get Ss to change partners and share their ideas again.

2 ▶ Get Ss to choose the one puzzle that they are most interested in and read the explanation on the appropriate page. Remind them not to tell each other the explanation at this stage. Get Ss to follow instructions 1–3.
1 Tell them to write two Yes/No questions about each of the other five puzzles.
2 Get Ss to ask each other the questions. Encourage them to answer only 'yes' or 'no' and not to give any more information away at this stage.
3 Get Ss to work with other Ss and to try to solve the puzzles again using their additional information.

> **OPTIONAL EXTENSION**
>
> Get Ss to find a puzzle (in a book or on the Internet) or create one themselves. E.g. they could make a wordsearch using vocabulary from this unit.

Review and practice

1▶

> **Answers:** 1 After travelling/Having travelled for hours to get to the village, she thought she should stay there for at least a couple of days.   2 After seeing/Having seen his neighbour struggling with a lot of heavy bags, he offered to help her.   3 After coming/Having come first in her university exams, she was approached by a top firm of lawyers.   4 After taking/Having taken home an injured cat she had found by the side of the road, she felt she had to keep it.   5 After seeing/Having seen a young man take a CD without paying, he told the security staff.   6 After speaking/Having spoken to his father, he told his boss he wanted a raise.   7 After getting/Having got a long letter from their cousin, they decided to go and see him.

2▶

> **Answers:** 1 He might have stayed late at the office. 2 I can't have left my gloves in the car.   3 She must have shown me her holiday photos at least ten times.   4 She can't have finished all her homework already.   5 They must have been really pleased to win the competition.   6 My letter might have got lost in the post.

3▶

> **Answers:** 1 No commas necessary.   2 I'm going to spend a few days in Seville, where I first met Raquel.   3 No commas necessary.   4 No commas necessary.   5 We decided to stay at the Regina Hotel, which some friends had recommended to us.   6 Tim, whose job involves a lot of travelling, has offered to let us use his flat for a few weeks.

4▶

> **Answers:** 1 Steve works for a small company **which/ that** makes kitchen equipment. 2 Correct   3 Did you hear exactly **what** he said?   4 The demonstration, **which** had been going on for several days, is finally over.   5 Correct   6 My sister, **who** speaks French and Italian fluently, wants to be an interpreter.

5▶

> **Answers:** 1 left-handed   2 aid   3 appeal   4 last-minute   5 Fair   6 guarantee   7 blaze

Notes for using the Common European Framework (CEF)

CEF References

9.1 Can do: tell a funny story

CEF B2 descriptor: Can give clear, systematically developed descriptions and presentations, with appropriate highlighting of significant points, and relevant supporting detail. (CEF page 58)

9.2 Can do: speculate about past events

CEF B2 descriptor: Can account for and sustain his/her opinions in discussion by providing relevant explanations, arguments and comments. (CEF page 77)

9.3 Can do: write an article

CEF B2 descriptor: Can write clear, detailed texts on a variety of subjects related to his/her field of interest, synthesising and evaluating information and arguments from a number of sources. (CEF page 61)

CEF quick brief

There are hundreds of Can do statements in the Common European Framework, which can make it difficult for a learner to assess their level. To simplify matters The CEF contains a 'self-assessment grid' containing brief descriptions of what a learner Can do at each of the six major levels. This grid is in the Total English Portfolio.

Portfolio task

Download the Total English Portfolio free from www.longman.com/totalenglish.

Objective: to reinforce student autonomy in updating the Portfolio.

This task can be done in Ss' own language.

1▶ For homework, ask Ss to update the Biography section of their Portfolio. They might like to reassess their language learning aims, history or significant experiences. They might also like to go over the Can do statements again and tick the new objectives at B1 and B2 level that they can now achieve.

2▶ Ask Ss to bring their Biography sections in and show them to other Ss.

10 Mind

Overview

Lead-in	**Vocabulary:** the power of the mind
10.1	**Grammar:** reflexive pronouns
	Can do: ask about and give your own beliefs and opinions
10.2	**Grammar:** gerunds and infinitives
	Vocabulary: advertising
	Can do: write the arguments for and against a point of view
10.3	**Grammar:** *if* structures (2)
	Vocabulary: speaking
	Can do: talk about your regrets and resolutions
Vocabulary	Commonly misspelt words
Com. Focus	How does your mind work?
Reference	
Practice	

Summary

Lesson 1: Ss read an article about the famous hypnotist Paul McKenna and his work. They listen to people giving opinions and then give their own opinions on a variety of topics.

Lesson 2: Ss listen to an extract from a radio programme about persuasion tactics in advertising and retail. They write an essay putting forward points for and against an argument.

Lesson 3: Ss read an extract from the novel *Brave New World* by Aldous Huxley focussing on brainwashing and conditioning. They also talk about their regrets in the past and resolutions for the future.

Vocabulary: Ss focus on commonly misspelt words.

Communication: Ss do a quiz and discuss different ways in which people think and approach life e.g. analytical people, interpersonal people, physical people.

Film bank: Yes, Prime Minister (4'10")

An extract from *Yes, Prime Minister,* one of Britain's most well-known political satirical TV series. In this series, which makes fun of political games, the newly-elected Prime Minister attempts to make various bold changes but these generally come to nothing, thanks to the manoeuvring of his manipulative Cabinet Secretary, who opposes action or change of any sort. In this extract, the Prime Minister is being given advice on how he looks and how he should behave before giving a political broadcast on TV.

Possible places to use this short film are:
► After Lesson 2 to extend the topic of persuasion (in politics, retail and advertising).
► At the end of the unit to round up the topic and language.

For ways to use this short film in class, see Students' Book page 161 and Teacher's Book page 187.

Lead-in

OPTIONAL WARMER

Write these expressions with *mind* on the board and ask Ss to discuss in pairs what they think they mean.

1 *I don't mind where we go.*
2 *Mind what you're doing with that!*
3 *I'm in two minds about it.*
4 *I'll bear it in mind.*
5 *It completely slipped my mind.*
6 *Are you out of your mind?*

(Answers: 1 **I don't care/it doesn't matter** where we go.   2 **Be careful** what you're doing with that!   3 I'm **undecided** about it.   4 I'll **remember it for reference**.   5 I completely **forgot**.   6 Are you **crazy/a bit mad**?)

1 ► Focus Ss on the photos and ask them to discuss the questions. Get whole class feedback.

> **Answers:** Connected with the (power of) the mind

2a ► Get Ss to work with a partner and match photos 1–3 with the quotes and explain to each other what they think the phrases in italics mean. Get class feedback.

> **Answers:** Picture 1: *the power of persuasion* = the skill of persuading someone to do something   Picture 2: *mind over matter* = using your thoughts to control physical feelings or an unpleasant situation   Picture 3: *willpower* = the ability to control your mind and body in order to achieve something you want to do

b ► Get Ss to discuss the questions in pairs and give details in their answers. Get whole class feedback.

3a ► Read the questions with the class but do not explain unknown words. Tell Ss they will listen to six people answering one question each. Play recording 10.1 and get Ss to make brief notes about each answer. Ss check answers in pairs. Then get class feedback.

> **Answers:** See transcript for recording 10.1 in Students' Book on page 175.

b ► In pairs, Ss write a short definition for each phrase in italics. Encourage them to think about the meanings in the context and to check their definitions in dictionaries.

> **Answers:** 1 a strange feeling that something bad is going to happen   2 a feeling that what is happening now has happened before   3 to use the ability to understand or know something because of a feeling rather than considering the facts   4 a special ability to know things without using your five ordinary senses   5 unable to see, move, feel, because you are not conscious   6 fears that are hidden in your mind and affect your behaviour, but you don't know are there

c ► Get Ss to ask and answer the questions in pairs.

10.1 Look into my eyes

Paul McKenna is a well-known hypnotist working in London with a variety of people, many of them rich and famous. He helps people with various different problems ranging from fear of flying to fear of your own fingernails. As well as his own private practice, McKenna has an incredibly successful TV career, with programmes like *The Hypnotic World of Paul McKenna*. His two-year contract with one television station is said to be worth about £2.5million. His private practice and his TV work have made McKenna into a 'household name' and given him almost guru-like status with a large following of satisfied customers. For more information go to: www.paulmckenna.com

In this lesson, Ss read an article about Paul McKenna and his work as a hypnotist and then focus on the grammar of reflexive pronouns. Ss then listen to people giving their opinions about McKenna and hypnosis and give their own opinions on a variety of topics.

OPTIONAL WARMER

Write the words below on the board and ask Ss to discuss this question: **Q: Which of these words mean (more or less) frightened and which mean (more or less) the opposite?** Give Ss dictionaries if necessary.

afraid brave intrepid nervous courageous terrified scared dauntless petrified daring bold anxious

(Answers: frightened = *afraid*, *scared*, *anxious*, *nervous*, *terrified*, *petrified*; not frightened = *brave*, *courageous*, *bold*, *intrepid*, *dauntless*, *daring*)

You could then get Ss to discuss these questions:
Q: Is there anything that you are particularly scared of? Why do you think this is?
Q: Do you know anyone who has a phobia? What is it and why?
Q: Do you think you are courageous person? Do you know anyone who is particularly daring or intrepid?

Reading

1a▶ Focus Ss on the photos and check they know what a hypnotist is (someone who puts people in a state similar to sleep and then influences their thoughts and actions).

▶ Get Ss to discuss the question in pairs. If you did the optional warmer, remind Ss they can talk about some of the fears they discussed here, but they should also think of other 'problems' e.g. trying to give up smoking. Get whole class feedback about their ideas.

b▶ Get Ss to read the text quickly and answer the questions. Remind them not to worry about unknown words at this stage but just to focus on answering the questions. Ss should check answers in pairs. Then get whole class feedback.

> **Answers:** 1 (giving up) smoking, (lack of) motivation, fear of flying, depression, phobias (e.g. someone who thought her fingernails were turning into knives)
> 2 impressed

2a▶ Get Ss to read the text again and decide if the statements are true, false or we don't know. After checking answers in pairs, get whole class feedback.

> **Answers:** 1 T 2 T 3 DK 4 F 5 T

OPTIONAL EXTENSION

You could do some more intensive vocabulary work here before moving on to the summary-writing exercise.
Get Ss to work in pairs and to find the following phrases in the text. Tell them to look at the context around each phrase and try to explain to each other what they mean. Give them dictionaries to help if necessary.

1 *modern-day guru* (para. 1)
2 *bustling with activity* (para. 2)
3 *eclectic band of followers* (para.3)
4 *completely at a loss* (para. 3)

(Answers:
1 someone who knows a lot about a particular subject, and gives advice to other people
2 very busy with lots of people doing different things
3 a group of people made up of a mixture of many different types
4 completely confused and uncertain about what to do or say)

b▶ Get Ss to write a paragraph summarising the main points of the text in about seventy-five words. If you think Ss need more guidance with this, you could tell them to start with these words: *Paul McKenna is an extremely successful hypnotist who …*, and to include details about the following three areas:

- What his job is (including who he deals with and why)?
- What he does when he hypnotises people?
- What makes him so successful?

c▶ Tell Ss to read their partner's paragraph and compare them. Get whole class feedback by asking Ss to say if they included the same points as their partner or how they were different.

3▶ Get Ss to discuss the questions in pairs or small groups. Get whole class feedback by asking each group to report back on one of their points.

Grammar

OPTIONAL GRAMMAR LEAD-IN

Write the three words below on the board and ask Ss this question: **Q: What is the difference grammatically between them?**

me myself I

(Answer: *me* = object pronoun; *myself* = reflexive pronoun; *I* =subject pronoun)

Then ask Ss to work together to list subject pronouns, object pronouns and reflexive pronouns.

(Answers:
Subject pronouns = *I, you, he, she, it, we, you, they*
Object pronouns = *me, you, him, her, it, us, you, them*
Reflexive pronouns = *myself, yourself, himself, herself, itself, ourselves, yourselves, themselves*)

4▶ Get Ss to complete the reflexive pronouns in the Active grammar box. Get whole class feedback.

> **Active grammar**
> 1 myself   2 himself   3 itself   4 ourselves
> 5 yourselves   6 themselves

5a▶ Get Ss to match the examples 1–6 with the correct rule A or B in the Active grammar box. Ss should check answers in pairs. Then, get whole class feedback.

> **Answers:** Rule A: 1, 3 and 5   Rule B: 2, 4 and 6

b▶ Read through the three sentences with the class. Then get Ss to discuss the question in pairs. Get whole class feedback.

> **Answers:** Sentence 1 means we taught tennis to both (or all) of us and nobody else helped us.   Sentence 2 means I taught you and you taught me.   Sentence 3 is wrong.

6▶ Ask Ss to complete the sentences. Remind them that they should use *each other*, a reflexive pronoun or an object pronoun as appropriate. Get them to check answers in pairs. Then get whole class feedback.

> **Answers:** 1 myself   2 each other   3 me   4 myself
> 5 each other   6 himself/herself   7 us   8 each other

Person to person

7a▶ Read through the questions with the class, making sure they understand difficult vocabulary e.g. *phobia*, *addiction*, *truancy* (*phobia* = a strong unreasonable fear of something; *addiction* = the need to take a harmful drug, e.g. smoking or alcohol, regularly without being able to stop; *truancy* = when students deliberately stay away from school without permission). Get Ss to work on their own and decide if they agree with the statements, making brief notes about their views.

b▶ Get Ss to compare their views with each other, encouraging them to give reasons to justify their opinions. Get whole class feedback and check how many Ss agree.

Listening

8▶ Tell Ss they are going to listen to three people talking about Paul McKenna and hypnosis. Play recording 10.2 and get Ss to choose which statement best summarises each person's opinion. Remind them that one statement cannot be used. After checking in pairs, get whole class feedback.

> **Answers:** Person 1: statement 4
> Person 2: statement 3   Person 3: statement 1

9a▶ Tell Ss that the gapped phrases in italics are all verb phrases about giving your opinion or stating your beliefs. Play recording 10.2 again and get Ss to complete the verb phrases. Ss should check their answers in pairs. Then get whole class feedback.

> **Answers:** 2 favour   3 believed   4 doubts
> 5 sceptical   6 against   7 doubt   8 convinced
> 9 suspect

b▶ Get Ss to work in pairs and answer the questions about the meaning of the verb phrases. Get whole class feedback.

> **Answers:** 1 I've always believed that/I'm convinced that   2 I have my doubts about/I'm sceptical that/I doubt   3 I reckon/I suspect   4 I'm in favour of   5 I'm against

Pronunciation

10▶ Play recording 10.2 again and get Ss to repeat the sentences in Ex. 9a. Remind them to pay particular attention to the pronunciation of the verb phrases in italics.

11▶ Get Ss to rewrite the sentences using the words in brackets and adding other words to complete the appropriate verb phrase. Ss should check their answers in pairs. Then get whole class feedback.

> **Answers:** 1 I've always believed that there is life on other planets.   2 I doubt that ghosts really exist at all.   3 I'm convinced that I knew what she was thinking.   4 I'm in favour of people trying all sorts of different treatments.   5 I reckon that some people have supernatural powers.   6 I have my doubts about the existence of UFOs.   7 I'm against paying someone for a service I don't understand.   8 I'm sceptical that anyone can predict the future.

Speaking

12▶ Read through the topics in the box with the class, checking that Ss understand them all. Then focus Ss on the How to ... box. You could ask them to add two more questions of their own to the list. Then get Ss to discuss the topics in the box with a partner. Remind them to use the language in the How to ... box and the phrases in Ex. 9 as appropriate.

13a▶ Tell Ss to choose one of the topics in Ex. 12 that they can talk about for one minute. Get them to prepare that they are going to say, using the notes 1–4 to help organise their ideas.

b▶ Get Ss in pairs or small groups to give their talks to each other.

> **OPTIONAL EXTENSION**
>
> You could get Ss to give their talks to the whole class after they have done them in pairs or small groups. Remind them to speak clearly and slowly enough. Get whole class feedback by asking Ss which of their views they heard were similar to theirs.
>
> You could also get Ss to write up their talks as short essays but there is more specific work on essay-writing in Lesson 10.2 so you may want to save it until then.

10.2 Persuasion

All around us, there are images on television, jingles on the radio, adverts in magazines, sound bites on the news, offers in the shops. Supermarkets and politicians, advertisers and salespeople are all hard at work using the power of persuasion to make us believe something or to persuade us to buy something. Huge amounts of money are spent on working out the best psychological tricks to guarantee that even the most cautious among us are open to manipulation.

Supermarkets, for example, play music or pump out the smell of freshly-baked bread to encourage us to spend more. They also use loyalty cards or reward cards to persuade us to shop at their store again. Advertisers too have a vast array of different ways of appealing to either the thinking part of our brain or to our emotions, encouraging us to feel safer, more attractive or to belong to a particular group.

In this lesson, Ss listen to an extract from a radio programme about persuasion tactics in advertising and retail. They then focus on the grammar of verb constructions with gerunds and infinitives. They finish by writing an essay putting forward points for and against an argument.

OPTIONAL WARMER

Write the word *persuade* on the board and ask Ss to explain to each other what it means (to make someone decide to do something, especially by giving them reasons why they should do it, or asking them many times to do it).

Elicit/tell them what part of speech *persuade* is and what the noun and adjective forms are (*persuade* = verb; *persuasion* = noun; *persuasive* = adjective).

Get Ss to work in pairs and write a list of as many words as possible using the letters in the word *persuade*. Each word should have at least three letters and must not be a name. Give them a time limit of two minutes.

(Some possible answers: ape apes are dare dear deep dear due ear ears era erase pause pea peas pear pears peer peruse pure purse read red sad see sea spade spare spear speed spread sue super sure use used user).

Listening

1 ▶ Focus Ss on the photos and get them to discuss the questions in pairs. Get whole class feedback about their ideas.

2 ▶ Tell Ss they are going to listen to an extract from a radio programme. Play recording 10.3 and tell them to answer the question. After checking answers in pairs, get whole class feedback.

Answers: advertising and supermarkets

3 ▶ Give Ss time to read through the notes. Play recording 10.3 again and get them to complete the notes. Ss should check their answers together. Then get whole class feedback.

Answers: 1 television, radio, magazines, news, shops   2 working out the best psychological tricks to manipulate and persuade people to do/buy things   3 playing music and pumping the smell of freshly-baked bread into the store   4 they tempt you back into the store and they provide the supermarket with information about shopping habits   5 adverts that appeal to the emotions and adverts that appeal to the thinking part of the brain   6 appeal to the thinking part of the brain by giving information because cleaning products hold little emotional appeal   7 those that appeal to our emotions   8 work on making us feel good and showing us lifestyles we can aspire to   9 very popular and a good way of getting message across quickly and powerfully

4 ▶ Get Ss to discuss the questions in pairs or small groups. Get whole class feedback about their ideas.

Vocabulary

5 ▶ Get Ss to work in pairs and choose the correct alternatives. Give them dictionaries to help if necessary. Do not get whole class feedback at this stage.

Answers: 1 advertisements   2 makes   3 marketing   4 slogans   5 commercial breaks   6 classified ad   7 hype   8 target market

Pronunciation

6a ▶ Get Ss to look at the three words and see if they know how to pronounce them. Play recording 10.4 and get them to mark where the main stress is on each word. Ss should check in pairs and decide if the stress is on the same syllable in each word or not. Get whole class feedback.

Answers: 1 ad<u>ver</u>tising   2 ad<u>ver</u>tisement   3 <u>ad</u>vert

OPTIONAL EXTENSION

You could ask Ss to look at the words in Ex. 5 and decide together where the stress is on each of them. (Answers: <u>makes</u>, <u>mar</u>keting, <u>slo</u>gans, com<u>mer</u>cial breaks, <u>clas</u>sified ad, <u>hype</u>, <u>tar</u>get market).

b ▶ Get Ss to work in pairs and to choose four questions in Ex. 5 to ask and answer together. Get whole class feedback by asking two or three Ss to report back about one of their partner's answers.

OPTIONAL EXTENSION

You could ask Ss to work in pairs or small groups and create their own advert. It could be a TV advert, a radio advert or an advert in a magazine. They need to think of a product and a slogan and then how to put them in a context.

Ss could present them to the class and then decide which ones were particularly persuasive and why.

Grammar

> **OPTIONAL GRAMMAR LEAD-IN**
>
> Write these two sentences on the board.
>
> 1 *I want seeing that new film.*
>
> 2 *I want to see that new film.*
>
> Ask Ss which one is correct and why. (Answer: 2 is correct because after the verb *want* we use the infinitive (*to see*) not the gerund (*seeing*)).
>
> You could briefly explain/elicit that there are certain verbs which use particular constructions – some are followed by the gerund, others by the infinitive and others by both, with a subsequent change of meaning.

7a ▶ Tell Ss to look at the verbs in bold in sentences 1–5 in the Active grammar box and choose the correct alternatives. Ss should check in pairs, but do not get whole class feedback at this stage.

b ▶ Play recording 10.5 and tell Ss to check their answers. Get whole class feedback if necessary.

> **Active grammar**
>
> 1 to buy   2 using   3 to make
> 4 to resist   5 leaving

c ▶ Get Ss to write the verbs in bold in the correct place in the Active grammar box. After checking in pairs, get whole class feedback.

> **Active grammar**
>
> (For Ex. 7c and Ex. 8a)
>
> | | |
> |---|---|
> | verb + gerund | ***carry on**, avoid, practise, suggest* |
> | verb + infinitive | ***want**, agree, arrange, hope* |
> | verb + object + infinitive | ***persuade**, advise, allow, encourage* |
> | verb + gerund OR verb +infinitive with a different meaning | ***try**, regret, remember, stop* |

8a ▶ Get Ss to work in pairs. Tell them to check the meanings of the words in the box and to write them in the correct place in the Active grammar box. Give Ss dictionaries to help if necessary and remind them that dictionaries can help not only with meaning, but with verb constructions (i.e. gerund or infinitive). Get whole class feedback.

> **Answers:** See box above (Ex. 7c)

b ▶ Remind Ss that some verbs can take both gerund and infinitive (last part of the table in the Active grammar box), and this affects the meaning. Get Ss to look at the pairs of sentences and discuss the question together. Get whole class feedback.

> **Answers:** 1a It's one option that I tried in order to solve a problem.   *Try* + gerund: when you try a number of different things to get something done/ solve a problem. The things you try are not difficult to do in themselves.   b I made an effort to do something that was quite difficult. *Try* + infinitive: when you make an attempt at doing something which is difficult to do   2a You remembered first and then you bought it.   b You bought it first and then you remembered the action of buying.   3a I'm sorry that I have to tell you.   b I did it and now I'm sorry about it.   4a We were watching and then we stopped so we could do something else.   b We were doing something else when we stopped in order to watch.

9 ▶ Read through the example with the class. Tell Ss to complete the second sentence in each pair, so that it has the same meaning as the first. Remind them to use between two and four words including the word in bold. Ss check answers in pairs. Get whole class feedback.

> **Answers:** 1 suggested going   2 encouraged me to get   3 tried to speak   4 agreed to give   5 remember coming   6 advised me to   7 avoid getting   8 persuaded me to buy

Person to person

10 ▶ Tell Ss that they are going to ask each other questions. Do the first one as an example by asking Ss to form the question for number 1. (Were you allowed to watch as much TV as you wanted as a child?). Get Ss to stand up and walk around the classroom and ask the questions to different Ss until they have one name for each question. Get whole class feedback by asking two or three Ss to report back on one of their questions.

Writing

11a ▶ Get Ss to discuss the statement in pairs, encouraging them to give reasons to justify their opinions. Get whole class feedback about their ideas.

b ▶ Read through the paragraph plan with the class. Tell them that the sentences in the box are all taken from an essay. Then get Ss to complete the table with the correct paragraph number 1–4. After checking answers in pairs, get whole class feedback.

> **Answers:** B para. 4;   C para. 4;   D para. 1;   E para. 3;   F para. 4;   G para. 2;   H para. 1

12 ▶ Get Ss to read through the statements and to choose one of them to write an essay about, or to choose something else they feel strongly about. Tell them to write down arguments in favour and arguments against the statement. Remind them that they should just write notes at this stage.

13a ▶ Get Ss to write an essay about their statement using the plan and the language in the table in Ex. 11b and their notes to help.

b ▶ Tell Ss to read another student's essay and say whether they agree with the final conclusion, giving reasons for their answer.

10.3 Brave New World

Aldous Huxley wrote *Brave New World* in 1932. It remains one of the most powerful science fiction stories ever. It is set in a future where peace and good health are compulsory but love and parenthood are obsolete. Thinking for yourself, being an individual and being unhappy are not allowed. Babies are produced and 'brought up' scientifically in 'Hatchery and Conditioning Centres'. But one of the main characters, Bernard Marx, refuses to be happy and to fit in. He is haunted by the feeling that there must be more to his life than this. *Brave New World* is available in the Penguin Readers series (Level 6). For more information go to: www.penguinreaders. com and http://en.wikipedia.org/wiki/Brave_New_World

In this lesson, Ss read an extract from *Brave New World*. The extract focuses on the brainwashing and conditioning of babies as they lie asleep in the 'Hatchery and Conditioning Centres'. Ss also focus on the grammar of *if* structures, including so-called first, second, third, zero and mixed conditionals. Ss finish by talking about their regrets in the past and resolutions for the future.

OPTIONAL WARMER

Get Ss thinking about some famous novels and authors. Write these novels and authors on the board and get Ss to work together and match them up.

Titles:	Authors:
The Hound of the Baskervilles	Charles Dickens
Pride and Prejudice	Charlotte Brontë
Great Expectations	Jane Austen
Jane Eyre	John Steinbeck
Brave New World	E.M. Forster
Anna Karenina	Arthur Conan Doyle
A Room with a View	Aldous Huxley
The Grapes of Wrath	Leo Tolstoy

(Answers: Level 5 (Upper Intermediate): *The Hound of the Baskervilles* – Arthur Conan Doyle; *Pride and Prejudice* – Jane Austen; *Jane Eyre* – Charlotte Brontë; *The Grapes of Wrath* – John Steinbeck.   Level 6 (Advanced): *Great Expectations* – Charles Dickens; *Brave New World* – Aldous Huxley; *Anna Karenina* – Leo Tolstoy; *A Room with a View* – E.M. Forster)

You could ask Ss to say which, if any, they have heard of/read and to tell other Ss about them. You could also tell them that all these titles are available as Penguin Readers (Levels 5 and 6 – see Answers above) and encourage them to read any that take their interest.

Reading

1 ▶ Get Ss to read the short text (starting 'Aldous Huxley …') and answer the questions in pairs. Get whole class feedback.

Answers: 1 He isn't happy and doesn't feel he fits in to the society he lives in   2 Because everyone is supposed to be happy and fit in completely

2 ▶ Read the three statements through with the class. Then get Ss to read the extract from the novel *Brave New World* and answer the question. Ss should check their answer in pairs. Then get whole class feedback.

Answer: Statement 3

3 ▶ Focus Ss on the first item in the exercise as an example. Tell them to read the text again and write a question for each of the answers. After checking answers in pairs, get whole class feedback.

Answers: 2 What did they hear when they went into the room?   3 What did the babies look like?   4 Why did the Director turn up the volume on the loudspeaker?   5 Which type of children does the loudspeaker say are the most stupid?   6 Which type of children are the babies in the room?   7 How many times is the message repeated every week?   8 At what age do the children start the more advanced lesson?   9 What does 'The child's mind becomes these suggestions' mean?   10 What is the Director so enthusiastic about?

4 ▶ Get Ss to discuss the questions in pairs or small groups. You could give them further guidance for question 3 and give them these possible ways that we are conditioned to consider:

- to get married and have children
- to expect to work long hours
- to be competitive with each other
- to expect men and boys not to cry
- to view success mostly in financial terms
- to smile at someone if he/she smiles at you

▶ Get whole class feedback about their ideas.

OPTIONAL EXTENSION

Remind Ss that *Brave New World* is available as a Penguin Reader (Level 6) and encourage Ss to read it, or any other books that take their interest. They could then report back to the class about what they thought of the book.

Vocabulary

5a ▶ Get Ss to work in pairs. Half the class (Student As) should look at the words in Group A, and the other half (Student Bs) should look at the words in Group B. Give them dictionaries and tell them to find the meaning, pronunciation and an example sentence for each word/phrase.

b ▶ Reorganise Ss into different pairs (one A and one B). Get them to tell each other the meaning, pronunciation and example sentence for each word/phrase. Get whole class feedback if necessary.

Answers:
Meanings – *to whisper* = to speak or say something very quietly using your breath rather than your voice   *to shriek* = to make a very high loud sound, especially because you are afraid, angry, excited or in pain   *to blurt out* = to say something suddenly and without thinking, usually because you are nervous or excited   *to be lost for words* = to be unable to say anything because you are very surprised/upset.   *to mumble* = to say something too quietly or not clearly enough, so that other people cannot understand you   *to interrupt* = to stop someone from continuing what they are saying or doing by suddenly speaking to them, making a noise.   *to speak your mind* = to tell people exactly what you think, even if it offends them   *to have a word with* = to talk to someone quickly, especially because you want to tell them to do something or you want their advice about something

6a ▶ Get Ss to complete the quotes with the correct form of the words/phrases from Ex. 5. Ss check answers in pairs but do not get whole class feedback yet.

b ▶ Play recording 10.6 and get Ss to check their answers. Get whole class feedback if necessary.

Answers: 1 blurted out/was lost for words
2 whispering/had a word with   3 shrieks/interrupts
4 mumbling/speak his mind

7 ▶ Get Ss to choose three of the words/phrases from Ex. 5 and to tell each other about different situations in which they or someone else spoke in each of the ways. Remind them to look back at Ex. 6 for ideas if necessary.

Grammar

OPTIONAL GRAMMAR LEAD-IN

Get Ss thinking about different kinds of *if* structures. Write these three beginnings of sentences on the board and ask Ss to work together and complete them in an appropriate way:

1 *If parents always speak two languages to their children, ...*

2 *If she works really hard, ...*

3 *If I won a lot of money, ...*

You could also ask Ss to complete these beginnings of sentences in the same way:

1 *If she had studied harder, ...*

2 *If she didn't study as hard as she does, ...*

3 *If he had memorised his verbs, ...*

8a ▶ Get Ss to match examples 1–3 with the correct uses A–C in the Active grammar box. After checking answers in pairs, get whole class feedback.

Answers: 1 C   2 A   3 B

b ▶ Get Ss to match examples 4–6 with the correct uses D–F in the Active grammar box. Ss should check answers in pairs. Then get whole class feedback.

Answers: 4 E   5 F   6 D

9a ▶ Tell Ss to look at the rules of form a–e in the Active grammar box and to write the correct type of conditional next to each one. You might want to remind Ss that this is one way of referring to the different *if* structures, but that different grammar books do it in different ways. After checking answers in pairs, get whole class feedback.

Active grammar

a First conditional   b Second conditional

c Third conditional   d Zero conditional

e Mixed conditional

b ▶ Tell Ss to work together and look at the three examples in this exercise. They should choose the correct alternatives from rules 1 and 2. Get whole class feedback.

Answers: 1 provided   2 unless

10 ▶ Get Ss to look at the sentences and say what type of conditional each one is. Tell them to correct the grammar mistake in each one. After checking answers in pairs, get whole class feedback.

Answers: 1 Second: If I had more time, **I'd** go and study English abroad.   2 Zero: If parents **shout** at their children, they become aggressive.   3 Mixed: **I'd** speak English fluently now if I'd learned it as a child.   4 Zero: I usually remember vocabulary, provided **I write** it down.   5 First: **If you repeat** a word enough times, you'll probably remember it.   6 Third: If I'd attended more lessons, I **would have** passed my exams.   7 Mixed: I'd have a better job if **I'd** passed my exam.   8 Zero: If a student reads books in English, his/her vocabulary **improves**.

Person to person

11 ▶ Get Ss to work together and discuss the question with each other. Get whole class feedback by asking two or three Ss to report back one fact about their partner.

Speaking

12a ▶ Check Ss understand the meaning of *regrets* (a sadness that you feel about something, especially because you wish it had not happened) and *resolutions* (a promise to yourself to do something). Get Ss to work together, to look again at the sentences in Ex. 10 and to decide which could be regrets and which resolutions. (Some are neither). Get whole class feedback.

Answers: Regrets: 3, 6, 7; Resolutions: 1

b ▶ Get Ss to think about their language learning or their school/work life. Get them to make a note of one or two regrets and resolutions using appropriate *if* structures.

c ▶ Tell Ss to compare their regrets and resolutions with other Ss. Get whole class feedback by asking Ss if they have any of the same resolutions as any other Ss.

Vocabulary: Commonly misspelt words

In this lesson, Ss focus on commonly misspelt words including *believe, accommodation* and *successful*.

> **OPTIONAL WARMER**
>
> Write the following words on the board. Ask Ss to discuss in pairs which ones are correct/incorrect.
> 1a *acomodation*   b *accomodation*   c *accommodation*
> 2a *there*   b *they're*   c *their*
>
> Answers: 1 c only is correct.   2 a, b and c are all correct depending on the context/meaning.

1a ▶ Get Ss to discuss the questions in pairs or small groups. Get whole class feedback about their ideas but do not accept or reject any ideas at this stage.

b ▶ Tell Ss to read the text and check their answers. Get whole class feedback.

> **Answers:** 1 c   2 c   3 a

2 ▶ Get Ss to decide which is the correct spelling for each pair of words. After checking answers in pairs, get whole class feedback.

> **Answers:** 1 believe   2 intelligence   3 subconscious
> 4 psychologist   5 doubt   6 existence   7 successful
> 8 responsibility

3a ▶ Tell Ss to find eighteen common spelling mistakes in the email. Remind them that they may be actual mistakes or they may be words which are spelt wrong because of the context (e.g. *there/their, where/wear*).

b ▶ Get Ss to compare their answers with a partner. Then get whole class feedback.

> **Answers:** great, generous, foreigner, weird, beginning,
> weather, definitely, changeable, accommodation,
> interesting, restaurants, library, necessary, usually,
> occasionally, friends, their, separate

4a ▶ Read the questions through with the class. Tell Ss that they are going to listen to a student of English talking about spelling in English. Play recording 10.7 and get Ss to say which of the questions the student does not talk about. After checking in pairs, get whole class feedback.

> **Answer:** The student does not talk about question 1.

b ▶ Tell Ss to discuss the questions in pairs or small groups. Get whole class feedback by asking each group to report back on one of the questions.

Lifelong learning

▶ Read the list of tips in the box through with the class. Get Ss to work in groups and add any more tips to the list. Get whole class feedback. Ask them which tips they think are the best for them and why.

Communication: How does your mind work?

In this lesson, Ss do a quiz and discuss different ways in which people think and approach life. The quiz is based on the idea that there are at least five types of thinkers/learners and that each type approach life and its problems in slightly different ways. The five that are used in this quiz are:
1 Linguistic thinkers/learners who tend to think in words and like to use complex ideas.
2 Logical-mathematical thinkers/learners who like to understand patterns and to analyse and understand the rules.
3 Interpersonal thinkers/learners who like to think about other people and are often peacemakers.
4 Existential thinkers/learners who like to spend time thinking about philosophical issues and don't like to be bothered with trivial questions.
5 Kinaesthetic thinkers/learners who like to think in movements and find it difficult to sit still for long.

1 ▶ Focus Ss on the photos and get them to discuss the questions in pairs or small groups. Get whole class feedback.

Albert Einstein (1879–1955) is generally regarded as the greatest scientist of the 20th century. He proposed the theory of relativity and also made major contributions to the development of quantum mechanics, statistical mechanics and cosmology.

William Shakespeare (1564–1616) was an English poet and playwright. He is considered by many to be the greatest writer in the English language, as well as one of the greatest in Western literature.

Madonna (born 1958) is a famous pop singer, actress, composer and producer. She is widely regarded as the Queen of Pop music. According to *The Guinness Book of World Records* she is the most successful female recording artist in the World.

Nelson Mandela (born 1918), was the first democratically-elected President of South Africa, having previously been a prominent anti-apartheid activist there. Mandela's twenty-seven-year imprisonment, much of which he spent in a tiny prison cell on Robben Island, became one of the most widely-publicized examples of apartheid's injustices.

Buddha is a title used in Buddhism for anyone who has discovered their enlightenment, although it is commonly used to refer to Siddhartha Gautama, the historical founder of Buddhism, who lived in India from about 623 BC to 543 BC.

2a ▶ Tell Ss that they are going to do a quiz to try to answer the questions: 'How does your mind work?', 'What kind of thinker/learner are you?' and 'What is your approach to life?'. Tell them to do the quiz individually and make notes about their answers, using the ideas in the boxes and their own ideas.

b ▶ Then, get Ss to do the quiz with a partner and to make a note of his/her answers.

3 ▶ Tell Ss to read the descriptions of the five thinker/learner types on page 150 and compare them with their notes about themselves and their partner. Then get Ss to discuss the questions in pairs. Get whole class feedback by asking Ss to report back on the most interesting point from their discussion.

Review and practice

1▶

> **Answers:** 1 burn yourself 2 felt 3 expresses herself 4 relax 5 hurt himself 6 meet 7 enjoyed ourselves 8 concentrated

2▶

> **Answers:** 1 We encourage all students **to do** some voluntary work. 2 I've arranged **to visit** my grandparents on Saturday. 3 Correct. 4 I remember **going** to the park every day after school when I was a child. 5 He persuaded me **to join** the new gym with him. 6 My teacher suggested **learning** ten new spellings every week. 7 Correct. 8 He advised **us to have** an early night before the exam.

3▶

> **Answers:** 1 hadn't gone 2 did 3 behave 4 had brought 5 doesn't arrive 6 press 7 would you do 8 would be lying

4▶

> **Answers:** 1 convinced 2 hype 3 interrupting 4 reckon 5 blurted 6 intuition 7 make 8 premonition

5▶

> **Answers:** 1 definitely 2 accommodation 3 responsibility 4 Correct 5 separate 6 their 7 Correct 8 successful

Notes for using the Common European Framework (CEF)

CEF References

10.1 Can do: ask about and give your own beliefs and opinions

CEF B2 descriptor: Can take an active part in informal discussion in familiar contexts, commenting, putting point of view clearly, evaluating alternative proposals and making and responding to hypotheses. (CEF page 77)

10.2 Can do: write the arguments for and against a point of view

CEF B2 descriptor: Can write an essay or report which develops an argument, giving reasons in support of or against a particular point of view and explaining the advantages and disadvantages of various options. (CEF page 62)

10.3 Can do: talk about your regrets and resolutions

CEF B2 descriptor: Can highlight the personal significance of events and experiences, account for and sustain views clearly by providing relevant explanations and arguments. (CEF page 74)

CEF quick brief

One of the implications of the Common European Framework and the Can do statements is that Ss are assessed in terms of how well they can achieve a communication objective. The aim is not to perform the task with perfect accuracy but to perform well enough at that particular reference level. The Can do statements set appropriate objectives for each reference level.

Portfolio task

Download the Total English Portfolio free from www.longman.com/totalenglish.

Objective: to reinforce student autonomy in updating the Portfolio.

This task can be done in Ss' own language.

1▶ For homework, ask Ss to update the Dossier section of their Portfolio. They might like to add another piece of work to their folder or choose another task to work on with the aim of adding it to their Biography.

2▶ Ask Ss to bring their Biography sections in and show them to other Ss.

photocopiable worksheets

contents

Three in a row

Game 1

1 Everybody was pleased when he was promoted, but I just felt j_____.	2 I hid under the bed covers in terror as the bedroom door c_____ slowly open.	3 I got divorced five years ago, but I still see my e_____ from time to time.
4 Kelly's promotion means she gets more money, and she also has more r_____.	5 Mrs Jackson is a w_____: her husband died five years ago.	6 Jan is my sister and Ann is her daughter, so that means that Ann is my n_____.
7 She s_____ at the top of her voice when the large spider ran across her hand.	8 Many jobs today require the applicant to have good computer s_____.	9 I couldn't sleep last night because my neighbours dog b_____ all night.

Game 2

1 I heard him s_____ and knew he had fallen asleep at last.	2 Andrew isn't really a friend, just an a_____: we play golf twice a year.	3 I get really f_____ when people don't understand what I'm trying to say.
4 Jo is my mother's daughter from her second marriage, so that makes Jo my h_____.	5 I've tried to contact him twice this morning, but without any s_____. He must have gone out.	6 There was a sudden loud b_____ as the door blew shut in the wind.
7 Kathy is my s_____: we're not related, but we share and understand the same emotions and interests.	8 Tom is rather i_____. He'd rather read a book on science or literature than go to the cinema.	9 This is my sister Liz, and this is her husband Charlie, my b_____.

Game 3

1 I haven't managed to do any work because the phone hasn't stopped r_____ all day.	2 Doctors and other health experts are always telling us about the i_____ of taking regular exercise.	3 This is my f_____ Andrea. We're going to get married next year.
4 You don't need to s_____: I'm not deaf, you know.	5 The dust made her s_____ violently. 'Bless you,' I said, passing her a tissue.	6 John is very a_____, and has just held his first exhibition of paintings.
7 I don't like the people I work with. It's a shame you can't choose your c_____ like you choose your friends.	8 It must be very l_____ being on your own all day.	9 This is my f_____ Jason. We share an apartment in Shepherd's Bush.

© Pearson Education Limited 2006 – Photocopiable

Tag dialogues

Student A

Part 1

1   Alison is hardly ever on time...

2   You've got two sisters,...

3   You can't speak German or French,...

4   You went to John's at the weekend,...

5   You don't like me very much,...

6   You know you're wrong,...

7   Let's go for a picnic,...

8   She never says anything in her English lessons,...

9   Help yourself to a piece of cake,...

10 Nothing exciting happened last night,...

11 I'm sorry, I'm not late ...

12 It's so peaceful here,...

A	...can you?	G	...won't you?
B	...shall we?	H	... does she?
C	... haven't you?	I	... do you?
D	...didn't you?	J	... did it?
E	... is she?	K	... isn't it?
F	... am I?	L	... don't you?

Part 2

i)   Yes, I'm really sorry. I was in a bad mood.

ii)   I tried, but it was really difficult.

iii) No, but we spoke on the phone this morning.

iv)   No, it's far too nice to be stuck in the classroom.

v)   Yes, but only because my bus didn't come on time.

vi)   No, it was cold, wet and miserable all day.

vii) Sorry, I've got a really bad back.

viii) Actually we get some lovely weather, even in the winter.

ix)   No, there's always something to do.

x)   No, everyone said they had better things to do than sit around in a hot office.

xi)   No, I received some bad news this morning which has really upset me.

xii) Yes, the living room looks really good now.

Student B

Part 1

1   You didn't do your homework,...

2   You haven't seen Jill today,...

3   It's hardly ever sunny in England,...

4   Nobody wants to work today,...

5   Help me lift this heavy suitcase,...

6   The weather wasn't very good yesterday,...

7   Nobody came to the meeting,...

8   You're late again,...

9   You were very rude to us,...

10 You aren't very happy today,...

11 They've done a great job...

12 We never time to ourselves...

A	... have you?	G	... weren't you?
B	... was it?	H	... do they?
C	...did you?	I	... will you?
D	...did they?	J	... do we?
E	...are you?	K	...aren't you?
F	...haven't they?	L	... is it?

Part 2

i)   No, it was very boring.

ii)   That's rubbish! You're the one who's never right!

iii) No, she's the least punctual person I know.

iv)   No thanks, I'm trying to lose a bit of weight.

v)   Yes, and a brother. They're all older than me.

vi)   Well I wouldn't exactly say you're my best friend.

vii) Yes, it's lovely to relax in the countryside.

viii) Actually I'm fluent in both of them.

ix)   Why not? According to the weather forecast it's going to be a lovely day.

x)   Yes, that's why we moved here.

xi)   Well, she's a bit shy and worried about making mistakes.

xii) No, it's alright. The meeting hasn't started yet.

© Pearson Education Limited 2006 – Photocopiable

Eliminator

```
A A A A A A A A A B B D D E E E E E E E E E E E E E E E E E E E E E G G G G H H H H H H H I I
I I L L L L L L M M M M N N N N N N N N N N N O O O O O O R R R R R R R R S S S T T T T
            V V V V V V W W W W Y Y Y Y Y Y Y Y Y Y Y Y Y Y
```

1   Sue, you'd like __some__ coffee, wouldn't you?

2   My boss is never happy with my work: _____ I do seems to please her.

3   You look really hungry. Do you want _____ to eat?

4   The weather is terrible today: it's been raining _____ day.

5   I don't suppose you have _____ I can leave my luggage for a few hours?

6   I didn't know _____ at the party, so I left early.

7   I've left my glasses _____, and I can't think where!

8   _____ the tea is gone, I'm afraid. Would you like a coffee?

9   You can visit me _____ time you like.

10 _____ time I go out, it rains!

11 The exam was so difficult that _____ failed.

12 I'm sorry, but there's _____ I can do to help you.

13 I can't go out because I haven't got _____ money.

14 I've looked _____ but I can't find her.

15 I'm bored because I haven't got _____ to do.

16 I don't suppose you have _____ sugar I could borrow, do you?

17 We go to France for our holiday _____ year.

18 We have to get up early _____ day.

19 She speaks to _____ of us like we are young children.

20 _____ student in the class was late this morning.

© Pearson Education Limited 2006 – Photocopiable

Modal dominoes

Start ➡	**A** Does Harry know what he's going to do when he leaves school?
B Poor you! You _____ really tired!	**A** Your boss seems like a really nice person.
B They're not sure. They think they _____ to the cinema instead.	**A** Boyd is really overweight, isn't he?
B We're not sure yet. We _____ our relatives in Australia.	**A** Heidi lives in a huge house and drives an expensive sports car.
B It _____ very cold and grey, and the days are very short.	**A** I've tried phoning Rick at home, but there's no reply.
B That's true. She _____ a lot.	**A** My cat died this morning.
B Well, he said he has other plans, but he _____ his mind.	**A** Ellen phoned to say she isn't coming to work because she's ill in bed.
B Well, the buses _____ very slow during the rush hour.	**A** I'm going out for a walk.
B No, and as a result she _____ her exams this summer.	**A** I think there's a possibility the government will lose the next election.

B He's not sure, but he _____ to university.	**A** My neighbour played music really loud all night, and I didn't get a moment's sleep.
B Yes, but at times he _____ quite rude.	**A** Are Tom and Angie coming round later?
B Yes. He _____ much exercise.	**A** What are you going to do for your holiday?
B Lucky her! She _____ a really good job.	**A** What's the weather like in Britain in winter?
B He _____ out. Try calling his mobile.	**A** Vicky's a fantastic tennis player, isn't she?
B Oh dear, I am sorry. You _____ really upset.	**A** Joe isn't coming to your party, is he?
B But she _____! I saw her in the supermarket on my way in.	**A** Does it take long to get to your house from here?
B You _____ mad! It's snowing and it's the middle of the night!	**A** Heather isn't doing very well at school, is she?
B You _____ right. They're not very popular at the moment.	➡ **Finish**

© Pearson Education Limited 2006 – Photocopiable

Phrasal verbs crossword

Complete the crossword puzzle by deciding what the missing phrasal verbs are in the text and writing the answers in the appropriate spaces in the crossword. Use the correct form of the verb in each case.

My best friend

Laurence is my best friend and I've known him all my life. We _____ (8 down) together, we went to school together and we even went to the same university. He's only a year older than me, but I suppose I've always _____ (6 across) him as someone older and wiser than myself. However, I must admit that he isn't always the easiest person to _____ (9 across) with: he was an only-child in a single-parent family, _____ (10 across) by his mother (a wonderfully kind and generous woman), but unfortunately he _____ (3 down) his father, who we both vaguely remember as being rather rude and selfish.

I suppose what I like most about Laurence is that he's so entertaining, and great fun to be with. He's loves being the centre of attention and so can _____ (2 down) a lot, which many people find a bit irritating. Also he's not always particularly reliable and, to be honest, not very responsible.

In all the time we've known each other, we've only _____ (4 down) with each other once, and that was when he started _____ (5 down) with a girl I really liked. However, it was only a matter of time before they _____ (7 down), and it wasn't long after that Laurence and I _____ (1 down) with each other.

© Pearson Education Limited 2006 – Photocopiable

Problems, problems!

Andrea Noble is a young professional lawyer in Oxford. She enjoys a good salary and varied social life, and is a member of the local cycling and rowing club. However, she does have three problems in her life at the moment:

a) She gets on really well with everyone in the office, but she is bored and frustrated with her job, and wants to leave and perhaps retrain to be a landscape gardener. Her job offers so much financial security, but is this the most important thing? What should she do?

b) She has two close friends who she really clicks with. The problem is that they do not see eye to eye at all, and both want to go on a safari holiday with her. She can only afford one holiday, but doesn't want to let either friend down. One friend she has known since childhood, the other is in the landscape gardening business....What should she do?

c) She has been asked to join the committee of her rowing club. Her ex-husband is on the committee and they don't really get on at all. Being on the committee would mean more opportunities to influence decisions at the club, but can she put up with her ex-husband?

James Davies is Andrea's new partner. He thinks she's fabulous and is very proud of her being a lawyer as he didn't manage to stick to any studying. He can't wait to go on holiday with her very soon, and has saved some money to spring a surprise holiday on her. He belongs to the rowing club too, and would love to see the club improve.

Bill Cowan is an acquaintance of Andrea's at the rowing club. He is attracted to Andrea and would like to go out with her. He works at the local garden centre and is a very relaxed and artistic type of person.

Tessa Brown is a very close friend of Andrea's. She has a lot in common with Andrea's close friend in the landscape gardening business, and also is rather attracted to Andrea's ex-husband, although she wouldn't want to tell Andrea this.

Amanda Short is a very ambitious work colleague of Andrea's. She is very intellectual and totally committed to the law firm. She is rather a lonely person in her social life, and always offers a sympathetic ear to anyone who has a problem.

Johnny Noble is Andrea's half-brother. They are very close, and his main concern is that Andrea is happy. He can't stand anyone being nasty to her or taking advantage of her good nature. He has little patience with people who cause her worry or anxiety.

© Pearson Education Limited 2006 – Photocopiable

Work and play

1. At the weekend, I enjoy _____ with my friends.

2. Barbara works as an _____, keeping and checking financial accounts, etc.

3. Alan _____ almost £35,000 a year in his new job.

4. Amanda wasn't very happy in her new job, so _____ after only a few weeks.

5. Richard hoped to work until he was 65, but _____ early because of poor health.

6. Every day, Carol _____ from her home in Oxford to her office in London.

7. When the company ran into severe financial problems, some employees were made _____.

8. Robert is a _____ for a major British newspaper.

9. I have a full-time job as an engineer, but I also do a lot of _____ work for a local charity.

10. After only six months, Heidi was _____ from Sales Assistant to Sales Manager.

11. I usually _____ my parents if I'm not busy in the evenings.

12. 65 is the usual age of _____ in Britain, but many people choose or have to work for longer.

13. The British _____ Sir Richard Rogers has designed some of the world's most unusual buildings.

14. The company discovered he was stealing from his office, so they _____ him.

15. I like to _____ time with my family whenever possible.

© Pearson Education Limited 2006 – Photocopiable

Future forms risk

Read the dialogues, then decide if the future form in the second sentence of each dialogue is used correctly.
Decide how much you want to bet on your decision (minimum £1.00 maximum £10.00).

		✓ or ✗	Bet	Win	Lose
1	A: 'I'm not very hungry today'. B: 'Me neither. I think **I'm just having** a sandwich for lunch'.				
2	A: 'Is Toby coming out with us Friday night?' B: 'I hope **he'll come**. He's such good fun to be with.'				
3	A: 'I got stopped in my car by the police twice today'. B: 'I'm not surprised. You're such a bad driver. **You're going to have** a serious accident one of these days'.				
4	A: 'How are you getting to Italy next week?' B: 'We **take** a train from London to Paris, and another one from Paris to Milan'.				
5	A: 'It's really hot and humid at the moment'. B: 'I know. I'm sure **there's going to be** a big storm later'.				
6	A: 'My teachers say I'm making really good progress'. B: 'That's great. **You're passing** your exams easily if you keep it up'.				
7	A: 'I hate to complain, but this meal really wasn't very good'. B: 'Oh dear, I'm sorry to hear that sir. I **have** a word with the chef to find out what went wrong'.				
8	A: 'Sally's got a lot of work to do, hasn't she?' B: 'She certainly has. I **think she won't come** out tonight'.				
9	A: 'That jacket doesn't look very warm'. B: 'It's OK. I heard on the weather forecast that **it's being** really hot later'.				
10	A: 'Here's the new timetable for our English lessons'. B: 'Thanks. Oh no, look! Our first lesson **begins** at eight o'clock!'				
11	A: 'This homework is really difficult'. B: 'Is it? Well, let me finish the washing up and then **I'm helping** you'.				
12	A: 'Have you got any plans for Saturday afternoon?' B: 'Yes, **I'll meet** Basil for an early supper, but I'm not sure where yet'.				
	Your final score:				

© Pearson Education Limited 2006 – Photocopiable

From start to finish

Start ➡	**1** A: 'I'm really hungry'. B: 'Are you? OK, I'm making you a sandwich when I finish watching the news'.	**2** A: 'You're not very happy in this job, are you?' B: 'Not really. I hope I won't still work here this time next year'.	**3** A: 'What are you going to do after work?' B: 'I'm not sure yet, but I'm going to go to the cinema'.
6 A: 'Shall we go for a walk?' B: 'I don't think that's a good idea. Look at those clouds building up: it's raining soon'.	**FREE SQUARE**	**5** A: 'What are your plans for Saturday?' B: 'Oh, not much. I'll meet my friends for lunch in the city centre'.	**4** A: 'Venice is very expensive and we're spending too much money'. B: 'Yes it is. At this rate we spend all our money before the end of the holiday'.
7 A: 'Roger retires next year, doesn't he?' B: 'Yes. By the time he leaves, he is going to be with the company for 35 years!'	**8** A: 'What's for dinner?' B: 'I haven't really thought about it, but I think I make pasta in cheese sauce'.	**9** A: 'How's the work going?' B: 'Rather slowly. I'm afraid I will finish it by tomorrow morning'.	**10** A: 'Shall we go to the café for lunch?' B: 'We haven't got enough time. Our afternoon lesson is beginning at 1.15'.
13 A: 'What are you doing at eight o'clock tonight?' B: 'Well, the football begins at half past seven, so at eight I am probably going to watch the match'.	**12** A: 'Have you decided what your plans are when you finish school?' B: 'Yes, I will start a course in Economics at the University of North London in September'.	**11** A: 'Robert was really rude to me earlier'. B: 'Me too. I think I won't go to his party tomorrow'.	**FREE SQUARE**
14 A: 'Karen seems very excited. What's up?' B: 'Haven't you heard? She's just found out she has a baby next April'.	**15** A: 'You're going on holiday on Tuesday, aren't you?' B: 'I certainly am! This time next week I'm lying on a beach in Croatia'.	**16** A: 'Here's £20. I'm sorry I can't lend you any more'. B: '£20 is fine, thanks. I'm returning it to you tomorrow'	**➡ Finish**

© Pearson Education Limited 2006 – Photocopiable

Just in case ...

Fire extinguisher	Dictionary	Football	Inflatable dinghy
Teddy bear	Swimming costume	Spade	Credit card
Motorcycle helmet	Portable television	Iron	First aid kit
Fish	Laptop computer	Golf club	Pair of socks
Camera	Passport	Champagne	Hair dryer
Penknife	Scissors	Guitar	Tape measure
Padlock	Soap and shampoo	Scarf and gloves	Vacuum cleaner
Torch	Cat	Parachute	Handcuffs

© Pearson Education Limited 2006 – Photocopiable

Beginnings and endings

Student A

1   … from my new job after only two weeks.
2   … about the terrible service in this hotel.
3   … for job interviews
4   … to yours, isn't it?
5   … in losing weight so quickly.
6   … in doing a course at college.
7   … at painting.
8   … from my last one.
9   … of missing the train.
10   … for the meal yet.

Student B

1   … of your achievements.
2   … in ghosts and other superstitious rubbish.
3   … on camping and other outdoor activities.
4   … on my exam results.
5   … for breaking my camera.
6   … on going to the station with me.
7   … about winning a medal in the Olympics.
8   … for a holiday job.
9   … about the theatre, and want to be an actor.
10   … about my father's illness.

Student B's sentences:

1 **I'm a little worried** (*about my father's illness*).

2 **He insisted** (*on going to the station with me*).

3 **I've decided to apply** (*for a holiday job*).

4 **I'm keen** (*on camping and other outdoor activities*).

5 **Well done! We're all very proud** (*of your achievements*).

6 **He didn't apologise** (*for breaking my camera*).

7 **I'm really passionate** (*about the theatre, and want to be an actor*).

8 **The job I get after school depends** (*on my exam results*).

9 **I don't believe** (*in ghosts and other superstitious rubbish*).

10 **She was very modest** (*about winning a medal in the Olympics*).

Student A's sentences:

1 **Everyone says that I'm good** (*at painting*).

2 **She was pleased when she succeeded** (*in losing weight so quickly*).

3 **I'm quite interested** (*in doing a course at college*).

4 **We can't leave: I haven't paid** (*for the meal yet*).

5 **This mobile phone is different** (*from my last one*).

6 **I'm sorry, but I'd like to complain** (*about the terrible service in this hotel*).

7 **I left early because I was afraid** (*of missing the train*).

8 **It's very important to prepare** (*for job interviews*).

9 **My computer is very similar** (*to yours, isn't it?*)

10 **My boss was so horrible, that I resigned** (*from my new job after only two weeks*).

© Pearson Education Limited 2006 – Photocopiable

The right response

Student A

A Hello, it's (your partner's name), isn't it?

B Hello, (your partner's name). I'm (your name and surname). Pleased to meet you.

C Come in and take a seat.

D Did you have a good journey here today?

E First of all I'd like to ask you some questions about your experience, if that's all right.

F I understand you've worked in a similar position before. Tell me about that.

G And what exactly did you do there?

H Did you enjoy the work?

I What qualities do you think you possess that make you suitable for this kind of work?

J What are your plans for the future?

K That sounds interesting. I hope things work out the way you want them to.

L Finally, is there anything you'd like to ask me?

M It lasts from the beginning of July to the middle of September, and you would be expected to be here from 10 in the morning until 6 in the evening.

N Yes, you would be needed on the first Sunday of each month. Is that all right?

O Good. Well, thank you for coming in today. We'll let you know by tomorrow morning. Goodbye (+ your partner's name).

✂ -

Student B

1 You must be joking. I'm not a slave, you know.	2 No, nothing at all. Can I go now, please?	3 Yes, please do.
4 Well, I'm very much a people person, I work well in a team and I'm good at using my own initiative.	5 Well, it was all right, you know, but at the end of the day it was just a job.	6 Yes, I was wondering how long this position is for, and the hours I would need to be here every day.
7 If you must, but I'd rather you didn't.	8 I organised sporting and social activities for the students, and accompanied them on trips in the city.	9 When I leave school, I'd like to do some voluntary work overseas, then train to be a vet.
10 Who knows. To tell the truth, I really don't care either way.	11 Yes, very much. I enjoyed meeting and working with students from around the world.	12 No, your school is in the middle of nowhere, and the bus service is rubbish.
13 Thank you. It will be good if they do.	14 Of course it is.	15 Thank you very much for seeing me. Goodbye.
16 Yes, thank you. There's a very good bus service from my home.	17 Well, last summer I worked as a social activities organiser at the Bradfell School of English.	18 I don't know really. I suppose I can work hard if I have to, when the money is good.
19 I'd rather stand, thanks.	20 Oh yes, I don't have a problem working weekends.	21 And you too, (Mr / Ms + your partner's surname).
22 That sounds fine. What about weekends?	23 Yes, I did, but there's really not much to tell you.	24 Yeah, bye. See you around.
25 Oh, this and that. Nothing much in particular.	26 Not a chance. My weekends are for me and nobody else.	27 I have absolutely no idea. I might become a rock star or something like that.
28 Hi there. And the same to you.	29 Yes, that's right.	30 Thank you.

© Pearson Education Limited 2006 – Photocopiable

Trading words

Student A

1	I couldn't afford a new computer, so I bought a cheap antique one from my friend.
	We'd like to change the word/expression: _____ for _____ (from student B)
2	During I was walking to school, I was stopped by the police.
	We'd like to change the word/expression: _____ for _____ (from student B)
3	The furniture in my bedroom is very modern, but the rest of the furniture in the house is more ancient.
	We'd like to change the word/expression: _____ for _____ (from student B)
4	This watch must be worth a lot of money: it's made of solid silk.
	We'd like to change the word/expression: _____ for _____ (from student B)
5	He didn't thank me for the work I had done, so up until that point I didn't offer to help him again.
	We'd like to change the word/expression: _____ for _____ (from student B)
6	My exams were at the beginning of June. Since then I went for a long holiday to recover.
	We'd like to change the word/expression: _____ for _____ (from student B)
7	We don't have any lessons at the afternoon this Friday so let's go to the cinema.
	We'd like to change the word/expression: _____ for _____ (from student B)
8	Andy refuses to wear porcelain shoes and anything else made from dead animals.
	We'd like to change the word/expression: _____ for _____ (from student B)
9	The shirt I bought was so slippery that it gave me a red rash around my neck.
	We'd like to change the word/expression: _____ for _____ (from student B)
10	Environmental groups often criticize supermarkets for giving away free rubber bags to their customers.
	We'd like to change the word/expression: _____ for _____ (from student B)

✂ --

Student B

A	The shirt she gave me was made of pure gold and felt really comfortable.
	We'd like to change the word/expression: _____ for _____ (from student A)
B	The aeroplane was invented in the beginning of the 20th century.
	We'd like to change the word/expression: _____ for _____ (from student A)
C	She threw the ball to me, but I couldn't catch it because it was wet and itchy.
	We'd like to change the word/expression: _____ for _____ (from student A)
D	Car tyres are made of plastic, which is produced in many tropical countries.
	We'd like to change the word/expression: _____ for _____ (from student A)
E	I inherited a wonderful set of leather plates and cups from my grandmother.
	We'd like to change the word/expression: _____ for _____ (from student A)
F	I didn't go anywhere while my last holiday: I just stayed at home and studied.
	We'd like to change the word/expression: _____ for _____ (from student A)
G	I bought a digital camera last month. After that I've taken hundreds of photographs.
	We'd like to change the word/expression: _____ for _____ (from student A)
H	Our town opened its first restaurant last year. From that point on, you had to go to the next town to eat out.
	We'd like to change the word/expression: _____ for _____ (from student A)
I	At the Museum, my teacher accidentally knocked over a valuable second-hand vase.
	We'd like to change the word/expression: _____ for _____ (from student A)
J	I'm very interested in history, and especially in the history of traditional Rome.
	We'd like to change the word/expression: _____ for _____ (from student A)

© Pearson Education Limited 2006 – Photocopiable

Correction connections

1 I was going out with her for 5 years when she asked me to marry her.	**2** He walked down the street when suddenly he slipped on a banana skin.	☺	**3** I didn't want another coffee because I already drunk four cups.	**4** What you do last Saturday?
5 Where had you worked this time last year?	**6** We were winning the game when the referee was deciding to send off two of our players.	**7** My teacher was really angry because I hadn't been finishing my homework.	**8** As I was driving to work, a dog was running into the road right in front of me.	**9** By the time I got to the party, most people already leave.
☺	**10** My computer was working perfectly, and then all of a sudden it had started making a strange noise.	**11** When I arrived at the station, I discovered that the train was leaving half an hour before.	**12** Had you seen Thomas yesterday afternoon?	☺
13 I'm sorry to disturb you. Did you work?	**14** I made some really good friends when I work in Aberdeen last year.	**15** I didn't need to post the letter because Sam already post it.	**16** I had drove for almost twelve hours when I fell asleep.	**17** I had only work for the company for six months when I was promoted.
18 What had you done for your holiday last summer?	☺	**19** I played tennis when it started to rain.	**20** My mobile phone stopped working when I had been in the middle of a conversation.	**21** I told her to come after dinner, but she arrived before I was finishing.
22 During the lesson my phone was suddenly ringing.	**23** Last year our football team had been winning every game we played.	**24** When I had got to the airport, I realised I had left my tickets at home.	☺	**25** By the time the film ended, half the audience fell asleep.

© Pearson Education Limited 2006 – Photocopiable

Your rule, my rule

Student A

		Student B's sentence
1	The Bahamas are an ideal place to go for a winter holiday.	
2	My friend Ruud comes from the Netherlands.	
3	I generally eat a lot of the pasta because it's cheap and nutritious.	
4	I ordered a pizza and a salad. The pizza was nice but the salad was horrible.	
5	The Black Mamba is more poisonous than any other snake.	
6	I would love to go walking in the Himalayas.	
7	I live in the Eynsham, a small town in Oxfordshire.	
8	Can you imagine what life would be like without the mobile phone?	
9	The Chinese are considered to be very industrious.	
10	The sky suddenly turned black and it started raining heavily.	
11	Just before Christmas, you can hardly walk along the Regent Street in London because there are so many people.	
12	Every year there is a big boat race between Oxford and Cambridge on the Thames.	
13	This is the most disgusting thing I've ever eaten!	
14	It's so hot in here because the window is closed.	
15	I haven't been to the theatre for ages.	

✂ -

Student B

		Student A's sentence
A	Only very rich people can afford to live on the Park Lane.	
B	Can you turn the heating on? I'm freezing.	
C	The Ancient Romans invented a lot of things that we still use today.	
D	I'd love to go on a cruise along the Nile.	
E	I'm bored. Let's go to the cinema.	
F	When the sun went down, it became very cold.	
G	Bob is the laziest person I know.	
H	The USA causes more pollution than any other country.	
I	She spent four months relaxing in the Maldives.	
J	The computer has changed everyone's lives in so many ways.	
K	Strict national laws have been introduced to protect the African elephant.	
L	I've never been to the New York, but I'd love to go there.	
M	There's a documentary on Channel 4 and a film on BBC1. The documentary sounds good, but I'd rather watch the film.	
N	The Alps stretch across western Europe from France to Austria.	
O	I never drink the coffee before I go to bed in case it keeps me awake.	

© Pearson Education Limited 2006 – Photocopiable

Adverb additions

heavily	colourfully	definately	badly	late
slowly	suprisingly	probably	closely	hard
beautifully	increasingly	completely	strongly	fast

1   He found his new job challenging and at times he considered leaving the company, but he worked and was promoted to manager after only six months.

2   We wanted to get out of the house for some fresh air, but in the end we decided to stay in and watch television because it was raining.

3   Carl had the measles for several weeks last term and so missed most of his lessons. As a result, everyone thought he would fail the exam, but he did well.

4   It was a lovely day, and we walked through the park, looking at the flowers and enjoying the beautiful weather.

5   Roger is a talented musician and he plays the piano and the guitar, but he only knows two or three songs!

6   I don't believe it! Look at the time! You've come again. Why don't you try catching an earlier bus.

7   He works for an environmental group because he feels that we need to do something about the damage we are doing to the earth's atmosphere.

8   I would love to have a job that pays me lots of money and gives me lots of benefits, but I have to admit that it's becoming difficult to find a well-paid job these days.

9   Amanda likes to dress, and always wears bright and unusual clothes that she's found in markets and charity shops in the town.

10   I can't believe how I did in the exam, especially after all the work I did and the extra lessons I went to.

11   The man who stole my wallet was older and shorter than me, but to my surprise he ran and I couldn't catch up with him.

12   'Please don't be late. Make sure you come on time', he said. 'Don't worry, I'll be there at nine,' I replied.

13   I would love to go out with you tonight, but our teacher gave us a lot of homework this morning and I won't finish until at least 10 or 11.

14   I keep telling Brian that being interested in politics and joining a political party are two different things, but he won't listen to me.

15   There was a lot of noise outside in the hall, then the door opened and Christine ran into the room, followed by her dog.

© Pearson Education Limited 2006 – Photocopiable

The same suffix

⇒	I	N	V	O	L	V	E	F	O	R	G	I	V	⇘
⇙	N	T	I	M	D	A	D	N	E	I	R	F	E	⇓
⇘	O	V	E	L	D	O	N	A	T	E	R	E	P	⇘
⇙	E	V	N	I	O	N	A	I	P	E	C	A	L	⇓
⇘	N	T	M	E	M	B	E	R	J	O	U	R	N	⇘
⇙	R	A	E	T	A	L	S	N	A	R	T	L	A	⇓
⇘	R	A	N	G	E	C	A	L	C	U	L	A	T	⇘
⇙	R	E	N	T	R	A	P	Y	D	A	E	R	E	⇓
⇘	F	O	R	G	E	T	P	R	O	D	U	C	E	☺

1   _____ to the museum is free for students on _____ of a student card, but they are encouraged to make a small _____ to help pay for the museum.

2   When our manager, Mr Beckham, was fired because of his illegal _____ in another company, his _____, Ms Jenkins, had to cancel our _____ with the company that supplied our equipment.

3   She was able to get _____ of the local golf club because of her long _____ with the club's director, and because of the club's _____ with the company she worked for.

4   He's well-known for his _____ (he never remembers to do what he's told), but also for his _____ to do anything people ask him to, and his qualities of _____ when they shout at him for not doing it!

5   She started her long career working as a _____ for the _____ of the pocket _____.

6   My father was not only a famous concert _____, but also worked for a time as a _____ on a national newspaper, and was also a best-selling _____, with several books to his name.

© Pearson Education Limited 2006 – Photocopiable

Communicative crossword

Student A

Give your partner a clue for the school subjects given in the crossword. Tell them how important, useful or interesting you think the subjects are and why.

I think that 1 across is a useful subject because it helps you to understand how living things work. Also it's very important if you want to train to become a doctor.

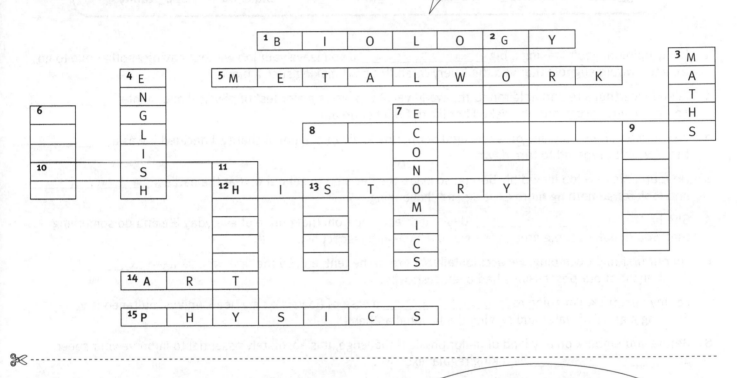

Student B

Give your partner a clue for the school subjects given in the crossword. Tell them how important, useful or interesting you think the subjects are and why.

I think that 1 across is a useful subject because it helps you to understand how living things work. Also it's very important if you want to train to become a doctor.

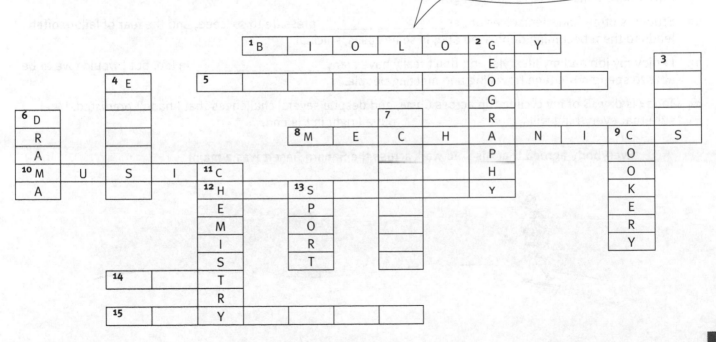

© Pearson Education Limited 2006 – Photocopiable

Add a letter, add a word

Complete sentences 1-14 with a word from the box, then rearrange the missing letters to make a word that can complete the sentence at the bottom of the page.

> ac_ievements   ambitio_s   ba_ance   chan_e   consu_ing   enduran_e   extre_e
> g_mble   int_nse   ob_ession   _urn   _ut   stam_na   opp_rtunity

1   In my opinion, you're taking a big _____ if you leave your job without having another one to go to, and I would suggest that you think very carefully about making such a move.

2   Ellen Macarthur's remarkable round-the-world yacht trip was a major test of physical and mental _____, and on several occasions she risked her life to fulfil her dream.

3   When I was offered a place on a cycling tour of Cuba in aid of a national charity, I decided it was a _____ that I wasn't prepared to turn down.

4   He found his new job incredibly boring, so made the decision to get out of it at the earliest _____ and look for something more exciting and challenging.

5   She had an all _____ desire to break free from the routine of everyday life and do something that would make people around the world admire and respect her.

6   On our first night camping, we accidentally set fire to the tent, and by the time we managed to _____ it out, most of our possessions had been destroyed.

7   For my next trick, I'm going to _____ a vase of flowers on my head while simultaneously drinking a glass of water and singing the national anthem!

8   Before you embark on any kind of major physical challenge, it is absolutely essential to improve your speed and _____ by taking regular exercise.

9   For many people, the desire to do something challenging and different can become a major _____ which can take over, and even ruin, their lives.

10 Putting a man on the moon was one of the 20th century's most remarkable _____ , and set the standards for scientific excellence for years to come.

11 I've never been keen on _____ sports such as parachuting and white-water rafting, and would rather have a nice relaxing game of golf.

12 Students often find themselves under _____ pressure to succeed, and the fear of failure often leads to them becoming depressed and, in some cases, suicidal.

13 I enjoy my job and my lifestyle, and don't really have many _____ in life, but I would love to be able to spend more time travelling and meeting people.

14 Today is day 18 of my cycling trip across China, and despite several challenges that I hadn't predicted, I feel sure that everything will _____ out all right in the end.

'Everybody agreed that his solo walk across the Sahara Desert was a major _____ '.

© Pearson Education Limited 2006 – Photocopiable

Just 45 seconds

✂

1 *advice*, any help or need I you give If **call** a I'll.	**2** car If *year*, and go to I next around Peru **country** I'll a hire the travel.
3 have If any you I'll ask to **you** help *problems*, someone.	**4** have take want If you **risks** to in *life*, you'll succeed to a few.
5 won't you **certificate** miss many If too English, you get a *classes*,.	**6** **money** *competition*, prize you If the, how will win you spend the?
7 lend If I you soon **possible** the return promise will you to it as as *money*,?	**8** accept what If *job*, don't you **instead** the will you do?
9 we If **boring** take risks life be would very *occasionally*, didn't.	**10** probably **climbing** *braver*, I was bit a I would go mountain If.
11 **world** I a off *work*, year I might travel If took the around.	**12** more If I **charity** had I some could work for do an *time*, international voluntary.
13 wouldn't If all job was more **time** I be so *exciting*, bored my the.	**14** eat I less take If were more and **exercise** *you*, I'd.
15 *wanted*, money had as as If you what would with do **it** much you you?	**16** **do** choose you any job could in the *world*, If would you what?
17 wouldn't I had more *carefully*, I **accident** had the If have driven.	**18** **train** have we we left hadn't so wouldn't If missed the *late*,.
19 careless you *camera*, **it** hadn't been have dropped so with your you wouldn't If.	**20** **it** I known how If skiing had done I dangerous have *was*, wouldn't.
21 had If *properly*, you the chicken have become we **ill** cooked wouldn't.	**22** to gone I had harder at worked I could **university** have If *school*,.
23 *university*, you hadn't have to If what gone would you **instead** done?	**24** we have map we had **lost** taken If a *us*, with wouldn't got.

123

© Pearson Education Limited 2006 – Photocopiable

Modal chase

		Student A + B START ▼					
mustn't wear	must take	mustn't be making	should have cooked	should have taken	ought to call	have got to make	ought have called
	needn't take	should attend	have to stay out	shouldn't have to borrow	don't need to leave	don't have need to wear	
should has arrived	shouldn't have cooked	did have to call			ought to make	should be cooked	ought to leave
had to call		didn't need to apply	must remembers to send	shouldn't have gone on	should have attend		have to wear
has to apply		don't need to wear	needn't borrow	ought to calling	has to wear		mustn't not stay out
don't must leave	mustn't attend	should take			mustn't make	needn't call	should have arrived
	shouldn't have borrowed	had to remember to send	mustn't call	shouldn't have taken	should have borrowed	shouldn't have arrived	
must go on	should wear		must have arrived	should have worn		don't have to go on	must have worn
needn't remember to send	don't need to call		should have applied	mustn't cook		had taken	must remember to send
mustn't stay out	had to attend	shouldn't have left	must to go on	had to take	must stay out	have to apply	should to take

1 I've put on a lot of weight recently. I really _____ a diet.
2 Men _____ a tie to that restaurant, otherwise they won't let you in.
3 You _____ an umbrella with you when you go out later, in case it rains.
4 The children are asleep, so we _____ too much noise.
5 When I started my first job, I _____ my boss 'Sir'.
6 The film doesn't start until nine o'clock, so we _____ too early.
7 I've got a long day tomorrow, so I _____ late tonight.
8 We _____ Jim and arrange to meet tonight. Have you got his number?
9 Before you get a job abroad, you _____ for a work permit.
10 You _____ the food more carefully; this chicken could kill someone!
11 It's my father's birthday in two weeks. I _____ him a card.
12 It's a very informal dinner party, so you _____ a suit.
13 Our flight left early, so we _____ an early bus to the airport.
14 If you want to pass your exams this year, you _____ more of your classes.
15 He really _____ earlier: he's missed half his lesson.
16 You _____ his camera without asking his permission. Now he's really angry, you know.

© Pearson Education Limited 2006 – Photocopiable

Who said what?

Write sentences for **eight** of the subject areas below. Use language of emphasis in each of your sentences. Do not show your paper to anyone else in the class.

Your name: _____

1   An object that you would like to possess.

2   A school subject that you do/did or don't/didn't enjoy.

3   A job that you would like to have.

4   An animal that you don't like.

5   A bad habit that annoys you.

6   A pop or rock group that you like.

7   A country you would like to visit.

8   Something that worries or frightens you.

9   A famous person that you don't like.

10   A book you have read recently that you enjoyed.

11   A film you have seen recently that you didn't enjoy.

12   Food that you would never eat.

13   A sport that you either like watching or playing.

14   An activity that you would never do.

© Pearson Education Limited 2006 – Photocopiable

Hot rocks

✂

1 House prices have now become so _____ that nobody can afford them any more. *(high)*

2 When two of its engines stopped, the aircraft rapidly began to lose _____. *(height)*

3 I want to make a _____-distance call to my sister in Australia. Is it expensive from London? *(long)*

4 Bill is usually an easy-going person, but when I broke his new camera he went off at the _____ end. *(deep)*

5 The bed in my hotel was so _____ that my head was pressed up against the wall and my feet hung over the end. *(short)*

6 The cave descends to a _____ of almost 200 metres, and parts of it have never been explored. *(depth)*

7 She fell from such a great ___ that it's a miracle she didn't break anything or seriously hurt herself. *(height)*

8 This exercise is designed to _____ your awareness of the construction of nouns and verbs. *(heighten)*

9 The hotel pool, which is open to both residents and non-residents, is an impressive 60 metres in _____. *(length)*

10 I really recommend this shop, as it sells a range of _____-quality computer equipment at excellent prices. *(high)*

11 House prices are extremely _____ at the moment, and are expected to drop even further. *(low)*

12 His name is Richard, but most people _____ his name to Rick. *(shorten)*

13 The new Spielberg film goes on for almost 3½ hours: films of this _____ are quite rare these days. *(length)*

14 The airport authority have said that they plan to _____ the runway at the airport from 2.5km to over 3km. *(lengthen)*

15 She was so _____ in thought that she didn't even hear us come into the room. *(deep)*

16 This is quite a _____-risk strategy, so we don't have much to lose if things go wrong. *(high)*

17 I asked him if he could _____ his price from £150 to £130, but he said it wouldn't be possible. *(lower)*

18 The road is too narrow for two cars to pass each other safely, so the council are going to _____ it by two metres *(widen))*

19 The window is three metres high and almost 5 metres in _____. *(width/breadth)*

20 As summer approaches, the days begin to _____. *(lengthen)*

21 The government is worried that unless major steps are taken, the economic crisis will _____. *(deepen)*

22 My father is about two metres tall, with _____ shoulders and a thick neck. *(broad)*

23 A lot of people like to _____ their horizons by travelling and meeting other people. *(broaden)*

24 She seems to know so much: her _____ of knowledge is amazing. *(breadth)*

25 It'll take us an hour to walk there along the main road, but I know a _____-cut that will only take about half an hour. *(short)*

26 The shop sells a _____ variety of camera equipment at very good prices. *(wide)*

27 We couldn't get the new cupboard into the room because the door wasn't _____ enough. *(wide)*

28 In the next two weeks I want to pass my exams and look for a job, but I don't have any _____-term plans yet. *(long)*

29 Does travel _____ the mind? I think so – you learn so many new things about the world around you. *(broaden)*

30 The longest day of the year in Britain is 21 June. After that, the days begin to _____. *(shorten)*

© Pearson Education Limited 2006 – Photocopiable

What would you do?

The coffee you have just seen in the supermarket only costs £2.00, but the company who makes it gives the farmers who grow the coffee beans very low prices for their product. There is another coffee next to it for £3.50; all of the profits from this go directly to the farmers and their families. Both coffees taste the same. Which coffee would you buy?	Your best friend's boyfriend/ girlfriend has just told you that he / she really likes you and wants to go out with you. You also really like him / her, but you already have a boyfriend/ girlfriend. Do you: (a) accept his / her offer? (b) tell your best friend? (c) tell your boyfriend/girlfriend?	You accidentally drive your car into another car that is parked by the side of the road. The car you have hit now has a big dent in the door. Nobody has seen the accident. Would you leave a note on the car explaining what you have done and offering to pay for the damage you have done?
Next week you are going to take a very important English exam. You have just found out that somebody has illegally put a copy of the exam onto the Internet, and for £20 you can download the papers. Would you?	You urgently need some money and have decided to sell your stereo. A colleague or schoolmate has offered you £200 for it, and you have agreed to sell it to her for that price. Somebody else then offers you £350 for the same stereo. Would you accept the second offer?	You are at the airport and waiting to check in for your flight. An old lady on the same flight approaches you and asks if you would carry something onto, and off, the plane for her, as she already has too much hand-luggage. Would you refuse to help her?
You really want an MP3 personal stereo. Somebody who you do not know very well offers you a brand-new one (still in its box) for a very cheap £35. You suspect, but cannot prove, that it has been stolen. Would you buy it?	You have just used a cash machine outside a bank. You wanted to take out £100, but the machine has given you £200. Your receipt shows that you have taken out £100. Would you inform your bank of the mistake?	Your neighbour, who you do not get on with, claims that he is unable to work because of a medical condition, and so is claiming large financial benefits from the government. However, you know that he is working full-time as a taxi driver. Would you report him to the authorities?
The police have arrested your best friend because they claim he started a fight in a nightclub and seriously injured someone. Your friend has denied this, and has asked you to tell the police that he was with you somewhere else that night. Do you lie to the police to support your friend? (remember: this is your *best* friend!)	You have just eaten a meal in a restaurant where the food was poor, the service was slow and the staff were rude. The staff are very busy, and nobody would notice if you walked out without paying the bill. Would you leave without paying?	You have a colleague at work who you really do not like. You know that he / she frequently drives his / her car after drinking alcohol, and also uses his / her mobile phone while driving. Both of these are illegal in your country. Would you report him / her to the police?
You see an adult shouting at a small child in the street. The child is screaming and is clearly very upset. The adult then starts hitting the child very hard. Would you say something to the adult?	There is a car on the market that you have wanted for a long time You have finally saved up enough money to buy it. However, you then discover that the company which makes the car also makes weapons, including landmines, which they sell to countries with aggressive foreign policies. Would you still buy the car?	You have found a wallet containing over £500 in cash. You are currently short of cash, and there is no name or contact address in the wallet. Would you hand the wallet over to the police or would you keep the money?

© Pearson Education Limited 2006 – Photocopiable

From top to bottom

START HERE

1 You can't go to your interview in those jeans and that old T-shirt: you look really **fsryufc**.	2 His hair is so **yvwa** that it looks like he is standing in a very strong wind.	3 She didn't explain the rules very clearly, and as a result we were all really **fcoudnse**.	4 Could you **edinmr** me to get some money from the bank when we go to town?	5 I had thought that she would like to hear all about my latest job, but she seemed rather **tesiuterednn**.	6 The town council want to build a **roaemlim** for everyone who died in the war.
7 I'm sorry, but I didn't **bermeerm** to get you any milk when I was in town.	8 I'm quite an **stimpotici** person, and always believe that good things are about to happen.	9 I'm so **grotflfeu** that I can see people I met only a few hours before, and have no idea who they are!	10 I'm not short and fat: I'm **oksytc**. There's a difference, you know!	11 My sister is the girl over there with the long, **thagsirt**, black hair.	12 He's not a very friendly man, and I always feel a bit **sayuen** when he's in the room.
13 Children are naturally **ircusou**: they always want to know what is going on.	14 Her hair isn't brown and it isn't red, it's something between the two: a sort of **nuurba** colour.	**You automatically win this space if you win the space above**	15 I felt rather **edaynon** when he arrived late for the third time that week.	16 April 27th 1998 was a particularly **baoermlem** date for me, as that was when I started my first job.	17 My brother has got a beard and moustache, but my father is **encla-evsnha**.
You automatically win this space if you win the space above	18 I don't think that newspapers always tell the truth, and I'm quite **sticpacle** about some of the stories they report.	**You cannot cross this space!**	19 I'm a bit **vgehorietw** at the moment, so plan to start a diet tomorrow. Or maybe next week. Or perhaps next month...	20 My mother has an excellent **eymmro** for names and faces, and always knows who people are when she meets them.	**You automatically win this space if you win the space above**
21 There was a tall, **gentlea** woman in a long dress standing in the corner.	22 As soon as my uncle begins to **semeiicrn** about his days in India, everyone leaves the room!	23 Some people believe that the best way to avoid **enkwrlsi** appearing on your face is to eat lots of fruit.	**You automatically win this space if you win the space above**	24 I'm rather **pucssisoui** of people who smile too much: I don't really trust them.	25 With his **kpyis** hair and the studs in his nose and ears, Toby looks like a punk rocker.
You cannot cross this space!	26 The children are really **cedeitx** about their holiday: they can't wait to go!	27 She wrote her number down, then told me to **zioeremm** it before destroying the paper.	**You cannot cross this space!**	28 The head of our athletics team at school is fast and strong, with a slender, **aruscuml** body.	**You cannot cross this space!**
29 She's not fat, but she is a little **bucbyh** because of all the chocolates she eats.	**You automatically win this space if you win the space above**	30 I really needed to pass my maths exam, so as you can imagine, I was very **delrevie** when I did.	31 He has long, blond, **yrclu** hair which makes him look slightly feminine.	**You automatically win this space if you win the space above**	32 I felt really **igcasnotl** when I visited the town I had grown up in 20 years before.
33 I bought a model of the Eiffel Tower as a **insorevu** of my visit to Paris.	**You cannot cross this space!**	34 My father used to have really thick hair, but recently he's started going a bit **dbal**.	35 After sailing around the Mediterranean for six weeks, he was really **dtnena**.	**You cannot cross this space!**	36 Your new boyfriend is very **dogo-ginloko**, isn't he?

FINISH HERE

© Pearson Education Limited 2006 – Photocopiable

Fill the boxes

Complete the sentences using the verbs and expressions in the boxes. You will need to change the verb form in some sentences.

> use to   used to   would   get used to   getting used to

> be change correct destroy drive eat go leave move
> speak spend take visit work read

1   Our teacher didn't _____ so strict, but now he really makes us work hard.

2   We didn't _____to the cinema very often, but now we're there almost every night.

3   Did you _____ lots of sweets when you were younger?

4   As children, we _____ all our pocket money on sweets and toys.

5   When she was younger, our aunt _____ us three or four times a week.

6   At school, our history teacher _____ all our homework in class, so we never got any real work done.

7   Our maths teacher _____ any homework that he thought wasn't good enough, and throw it into the bin in front of all the other pupils in the class!

8   When we first hired a car in England, it was a bit strange, but now we're _____on the left side of the road.

9   Many children are _____ a bedtime story every night.

10 I'm _____ English as I go to London quite a lot.

11 He's _____ jobs: he's had five in the last year!

12 I can't _____ home for work so early every morning.

13 I don't think I'll ever _____ in such a noisy environment.

14 I think I'm gradually _____ the train to work, but I'd rather go by car.

15 My husband is a diplomat, and I'm slowly _____ from one country to another on a regular basis.

© Pearson Education Limited 2006 – Photocopiable

Abilities crossword

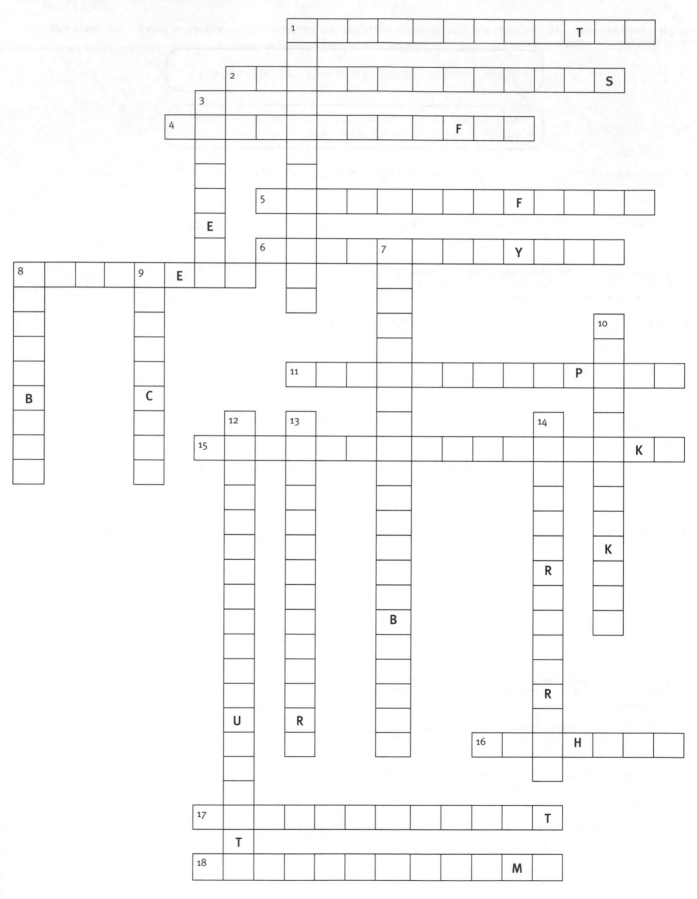

© Pearson Education Limited 2006 – Photocopiable

Paragraph auction

Before you do this activity, decide which sentences contain a mistake.

1	I really enjoy my English lessons, and I think I'll be able to pass my FCE exam next year, but I do wish our teacher would make it a bit more challenging for us.
2	Although Antonio is an excellent student, and works well in the lessons that he attends, however he should try to be more punctual and attend more of his classes.
3	On our last holiday, the weather was awful, the hotel was terrible and the food was almost inedible. Nevertheless, we managed to enjoy ourselves as there was so much to do and the nightlife was fantastic.
4	We used to live in the countryside, but last year we moved to the city. We're slowly getting used to being surrounded by people and noise, although I must say that I often miss the peace and quiet of our old home.
5	As children, we would often steal apples from our neighbour's garden, and we used to throw any that we didn't eat at the local policeman. However, on the whole we would be quite well-behaved and respectful.
6	Thank you very much for your letter of 16 July and for letting us know that you've managed arranging a meeting for next week. However, our offices are currently being redecorated, and we were wondering if we could hold the meeting in your office instead.
7	I think that I'm very good at cooking and could get a job in a restaurant if I wanted to, although I don't think I would enjoy it very much as I don't think I could get used to working late every night.
8	Although I'm used to getting up early and usually manage to get to work on time, I nevertheless find it difficult to concentrate so early in the morning, and wish I had a job that started a bit later in the day.
9	Mike is very hardworking, and everyone thinks he'll do very well when he eventually leaves school. However, he didn't used to be like that, and I can clearly remember the time when he was really lazy and would spend all his time in front of the television.
10	I used to spend all my time playing computer games and listening to loud music, but I've changed a lot since then. Nevertheless I still enjoy relaxing from time to time, I now find that I enjoy the challenge of work, and am working hard for my future.
11	When I was much younger I used to believe in ghosts and was scared to sleep with the lights off. As I grew older, however, I naturally became more sceptical of such things, although to tell you the truth I still believe that there are many things that can't really be properly explained.
12	I was a terrible language learner at school and could never manage to pass any of my exams. When I first went travelling, however, I discovered that I was able to communicate quite well using just a few key words and gestures. Nevertheless, there were occasions when I wished that I had had better language-learning skills when I was younger.

© Pearson Education Limited 2006 – Photocopiable

Personality bingo

He/She's a cold fish.	He/She's the salt of the earth.	His/Her heart's in the right place.
He/She's as stubborn as a mule.	He/She's a killjoy.	He/She's a loner.
He/She's a slave driver.	He/She's a trouble-maker.	He/She's a windbag.

✂ -

He/She's an awkward customer.	He/She's a windbag.	He/She's a couch potato.
He/She's the salt of the earth.	He/She's got a chip on his/her shoulder.	He/She's a pain in the neck.
He/She's a slave driver.	He/ She's a real know-all.	He/She's an early bird.

✂ -

He/She's a windbag.	He/She's a trouble-maker.	He/She's a busybody.
He/She's a pain in the neck.	He/She's a killjoy.	He/She's as hard as nails.
He/ She's a real know-all.	He/She's a loner.	He/She's a cold fish.

✂ -

He/She's a loner.	His/Her heart's in the right place.	He/She's a couch potato.
He/She's got a chip on his/her shoulder.	He/She's an early bird.	He/She's an awkward customer.
He/She's the salt of the earth.	He/She's as stubborn as a mule.	He/She's a slave driver.

✂ -

He/She's a stick in the mud.	He/She's a windbag.	He/She's a pain in the neck.
He/She's a high-flyer.	He/She's an awkward customer.	He/She's a trouble-maker.
He/She's a slave driver.	He/She's as hard as nails.	He/She's a cold fish.

✂ -

He/She's a killjoy.	He/She's a busybody.	He/She's as stubborn as a mule.
He/She's an early bird.	He/She's got a chip on his/her shoulder.	His/Her heart's in the right place.
He/She's as hard as nails.	He/She's the life and soul of the party.	He/She's a couch potato.

© Pearson Education Limited 2006 – Photocopiable

Personal time capsule

1 What your partner looks like:

_____

2 How he/she would describe his/her character and personality:

_____

3 Three personal possessions that are very important to him/her:

_____

4 A book that he/she has particularly enjoyed:

_____

5 A favourite music group, its style of music and a song or album they have made:

_____

6 A film that he/she has particularly enjoyed:

_____

7 Something he/she used to do but doesn't do any more:

_____

8 Something he/she didn't use to do, but does now:

_____

9 Something he/she has got used to doing, or something he/she is getting used to doing:

_____

10 A particular memory he/she has from his/her past:

_____

11 A person who is very important to him/her:

_____

12 Three things that he/she is able to do:

_____

13 Something that he/she hopes he/she will be able to do in the future:

_____

133

© Pearson Education Limited 2006 – Photocopiable

DIY travel survey

itchy feet	independent traveller	petrifying
emigrating	uncharted territory	challenging
disgusting	wander around	fascinating
annoying	culture shock	homesick
roam	subzero temperatures	

1 When was the last time you felt really _____? What did you miss about home?
Your partner's answer: _____

2 The next time you have _____, where do you think you'll go?
Your partner's answer: _____

3 In your opinion, what's the biggest difference between a tourist and an _____?
Your partner's answer: _____

4 Would you feel nervous about going into _____ or would you enjoy experiencing the unknown?
Your partner's answer: _____

5 Have you ever experienced _____, and where were you when it happened?
Your partner's answer: _____

6 Some people say that one of the most enjoyable things you can do in a foreign city is simply _____. Do you agree with them, or would you do something different?
Your partner's answer: _____

7 What things have you found _____ when you have visited foreign countries? Why are you irritated by them?
Your partner's answer: _____

8 What's the most _____ thing you have ever eaten when travelling? Why was it so unpleasant?
Your partner's answer: _____

9 What's the most _____ or inspiring place you have ever visited (or would like to visit)?
Your partner's answer: _____

10 Have you ever had a really _____ experience while travelling? What was frightening about it and what happened?
Your partner's answer: _____

11 If you could set yourself a really _____ journey, what would you do, where would you go, and why would you do it?
Your partner's answer: _____

12 Have you ever been anywhere where you experienced _____ or where it was extremely hot? Where did you go, and how did you manage in such extremes of heat or cold?
Your partner's answer: _____

13 In Britain, many young people can't wait to leave home and set off to _____ around the world. Is this the same in your country?
Your partner's answer: _____

14 Would you ever consider _____ or living abroad for a while, and if so, where would be your first choice?
Your partner's answer: _____

© Pearson Education Limited 2006 – Photocopiable

Perfect proverbs

A   I _____ a practice test for my English exam and I got 85%, so I'll definitely pass the real exam next week. *(just do)*

B   Thanks for the invitation to your party on Saturday, but my cousin _____ me and said me he's coming over this weekend. Can I bring him with me? *(just call)*

C   Ana _____ late to her lessons all this term, and she always seems to be late, but she promises to improve from now on. *(come)*

D   I'm very worried. My son went on holiday last week and I _____ to hear from him since then, but so far nothing. *(wait)*

E   I _____ German for three months, but I don't seem to be making much progress. *(learn)*

F   I only joined this company last week, and my new boss _____ at me four times since then. *(already shout)*

G   Originally there were just three of us in the office, and we got a lot of work done. However, three more people _____ us, and we're not working as well as we did. *(just join)*

H   Our teacher gave us lots of homework this afternoon. I_____ it, but because I did it so quickly, it's full of mistakes. *(already finish)*

I   All week, Mr Johnson _____ everybody in the office that he's really pleased with our work, but it would be nice if he gave us all a pay rise as a result. *(tell)*

J   I _____ at this essay I wrote last night, and it's full of spelling mistakes. There must be something wrong with my computer. *(just look)*

K   We _____ to solve this problem for ages now. Perhaps if we asked some of our friends to help, we might be more successful. *(try)*

L   Remember when I helped fix your computer? Well, I _____ some problems with my car recently, and I was wondering if you could look at it. *(have)*

M   I don't believe it! Emma _____ my favourite cup. The stupid, careless woman! I'm never going to speak to her again. *(break)*

N   Our boss _____ on a two-week holiday, so there's a really relaxed atmosphere in the office, and we aren't getting much work done. *(just go)*

O   What a terrible morning! First of all I overslept, then I missed the bus, then I fell over and hurt my leg, and finally I _____ that the company is going to cut our salary by 15%. *(just hear)*

P   I started applying for a job last week, and I _____ three offers to attend an interview. I'm going to make an appointment to see all three companies as soon as possible. *(already receive)*

1   Don't worry. His bark is worse than his bite.

2   That's true. Actions speak louder than words.

3   Well, you shouldn't count your chickens before they're hatched.

4   Why not? Many hands make light work.

5   Oh dear. Well, you know what they say: too many cooks spoil the broth.

6   Oh dear. It never rains but it pours.

7   Sure. The more the merrier.

8   Are you sure? A bad workman always blames his tools, you know.

9   Oh come on! You shouldn't make a mountain out of a molehill.

10   I see. When the cat's away, the mice will play, right?

11   Relax. No news is good news.

12   Good idea. You should strike while the iron is hot.

13   Oh well, more haste, less speed.

14   Of course. One good turn deserves another.

15   I suppose it's never too late to mend.

16   Give it time. Rome wasn't built in a day.

135

© Pearson Education Limited 2006 – Photocopiable

Something in common

You are 19 years old, you live with your mother, father and younger brother in a big city, and you're a student. Your favourite hobby is playing football. You also enjoy going to nightclubs with your friends. For your last holiday, you went skiing. In the future, you'd like to go walking in the Himalayas. Your favourite personal possession is your mobile phone.	You are 19 years old, you live with your mother, father and older brother in the country, and you're a shop assistant. Your favourite hobby is playing tennis. You also enjoy going for walks with your friends. For your last holiday, you went camping. In the future, you'd like to go skiing. Your favourite personal possession is your computer.
You are 20 years old, you live with your mother, father and younger brother in a small village, and you're an office assistant. Your favourite hobby is photography. You also enjoy watching television. For your last holiday, you went sailing. In the future, you'd like to travel around the Caribbean. Your favourite personal possession is your camera.	You are 20 years old, you live with your mother, father and older brother by the sea, and you're unemployed. Your favourite hobby is going to the cinema. You also enjoy watching television. For your last holiday, you went to Venice. In the future, you'd like to visit Paris. Your favourite personal possession is your motorbike.
You are 21 years old, you live with your elder brother in a big city, and you're a musician. Your favourite hobby is listening to music. You also enjoy going to nightclubs with your friends. For your last holiday, you went walking in the countryside. In the future, you'd like to visit Australia. Your favourite personal possession is your bicycle.	You are 21 years old, you live with your mother in the country, and you're a student. Your favourite hobby is playing tennis. You also enjoy playing the guitar. For your last holiday, you stayed at home. In the future, you'd like to travel around the Caribbean. Your favourite personal possession is your car.
You are 22 years old, you live with your elder brother in a small village, and you're a shop assistant. Your favourite hobby is playing football. You also enjoy gardening. For your last holiday, you went to a small island in the Indian Ocean. In the future, you'd like to visit China. Your favourite personal possession is your computer.	You are 22 years old, you live with your sister by the sea, and you're a nurse. Your favourite hobby is travelling. You also enjoy reading. For your last holiday, you went to Venice. In the future, you'd like to visit Australia. Your favourite personal possession is your personal stereo.
You are 23 years old, you live with your mother by the sea and you're unemployed. Your favourite hobby is photography. You also enjoy gardening. For your last holiday you went skiing. In the future, you'd like to visit Paris. Your favourite personal possession is your car.	You are 23 years old, you live on your own in a medium-sized town and you're a musician. Your favourite hobby is travelling. You also enjoy playing the guitar. For your last holiday you went to a small island in the Indian Ocean. In the future, you'd like to go walking in the Himalayas. Your favourite personal possession is your bicycle.
You are 24 years old, you live with your sister in a medium-sized town and you're an office assistant. Your favourite hobby is listening to music. You also enjoy reading. For your last holiday, you stayed at home. In the future, you'd like to go skiing. Your favourite personal possession is your personal stereo.	You are 24 years old, you live on your own in a small village, and you're a nurse. Your favourite hobby is going to the cinema. You also enjoy going to walks with your friends. For your last holiday you went camping. In the future, you'd like to visit China. Your favourite personal possession is your camera.
You are 25 years old, you live with your elder brother in the country and you're a student. Your favourite hobby is travelling. You also enjoy reading. For your last holiday, you went sailing. In the future, you'd like to visit Australia. Your favourite personal possession is your motorbike.	You are 25 years old, you live on your own in a small village and you're an office assistant. Your favourite hobby is photography. You also enjoy watching television. For your last holiday, you went walking in the mountains. In the future, you'd like to go walking in the Himalayas. Your favourite personal possession is your motorbike.

© Pearson Education Limited 2006 – Photocopiable

Just 15 questions

© Pearson Education Limited 2006 – Photocopiable

Go on, go on!

1 Is the Internet a good place to go shopping? Well, obviously, **it goes...**	...**for it.** There are lots of things to do there.	...**go** since seven this morning. That's the trouble with working in a hotel. It's **all...**
...**down** again. I don't know how long it will be before they fix it.	...**around** the school at the moment.	...**a go** if you can't find what you want locally.
2 The thing I like the most about Penelope and Jim is that once they promise something, they never **go...**	5 There's such a choice of wonderful things to eat here. I think I'll **go...**	...**back** on their word. **We go...**
3 I'm really quite excited because I'm **going...**	...**back** a long time, you know. I've known them both for years.	9 I've been trying to access the Internet all day, but without success. I'm not sure what's **going...**
...**back** now! You never know, it may work out for them.	6 I'm not particularly adventurous, but I'd love to **have a ...**	...**for** the fruit starter followed by the pie. I would try the lobster, but I **went...**
4 They were both dedicated, hardworking students, and they **went...**	...**without saying** that you can find just about anything you want there. It's certainly **worth...**	...**go** at parachuting. However, at almost £150 **a...**
...**go** day and night.	7 Their parents said they were not really suited for marriage, but they decided to **make...**	...**to show** that hard work and dedication can pay off.
...**down with** some sort of horrible stomach bug. Apparently, there's a **lot of it going...**	8 I'm not surprised they're both so tired. They've been **on the...**	...**a go of** it. Anyway, the wedding is next week, so I suppose **there's no going...**
...**on,** but I have a feeling that the network has **gone...**	...**go,** it's not exactly a cheap way of having fun.	10 Andrea and Graham can't come to the party tonight, as they've **gone...**
...**off** seafood a while ago.	...**away** for a few months. I've got a temporary job in Melbourne. Everyone says it's a city that's **got a lot going...**	...**to great lengths** to make sure they got good results. Of course they did extremely well, which just **goes...**

© Pearson Education Limited 2006 – Photocopiable

Quotes and proverbs

✄

Nobody should travel until he has learned the language of the country he visits. Otherwise he is like a baby: helpless and ridiculous.	People travel around the world to search for what they need, and they return home to find it.
A journey of a thousand miles begins with a single step, and the most difficult step of any journey is the first.	Everybody should love travelling, but they shouldn't make the road their home.
The best journeys that we make do not always go in a straight line.	The world is a book, and those who do not travel read only a page of it.
Somewhere on your journey, don't forget to turn around and enjoy the view.	Travelling makes an intelligent person more intelligent, and a stupid person more stupid.
I can't think of anything more wonderful and exciting than to be in a country where you are ignorant of almost everything.	One of the happiest moments of your life is the departure on a distant journey to places you have never been before.
Sometimes you need to get away from your family and friends for a while, and go to new places. That way, you will be more open to influence and to change.	It is better to travel than to arrive at your destination. The journey, and not the arrival, is what matters.
Travelling thousands of miles around the world is better than reading thousands of books.	When you travel, you leave everything that you are familiar with at home. This may not always be very comfortable for you, but it is certainly always exciting.
A traveller who does not observe what is happening around him, and who does not behave like the people around him, is like a bird without wings.	Don't tell me how educated you are; tell me about how much you have travelled and about the places you have seen.
When you travel, do it like Gandhi, with simple clothes, open eyes and an open mind.	The best way of finding out if you like someone or if you hate them is to go travelling with them.

© Pearson Education Limited 2006 – Photocopiable

Wrong word crossword

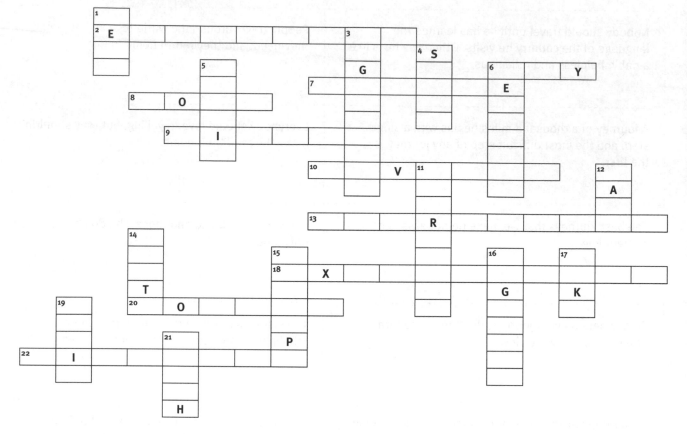

Across:

2 It cost us £10 for a hamburger and a plate of fries, which I thought was a bit far-fetched.
6 Put some vegetable oil in the pan, and grill the meat in it for five minutes on both sides.
7 I've got a wonderful receipt for crispy Chinese duck which I can let you have.
8 My friend Bill is an excellent cooker, and can make you almost anything you want.
9 This coffee is really sweet. Could I have some milk and sugar in it please?
10 The cafe serves a variety of pancakes, some with sweet fillings and some with salty fillings.
13 This pen was a bit luxury. It cost me £25, and although it's quite a good pen, it's not that good.
18 My brother is really overpriced. He spends so much that he always has to borrow money from the bank.
20 The silence was interrupted by the noise of horse's paws coming rapidly towards us.
22 This television normally sells for £1200, but I got a 25% bargain because I offered to pay cash.

Down:

1 What's the matter with you? You're like a horse with a sore head this morning. Did you sleep badly last night?
3 Jan is a vegetable, so when she comes to dinner, make sure you don't give her any meat.
4 Before you cook the meat, you should thinly grate it and then add salt and pepper.
5 I bought the car for £1500, repaired it and sold it for £1820, giving me a loss of over £300.
6 There was a terrible noise during the night, and this morning there were fins all over the garden. I suppose my cat must have caught a bird.
11 My job doesn't pay me much, so by the end of the month I'm always overcooked at the bank.
12 You should only cook the steak for two minutes on each side. It needs to be quite raw when you serve it.
14 How do I know that John is going out with Sue? I got it straight from the horse's beak. John told me last night.
15 When you go to the shop, don't forget to get a refund in case you need to return anything.
16 The market traders will always overcharge you, so try bidding with them to bring the price down.
17 Beat the eggs, then add them to the cake mixture, put the mixture into a tin and roast it for 45 minutes.
19 Sometimes it's really nice to boil yourself and spend some money on a special treat.
21 My last holiday cost over £1000, but it was afford it as I had such a wonderful time.

© Pearson Education Limited 2006 – Photocopiable

The same mistake

Student A

Do not show your paper to your partner.

1 How many time have I told you not to leave the door open when the dog's in the room?

2 Could you give me some informations about train times to Cardiff, please?

3 I like eating most meats, but I refuse to eat a chicken unless I know it's been really well cooked.

4 There was a party last night, so there weren't much students in the class today.

5 If you want to know how many luggage you can take onto the aircraft, call the airline.

6 We should probably go now. There's a little reason to stay.

7 We've got little time left before our next lesson begins. Shall we get a coffee?

8 Don't go into the kitchen yet. I accidentally dropped egg, and the floor is really sticky.

9 There were a lots of people in town today. I think there must have been a demonstration or something.

10 The meal was very expensive, but we've got a bit money left. Let's go for a drink.

11 I don't have much for breakfast. I usually just have a loaf of toast with butter and marmalade.

12 I don't believe it! You've eaten a whole tube of chocolate by yourself. I hope you're sick!

✂ ---

Student B

Do not show your paper to your partner.

A One of the problems with living in a big city is that there are too much cars on the road.

B We can't go yet. I need few minutes to pack my bags, and then we can leave.

C You can't go to your interview in that shirt. It looks like you've been sleeping in it! Let me get iron and press it for you.

D I don't like vegetables much, but I eat a lots of fresh fruit, so I suppose my diet must be fairly healthy.

E Be careful when you go into the room. I dropped a bottle of wine, so there's a glass all over the floor.

F Let me give you a piece good advice: lobster really doesn't taste good with tomato ketchup all over it.

G I've had a horrible morning. First of all I overslept, then I slipped over on a slice of soap in the shower, and then I missed my bus.

H The shop sells many different wine, but they're all very expensive and none of them are very good.

I My sister made this cake and it's absolutely delicious. Would you like a lump to go with your coffee?

J This smells delicious! But I'm on a diet, so don't give me too many spaghetti, please.

K Adam has a few interests outside work. He prefers to spend all his time in the office.

L We can't repair the computer ourselves because we haven't got the right equipments.

© Pearson Education Limited 2006 – Photocopiable

141

Passive verb swap

Student A

1 The school has received a lot of money from the government, and in my opinion it _____ _____ _____ on building a new library. Do you agree?

2 The living room smells of paint because it _____ _____ last week.

3 Much of the town of Argostoli _____ _____ by an earthquake in 1953.

4 He's still here because we _____ _____ _____ permission to leave the country yet.

5 Have you heard the news? A new sports centre_____ _____ _____ _____ _____ by the river next year.

6 When we got to the airport, we discovered that our flight _____ _____ _____ two hours earlier.

7 The head teacher can't see you at the moment. He _____ _____ _____ by someone from the local paper.

8 The last time we came here, the underground train system _____ _____ _____. We had to use the buses instead.

9 Every day, 46 million meals _____ _____ at McDonald's around the world.

10 The hotel manager accused us of damaging the bedroom, and we _____ _____ ten minutes to pack our bags and leave.

11 Do you think that Tim _____ _____ _____ to join the football team next season?

12 You idiot! Always look both ways before crossing the road! You _____ _____ _____ _____!

> **These are your partner's verbs.**
> catch   close   discover   distribute   meet   promote
> punish   sack   tell (x2)   use   watch

Student B

1 As soon as the fire broke out, we _____ _____ to leave the building immediately.

2 As I walked along the street, I had a strange feeling that I _____ _____ _____ by someone.

3 By the time we saw the news on TV, the men responsible for the bank robbery _____ already _____ _____ by the police.

4 The temples _____ _____ after a violent storm in the mid-1950's removed the earth that was covering them.

5 The students still _____ _____ _____ when their exam will be. Their teacher is keeping very quiet about it.

6 If you need somewhere to work quietly, you can go to room 15. It _____ _____ _____ at the moment.

7 The magazine 'Get a Life' _____ _____ free of charge to over 2 million homes in the city every week.

8 The main road into town _____ _____ _____ _____ _____ for two months from next week for repairs. We'll have to find another way into the city.

9 I won't need to get a taxi from the airport because I _____ _____ _____ there by my uncle.

10 It was very brave of you to call your boss an idiot. You _____ _____ _____ _____!

11 I think that students who break the rules _____ _____ _____. What's your opinion?

12 Laura is an excellent worker. I have a feeling she _____ _____ _____ very soon.

> **These are your partner's verbs.**
> ask   build   cancel   decorate   destroy   give (x2)
> interview   kill   modernise   sell   spend

© Pearson Education Limited 2006 – Photocopiable

10-minute trade-off

Student A

These are your statements. You need to get a follow-on sentence for each one from your partner. Write the letter of the follow-on sentence after each statement.

1 We don't buy our vegetables from the supermarket.
2 The advantage of a digital camera is that you can view the photographs on your computer.
3 The winner of the competition will receive a wonderful treat.
4 Thanks to your dog, the carpet is absolutely filthy.
5 I can't get back home because I haven't got a passport.
6 The living room is really dark, even on a bright day.
7 This room is in a terrible mess.
8 It's very important to keep your car in good working order.
9 I always find that the clothes I buy in the shops don't fit me very well.
10 I've written a cheque to pay for my credit card bill, but I keep forgetting to post it.

Student B

These are your statements. You need to get a follow-on sentence for each one from your partner. Write the letter of the follow-on sentence after each statement.

1 My computer keeps losing data and crashing on me.
2 The room smells a bit strange at the moment.
3 I've always wanted a decent photograph of me and my family to put on the wall.
4 Our old kitchen is really old-fashioned and all the cupboard doors keep falling off.
5 My hair looks a right mess; it's too long and almost impossible to do anything with.
6 I'm having real problems seeing things properly.
7 This jacket is made of leather, so I can't put it in the washing machine.
8 When you see me, you might get a bit of a surprise.
9 My mum is really angry with me.
10 We've got some friends coming to dinner tonight.

These are your partner's follow-on sentences.

A I'm having a photograph made of us at a studio in town.	B We're having it destroyed soon.	C I've had my hair cut really short!
D I had her removing from the room.	E Maybe I should have it checked for viruses.	F I need to get it dry-cleaned.
G I must get them removed when I have the chance.	H I think I should have it looked at by a doctor.	I We're having a new one fitted next week.
J I got my ears pierced without telling her.	K I'm going to have it decorated tomorrow.	L That's because we've just had it painted.
M I must get the housework done before they arrive.	N I'm having them cooked for dinner.	O I've finally decided to have our picture taken by a professional.
P We're having re-paired it next week.	Q I ought to have it cut as soon as possible.	R I must get my eyes tested.

These are your partner's follow-on sentences.

A I must get it tidied before I go away this weekend.	B We get it sent to our house.	C I have mine serviced once a year.
D We should have the trees outside cut down to let in more light.	E We have ours repairing at a shop in town.	F I had it stolen last night.
G I had it painted before you got home.	H We're going to have the windows removed to give us more air.	I I really need to get it sent off as soon as possible.
J We have them cooked by a professional chef.	K I like to have mine specially designed instead, although it is very expensive.	L They will have a meal cooked for them at home by a famous chef.
M We must get wash before it begins to smell.	N We ought to get it cleaned before things start living in it.	O I need to get it written before tomorrow.
P We have ours destroyed on a regular basis.	Q You don't need to have the pictures developed.	R We always have them delivered to the house.

© Pearson Education Limited 2006 – Photocopiable

Prefix predicament

1. This chicken is _____. It's still a bit pink inside. Put it back in the oven for ten minutes.

2. You look so exhausted. You're really _____ at the moment. You should consider taking a break.

3. Mrs Brown is divorced, but she still sees her _____ from time to time.

4. The company produces a _____ report which comes out in April and then in October.

5. A lot of _____ companies have set up divisions in China, where operation costs are often lower.

6. If you _____ cooked chicken that has been in the refrigerator, make sure that it is very hot before you eat it.

7. These mints are _____ and will make your mouth feel like it's on fire!

8. The village hall is a _____ building. It is used as a sports centre and nursery, and can be converted to a cinema.

9. I asked my teacher if I could _____ my last essay and try to get a better mark.

10. If you want a good _____ dictionary, I recommend the Longman Active Study Dictionary. Everything is in English, but the definitions and examples are very easy to understand.

11. I think you're being _____ for the work you do. Your company should be more generous.

12. Rawdon is an _____ name. I've never heard it before. Where does it come from?

13. My hotel bed was so _____ that I didn't get a moment's sleep all night.

14. We _____ the time it takes to drive to Wales. We thought it would take us four hours but it took us six!

15. I went to a fascinating _____ exhibition on Africa. There was a short film, followed by a Powerpoint computer presentation, and then we listened to some traditional music on CD.

16. Sorry I'm late. My alarm didn't go off and I _____.

17. We need to get started on the project as soon as possible. We can't afford to have any _____ delays.

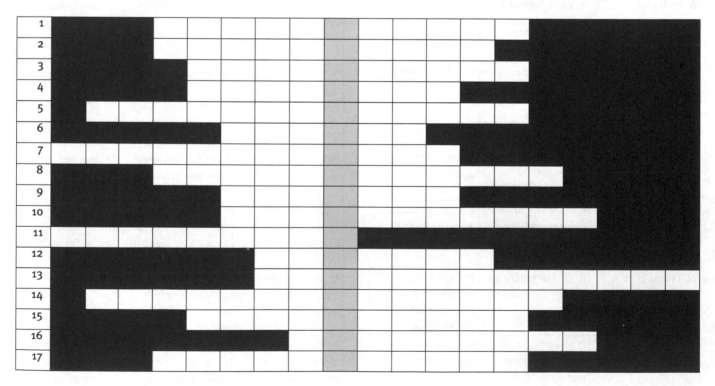

Use the word in the shaded vertical strip to complete this sentence.

'I think that sending young criminals to prison is _____. They just spend their time with other criminals, then come out and commit more crimes'.

© Pearson Education Limited 2006 – Photocopiable

I would like to complain about...

© Pearson Education Limited 2006 – Photocopiable

Join up three

Team A

1 It's absolutely _____ that we get this work finished on time. If we don't, the project will fail.

2 My girlfriend is really high-_____. She expects me to buy her extravagant presents all the time.

3 I find Mr Downing exremely arrogant and _____. In fact I think his op[inions can be quite offensive.

4 When he got the job, he was _____. I've never seen anybody so happy in all my life!

5 Mike is really friendly and down-to-_____. It's unusual to find somebody so practical, direct and honest.

6 I'm absolutely _____. I haven't eaten anything all day.

7 I don't think I'll win the competition, but I'm going to _____ a go.

8 After travelling for 24 hours, I was absolutely _____, and fell asleep almost immediately.

9 Everybody likes her because she's so _____-going. She never seems to get upset or annoyed.

10 He's the most _____ person in the company, and really manages to make things happen or change.

11 The film was a complete _____, and lost the production company millions of dollars.

12 Typewriters have had their _____: everybody uses computers now.

13 Beatrice loves being the centre of _____. She's not happy unless she's surrounded by an audience of enthusiastic listeners!

14 She's so _____. She's always determined to do what she wants, even if other people advise her not to do it.

Team B

1 Can you turn the heating on? It's absolutely _____.

2 Single minded people usually work extremely hard to acheive their aim.

3 He failed his driving test, but refused to _____ up, and continued taking lessons.

4 People with an _____ personality tend to like meeting and talking to people.

5 On the whole you're a good student, but unfortunately some of your written work isn't up to _____.

6 My line manager is very _____: he's always controlling and deceiving people in order to get what he wants.

7 She was really _____ when her husband died: he was the centre of her life.

8 I wouldn't describe myself as a party _____, although I do like going out and enjoying myself.

9 I saw an absolutely _____ documentary last night. I couldn't take my eyes away from the screen.

10 You're not just dirty, you're absolutely _____! Go and have a shower immediately!

11 Very few people _____ in losing weight and keeping it off.

12 You're so _____! Why don't you think about other people for a change?

13 The book is a _____-seller in the USA, where over two million copies have been sold.

14 Anne is always making people laugh with her amusing comments. She's so _____!

Team B's answers

1 vital/essential 2 opinionated 3 rude 4 ecstatic
5 earth 6 starving 7 have 8 exhausted 9 easy
10 proactive 11 flop 12 day 13 attention
14 headstrong/stubborn

Team A's answers

1 freezing 2 minded 3 give 4 outgoing
5 scratch 6 manipulative 7 devastated/
upset 8 animal 9 fascinating 10 filthy
11 succeed 12 selfish 13 best 14 witty

© Pearson Education Limited 2006 – Photocopiable

Sentence jumble

1   I've been a bit overworked recently. **holiday took high It's I a.**

_____

2   You used my computer when I was out, didn't you? **use I'd you permission my didn't rather without.**

_____

3   Our flight leaves in under three hours. **the Isn't airport time for left we?**

_____

4   I know you're worried about discussing your exams with your teacher. **you him rather I to them most spoke Would about?**

_____

5   It's getting dark. **we left home for It's and went beach the time.**

_____

6   Eddie rang and said he urgently needed to talk to you. **better possible You him as as call soon.**

_____

7   You've had that terrible cough for ages. **some it up Isn't smoking about gave time you?**

_____

8   You can't live with your parents forever. **a your high own you It's place of time looked.**

_____

9   I don't think I can wait until tomorrow for that money I lent you. **to returned rather today I'd me it.**

_____

10 Would you mind putting that cigarette out? **here I'd in rather smoke you.**

_____

11 We've been waiting here for twenty minutes. **arrived about bus all It's the time.**

_____

12 We've got an early start tomorrow morning. **late tonight stay We'd side better out not**

_____

13 Let's go out tonight. **meal rather or theatre go for a go to the you?**

_____

14 Our computer is old and slow. **got time new one we a It's buy high.**

_____

15 I know you're very busy at the moment. **you tonight come it didn't Would rather I over?**

_____

16 I really hate big cities; they're so noisy and busy. **York I'd with to New you go rather.**

_____

17 Tim and Samantha are coming to dinner tonight. **something better I'd to for shopping eat.**

_____

18 Angie obviously hates working here. **new it time looked a job Isn't she about?**

_____

© Pearson Education Limited 2006 – Photocopiable

Reported speech dominoes

	A	B	A
START ➡	'I'm trying to book us a place at that new bistro.'	**B** She _____ she _____ _____ to reserve a restaurant table.	'I lent you £20, didn't I?'
B He _____ that he _____ _____ me some cash.	'I waited for you for almost two hours.'	**B** She _____ me that she _____ _____ quite a long time.	'Can you help me push this into the living room?'
B He _____ me if I _____ _____ him move something.	'I want to stay at home.'	**B** He _____ me he _____ _____ to go out.	'This is the first time I've eaten fast food.'
B She _____ that she _____ never _____ hamburgers or pizza before.	'I've been working for On-Line Media since the beginning of last month.'	**B** He _____ he _____ _____ _____ for that company for about six weeks.	'I was driving back from work when the other car hit me.'
B He _____ us that he _____ _____ _____ home at the time of the accident"	'Let's go to that new bar on the High Street.'	**B** He _____ _____ out for a drink.	'A new department store is opening on Broad Street soon.'
B She _____ that a new shop _____ _____ in the near future.	'We will deliver the goods you asked for tomorrow.'	**B** She _____ me they _____ _____ my order the next day.	'I'll definitely come on time tomorrow, and that's a guarantee.'
B She _____ _____ _____ punctually the next day.	'What are you going to do on Saturday and Sunday?'	**B** She _____ us what we _____ _____ _____ _____ at the weekend.	'Who did you see last night?'
B She _____ me who I _____ _____ the previous evening.	'Don't forget to buy some chicken or we won't have anything to eat tonight.'	**B** She _____ me _____ _____ something for dinner.	'Remember to phone for a taxi this afternoon.'
B She _____ me _____ _____ and book a cab.	'I took your money. It was me. I'm so sorry.'	**B** She _____ _____ my cash, and apologised.	'Don't use my laptop, stereo or mobile phone without asking me first.'
B He _____ us not _____ _____ his things without his permission.	'Why don't we go out in the car for half an hour?'	**B** She _____ _____ for a drive.	*John*: 'Why don't we rent a film tonight?' *Alan:* 'OK, that's a good idea.'
B ...We _____ _____ _____ a movie.	'I'm afraid I dropped your laptop, which is why it isn't working.'	**B** She _____ _____ my computer and damaging it.	➡ **FINISH**

© Pearson Education Limited 2006 – Photocopiable

Race to the middle

1   I've tried _____ _____ _____ new friends at my new school, but it's very difficult.

2   Adam is almost always late. He _____ _____ _____ on time.

3   Giorgia was very quiet in today's lesson. She _____ _____ a word.

4   He has a very serious illness, and unfortunately there's _____ _____ the doctors can do.

5   Carol used to phone me every day, but now she _____ _____ _____ me anymore.

6   Her pronunciation is so bad and she speaks so quickly that I find it _____ _____ _____ anything she says.

7   My spoken English is very good, but my Spanish is terrible. In fact, I can _____ _____ a single word.

8   The supermarket was very quiet this morning. There were _____ _____ people there.

9   It was minus 8°C and snowing, but he went for a walk wearing only a pair of shorts and a T-shirt. I find it _____ _____ _____ that anyone could be so stupid!

10 There was so much smoke in the room that we could _____ _____ more than two metres in front of us.

11 When I say 'yes', he says 'no', and when I say 'no' he says 'yes'. In fact, he _____ _____ _____ with me about anything!

12 I didn't enjoy the party very much. There was _____ _____ I knew there.

13 My English hasn't improved since I came to the school. I've _____ _____ any progress since I got here.

14 Our teacher is terrible. He knows almost nothing about the language. For example, he can _____ even _____ how to use reported speech.

15 I used to really enjoy golf, but now I _____ _____ _____ it any more.

16 I don't really care if the weather is good or bad. I'm indoors working all day, so it _____ _____ _____ difference to me.

© Pearson Education Limited 2006 – Photocopiable

It's mine!

Student A

A   You should reduce the amount of fatty food and sugar you eat if you want to lose weight.

B   You should _____ _____ _____ the amount of fatty food and sugar you eat if you want to lose weight.

A   I've missed lots of lessons, so I don't think I'll ever reach the same standard as the other students.

B   I've missed lots of lessons, so I don't think I'll ever _____ _____ _____ the other students.

A   Our teacher refuses to tolerate students who come late and say nothing during the lesson.

B   Our teacher refuses to _____ _____ _____ students who come late and say nothing during the lesson.

A   I never eat breakfast, but I always compensate with a big lunch.

B   I never eat breakfast, but I _____ _____ _____ it with a big lunch.

✂ -

Student B

A   I've always admired and respected people who devote their lives to looking after others.

B   I've always _____ _____ _____ people who devote their lives to looking after others.

A   Some people admit that they break the speed limit on the roads if they think they can avoid being caught.

B   Some people admit that they break the speed limit on the roads if they think they can _____ _____ _____ it.

A   I had to walk quickly to stay at the same speed as him.

B   I had to walk quickly to _____ _____ _____ him.

A   I made an official application to be transferred from the company's office in London to its office in Bristol.

B   I _____ _____ _____ a transfer from the company's office in London to its office in Bristol.

✂

catch	come	up	on	with	get
up	cut	put	make	up	for
put	up	looked	keep	with	in
with	for	up	away	with	to
of	forward	from	give	by	go

© Pearson Education Limited 2006 – Photocopiable

The road to success

1 _____ (student's name) is _____ (character).
Key words and expressions that helped me to identify him/her were:

2 _____ (student's name) is _____ (character).
Key words and expressions that helped me to identify him/her were:

3 _____ (student's name) is _____ (character).
Key words and expressions that helped me to identify him/her were:

4 _____ (student's name) is _____ (character).
Key words and expressions that helped me to identify him/her were:

5 _____ (student's name) is _____ ((character).
Key words and expressions that helped me to identify him/her were:

6 _____ (student's name) is _____ (character).
Key words and expressions that helped me to identify him/her were:

7 _____ (student's name) is _____ (character).
Key words and expressions that helped me to identify him/her were:

8 _____ (student's name) is _____ ((character).
Key words and expressions that helped me to identify him/her were:

9 _____ (student's name) is _____ ((character).
Key words and expressions that helped me to identify him/her were:

10 _____ (student's name) is _____ (character).
Key words and expressions that helped me to identify him/her were:

© Pearson Education Limited 2006 – Photocopiable

Six convicts

Part 1

Complete the dialogues in the picture with a word from the box.

> appeal   brand   claim   convicted
> fair   pull   sentenced   sue

I'm trying to _____ the police for £5000.- they broke a window when they came to arrest me.

_____ enough. What did they arrest you for?

The Judge _____ me to 100 years.

I'm here because I filed a _____ for £10,000,000 that I didn't really lose. – What are you in for?

_____ the other one!

Setting fire to a _____ -new car

No, really. I was going to get 2 years, but I called the judge a mad monkey! I made an _____ but the court rejected it.

Me? I was _____ for stealing from a department store.

Part 2

Use the picture above and the information below to match the name of the criminal with the crime he committed.
The crimes committed are: fraud, bank robbery, shoplifting, forgery, arson and pick pocketing.

1   **Dick Kray** is in prison for fraud.

2   The arsonist is sitting next to a bank robber.

3   **Reg Black** doesn't believe the story he is listening to.

4   **Bert Adams** is sitting to the right of a man asking a question.

5   The man who is in prison for forgery is talking to someone who tried to change someone else's decision.

6   The man sitting next to **Dick Kray** has been sent to prison for shoplifting.

7   **Joe Biggs** thinks that the person he is speaking to is doing something reasonable and right.

8   The man sitting to the left of the pickpocket is talking to the man who destroyed something that had just come out of the factory.

9   **Ron Smith** is talking to the man who is next to the man with the beard.

10   **Jim Roberts** is sitting to the right of the man who illegally tried to get something from an insurance company.

© Pearson Education Limited 2006 – Photocopiable

Escape!

Student A start ▶										

Student B start ▶										

Student A

1 B_____ g_____ on holiday, I had to save up a bit of money.

2 O_____ a_____ at work, I made myself a coffee and checked my emails.

3 H_____ s_____ all my money, I decided to apply for a job.

4 A_____ s_____ my mobile phone, the thief tried to sell it – to my best friend!

5 W_____ w_____ to the bus stop, I slipped on a banana skin and twisted my ankle.

6 H_____ t_____ the thief's fingerprints, the police ran a check on their computer.

7 A_____ f_____ the thief guilty, the judge sent him to prison.

8 H_____ w_____ for her outside the cinema for almost an hour, I eventually gave up and went home.

9 O_____ e_____ the classroom, I discovered that the lesson had already started.

10 H_____ already e_____ a big breakfast, I turned down his offer of lunch

11 B_____ p_____ someone in prison, a court must be sure that he/she is guilty beyond reasonable doubt.

12 H_____ o_____ to lend me his car earlier in the day, he suddenly decided that he needed it himself instead.

Student B

1 H_____ w_____ for the same company for 10 years, I decided to look for something completely different.

2 O_____ o_____ the classroom door, I discovered that there was nobody there.

3 H_____ s_____ to everyone that we all went out for dinner, I realised that I didn't have enough money to pay for it.

4 B_____ j_____ a class, all students have to take a test so we can put them in the right level.

5 A_____ p_____ all my exams, I decided to reward myself with a holiday.

6 O_____ s_____ the policeman coming towards us, we ran away as fast as possible.

7 H_____ r_____ the book, I couldn't wait to see if the film was as good.

8 A_____ a_____ to him for breaking his camera, I went out and bought him a new one.

9 W_____ w_____ the football match, I suddenly remembered I had left the oven on at home.

10 B_____ s_____ an email, you should check that it doesn't contain any viruses.

11 W_____ d_____ to work, I suddenly lost control of the car and drove into a tree.

12 A_____ d_____ where we wanted to go for our holiday, we started looking for cheap flights.

Student B's answers

1 Having worked 2 On opening 3 Having suggested 4 Before joining 5 After passing 6 On seeing 7 Having read 8 After apologising 9 While watching 10 Before sending 11 While driving 12 After deciding

Student A's answers

1 Before going 2 On arriving 3 Having spent 4 After stealing 5 While walking 6 Having taken 7 After finding 8 Having waited 9 On entering 10 Having ... eaten 11 Before putting 12 Having offered

© Pearson Education Limited 2006 – Photocopiable

Probability hit and miss

1 Let's go for a picnic.	2 Juan wasn't in class today.	3 Mary's in the USA, isn't she?	4 If you go out, take an umbrella with you.
5 Is Ferdinand at work today?	6 I saw Helen driving a brand-new sports car yesterday.	7 The police still haven't caught the man responsible for the robbery.	8 I wonder where Eve stayed when she went to London at the weekend.
9 Paul and Anne should be here by now.	10 How did Jim get to the airport?	11 Does anyone know who broke the computer printer?	12 I'm really surprised that Heidi didn't come to your party.
13 I wonder how my father found out that I had failed the test.	14 I asked Jan if I could take the day off work, and she started shouting at me.	15 That's strange. I can't get a signal on my mobile phone.	16 I haven't seen Alison since lunchtime.
17 I accidentally walked out of a restaurant without paying last night.	18 I'm sorry I missed yesterday afternoon's lesson. I was ill.	19 I wonder if Hitoshi passed his English exam.	20 Does Susie know you've got a new girlfriend?

A Well she can't have gone to a hotel: she hasn't got enough money.	B Yes. I suppose they might have got lost on the way over.	C That's because you haven't paid your bill. They must have cut you off.	D Yes. She must have forgotten about it.
E Really? He might have left the country to hide abroad.	F You can't have been. I saw you in town at lunchtime, and you looked fine then.	G Really? She must have made a lot of money recently.	H Well, he only took it yesterday, so he can't have got the results already.
I She can't be. She starts her new job today.	J I haven't told her yet, but she might have found out from someone else.	K It could have been anyone. We all use it.	L Your teacher must have told him. There's no other way he could know.
M That's not like her at all. She must have had a bad morning in the office.	N He could be. He often has to work at the weekend.	O That was careless. You could have got into trouble with the police.	P That's strange. He never usually misses his lessons. He must be ill.
Q I will. It looks like it could rain later.	R She wasn't feeling very well this morning, so she might have gone home.	S Is that a good idea? It's a bit cloudy. It might rain later.	T He can't have taken a bus. They don't run on a Sunday.

© Pearson Education Limited 2006 – Photocopiable

Find the five

1 William Shakespeare, who wrote *Oliver twist*, was born in Stratford-upon-Avon in England.

2 London is the city in where the 2012 Olympics will be held.

3 *Yesterday* which was recorded by the Beatles is one of the most-recognised songs in the world.

4 Bill Gates, who owns Microsoft, dropped out of Harvard before he finished his course.

5 Salzburg is the Austrian city, where the composer Mozart was born.

6 The Internet, which allows people to access websites all over the world, was invented by an American.

7 Bill Clinton, who came from Texas, was US President for 8 years.

8 *Total English*, what was written by Acklam and Crace, was first published in 2006.

9 Singapore is a small republic in South-East Asia where became independent in 1965.

10 *The Titanic*, which sank in the Pacific Ocean in 1912, was the largest ship in the world at the time.

11 Arthur Conan Doyle, whose created the character of Sherlock Holmes, was inspired by a man called Dr Joseph Bell.

12 Elephants, which are the second largest mammal in the world, are unable to jump.

13 Liverpool United, which is one of Britain's most successful football teams, was the first professional team that David Beckham played for.

14 Gandhi was the man he was largely responsible for Indian independence in 1947.

15 Pasta, which is widely eaten in Italy, was brought to the west from China by Marco Polo.

16 France, which won the European Cup in 1998, is one of the world's most popular tourist destinations.

17 The Cambridge First Certificate, is an international English exam, which takes places three times every year.

18 Neil Armstrong was an American astronaut who became the first man to go into space in 1969.

19 The airliner Concorde, which flew passengers across the Atlantic at twice the speed of sound, stopped making commercial flights in 2004.

20 Christopher Columbus, who was the first man to go to Cuba, originally came from Italy.

21 The television, who's inventor came from Scotland, is considered to be one of the most important inventions of the 20th century.

22 Mel Gibson, whose films include *Lethal Weapon* and *Mad Max*, originally comes from Australia.

23 Antarctica, when temperatures can be as low as -90°C, has a permanent population of about 1000 people.

24 Polar bears, which live in Antarctica, are all left-handed.

25 Leonardo da Vinci was a great artist that was mainly interested in engineering and technology.

26 The Great Wall of China, which is the longest human structure in the world, can be seen from space.

27 Turkey is a bird which originally came from North America and is now traditionally eaten at Christmas in many countries around the world.

28 Washington DC, which is the capital of the USA, is in Washington State.

29 Apart from the United Kingdom, Australia and New Zealand are the only other countries where people drive on the left.

30 Vincent Van Gogh, whose paintings include *Sunflower* and *Starry Night*, cut off his own nose.

© Pearson Education Limited 2006 – Photocopiable

In the news

aid   axe   back   bid   blast   blaze   clash   drama   hit   key   plea   quit

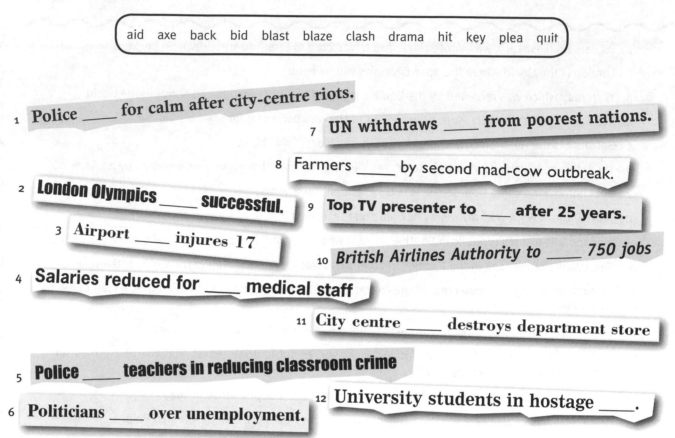

1 Police _____ for calm after city-centre riots.

7 UN withdraws _____ from poorest nations.

8 Farmers _____ by second mad-cow outbreak.

2 London Olympics _____ successful.

9 Top TV presenter to _____ after 25 years.

3 Airport _____ injures 17

10 British Airlines Authority to _____ 750 jobs

4 Salaries reduced for _____ medical staff

11 City centre _____ destroys department store

5 Police _____ teachers in reducing classroom crime

12 University students in hostage _____.

6 Politicians _____ over unemployment.

a   How can they do this? These people play a vital role. If they don't get paid enough, they'll just leave and look for work elsewhere.

b   They showed it on the television last night. It was very tense, but eventually they were all released.

c   Why are they always arguing? They always seem to be in dispute about something. It's time they all worked together on the problem for a change.

d   At least the fire happened at night, so nobody was injured. I wonder if it was arson?

e   I think it's good that they're getting some support, especially considering the problems that some city schools face.

f   I know that they're making people redundant to save money, but that's not much help or comfort to the people who are going to be unemployed as a result.

g   I think it's disgusting that they're doing this. Without international help, how can people in those countries lead a normal life?

h   This is wonderful news. A lot of people said their attempt would fail, but I always knew they would get it.

i   I think it's going to take more than a strong request to stop this. The people are angry, and the violence is just a reflection of this.

j   It's terrible. So many of them have been badly affected by it that they are going out of business. And we have to pay for expensive imported beef.

k   It could have been worse, I suppose. Apparently, the bomb was hidden behind a pile of suitcases, and that helped to reduce the effect of the explosion.

l   What a pity. He's done such a good job. I wonder who will replace him when he resigns.

© Pearson Education Limited 2006 – Photocopiable

Four lawsuits

Card A

- He was hit by lightning but fortunately, he wasn't killed, although he suffered some serious injuries.

- His neighbour also didn't know that someone was trying to steal part of his vehicle, started the engine and drove off.

- Ms Carson then stood up to leave, but slipped on the spilt drink, fell down and badly hurt her back.

- As a result, she tried to enter by climbing in through the toilet window.

Card B

- 19-year-old thief Cark Truman decided to steal the wheels off his neighbour's car so that he could sell them for a bit of cash.

- He tried to sue the amusement park because they hadn't warned people not to be outside during a storm.

- Ms Amber Carson went to a fast food restaurant with her boyfriend but while they were there, they had a big argument.

- She filed a lawsuit against the club and was awarded $12,000.

Card C

- One evening, Ms Kara Walton from Delaware went out to a nightclub with some friends but didn't want to pay the $3.50 entry charge.

- She sued the restaurant because they had failed to clean up the spilt drink quickly enough, and was awarded over $100,000.

- Mr Truman sued him for $74,000 plus medical expenses for the injuries he received as a result.

- While he was there, there was a big storm but he didn't take shelter.

Card D

- Mr Shaun Perkins from Laurel in Indiana decided to take his family to an amusement park.

- In anger, she threw a full cup of orange juice at him, which missed and landed on the floor.

- He waited until it was dark, silently made his way to the car, and began trying to take one of the wheels off but didn't realise his neighbour was in the car.

- Unfortunately, she fell while trying to get in, and knocked out two of her front teeth.

© Pearson Education Limited 2006 – Photocopiable

Wordabout

willpower	déjà vu	doubt	reckon	commercial break
lost for words	sceptical	suspect	classified ads	slogan
whisper	shriek	mumble	powers of persuasion	blurt out
premonitions	subconscious	interrupt	speak your mind	sixth sense

1　Don't _____ like that. Try opening your mouth and speaking more clearly.

2　He was a friendly and relaxed man, but I could tell that there was a lot of anger buried in his _____.

3　Consider your answer carefully: don't just _____ the first thing that comes into your head.

4　Please don't _____ me when I'm trying to speak to the class.

5　He used all of his _____ to convince us that we had done the right thing.

6　It's very important that you tell us exactly how you're feeling. We want you to _____.

7　I couldn't see or hear anyone, but my _____ told me there was another person in the room.

8　I've had some strange _____ recently. One of these is that I'm going have a bad accident.

9　I know you're angry, but please don't _____ at me like that. If you lower your voice, I promise I'll listen.

10　If you want to lose weight, it takes a lot of _____ to avoid fatty and sugary foods.

11　I found my car in the _____ in the paper. The man selling it only wanted £800 for it.

12　When I walked into the room I had a strange feeling of _____. I was sure I had been there before.

13　When she told me she was going to get married, I was _____. I couldn't think of a thing to say.

14　I'm extremely _____ about people who say they can see into the future.

15　I seriously _____ whether he will pass his driving test; he hasn't had enough practice.

16　I strongly _____ that most people have broken the law a few times in their life.

17　I would have enjoyed the film on television last night, but there was a _____ almost every 10 minutes.

18　Do you _____ it's going to rain later? It looks a bit cloudy.

19　Speak up. You don't have to _____. No one can hear us.

20　The advertising _____ that most British people remember is 'Go to work on an egg'.

© Pearson Education Limited 2006 – Photocopiable

Up and down

▼ GO BACK ▼
yourself
us
ourselves
myself
you
themselves
him
no pronoun can be used
her
himself
yourselves
each other
them
me
itself
herself
▲ START ▲

Student A

1 Anne and I always help _____ with their homework every night.

2 My son didn't need my help with tying his shoelaces. He did it all by _____.

3 Peter doesn't seem happy at the moment. I wonder what's wrong with _____.

4 He looked at _____ really strangely. 'Stop staring!', I said angrily.

5 Mrs Ranscombe lives by _____ in a large house in the country.

6 I don't want to ask him what he's doing. Why don't you ask him _____?

7 I watched in terrified fascination as the door slowly opened all by _____.

8 Tony and Julie poured _____ a couple of large glasses of water.

9 It was strange seeing _____ on television: we all looked completely different!

10 I burnt _____ while I was making dinner. It really hurts!

11 You can't go home by _____, girls: it's getting dark it isn't safe around here.

12 Take it easy. Sit down, put your feet up and relax _____.

Student B

1 We should take it easy for a while. If we work too hard, we'll tire _____ out.

2 'Stop fighting!' the teacher shouted, but the two boys continued hitting _____

3 My neighbour is a bit mad. He walks up and down all day talking to _____.

4 The washing machine turns _____ off when the washing cycle is finished.

5 Our boss told _____ that we could leave early that day.

6 I'm really hungry. I think I'll make _____ a sandwich.

7 You're going to Venice? If I were you, I'd take plenty of money with _____.

8 Please be quiet. It's so difficult to concentrate _____ with all that noise going on.

9 OK everybody, here's a cake I made. Help _____ to a slice.

10 Rachel looked at _____ in the old photograph. 'I look so young!' she thought.

11 Linda and John had the house to _____ while their parents were away.

12 Cristina decided to take a map with _____ in case she got lost.

© Pearson Education Limited 2006 – Photocopiable

10 Grammar 2

Mixed doubles

Mixed doubles

He needed the language for his new job, so he refused ...	In the end I tried ...	My new job involves ...	I wanted to ask Jo for some help with my work, but when I tried ...
We couldn't meet you at 3.00 as our teacher wouldn't allow ...	I really regretted ...	Naturally he's refused ...	We're short of money at the moment, so we can't afford ...
I've got to go back there tomorrow, so I promise ...	He had planned to change jobs after a few years, but he went on ...	I went to the post office but I'm afraid I didn't remember ...	After University, my grandfather went on ...
Perhaps for a change we should consider ...	It was really busy in the office, but I stopped ...	We both chatted about work, then arranged ...	We told him it was urgent, but we didn't manage ...
Although he found his Spanish classes difficult, he carried on ...	I don't like it very much, and have considered ...	I'm really scared of flying, so I try to avoid ...	However, I do enjoy ...

Activity grid

1A	... to talk to Bob in the Sales Department.	1B	... to go out for a drink when we both finished for the day.
2A	... to become an accountant for a major company.	2B	... working with them until he was 58.
3A	... to post your letter.	3B	... to do it first thing tomorrow morning.
4A	... to go abroad for our holiday.	4B	... spending time at home and decorating the house instead.
5A	... calling him stupid and useless.	5B	... to speak to me since then.
6A	... going anywhere by plane.	6B	... travelling by train, especially if it's a long journey.
7A	... flying to and from the USA on business a lot.	7B	... looking for a job that doesn't involve so much travel.
8A	... studying the language as hard as possible.	8B	... to give up, no matter how hard it was.
9A	... us to leave the lesson early.	9B	... to change his mind.
10A	... calling her, she was out.	10B	... to do it all by myself, but found it much too difficult.

160

© Pearson Education Limited 2006 – Photocopiable

A hidden message

1. If your coming on the trip tomorrow, please let me know the day before.

2. My parents will give me the money to go on holiday to English with my friends if I do well in my exams next week.

3. If I were you, I will spend less time watching television and more time studying.

4. It's quite strange, but if Andy gets worried or nervous, his pronunciation improve.

5. If I hadn't eaten so much sweets as a child, my teeth wouldn't be in such bad condition now.

6. If the weather was more warmer, we could all go to the beach for a picnic.

7. The teacher won't give you a certificate at the end of the course if unless you attend more lessons and come on time.

8. If you looked at you in a mirror, you'd realise how terrible you look in that dress.

9. If I hadn't spend so much money last month, I could take a holiday now.

10. He usually remembers what to do provided that you tell him several time.

11. Learning English is much more fun if you can practising it with a friend.

12. If I had seen Michael last night, I could have asked it to come out with us next Saturday.

13. The manager says he'll throw you outside of the restaurant unless you stop behaving so badly.

14. You'd be the much slimmer if you didn't eat so much chocolate.

15. I might have passed my exam if I had worked harder during my English classroom.

Write the <u>wrong</u> words in the table below to reveal the secret message.

1	2	3	4	5
6	**7**	**8**	**9**	**10**
11	**12**	**13**	**14**	**15**

© Pearson Education Limited 2006 – Photocopiable

Is it spelt right?

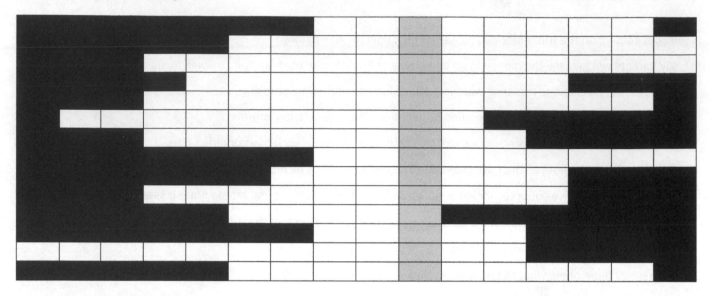

1	One of the problems with living in a city like London is that acommodation is really hard to find, and unless you live outside the city centre, it can be really expensive.	**2**
3	I don't beleive it! This is the fifth time you've been late this week. Why don't you get yourself an alarm clock or, even better, have an early night for a change!	**4**
5	I joined this course a couple of months ago, and I've made a lot of progress since then, although to be honest I nearly gave up at the begining when I realised how much work I would have to do.	**6**
7	At first I got on well with Rob, but we had a few arguments which made things difficult, and by the end things were so bad that when we went out for drinks with our friends we had to sit at seperate tables.	**8**
9	People usually keep unhappy memories buried in their subconsious, but these memories can often be awakened by stress or pressure, and can make a normally cheerful person very depressed.	**10**
11	Last week I met a really intresting man. He designs the magic tricks that are performed on television. He's so clever that apparently the police ask him for help when they have a difficult crime to solve.	**12**
13	If you want to be a sucessful English learner, you need to practise outside the classroom as much as possible, and you should try to use the language you learn every day so that you don't forget it.	**14**

2 I'm not sure whether Geoff will come on time tonight, but I know that he'll definitely come because he's hoping I'll return the money I borrowed from him last week!

4 It can be extremely hard being a foriegner living in a strange city, especially if you don't speak the language, you haven't got any friends and you don't have much money.

6 I'm generally quite careful with my money, but ocasionally I like to go out and really enjoy myself. I'm especially fond of shopping and eating out, which can be very expensive.

8 I stayed at my friend's house in the country at the weekend. During the night, something really wierd happened: I heard a strange noise, and opened my eyes to see the door opening all by itself!

10 When you read a piece of English text, it isn't necesary to understand every single word you read. The important thing is to get a general understanding of the text, and then to identify the main points.

12 Most British people go abroad for their holiday because they get fed up with the British weather. The problem is that it's so changable you never know what it will be like from one day to the next.

14 Will Mandy pass her driving test tomorrow? I seriously dout it. She's actually a very good driver, but she gets very nervous, especially if someone is watching her and judging her abilities.

© Pearson Education Limited 2006 – Photocopiable

The world's dustbin

Item 1: _____

because _____

Item 2: _____

because _____

Item 3: _____

because _____

Item 4: _____

because _____

Item 5: _____

because _____

© Pearson Education Limited 2006 – Photocopiable

Teacher's notes

UNIT 1 Vocabulary 1
Three in a row

Procedure

Divide the class into pairs and give each pair a copy of the activity. Tell them that they are going to play three games of noughts and crosses. They need to get three squares in a row, horizontally, vertically or diagonally. To do this, they choose a square, look at the sentence, and decide which word can be used to complete the sentence. They then write in the word. They should use the correct form of the word (e.g., singular/ plural, past simple, etc). When students have played all three games, they check their answers with you. The winner is the pair to get three squares in a row of correct answers.

Answers

Game 1: 1 jealous   2 creaked   3 ex-husband (or ex-wife)
4 responsibility   5 widow   6 niece   7 screamed   8 skills
9 barked

Game 2: 1 snore (or snoring)   2 acquaintance   3 frustrated
4 half-sister   5 success   6 bang   7 soul mate
8 intellectual   9 brother-in-law

Game 3: 1 ringing   2 importance   3 fiancée   4 shout
5 sneeze   6 artistic   7 colleagues   8 lonely   9 flatmate

UNIT 1 Grammar 1
Tag dialogues

Procedure

Divide the class into pairs, A and B. Cut the activity and give one section to each student. They should not show these to one another. Students look first at Part 1 and individually match the first part of the questions (1-10) with their question tags (A-J). Student A then reads his/her questions and student B looks at the Part 2 sentences and makes an appropriate response. Then, student B reads his/her questions and student A makes an appropriate response. One student in each group could be a 'secretary' who writes the complete dialogues on a separate sheet of paper. Get feedback from the class. The pair that forms the most correct dialogues is the winner.

Answers

Student A: 1 K iii   2 C v   3 A viii   4 D x   5 I vi   6 L ii   7 B
ix   8 H xi   9 G iv   10 J i   11 F xii   12 K vii

Student B: 1 C ii   2 A iii   3 L viii   4 H iv   5 I vii   6 B vi   7 D
x   8 K v   9 G i   10 E xi   11 F xii   12 J ix

UNIT 1 Grammar 2
Eliminator

Procedure

Students work in teams of two or three. Give each team a copy of the activity. Write the following words on the board: *all, any, anybody, anything, anywhere, every, everybody, everywhere, nothing, some, something, somewhere*. Explain that sentences 1–20 can all be completed with one of them. Allow your students a minute to look at these words and try to remember them (they should not write them down), and then rub them off.

Working in their teams, students complete each sentence with one of these words. Some of the words can be used more than once. Each time they write a word, they delete the letters that are used from the box at the top of their sheet. The first one has been done as an example. Allow them 10 minutes for this. Check

their answers in a class feedback. Students then add up the total number of letters left in the box and from any of the words they used incorrectly in the sentences. The team with the least number of letters left is the winner.

Answers

1 some   2 nothing   3 every   4 anywhere   5 all   6 everybody
7 somewhere   8 All   9 any   10 Every   11 anybody
12 nothing   13 any   14 everywhere   15 anything   6 any
17 something   18 every   19 all   20 Every

UNIT 1 Grammar 3
Modal dominoes

Procedure

Divide students into groups of three or four. Cut the sheet into cards and give each group a set. The cards contain sentences which form mini dialogues. Sentence B 'follows on' from sentence A. The aim of this activity is for students to join all the cards together in a line. The first and last cards are marked Start and Finish. However, the modal verb and main verb have been removed from the B sentences. Students must decide which verbs can be used to complete them (*might, may, could, must, can* or *can't* + main verb: in some cases, more than one option is possible). The first group to join all the cards together and correctly complete the B sentences is the winner.

Answers

might/may/could go   must be   can be   might/may/could go
can't take/get   might/may/could visit/see   must have
can be/get   must/might/may/could be   must practise/play
must be   might/may/could change   can't be   can be
must be   might/may/could fail   might/may/could be

UNIT 1 Vocabulary 2
Phrasal verbs crossword

Procedure

Divide the students into pairs or small groups. Give each pair/group a copy of the activity. Tell them that they need to complete the crossword grid with appropriate phrasal verbs. To do this, they read the text 'My best friend', decide what the missing phrasal verbs are and write them in the appropriate spaces in the crossword grid. There should be no gaps between the verb and particle on the crossword grid, and students should be careful that they use the correct form of the verb.

Answers

Down: 1 made up   2 show off   3 takes after   4 fallen
out   5 going out   7 split up   8 grew up   **Across:** 6 looked
up to   9 get on   10 brought up

UNIT 1 Communication
Problems, problems!

Procedure

Divide the students into pairs or small groups. Give each pair/ group a copy of the activity. Tell them that they are going to decide which of the central character's friends/relatives is best equipped to advise her on each of her three problems. They must come to a united decision! Students first read the character profile of the central character and then the profiles of the five other characters. Monitor students as they work

164

to check that all students are contributing orally and that all vocabulary is clear to them.

Write *problem a) b)* and *c)* on the board and ask each group who they think should offer Andrea advice on each problem, and write the names under the relative problems. Ask students to give reasons for their choices. Compare and contrast the groups' choices.

Possible advisers:

a) Johnny Noble could help. His main concern being her happiness, he could prioritise this rather than the financial and material benefits of her current job.
Andrea may be ill-advised to consult Amanda because of her ambition and commitment to the law firm. She may tell other colleagues of Andrea's feelings which could jeopardise Andrea's position if she decided to stay. Being so committed to the job, Amanda may not understand why Andrea is unhappy.

b) James could help Andrea here. Andrea could tell her friends that she can't go with either, as James has just told her he's booked a holiday for the two of them.
Andrea may be ill-advised to consult Tessa Brown, as she is close to one of the friends that wants to go on the holiday and could spill the beans over Andrea's dilemma.

c) Bill or Amanda could advise Andrea. Bill is someone she knows casually at the rowing club, and may offer an independent opinion. Amanda offers a sympathetic ear to friends, and as this doesn't relate to professional matters, could give wise advice. James could offer slightly biased advice as he would probably want Andrea to join the committee as a way improving the rowing club. He may not put her personal feelings first.

UNIT 2 Vocabulary 1
Work and play
Procedure

Divide students into pairs. Give each pair a copy of the worksheet. Explain that each of the sentences contains a missing word. Students must work together, read these sentences and decide what they think the word is. They then write it in the corresponding space on the grid. To help them, some of the letters are already in the grid. Explain to students that if they do this correctly, they will reveal (in the shaded vertical strip) something that many employers ask for when somebody applies for a job. The first pair in the class to reveal the missing expression is the winner.

Answers

1 socialising 2 accountant 3 earns 4 resigned 5 retired
6 commutes 7 redundant 8 journalist 9 voluntary
10 promoted 11 visit 12 retirement 13 architect
14 sacked 15 spend   The expression is *curriculum vitae*

UNIT 2 Grammar 1
Future forms risk
Procedure

Students work in pairs or small groups. Give each pair/group a copy of the activity. Students must look at dialogues 1–12, and decide if the future form in bold in the second sentence of each dialogue is being used correctly. They tick (✓) or (✗) accordingly. Then they bet on their answer, (minimum £1.00 and maximum £10.00) depending on how sure they are.

Allow them about 10–15 minutes for this, then tell them to stop and check their answers with you. If students have bet on a correct sentence, they write the amount in the win column. If they have bet on an incorrect sentence, they write it in the lose column. At the end, students add up the win column and the lose column and then subtract the lose column from the win column. The pair with the most money is the winner.

Answers

1 ✗ (I'll just have) 2 ✓ 3 ✓ 4 ✗ ('re taking) 5 ✓ 6 ✗
(You're going to pass/You'll pass) 7 ✗ (I'll have) 8 ✗ (I don't
think she'll come) 9 ✗ (it's going to be) 10 ✓ 11 ✗ (I'll
help) 12 ✗ (I'm going to meet or I'm meeting)

UNIT 2 Grammar 2
From start to finish
Procedure

Divide students into groups of three or four. Give each group a copy of the playing board and a dice. Explain that the squares on the grid contain a mini-dialogue. The second sentence of each dialogue contains a future construction that has been used incorrectly or doesn't sound natural. The students place a counter (coins will do) in the 'Start' square, take it in turns to roll their dice, move along the board and correct the mistake in each case. They can check their answers with you, but do not give them the correct answer if they are wrong. In some cases, more than one construction is possible.

If a student does not make a proper correction, s/he moves back along the board by the same number that s/he has moved forward, and then waits for his/her next turn. If a student lands on a sentence that has already been corrected, s/he rolls his/her dice again. If s/he lands on a 'Free square', s/he waits for his/her next turn. The winning student is the first student to reach the finish.

Answers

1 ... I'll make ... 2 I won't still be working ... 3 ... I'll probably
go ... 4 ... we'll have spent ... 5 ... I'm meeting .../... I'm going
to meet ... 6 ... it's going to rain ... 7 ... he will have been
... 8 ... I'll make ... 9 ... I won't have finished .../I won't finish
... /I'm not going to finish ... 10 ... begins ... 11 ... I don't
think I'll go ... 12 ... I'm starting .../I'm going to start /I start
... 13 ... I'll probably be watching ... 14 ... she's going to have
a baby ... 15 ... I'll be lying ... 16 ... I'll return ...

UNIT 2 Grammar 3
Just in case ...
Procedure

Divide the class into two or three small teams. Write a list of situations on the board: *a cinema, the office, a church, a train station, a supermarket, a dinner party, a library, an airport, an art gallery, a circus, a birthday party, a skiing holiday, a toilet, a football match* and *a café*. Copy the activity and cut into cards. Put the cards in a pile face down between the teams. One student from the first team takes an object card and shows it to the other team(s). Give the teams thirty seconds to think of a reason why they are taking the object to the first situation listed on the board, using *in case* or *just in case* e.g. *I'm taking a scarf and gloves to the office in case the heating breaks down.* The teams and teacher listen to explanations from each team and decide which is the most logical or convincing, and a point is awarded to the winning team. Then the next team chooses a card and uses the next situation on the board. When the situations have been used up, students go back to the first one again. The winning team is the team that has the most points once all the cards have been used.

UNIT 2 Vocabulary 2
Beginnings and endings

Procedure

Divide the class into pairs, A and B. Give students either section A or B. The aim of the activity is to match the sentence beginnings with their endings. Student A starts by looking at Student B's *sentence beginnings* at the bottom of his/her sheet and reading out number 1, e.g. *I'm a little worried …* (S/he mustn't read the part in brackets as this is the answer). Student B listens and reads what s/he thinks is the correct *sentence ending* on his/her sheet e.g. *… about my father's illness*. If student B has found the correct *sentence ending*, s/he writes in the *sentence beginning* above the appropriate *sentence ending* in the grid. If student B reads the incorrect *sentence ending*, s/he must wait a turn to have another go. It is then student B's turn who reads out a *sentence beginning* for student A. The first student to complete their sentences is the winner.

UNIT 2 Communication
The right response

Procedure

Divide the students into pairs, A and B. Give students either section A or B. They should not show these to each other. Explain that student B has applied for a summer job as a social activities organiser (organising sporting events, evening activities, school visits, etc.) at a summer language school, and is going to be interviewed for the job by student A. Student A asks the questions on his/her paper and student B chooses the most appropriate response on his/her paper. Both students decide if this response is appropriate. Student A writes the number of student B's response next to the appropriate sentence on his/her paper. Allow the class about 10–15 minutes to do this, then check their answers. The pair which correctly matches the most appropriate prompts and responses is the winner.

Answers

A 29   B 21   C 30   D 16   E 3   F 17   G 8   H 11   I 4
J 9   K 13   L 6   M 22   N 20   O 15

UNIT 3 Vocabulary 1
Trading words

Procedure

Divide the students into pairs, A and B. Cut up and give students either section A or B. They should not show each other their papers. Explain that each of their sentences contains a word/expression that is wrong. They need to replace these with a more suitable words/expression, which the other student has in one of their sentences. To do this each student reads through their sentences and circle words they think are wrong. Then students take it in turns to read their sentences one by one to their partners, who look for the corresponding sentence. They then make a direct exchange (e.g., In student A's sentence 1: *antique* should be replaced with *second-hand*, in student B's sentence I, which in turn should be replaced with *antique*).

Students make a note of this in the space provide on the activity sheets. Allow them about 10 minutes to do this. The pair which made the most correct exchanges is the winner.

Answers

1 antique = I second-hand   2 During = F while   3 ancient = J traditional   4 silk = A gold   5 up until that point = H From that point on   6 Since then = G After that   7 at = B in   8 porcelain = E leather   9 slippery = C itchy   10 rubber = D plastic

UNIT 3 Grammar 1
Correction connections

Procedure

Divide the students into groups of four. Give each group a copy of the activity. Two students within each group take it in turns to choose a sentence on the grid and identify, then correct, the mistake in each one. These mistakes all involve misuse of a past form. The aim of the activity is to collect rows of four squares, either horizontally, vertically or diagonally, while at the same time trying to prevent the other pair from doing the same (see 'Three in a row' Unit 1). The squares marked with ☺ are bonus squares. If a pair corrects a sentence directly above, below, to the left or right of one of these squares, they automatically win that square as well. When one pair gets a row of four squares, they ask you to check their answers. If they are correct, they win 1 point. If they are wrong, the point is awarded to the other pair. Once a square forms part of a row of four, it cannot be used again to help form another row of four. The winning pair is the pair in each group who wins the most rows of four squares after about 15 minutes of play.

Answers

1 I had been going out …   2 … was walking …   3 … I had already drunk …   4 … did you do …?   5 … were you working …?   6 … referee decided …   7 … I hadn't finished …   8 … a dog ran …   9 … had already left /… were already leaving   10 … it started making …   11 train had left …   12 Did you see …?   13 …Were you working?   14 … I was working …/… I worked …   15 … had already posted it.   16 I had been driving …   17 I had only been working …/ I had only worked …   18 … did you do …   19 I was playing …   20 … I was in the middle …   21 … I had finished. /…I finished.   22 … suddenly rang.   23 … team won …   24 … I got to the airport …   25 … had fallen asleep /… were falling asleep.

UNIT 3 Grammar 2
Your rule, my rule

Procedure

Divide the class into pairs, A and B. Cut up and give students either section A or B. Explain that each of their sentences contains the definite article *the*. Most of the sentences are correct, but three use *the* when they shouldn't. Working together, but without looking at each other's papers, they match their sentences by identifying a common rule for the use of *the*. They must also match the sentences which use *the* incorrectly. To do this they first individually read through their sentences deciding where and how *the* is used correctly or incorrectly. They then take it in turns to read out their sentences while their partner looks for the matching sentence. They write down the number or letter of their partner's matching sentence, in the right-hand column. The winning pair is the first pair to correctly match all their sentences.

Answers

1 I   2 H   3 O (*pasta* and *coffee* are not preceded by *the*)   4 M   5 K   6 N   7 L (*Eynsham* and *New York* are not preceded by *the*)   8 J   9 C   10 F   11 A (*Regent Street* and *Park Lane* are not preceded by *the*)   12 D   13 G   14 B   15 E

UNIT 3 | Grammar 3
Adverb additions

Procedure

Divide the class into pairs. Copy one activity sheet for each pair. Explain that each sentence has had an adverb removed from it, which can be found in the box. Sometimes the sentence retains its meaning without the adverb, and sometimes the adverb is required to give the sentence meaning. Working in their pairs, they decide what the missing adverb is, and then decide where in the sentence that adverb goes. Allow them about 10-15 minutes to do this. There may be several possible answers, but all the words in the box must be used once.

Students then decide how certain they are that their sentences are correct, and award themselves points as follows: Very certain: 3 points. Quite certain: 2 points. Not very certain: 1 point. Review the answers with them. For each correct sentence, they win the points that they awarded themselves (the adverb must be placed in the right place in the sentence). If their sentence is wrong, they lose the points that they awarded themselves. The winner is the pair who wins the most points.

Possible answers

1 … worked **hard** …   2 … raining **heavily**.   3 … did **surprisingly** well.   4 … walked **slowly** …   5 … plays the piano and the guitar **beautifully** …   6 … come **late** …   7 … feels **strongly** …   8 … **increasingly** difficult …   9 … dress **colourfully** …   10 … how **badly** I did …   11 … ran **fast** …   12 … **definitely** be there …   13 … **probably** won't finish …   14 … **completely** different …   15 … **closely** followed … / … followed **closely** …

UNIT 3 | Vocabulary 2
The same suffix

Procedure

Divide the class into pairs. Give each pair a copy of the activity. The box at the top of the page contains 18 words which have been joined together, and which students have to identify. They do this by following the direction of the arrows, reading from left to right or from right to left. They then use the words from the box to complete sentences 1–6. They will need to change the form of the words by adding an appropriate suffix (and making any other necessary changes, e.g., changing -*y* to -*e*, etc.). In each sentence, the suffix should be the same (e.g., all the words in sentence 1 end with the suffix -*ion*). Students can use dictionaries if necessary. The first pair to complete all the sentences is the winner.

Answers

In the grid: involve, forgive, friend, admit, novel, donate, replace, piano, invent, member, journal, translate, arrange, calculate, ready, partner, forget, produce

1 admission, production, donation   2 involvement, replacement, arrangement   3 membership, friendship, partnership

4 forgetfulness, readiness, forgiveness   5 translator, inventor, calculator   6 pianist, journalist, novelist

UNIT 3 | Communication
Communicative crossword

Procedure

Divide the class into pairs, A and B. Give each student section A or B. They should not show each other their sections. Explain that they both have the same crossword grid, but with different words filled in. These are all academic or vocational school subjects. They must help each other to complete their grid by saying how important, useful or interesting they think the subjects are, and why. They must not say what the subjects are. The first pair to complete their grids is the winner.

UNIT 4 | Vocabulary 1
Add a letter, add a word

Procedure

Divide the class into pairs. Give each pair a copy of the activity sheet. Explain that sentences 1-14 each contain a missing word. These words are in the box at the top of the activity sheet. However, each word has had a letter removed. In pairs, students identify which word should be used to complete each sentence, and also decide which letter is missing from those words. They write their complete words in the sentences, then use the missing letter from each word to complete the sentence at the bottom of the page. The first pair to do this is the winner.

Answers

1 gamble   2 endurance   3 chance   4 opportunity   5 consuming   6 put   7 balance   8 stamina   9 obsession   10 achievements   11 extreme   12 intense   13 ambitions   14 turn   The missing letters spell *accomplishment*.

UNIT 4 | Grammar 1
Just 45 seconds

Procedure

Organise the class into groups of four and divide each group into two teams, A and B. Copy one activity sheet for each group, and cut these into cards. Students shuffle the cards and place them face down on the desk between them. Explain that each card contains a conditional sentence in which the words have been mixed up. Each team takes it in turns to take a card, and rearrange the words to make conditional sentences. They should write their sentences down on a separate sheet of paper. They have 45 seconds to do each one (the other team times them). Each sentence begins with *If*, the conditional clause ends with the word in *italics*, and the main clause ends with the word in **bold**. When all the groups have used up all their cards, check their answers. The winning team is the team in each group who correctly rearranges the most sentences.

Answers

1 If I need any help or advice, I'll give you a call.   2 If I go to Peru next year, I'll hire a car and travel around the country.   3 If you have any problems, I'll ask someone to help you.   4 If you want to succeed in life, you'll have to take a few risks.   5 If you miss too many English classes, you won't get a certificate. 6 If you win the competition, how will you spend the prize money?   7 If I lend you the money, will you promise to return it as soon as possible?   8 If you don't accept the job, what will you do

instead? 9 If we didn't take risks occasionally, life would be very boring. 10 If I was a bit braver, I would probably go mountain climbing. 11 If I took a year off work, I might travel around the world. 12 If I had more time, I could do some voluntary work for an international charity. 13 If my job was more exciting, I wouldn't be so bored all the time. 14 If I were you, I'd eat less and take more exercise. 15 If you had as much money as you wanted, what would you do with it? 16 If you could choose any job in the world, what would you do? 17 If I had driven more carefully, I wouldn't have had the accident. 18 If we hadn't left so late, we wouldn't have missed the train. 19 If you hadn't been so careless with your camera, you wouldn't have dropped it. 20 If I had known how dangerous skiing was, I wouldn't have done it. 21 If you had cooked the chicken properly, we wouldn't have become ill. 22 If I had worked harder at school, I could have gone to university. 23 If you hadn't gone to university, what would you have done instead? 24 If we had taken a map with us, we wouldn't have got lost.

Unit 4 Grammar 2
Modal chase

Procedure

Divide the class into pairs. Give each pair a copy of the activity sheet. They will need a dice and a counter each (coins will do). They should place their counters in the box marked 'Student A + B start' at the top of the grid. Explain that sentences 1–16 have had some words removed which can be found somewhere in the grid. These sentences express past, present and future obligation, using modals. Some of the options in the grid either do not fit any of the sentences or are grammatically incorrect. Both students first look at sentence 1, and then look for the box on the grid containing the missing words for that sentence. When they find it, they should not tell each other what they think those words are. They then take it in turns to roll their dice and move their counter towards the box they have chosen. They can move their counter up and down or left and right but not diagonally or across the black areas. As soon as they land on the box they have chosen, they 'claim' it by putting either a circle or a cross in that box and writing the correct words in the appropriate sentence. The box cannot then be claimed by the other student on this round. Both students then look at the next sentence and move their counters on from the squares they are already on. Allow them about 15 minutes to complete all the sentences, and then check their answers. The winner is the student in each pair who claims the most correct boxes/completes the most sentences.

Answers

1 must go on   2 have to wear   3 should take   4 mustn't make   5 had to call   6 don't need to leave   7 mustn't stay out   8 ought to call   9 have to apply   10 should have cooked   11 must remember to send   12 don't need to wear   13 had to take   14 should attend   15 should have arrived   16 shouldn't have borrowed

Unit 4 Grammar 3
Who said what?

Procedure

Give each student a copy of the activity sheet. Explain that they should choose eight of the subject areas and write a sentence for each one that is true for them using language of emphasis

(lesson 4.3). They should not show their sentences to anyone else. Allow them about 10 minutes for this.

Collect in all the papers. Tell them that you are going to read the sentences out to them, but will not say who wrote them. If a student thinks they know whose sentence is being read out, they must put their hand up and tell you. Take one student's sheet and read out the sentences one by one. If a student correctly guesses who wrote the first sentence, they win 8 points. However, if they are wrong they are eliminated from this round and have to wait for the next student's sentences to be read out before they can re-join the activity. You then read out the second sentence from the same sheet. If another student guesses this sentence correctly, they win 7 points. The number of points they can win is reduced by 1 with each sentence you read. The winner is the student who has the most points after all the students' sentences has been read out.

Unit 4 Vocabulary 2
Hot rocks

Procedure

Divide the class into groups of four. Copy and cut the activity sheet into cards, and give each group a set of cards, which they place face down on the desk between them.   Put the adjectives, *long*, *short*, *wide*, *broad*, *high*, *deep*, *low* on the board. Explain that the aim of the activity is for them to collect as many cards as possible. To do this, students in each group take it in turns to pick up a card and read out the sentence using the word 'BLANK' in place of the gap in each sentence, e.g. *House prices have now become so BLANK that nobody can afford them anymore.* They must not read the answer, which is written in brackets after each sentence. The other students in the group must try to identify the missing word. They can use the root adjectives on the board to help them. The student who says the correct answer gets the card. If no student gets the correct answer, the card can be discarded and looked at again after the game. The winner is the student in each group who has the most cards after about 15 minutes of play.

Unit 4 Communication
What would you do?

Procedure

Students do the activity in groups of four or five. Cut the sheet into cards and give each group a set, which they should place face down on the desk. Explain that each card contains a moral or ethical dilemma that they might face in real life. Students take it in turns to take a card from the set and read the dilemma out to the group. The student who read the card notes down what they think they would do in that situation. The other students in the group also note down what they think that student (the reader) would do. When they are ready, students in turn reveal how they thought the reader would behave. Those who were right can be awarded a point. Students can then discuss what they would do. When they have discussed all of their cards (give students 20 minutes for this), some of the situations can then be extended into a whole-class discussion.

UNIT 5 · Vocabulary 1
From top to bottom

Procedure

Divide the class into pairs. Give each pair a copy of the activity sheet. Explain that each sentence contains a jumbled word in bold. The two players take it in turns to choose a sentence anywhere at the top of the grid, and rearrange the jumbled letters to make a word. The first letter of each word is underlined. If they are unsure or if they are challenged by their opponent, they can check their answers with the teacher. If they are correct, they can then move down to the next space on the grid (either vertically or diagonally). The aim of the activity is to be the first student to reach the bottom of the grid. If they are wrong, that space then becomes 'dead' and students have to choose the space to the left or right of their previous correct answer before continuing their descent. The other student, however, can still try that square. There are also 'free' spaces which they automatically win if they win the space above, and also 'blocked' spaces, which they cannot cross, and have to go round instead. (The numbers do not dictate the order in which the sentences should be completed.) The winner is the student who has got the furthest down the grid in 15 minutes of play.

Answers

1 scruffy   2 wavy   3 confused   4 remind   5 uninterested
6 memorial   7 remember   8 optimistic   9 forgetful
10 stocky   11 straight   12 uneasy   13 curious
14 auburn   15 annoyed   16 memorable   17 clean-
shaven   18 sceptical   19 overweight   20 memory
21 elegant   22 reminisce   23 wrinkles   24 suspicious
25 spiky   26 excited   27 memorize   28 muscular
29 chubby   30 relieved   31 curly   32 nostalgic
33 souvenir   34 bald   35 tanned   36 good-looking

UNIT 5 · Grammar 1
Fill the boxes

Procedure

Divide the class into pairs. Give each pair a copy of the activity. Each sentence on their activity sheet has had some words removed which can be found in the two boxes at the top of the activity. They should choose a phrase from the first box and a verb in the second box (in its correct form) to complete each of their sentences. The pairs write their answers in the grid allocated for each sentence. Each space on the grid should have 1 letter, and there should be no gaps between words. There may be more than one alternative to complete each sentence, but only one of these will fit into the grid. The winning pair is the pair to correctly complete the worksheet first.

Answers

1 use to be   2 use to go   3 use to eat   4 would spend
5 would visit   6 would correct   7 would destroy   8 used to
driving   9 used to reading   10 used to speaking   11 used to
changing   12 get used to leaving   13 get used to working
14 getting used to taking   15 getting used to moving

UNIT 5 · Grammar 2
Abilities crossword

Procedure

Divide the class into pairs. Give each pair a copy of the crossword grid. Explain that you are going to read some sentences out to the class which contain some missing words. Students have to decide what these words are and use them to complete the crossword. The missing words are expressions used to talk about ability. To help them, one or two letters of each main verb are already in the crossword. In some cases, the sentences can be completed in more than one way, but there is only one possible answer that will fit in the crossword. There should be no gaps in the crossword for spaces between words or for apostrophes.

Begin by asking one pair to choose a line on the crossword (e.g., 1 across), then read the appropriate clue/sentence out to them. Do not read out the words in brackets, as these are the answers. Pause for a few seconds/tap your desk/say 'blank' the same number of times as there are words. Allow the class a few moments to discuss the answer in their pairs, and write in their answers. Then ask another pair to choose another line on the crossword, and so on. The winning pair is the pair who have most completed their crossword after all the clues/sentences have been read out.

Answers

Across: 1 How do you (*manage to stay*) so slim? Do you stick to a special diet?   2 After three attempts, I finally (*managed to pass*) my driving test.   4 I (*managed to fix*) your computer, but the printer is still making a funny noise.   5 I knew I (*couldn't afford*) to pay the rent on my house, so I offered to decorate the place instead.   6 I'm really (*bad at playing*) tennis. I haven't won a game for years!   8 I know you're having a few problems with your homework, but I'm afraid I (*can't help*) you at the moment.   11 I used to (*be able to speak*) French fluently, but now my pronunciation isn't as good as it used to be.   15 We (*weren't able to take*) a holiday last summer because we didn't have enough money.   16 My laptop computer is very small, but it (*can hold*) a huge amount of information.   17 I've (*managed to get*) some tickets for the show tonight.   18 Thanks for the invitation to your party, but I'm afraid I won't (*be able to come*), as I've got too much work.

Down: 1 Did you (*manage to talk*) to Bob earlier and ask him about his plans for the weekend?   3 I've got a terrible sense of taste. I (*can't tell*) whether something is sweet or salty.   7 I've always been (*terrible at remembering*) people's names. What's yours again?   8 By the time my daughter was eight, she (*could beat*) me at chess.   9 Do you know (*how to cook*) Japanese food?   10 Samantha is (*great at making*) people feel relaxed. Within minutes, she has complete strangers smiling and laughing.   12 By the time we finish this course, we should (*be able to communicate*) quite effectively in English.   13 Although I haven't (*been able to work*) recently because of my bad back, my company is still paying me my regular salary.   14 My brother is really (*good at repairing*) broken electrical items. Why don't you ask him to look at your TV?

UNIT 5   Grammar 3
Paragraph auction

Procedure

Divide the class into groups of three or four. Give each group a copy of the activity sheet. Explain that you are 'giving' each group £500, and that they are going to use this money to buy the paragraphs on their sheet in an 'auction'. However, some of the paragraphs contain mistakes, and they should avoid buying these, as they are 'worthless'. The aim of the activity is for one group to 'buy' more correct paragraphs than the other groups. They shouldn't spend too much money on one paragraph, as once they have spent all their money, they won't be able to buy any more. Allow the groups a few minutes to look at their paragraphs to decide which ones are good and which are bad, then begin the activity.

You are the auctioneer, and you begin by trying to sell paragraph one to them. Start the bidding at £20. If a group offers you this amount of money, raise the amount to £30. If none of the other groups are willing to pay this, then the group who offered you the £20 'wins' that paragraph, and the £20 is deducted from the amount they hold. If, however, another group offers you £30, then raise to £40, and so on until the paragraph is sold. Do this for the other paragraphs. The winning group is the group who has bought the most correct paragraphs. If there is a tie, the winning group is that with the most money still unspent.

Answers

1 Correct   2 Wrong (*however* should not be in the sentence, as it begins with *Although*)   3 Correct   4 Correct   5 Wrong (*would be quite well-behaved* is wrong as *would* is followed by an action, not a situation, when used to talk about past habits)   6 Wrong (*managed* should be followed by the infinitive *to arrange*)   7 Correct   8 Correct (the use of *nevertheless* is acceptable as it adds emphasis to the contrast. We could use *still* instead)   9 Wrong (should be *didn't use to be*)   10 Wrong (*Nevertheless* should be *Although*)   11 Correct   12 Correct

UNIT 5   Vocabulary 2
Personality bingo

Procedure

Briefly demonstrate the game of bingo on the board. Divide the class into teams of two students, and give each team a bingo card. Give the students a few minutes to and discuss what they think the words/expressions on their cards mean. Tell them that you are going to read them some sentences. Each sentence describes personality types or features that are expressed with an idiom on their cards. Read out the sentences below, at random, and allow a few moments between each sentence for students to look for an appropriate idiom on their card. Read each sentence out twice. If they find the appropriate idiom, they tick the box that it's in. The first team to tick all their boxes calls *Bingo!* and wins the game.

Sentences

1 David seems to enjoy deliberately causing problems or starting arguments. (*a trouble-maker*)   2 Jennifer seems to spend all her time sitting in front of the television. (*a couch potato*)   3 My boss Mr Walton makes us all work very hard. (*a slave driver*)   4 The problem with Stan is that he behaves as if he knows everything. (*a real know-all*)   5 Martina doesn't really enjoy spending time with other people: she prefers to be

on her own a lot. (*a loner*)   6 The annoying thing about Jane is that she talks too much all the time. (*a windbag*)   7 Patricia is a nuisance, and is always annoying people. (*a pain in the neck*)   8 Freddie is rather unfriendly, and seems to have no strong feelings. (*a cold fish*)   9 Harriet is very kind and has the right feelings about important things. (*Her heart's in the right place.*)   10 Nellie is rather tough, and doesn't really care about the effects of her actions on other people. (*She's as hard as nails.*)   11 Mrs Manser is a very difficult and unhelpful person, and nobody likes dealing with her. (*an awkward customer*)   12 Mike never changes his mind, even when everybody tells him he is being unreasonable. (*as stubborn as a mule*)   13 Chaz often becomes offended or angry because he thinks he's been treated unfairly the past. (*He has a chip on his shoulder*)   14 Brian is very old-fashioned and refuses to try anything new. (*a stick in the mud*)   15 Mr Ford shows too much interest in other people's private activities. (*a busybody*)   16 Peter really enjoys social occasions and is fun and exciting to be with. (*the life and soul of the party*)   17 Gregory works hard and is always extremely successful in anything he does at work. (*a high-flyer*)   18 John always wakes up at half past five and is at work by seven o'clock. (*an early bird*)   19 Caroline hates to see people having fun and always tries to spoil other people's pleasures. (*a killjoy*)   20 Nigel is a good and honest man who will always help you if you have problems. (*the salt of the earth*)

UNIT 5   Communication
Personal time capsule

Procedure

Students do the activity in pairs. Give each student a copy of the activity sheet. Tell them to imagine that they are going to bury a time capsule. In addition to the objects that they chose in lesson 5 Communication focus, they need to include some information about somebody in their class (their partner), so that future generations get an idea of a 'typical' early 21st century person: what they were like, their abilities, likes, preferences, etc, and how they lived their lives. Students ask their partner questions based on the prompts on the activity sheet, and write their answers in the spaces provided. Allow them about 10–15 minutes for this. Then collect in all the activity sheets and redistribute them to different pairs. The pairs read the answers on the two new activity sheets they been given and guess whose time capsule they are for.

UNIT 6   Vocabulary 1
DIY travel survey

Procedure

Divide the students into pairs. Give each pair a copy of the activity sheet. Explain that each sentence has words or expressions related to travel that are missing. Working in their pairs, students complete the sentences using the words/phrases in the box. They then ask each other the questions and write down their partner's answers to the survey. Get feedback.

Answers

1 homesick   2 itchy feet   3 independent traveller 4 uncharted territory   5 culture shock   6 wander around 7 annoying   8 disgusting   9 fascinating   10 petrifying 11 challenging   12 subzero temperatures   13 roam 14 emigrating

Unit 6 | Grammar 1
Perfect proverbs

Procedure

Divide the class into pairs. Give each pair a copy of the activity sheet. Students take it in turns to choose one of the sentences in the left-hand column, and complete it using the verb in brackets. They must decide whether to use a Present Perfect Simple or Continuous form to complete the gap in the sentence. They then match the sentence with an appropriate response in the right-hand column. These responses all include a well-known English proverb. Set a time limit of about 10–15 minutes for this, then stop the activity. The student in each pair who made the most correct matches is the winner.

Answers

A 've just done (3)   B has just called (7)   C has been coming (15)   D 've been waiting (11)   E 've been learning (16)   F has already shouted (1)   G have just joined (5)   H 've already finished (13)   I has been telling (2)   J 've just been looking (8)   K 've been trying (4)   L 've been having (14)   M has broken (9)   N has just gone (10)   O 've just heard (6)   P 've already received (12)

Unit 6 | Grammar 2
Something in common

Procedure

Cut the activity sheet into cards, and give one card to each student. If you have fewer or more than 14 students in your class, either use fewer cards or get students to share cards. They should not show their cards to one another. This activity works best if the students can mingle. Tell them to imagine that the information on their cards is true about them. The aim of the activity is to find other students in the class with whom they have something in common. They do this by walking around the class and asking the others questions. They should use a combination of direct and indirect yes/no and information questions. They will find it helpful to have a separate sheet of paper on which they can write down the students' names and the feature that they have in common. Allow them about 10–15 minutes for this. The winner is the student who makes the most 'matches'.

Unit 6 | Grammar 3
Just 15 questions

Procedure

Divide the class into groups of four. Give each group a set of cards, which they should place in a pile face down on the desk. Students take it in turns to take a card from the top of the set. They should not show this card to the others in the group. The others have to find out what is on the card by asking questions. These can only be yes/no questions, and they should try using language of comparison e.g., *Is it bigger than a car? Is it as fast as an aeroplane?* The student with the card can only answer yes or no, but s/he can elaborate slightly using language of comparison e.g., *Yes, it's much bigger than a car. No, it's a little slower than an aeroplane.* Students are allowed to ask a maximum of 15 questions for each card. If they guess what is on the card before they have asked 15 questions, they 'win' that card. A guess counts as a question. If they do not guess what is on the card, it is put aside and another student takes another card from

the top of the set. Allow about 15 minutes for the activity. The winner is the student who wins the most cards.

Unit 6 | Vocabulary 2
Go on, go on!

Procedure

Divide the class into pairs. Cut up and give each pair a set of cards, which they should spread out between them, face up. Explain that the 30 cards form 10 short monologues. Each monologue can be made up by joining three of the cards. Each section of the monologue is joined by an expression using *go*. The expression joining parts 1 and 2 of the monologue appears in their course book, but the expression joining parts 2 and 3 might be new to them but tell students they can use the context to work out the answer. Working in their pairs, they form the 10 monologues (using a monolingual dictionary, if they like). The first part of each monologue is on one of the shaded cards. The first pair to correctly complete all 10 monologues is the winner.

Answers

1 … **it goes without saying** that … … certainly **worth a go** if you can't …   2 … **go back** on their word. We **go back** a long way …   3 … **going away** for a few months … … a city that's **got a lot going for it**. There are …   4 … **went to great lengths** to make sure … … which just **goes to show** that hard work …   5 … **go for** the fruit starter … … but I **went off** seafood …   6 … **have a go** at parachuting … … £150 **a go**, it's not exactly …   7 … **make a go of** it. … suppose **there's no going back** now! …   8 … **on the go** since … … It's **all go** day and night.   9 … **going on**, but … … has **gone down** again …   10 … **gone down with** … … a lot of it **going around** the school …

Unit 6 | Communication
Quotes and proverbs

Procedure

Divide the class into groups of three or four. Give each group a set of cards which they place in a pile in front of them. Explain that each card contains a proverb or a quote about travel (these have been slightly abridged/simplified). Each student in the group takes it in turns to pick up a card and read their proverb/ quote out to the rest of the group. For each one, the students decide what it means. They can use a dictionary to help them with any unfamiliar words. Each student then says whether they agree or disagree with the proverb, and why. Make sure students justify their views. Also encourage the students to draw on and describe their own experiences when expressing their views. Finally, students as a group decide whether they agree or disagree and put cards in an 'agree' or 'disagree' pile. Then they each pick up a new card and discuss that proverb. At the end, you can get feedback and have a class discussion about those proverbs the groups have disagreed with. In a multi-national class, you could also ask them if there are any famous proverbs and quotes about travel in their country.

Unit 7 | Vocabulary 1
Wrong word crossword

Procedure

Divide the class into pairs. Give each pair a copy of the activity sheet. Explain that the sentences below the crossword grid all contain a wrong word. Students work together and must decide what the wrong word is and what it should be, then write the correct word in the crossword grid. In some cases, more than one replacement word may be possible, but only one will fit in the grid. Allow about 15 minutes for this, then check their answers.

Answers

Across: 2 far-fetched = excessive   6 grill = fry   7 receipt = recipe   8 cooker = cook   9 sweet = bitter   10 salty = savoury   13 luxury = overpriced   18 overpriced = extravagant   20 paws = hooves   22 bargain = discount

Down: 1 horse = bear   3 vegetable = vegetarian   4 grate = slice   5 loss = profit   6 fins = feathers   11 overcooked = overdrawn   12 raw = rare   14 beak = mouth   15 refund = receipt   16 bidding = haggling   17 roast = bake   19 boil = spoil   21 afford = worth

UNIT 7 | Grammar 1
The same mistake

Procedure

Divide the class into pairs. Give each student in the pair a copy of the Student A or Student B section. They should not show these to each other. Explain that they have a different set of sentences, but each set contains the same kinds of mistakes which are all connected with countability/uncountability of nouns. E.g. the mistake in sentence 1 on Student A's list matches the mistake in sentence H on students B's list. The students should first look through their own sentences to identify and correct the mistakes in their sentences. Then they work together to match equivalent mistakes in the sentences. To do this, students take it in turns to read their sentences while their partner looks for the corresponding sentence. They should not look at each other's papers. Allow them about 15 minutes for this, then review the answers with the class.

Answers

1 How many **times** ... H ... many different **wines**, ...   2 ... some **information** ... L ... the right **equipment**.   3 ... eat chicken ... E ... there's glass ...   4 ... **many** students ... A ... **many** cars ... 5 ... **much** luggage ... J ... **much** spaghetti ...   6 ... very little time ... K ... few interests ...   7 ... **a** little time... B ... **a** few minutes ...   8 ... **an** egg, ... C ... **an** iron ...   9 ... lots of (or a **lot** of) D ... lots of (or a **lot** of) ...   10 ... a bit **of** money ... F ... a piece **of** good advice   11 ... a **slice/piece** of toast ... I ... a **slice/piece** to ...   12 ... bar of chocolate (or **box** of chocolates) ... G ... **bar** of soap ...

UNIT 7 | Grammar 2
Passive verb swap

Procedure

Divide the class into pairs, A and B. Give each student either an A or B section.   Explain that each of their sentences can be completed by making a passive construction. Their partner has the verbs needed to complete their sentences in a box at the bottom of their section. Give students a few minutes to read through their sentences before they start the activity and to try and guess what verbs might fit. Students take it in turns to tell their partner a verb from the verb box on their paper. Their partner looks at his/her sentences and completes a sentence using that verb. They will need to put the verbs into their correct form, and decide what other words are missing from the sentences (these could include modal verbs, and some of the auxiliary verbs could be negative). The number of words missing is indicated by the spaces in each sentence. Negatives (e.g.,

isn't) count as one word. Review the answers with the class.

Answers

Student A: 1 should be spent   2 was decorated   3 was destroyed   4 haven't been given   5 is going to be built 6 had been cancelled   7 is being interviewed   8 was being modernised   9 are sold   10 were given   11 will be asked 12 could/might have been killed

Student B: 1 were told   2 was being watched   3 had ... been caught   4 were discovered   5 haven't been told   6 isn't being used   7 is distributed   8 is going to be closed   9 am being met   10 could/might have been sacked   11 should be punished   12 will be promoted

UNIT 7 | Grammar 3
10-minute trade-off

Procedure

Divide the class into pairs, A and B. Give each student an A or B section. Explain that statements 1–10 all have a follow-on sentence using *get/have something done* which their partner has in the grid at the bottom of their sheet. Working together, they have ten minutes to try to obtain their follow-on sentences from their partner, but without looking at their partner's paper. Student B starts by choosing a follow-on sentence from the grid at random and reading it out for student A. Student A looks at his/her statements 1-10 and decides if student B's sentence follows on from any of them. There are several 'trick' sentences which don't follow on from any of the statements (the context/grammar is wrong). If student A thinks it doesn't fit any of the statements, student B must read out another follow-on sentence until student A finds one which matches. Student A then writes the letter of that follow-on sentence after their numbered statement. It is then student A's turns to read out a follow-on sentence for student B. The student who matches the most statements with the correct follow-on sentences is the winner.

Answers

Student A: 1 R   2 Q   3 L   4 N   5 F   6 D   7 A   8 C   9 K   10 I

Student B: 1 E   2 L   3 O   4 I   5 Q   6 R   7 F   8 C   9 J   10 M

UNIT 7 | Vocabulary 2
Prefix predicament

Procedure

Divide the class into pairs. Give each pair a copy of the activity sheet. Explain that each sentence contains a missing word that contains a prefix. Students must work together, reading these sentences and deciding what they think the word is. To help them, you could put a list of prefixes on the board: *un, ex, multi, over, under, bi, mono, re, extra*. Students write each word in the corresponding space on the grid.   Explain to students that if they do this correctly, they will reveal (in the shaded vertical strip) a word that will complete the gap in the sentence below. The first pair in the class to reveal the missing expression is the winner.

Answers

1 undercooked   2 overworked   3 ex-husband   4 biannual 5 multinational   6 reheat   7 extra-strong   8 multipurpose 9 rewrite   10 monolingual   11 underpaid   12 unusual 13 uncomfortable   14 underestimated   15 multimedia 16 overslept   17 unnecessary. The word: *counterproductive*.

UNIT 7 | Communication
I would like to complain about...

Procedure

Divide the class into two groups. Make two copies of the activity sheet and cut out the cards. Give out a set of cards to each group so that each student gets one card. You do not need to give out all of the cards but ensure that for each card handed out, a student in the other group has the same card. Students should not show these to the others in the class. If there are an odd number of students, two students in one of the groups can share a card. Large classes can be split in half with two groups in each half.

Tell your students to look at their card, and explain that it illustrates a problem. One group of students are the 'complainers'. The other group are the managers of the company, service, shop, etc., that is responsible. Students should decide what has happened, and then spend two minutes deciding what they might say in a small role play. 'Complainers' take it in turns to start a role play by saying, e.g. *Excuse me, I'd like to speak to the pet shop owner about this parrot.* The student in the other group holding this card must step forward and give a response. The 'complainer' should be adamant that the manager and/or his company is at fault, while the manager/owner should try to make excuses and, if possible, pass the blame back onto the person complaining. Each role play should last at least one minute. The other students listen to the role plays and decide who they felt dealt with the problem most effectively.

UNIT 8 | Vocabulary 1
Join up three

Procedure

Divide the class into teams, A and B, of two students each team. Copy and cut up the activity sheet so that each team is given their section of sentences as well as the other team's answers, which they should not show to the other team. Both teams share the grid.

Tell the students that they are going to play a version of noughts and crosses on the grid. The aim of the activity is for each team to get as many rows of three noughts or crosses (vertically, horizontally or diagonally) as possible. The teams take in turns to choose a sentence from their list and say which word they think fits the gap. If they are correct (they check their answer with the other team) they can place a nought or cross on any of the squares in the grid. If they are wrong, they miss a turn. When it is their turn again, they can try again with that sentence or choose another one. The teams continue until they have run out of squares on the grid or one of the teams has run out of sentences. The team with the most number of rows of three noughts or crosses is the winner.

UNIT 8 | Grammar 1
Sentence jumble

Procedure

Divide the class into pairs. Give each pair a copy of the activity sheet. The pairs work together through the sentences. The second sentence in bold is jumbled up; the first sentence gives them a clue as to what that second sentence should be. They need to rearrange the jumbled sentence into a correct sentence (but they should be careful: in some of the jumbled sentences

there is one *missing* word, and in others there is an *extra* word that they do not need). They write their complete sentence, properly rearranged, in the space provided. You could put the extra words on the board or around the room. The first pair to correctly rearrange all the sentences is the winner.

Answers

1 It's high time I took a holiday. 2 I'd rather you didn't use it without my permission. 3 Isn't it time we left for the airport? 4 Would you rather I spoke to him about them? (*most* is not needed) 5 It's time we left the beach and went home. (*for* is not needed) 6 You had better call him as soon as possible. 7 Isn't it about time you gave up smoking? (*some* is not needed) 8 It's high time you looked for a place of your own. 9 I'd rather you returned it to me today. 10 I'd rather you didn't smoke in here. 11 It's about time the bus arrived. (*all* is not needed) 12 We'd better not stay out late tonight. (*side* is not needed) 13 Would you rather go for a meal or go to the theatre? 14 It's high time we got a new one. (*buy* is not needed) 15 Would you rather I didn't come over tonight? (*it* is not needed) 16 I'd rather not go to New York with you. 17 I'd better go shopping for something to eat. 18 Isn't it about time she looked for a new job?

UNIT 8 | Grammar 2
Reported speech dominoes

Procedure

Divide the class into groups of three or four. Cut the sheet into cards and give each group a set. The aim of this activity is for students to join all the cards together in a line. To do this, students join an 'A' card showing a direct speech sentence with a 'B' card showing a reported speech version of that sentence. In the 'B' sentences, the reporting verb and the main verb (in its relevant construction) have been removed. Students must complete the sentences. The first group to join all the cards together and complete the B sentences with a relevant reporting verb and accompanying main verb construction is the winner.

Suggested answers

said/was trying said/had lent told/had waited asked/could help told/didn't want said/had eaten said/had been working told/had been driving suggested going said/was opening told/would deliver promised to come asked/were going to do asked/had seen reminded/to buy reminded/to phone admitted taking warned/to use suggested going decided to rent admitted dropping

UNIT 8 | Grammar 3
Race to the middle

Procedure

Divide the class into pairs or small groups. Give each pair/group a copy of the activity sheet. Explain that sentences 1–16 can all be completed with expressions using *hard* or *hardly*. These expressions can then be written into the spiral, starting at the arrow and moving in to the middle. The different shadings show the amount of space available for each expression and some letters have already been put into the spiral. In some sentences, more than one answer may be possible, but only one will fit into each section of the spiral. The first pair/group to complete all the sentences is the winner.

Teacher's notes

Answers

1 hard to make   2 hardly ever comes   3 hardly said
4 hardly anything   5 hardly ever calls   6 hard to
understand   7 hardly speak   8 hardly any   9 hard to
believe   10 hardly see   11 hardly ever agrees   12 hardly
anyone   13 hardly made   14 hardly ... explain   15 hardly
ever play   16 hardly makes any

Unit 8 — Vocabulary 2
It's mine!

Procedure

Divide the class into pairs. Give each student an A or B section.
They should not show these to one another. Cut up and give
each pair a set of the word cards at the bottom of the page,
which students place face down in a pile between them. The
sentence 'B's on their cards can be completed with a 3-word
phrasal verb so that sentence B has the same (or a very similar)
meaning as sentence A. The word cards contain the verbs and
particles that make up the phrasal verbs needed to complete
the students' sentences. There are a few extra verbs and
particles which do not fit any sentences.

Students take it in turns to pick up a word card from the top of
the set, which they should not show their partner. If they think
the word can be used to form one of their missing phrasal verbs,
they keep the card. If they don't think it can be used, it is placed
to one side. When one student thinks s/he has all the words to
make all of his/her phrasal verbs, the cards that have been put
aside should then be shuffled and picked up in the same way. A
word card can only fill one gap in their sentences.

The first to 'win' all his/her cards announces this and then
checks his/her answers with you. Tell the student if there
mistakes but do not say what they are. The student can then
decide what cards to put down. The game continues until one of
the students 'win' with no mistakes.

Answers

Student A: cut down on / catch up with / put up with / make
up for   **Student B:** looked up to / get away with / keep up with
/ put in for

Unit 8 — Communication
The road to success

Procedure

Divide the class into pairs. Give one copy of the activity sheet
to each student (two copies if there are more than 10 students
in the class). Tell your students to imagine that they are
somebody well-known, locally, nationally or internationally. The
person should be/have been successful in some way, and be
familiar to the majority of students. They can be living or dead,
or a well-known fictional character (e.g. Superman). Students
tell their partner who they are pretending to be, but they should
make sure that nobody else hears them. Their partner then
prepares a list of six interview-style questions to ask them. At
least three of these questions must include a form of the word
success e.g., *How have you become so successful?*, *What's the
best way to succeed in life?*, *What's your greatest success so
far?* Allow them 5–10 minutes for this.

Ask the student pairs to conduct their interviews in turn while
other students in the class listen. The interviews should be no
more than 3 minutes long and they should not mention their

interviewee's assumed character name. The other students
should decide who is being interviewed. They write the
student's name and who they think his/her assumed character
is on their activity sheet. They also make a note of any key
words and expressions that helped them to identify
the character. The student who identifies the most people is
the winner.

Unit 9 — Vocabulary 1
Six convicts

Procedure

Divide the class into pairs. Give each pair a copy of the activity
sheet. In part 1, students have to complete the dialogues with
words from the box. In part 2, they have to use a combination
of what they can see in the pictures, the speech bubbles and
the information given in the sentences, to match the men in the
pictures with their names and the crimes they have committed.
The first pair to do this correctly is the winner.

Answers

Part 1: Convicts 1 and 2: *sue/Fair/brand-*   Convicts 3 and 4:
sentenced/Pull/appeal   Convicts 5 and 6: *claim/convicted* (or
sentenced)

Part 2: 1 Ron Smith (arson) 2 Joe Biggs (bank robbery)   3 Bert
Adams (pick pocketing)   4. Reg Black (forgery)   5 Dick Kray
(fraud)   6 Jim Roberts (shoplifting)

Unit 9 — Grammar 1
Escape!

Procedure

Divide the class into pairs, A and B. Cut and give each student
their section of the activity sheet. The grid should be placed
between them. Tell them they are criminals and are trying to
escape. To do this, they must move from one side of the grid to
the other. The students take it in turns to read and complete
one of their sentences with one of the sequencing devices from
lesson 9.1 (the first letters of each word have been given to
them). If they do this correctly, they can put a cross in the start
square. Their partner can tell them if they are correct. With
each correct question they can put a cross in the next square
until they escape. If they make a mistake, they miss a turn. The
winner is the student who escapes first.

Unit 9 — Grammar 2
Probability hit and miss

Procedure

Divide the class into pairs. Cut up and give each pair both sets of
cards (shaded and unshaded). They should place all the cards
face down on the desk between them, the shaded cards to one
side and unshaded cards to the other. Explain that the cards
contain 20 mini dialogues. The shaded cards have the first part
of the dialogue, and the unshaded cards contain the second part
of each dialogue which contains a modal of deduction. The aim of
the activity is to match both parts of all the dialogues.

Students take it in turns to pick up one card from each set
(shaded and then unshaded) and read them aloud. If both
students agree that the cards match to form a mini dialogue, the
student keeps both cards as a 'trick'. If they don't match, s/he
places them back down where they were before and the next

student picks up two cards. This continues until all the cards have been played. The student to make most matches is the winner.

Answers

1 S   2 P   3 I   4 Q   5 N   6 G   7 E   8 A   9 B   10 T
11 K   12 D   13 L   14 M   15 C   16 R   17 O   18 F   19 H
20 J

Unit 9 Grammar 3
Find the five

Procedure

Divide the class into pairs. Give each pair a copy of the activity sheet. Explain that each of the 30 sentences on their sheet gives them an interesting fact about something. However, sometimes the fact or grammar (relative clause construction or relative pronoun) or punctuation is wrong. There are only five sentences on their sheet which are both grammatically and factually correct. They must identify which sentences these are. The first pair to identify the five correct sentences is the winner.

Answers

The correct sentences are: 4, 12, 19, 22 and 27

Grammatically incorrect sentences: 2 *in where* = *where* or *in which*   3 Should be commas after *Yesterday* and *Beatles*.   5 Shouldn't be a comma after *city*.   8 *what* = *which*   9 *where* = *which*   11 *whose* = *who*   14 *he* = *who*   17 There should be no commas after *Certificate* or *exam*.   21 *who's* = *whose*   23 *when* = *where*   25 *that* = *who*

Factually incorrect sentences: 1 Charles Dickens wrote *Oliver Twist*.   6 It was invented by a Briton (Tim Berners-Lee).   7 He came from Arkansas.   10 It sank in the Atlantic Ocean.   13 Manchester United was Beckham's first major league posting.   15 Italians had been eating pasta long before Marco Polo made his travels.   16 France won the World Cup in 1998.   18 Neil Armstrong was the first man to walk on the moon (Yuri Gagarin was the first man in space).   20 There were people on Cuba long before Columbus arrived.   24 Polar bears live in the northern hemisphere.   26 It cannot be seen from space.   28 Washington DC is in Virginia.   29 Several other countries drive on the left, including Japan, India and Malaysia.   30 Van Gogh cut off one of his ears.

Unit 9 Vocabulary 2
In the news

Procedure

Divide the class into pairs. Give each pair a copy of the activity sheet. Explain that each of the newspaper headlines have had a word removed. These words are all in the top box. Working together, they should decide on the appropriate word for each headline. To help them, there are some clues in the form of readers' comments on each story (a-l). However, these are not in the same order as the headlines. The first pair to correctly complete the headlines and match the headlines with the readers' comments is the winner. Optional follow-up: When students have matched the words with the headlines, they should then rewrite these headlines as complete sentences.

Answers

1 plea (i)   2 bid (h)   3 blast (k)   4 key (a)   5 back (e)
6 clash (c)   7 aid (g)   8 hit (j)   9 quit (l)   10 axe (f)
11 blaze (d)   12 drama (b)

Unit 9 Communication
Four lawsuits

Procedure

Divide the class into groups of four. Give a card to each student. They should not show these to one another. Explain that between them, your students have four stories about four people who have filed lawsuits against companies or individuals. These are all real cases from the USA, and the common factor is that in each case the lawsuit has been completely unreasonable. Each card contains one sentence from each story and the sentences are not in the correct order. Working together, but without looking at one another's cards, they should try to piece the stories together. Allow them about 15 minutes to do this, then review their answers. You can follow this up by discussing the cases, and asking them if they have heard of other, similar cases.

Answers

Mr Shaun Perkins, from … While he was there, … He was hit by lightning … He tried to sue …
One evening, Ms Kara Walton … As a result, … Unfortunately, she fell … She filed a lawsuit …
19-year-old thief Cark Truman … He waited until … His neighbour also … Mr Truman sued him …
Ms Amber Carson … In anger, she threw … Ms Carson then stood up … She sued the restaurant …

Unit 10 Vocabulary 1
Wordabout

Procedure

Divide your class into pairs, A and B. Cut up the sentence cards and deal them out between the students in each pair. Cut up the word cards and place them face down in a pile on the desk. Students take it in turns to pick up a word card from the pile and see if it can be used to complete one of their sentences. If it can, then the student puts the sentence and word cards together to one side as a 'trick'. If it cannot, the student puts the word card back at the bottom of the pile. The winner is the student who turns all of their sentences into tricks first. They can check their matching pairs with you. If any are incorrect, they must put the relevant word card(s) back at the bottom of the pile and the game continues until one student wins.

Answers

1 mumble   2 subconscious   3 blurt out   4 interrupt
5 powers of persuasion   6 speak your mind   7 sixth sense
8 premonitions   9 shriek   10 willpower   11 classified ads
12 déjà vu   13 lost for words   14 sceptical   15 doubt   16 suspect
17 commercial break   18 reckon   19 whisper   20 slogan

Unit 10 Grammar 1
Up and down

Procedure

Divide the class into pairs, A and B. Give each pair a copy of the playing grid on the left of the activity page, and each student either the A or B section. Each pair will also need a dice and two counters (coins will do). Explain that each of their sentences has a word removed. These words appear on their playing grid.

Students place their counters in the start space at the bottom of the grid. Taking it in turns, they roll the dice, and move their counter the appropriate number of spaces up the grid. When they land on a word, they look at their sentences to see if they can complete any of them with this word. If they can, they write the word in the gap in the appropriate sentence. If it doesn't fit any sentence, it is the next student's turn to roll the dice. When they reach the top of the grid they must go back down it again. The winner is the student who completes all their sentences first.

Answers

Student A: 1 them 2 himself 3 him 4 me 5 herself
6 yourself 7 itself 8 themselves 9 ourselves
10 myself 11 yourselves 12 no pronoun

Student B: 1 ourselves 2 each other 3 himself
4 itself 5 us 6 myself 7 you 8 no pronoun
9 yourselves 10 herself 11 themselves 12 her

UNIT 10 | Grammar 2
Mixed doubles

Procedure

Divide the class into pairs. Cut up and give each pair a set of cards and also a copy of the activity grid. The cards are placed face down in a pile between them. Explain that the cards contain the first part of 20 sentences. The second part of each sentence can be found on the activity grid. There are 10 situations, each of which is described by two sentences.

Working in their pairs, students take it in turns to pick a card and place it in the correct space on the grid, so that the second part of the sentence follows on from the first and also fits the context of the situation. Students can correct each other if they think they have made a mistake, but they should explain why they think their partner has got it wrong. Allow them about 10 minutes for this, then stop the activity and review their answers. The pair with the most correct sentence pairs is the winner.

Answers

1A It was really busy in the office, but I stopped … 1B We both chatted about work, then arranged … 2A After University, my grandfather went on … 2B He originally planned to do something different after a few years, but he went on … 3A I went to the post office but I'm afraid I didn't remember… 3B I've got to go back there tomorrow, so I promise … 4A We're short of money at the moment, so we can't afford … 4B Perhaps for a change we should consider … 5A I really regretted … 5B Naturally he's refused … 6A I'm really scared of flying, so I try to avoid … 6B However, I do enjoy… 7A My new job involves … 7B I don't like it very much, and have considered … 8A Although he found his Spanish classes extremely difficult, he carried on … 8B He needed the language for his new job, so he refused … 9A We couldn't meet you at 3 because our teacher wouldn't allow … 9B We told him it was urgent, but we didn't manage … 10A I needed to talk to Alison and ask her for some help with my homework, but when I tried … 10B In the end I tried …

UNIT 10 | Grammar 3
A hidden message

Procedure

Divide the class into pairs. Give each pair a copy of the activity sheet. Explain that each of the sentences 1–15 contains a wrong word. Either the word itself is wrong, or the wrong word form has been used or the word shouldn't be in the sentence at all.

Working in their pairs, students identify the wrong word in each sentence, and write it in the table at the bottom of their sheet. If they do this correctly, they will reveal a 'hidden' message. As a follow on task, work with them to correct the sentences.

Answers

'Your English will improve much more if you spend time practising it outside the classroom'.

Corrections: 1 you're 2 England 3 would
4 improves 5 many 6 ~~more~~ 7 ~~if~~ 8 yourself 9 spent
10 times 11 practise 12 him 13 out 14 ~~the~~
15 class(es)

UNIT 10 | Vocabulary 2
Is it spelt right?

Procedure

Divide the class into pairs or small groups. Give each group a copy of the activity sheet. Explain that each of the cards, 1-14, contains one word with a spelling mistake. They should identify the mistake in each case and correct it. They should then write the correctly-spelt words into the grid. The aim is to reveal another word in the shaded vertical strip that is often spelt incorrectly. To make this more challenging, there are no numbers on the grid so students will have to write in the words where they fit on the grid. They will find the word they reveal is spelt incorrectly. They should correct it. The first pair/group to identify and correct the spelling of the word in the shaded strip is the winner.

Answers

In the grid (top to bottom): separate, interesting, accommodation, beginning, occasionally, successful, foreigner, necessary, believe, changeable, doubt, weird, subconscious, definitely. In vertical strip: *pronunciation*

UNIT 10 | Communication
The world's dustbin

Procedure

Students do this activity in pairs. It is then extended into a whole-class discussion. Give each pair a copy of the activity sheet. Tell your students to imagine that a huge dustbin has been built, and they have been invited to choose some of the things that really annoy or irritate them and throw these into the dustbin. However, before they can throw them away, they have to persuade others that this is a good idea. They cannot throw away named people, countries, political parties or religions.

Working in their pairs, students try to agree on five things to throw in the bin. Allow them about 5–10 minutes for this. Each pair then takes it in turns to tell the class about one of the objects they would dispose of (encourage them to use sequencing language, i.e., *First of all, furthermore*, etc.). The rest of the class can challenge them or provide a counter-argument, using some of the key language from unit 10 (e.g., giving opinions, arguing for/against a point of view, using conditionals to talk about potential advantages/disadvantages, etc.). Everybody then votes on whether or not to throw the chosen object away. If a majority agree, the pair can get rid of their object. If the majority disagree, the pair has to keep their object. The process is repeated until all the student pairs have argued the case for all of their objects. The pair who has thrown away most of their objects by the end is the winner.

DVD worksheets

Before watching

1 Match the sentence halves in each column to form complete sentences.

1 He doesn't <u>take after</u>	a after he explained that this would be a good job to take.
2 They never saw <u>eye to eye</u>. In fact,	
3 They <u>made up</u>	b his Uncle at all. He's so charming!
4 My best friend really helped me when I <u>split up</u>	c he didn't respect her in any way.
	d with each other because he had no sympathy for her family.
5 They <u>fell out</u>	
6 He always <u>looked up to</u>	e his Uncle despite his Uncle being a fairly unpleasant character.
	f with my long-term boyfriend.

2 Discuss

If you had a problem, who would you go to for help? Would you choose particular friends or relatives to help you with specific problems?

While watching

3 The following events all take place in the film extract. Watch the film and number the events 1-8 according to the order they happen.

a Kate is described as the cleverest girl in her school. ☐

b Nicholas is asked by Uncle Ralph if he is willing to work. ☐

c Nicholas agrees to do anything Uncle Ralph wants. ☐

d Uncle Ralph is annoyed to hear of his brother's death. ☐

e Uncle Ralph reaffirms that Mrs Nicholas spent all the money she had left in coming to London. ☐

f Nicholas is concerned about his mother and sister if he gets the job. ☐

g Uncle Ralph is introduced to his brother's widow and children. ☐

h Uncle Ralph describes an advert for a job he has seen for Nicholas. ☐

4 Watch the film and complete the sentences.

1 **A:** 'You must _____ up against _____ ma'am. I always do.'
   B: 'Mine was no _____ loss.'   **A:** 'It was no _____ loss.'

2 'When my wife died ma'am, _____ years ago, I _____ to survive the _____. _____ , you will do the same.'

3 ...'but whenever a man dies without _____ he seems to think it gives him the _____ to _____ of other peoples.'

4 You may thank your _____ stars. An _____ assistant wanted.'

After watching

5 What is your impression of Uncle Ralph's personality? Write three sentences about him using examples from the film to support your thoughts.

6 Now think about Nicholas. What sort of person does he seem to you? Write three sentences using examples from the film to support your thoughts.

© Pearson Education Limited 2006 – Photocopiable

Before watching

1 Decide on five dream careers. Write the qualities needed for these careers.

Dream career	Qualities needed

2 Discuss.
What sort of qualities do you think you would need to be a fashion designer?

While watching

3 Watch the film and <u>underline</u> the correct word in each of the following sentences.

1 Lindsay's company produces a range of *country/urban* sportswear.
2 Lindsay started the company when she was *twenty-four/twenty-five*.
3 The highlight of her career so far was when they were in Top Shop in *Oxford/ Oxford Circus*.
4 Later this year, she'll be dealing directly with *small local shops/ large department stores*.
5 Her ambition started early when she used to make clothes for her *Sindy/Barbie dolls*.
6 It's an *easy/hard* business to break into.
7 You need lots of *energy/patience* for this business.
8 Lindsay ends up spending *four/three* days a week on her own.
9 A lot of *self-esteem/self-motivation* is required just to get out of bed in the morning.
10 Lindsay feels very *privileged/lucky* to be in her position.
11 Most of Lindsay's friends earn *more/less* money than her now.
12 But Lindsay has loads of *plans/potential* for the future which is what she's looking forward to.

After watching

4a Choose one of the dream careers from Ex.1 or any other career and write 8-9 sentences describing a typical working day. You can use the words/phrases in the box below to help you.

produce	deal (directly) with	responsibilities	qualities
work with/alone	earn	ideas	ambition/hopes for the future

b Read one line at a time of your typical working day to your partner. At the end of each line, your partner can guess which the dream career/typical day you are describing.

© Pearson Education Limited 2006 – Photocopiable

Before watching

1 Discuss.

1 What do you think are the ingredients of a successful adventure film?
2 Put these in order of importance in an adventure film:
 • special effects
 • plot
 • dialogue
 • which actors are in the film
3 Are there any differences between old adventure films and new adventure films?
4 Is it important that the hero or heroine has some romantic interest? Why/Why not?
5 Is it important to have a happy ending in adventure films?
6 What is the best adventure film you have ever seen? Why? How did it end?

While watching

2 The following phrases are all used in the film. Watch the film and fill in each gap.

a demons and _____
b _____ kingdoms
c legendary _____ hero
d world's most _____ sorcerer!
e This is Sinbad's _____ adventure!
f See the _____ battle ...
g The _____ magic of Dynarama ...
h ... recreate the _____ breathtaking adventure

3 How do you find the language used to describe the film 'Sinbad'? What kind of nouns and adjectives are used to create this effect? Discuss your thoughts with your partner.

4 Mark the following statements about the film Ben-Hur, true (T) or false (F).

a Ben-Hur was a slave who became a prince. ☐
b Ben-Hur talks about the day that Rome falls. ☐
c Quintas Arrias, Ben Hur's enemy is saved by Ben-Hur. ☐
d Ben-Hur and Quintas Arrias didn't become good friends. ☐
e Messala was once Ben-Hur's enemy and now his best friend. ☐
f The narrator says that nothing is better than actually watching the film. ☐

After watching

5 Now think of your own film hero. He/she can be from any era. Write 6-8 sentences to describe this person. You can use some of the words from Ex. 2.

© Pearson Education Limited 2006 – Photocopiable

Before watching

1   Imagine you are preparing to sail solo around the world. Write three sentences using *must/mustn' t*, *have to/have got to* and *should* to describe how you would prepare for the journey.

a _____

b _____

c _____

2   Now imagine the journey! Write a sentence to describe the trip using each of the words in the box.

(risk   endurance   fitness   gamble   substantial)

a _____

b _____

c _____

d _____

e _____

While watching

3   Watch the film and then answer the following questions.

a   By how many hours did Ellen break the previous world record?

b   What type of technology was in her boat? What do you think this means?

c   Which race prepared her well in 2001?

d   Which three roles did she need to play in this race?

e   What particular challenge faced her in the Southern Ocean?

f   One thing is particularly essential for solo sailing. What is it?

g   What does the narrator describe sleep as? A l _____ .

h   On average, how long does Ellen sleep a day?

4   Watch the film again and replace the <u>underlined</u> words with the actual words that are used in the film.

a   ... <u>packed with</u> space age technology.

b   ... racing yacht ever <u>constructed</u>.

c   ... strong both physically and <u>emotionally</u>.

d   ... <u>fix</u> a broken mast ...

e   'I'm just <u>so tired!</u>'

f   ... the middle of a <u>large</u> ocean ...

g   ... to give her <u>sufficient</u> energy ...

h   A solo sailor needs skill, determination, <u>bravery</u> and strength.

After watching

5   Imagine you are going to interview Ellen MacArthur. Prepare six questions to ask her. Roleplay the interview with a partner. Answer spontaneously to each question.

© Pearson Education Limited 2006 – Photocopiable

Before watching

1 The sentences below all involve reminiscing about the past. Fill in the gaps with one of the words below.

> remember   memory   souvenir   memorable   reminds   reminiscing   nostalgic   forgetful

a I like _____ about a family holiday we all loved in Cornwall.
b I can clearly _____ beautiful golden sandy beaches with lovely clear blue sea.
c I once bought a lovely _____ that always _____ me of the holiday.
d It's good to have _____ moments where you recapture happy childhood family holidays.
e One of the most _____ moments was when we all went out on a boat and saw dolphins.
f I think that my _____ serves me well, though I can be _____ about some things.

While watching

2 Watch the first half of the film and match the moments from the film with words and phrases said during these moments.

Moments from the film

1 People quickly found out about our top performance sports car.
2 The car manual was read in great detail.
3 Everyone counts down to the car starting.
4 The family enjoyed wonderful holidays.
5 Dad catered for everything the family needed.
6 People always noticed the family when they arrived at campsites.
7 Whatever happened, the family always knew that Dad was best.
8 Dad didn't know it couldn't go on for ever.

Words and phrases

a ... cover to cover ...
b ... here we go ..., 5,4,3 ...
c ... news spread quickly ...
d ... holidays of a lifetime ...
e ... despite the occasional setback.
f ... it couldn't last forever ...
g ... our arrival would raise eyebrows
h ... answer our every need ...

3 Watch the second half of the film and fill in the gaps below.
a We'd grown up and it finally _____ on us that our Dad ...
b We were beginning to _____ that the captain perhaps wasn't the best driver ...
c I guess my Dad _____ it quite _____ driving.
d Even though Dad _____ to work on the car, he no longer had the _____ to lift up the bonnet.
e If he had, he_____ realised that the engine was now a solid lump of rust.
f Even though the car hadn't _____ for 10 years, it had always been _____ and insured.

After watching

4 Discuss.
1 How did the tone change from the first half of the film to the second half?
2 How did the children view their Dad in the first half? And in the second half?
3 Why do you think that their Dad had made sure the car was insured for the last 10 years despite not even driving or moving it?
4 What did you like or dislike about this home movie?

© Pearson Education Limited 2006 – Photocopiable

Before watching

1 Discuss.

a What do you think are the advantages of travelling as an independent traveller?

b If you could choose two places, where would you travel independently?

c What sort of accommodation would you a) expect and b) be happy to settle for?

d If you only had a medium rucksack, how would you pack to cater for both subzero temperatures and scorching ones?

e Imagine you were bitten by the travel bug. In an ideal world, what would be the best way to organise each year so that you had both enough time to travel but could also earn enough money to travel?

While watching

2 Read the following statements about Bhutan. Now watch the film and mark the statements true (T) or false (F). If the statement is false, write the correct fact.

a Michael Palin uses stone imagery to compare the size of Bhutan with China and India. ☐

b There are hardly any mountains and forests in Bhutan. ☐

c Men are expected to wear national costume. ☐

d Michael Palin likes to look chic and smart when travelling. ☐

e Bhutan is the same size as Switzerland. ☐

f Its environmental policy is quite relaxed. ☐

g In at least 50% of the country's national parks, wood cannot be collected. ☐

h The King is not very popular. ☐

i Bhutan wants as much tourism as possible. ☐

j Mountain ranges divide the country into a series of steep valleys. ☐

After watching

3 Match the phrases from the film on the left with their meaning on the right

1 tiny pebble, ... between China and India

2 borders on Tibet....

3 favour the international dishevelled look

4 room to move...

5 strictest environmental policies..

6 not even fallen wood can be gathered

7 declared policy...

8 fled and left the valley

9 keep tourist numbers manageable

10 conditioned mentally and physically by...

a *governed*

b *able to cope*

c *ran away*

d *announced*

e *collected*

f *sternest*

g *space to*

h *like*

i *is on the edge of*

j *very small*

4 Use six of the underlined words above to write a short summary of the film.

© Pearson Education Limited 2006 – Photocopiable

Before watching

1 Read the following extract from a diary of a Viking Re-enactor and mark the statements below either true (T) or false (F).

I recently joined a Re-enactment society, as I'm really interested in that period of history and ignored all my friends telling me it's a very far-fetched idea! Some people have quite monotonous weekends, but you can't use that word to describe a weekend in a Viking camp! I decided not to worry about being excessive and bought a fabulous Viking costume to wear. My fellow Vikings were very impressed. Some of them had some really extravagant costumes. One man had what seemed like an extra-large Viking hat - I'm surprised he could walk in it! At the end of the weekend I thought it had definitely been worth it, and it's an experience I will enjoy again without doubt! Unusual perhaps, but great fun!

a The writer took notice of her friends' comments about Re-enactment societies. ___

b A weekend in a Viking camp couldn't be described as boring. ___

c The writer was anxious about going too far with her costume ___

d Her fellow Vikings liked her costume. ___

e It is doubtful as to whether she will do another Viking re-enactment weekend. ___

While watching

2 Watch the film and then answer the following questions.

a What is Old Sarum?

b What do these people wear in order to fight?

c Speaker one says he has had a long interest in three things. Which three things?

d Speaker one confirms that it is a c_____ environment where the Re-enactors try not to hurt each other when they fight.

e Speaker three has no problems switching from character back into his modern personality. What does he find it easy to do?

f How do the people here want their medieval camp to be?

g What does speaker four think of having to make your own Viking clothes?

h As a craftsman, what is the blacksmith responsible for?

i How does the final female speaker view the Dark Ages?

j Which words are used to describe what the re-enactors become when they leave behind their jobs as accountants, builders and shop keepers?

After watching

3 Look at some of the phrases below which are used in the film.

> obsessed with   go to such extremes   pointed me in the right direction   I haven't looked back ...   I got into this because of my love ...   I don't have any problem with ...   You get a lot of ... out of it   I find it easy to ...   ... to take it a bit far ...

Imagine you are interviewing the diary writer from Ex. 1 or one of the re-enactors from the film. Write out the dialogue and role play it with your partner. Write at least five questions and answers using as many of the words/phrases above as you can.

© Pearson Education Limited 2006 – Photocopiable

Before watching

1 What do you think are the secrets of succeeding in business? Work with your partner to decide on five key things that you must do/ways you must think to be successful.

1 _____
2 _____
3 _____
4 _____
5 _____

2 Rewrite or add to any of your five points above to include some of the vocabulary below.

> go under   have a go   give up   come up with   proactive   single-minded
> really   extremely   absolutely   important   vital

While watching

3 You are going to hear some advice on succeeding in business given by a milliner, web consultant, quantity surveyor, street performers, Indian takeaway owner, card maker and Internet entrepreneur. Watch the film and identify who says the advice below.

a You will find your own skill one day and you will do well.
b My advice to you is 'know your customer'.
c Choose your business partners very carefully!
d A good business is a good idea.
e Always remember you don't have to work for someone else.
f Find a professional body that deals with start up businesses who'll help you put your ideas into action.
g I'm already financially successful … I love what I do.

4 Watch the film again and answer the following questions.

a How does the milliner comment on his financial success?
b What is the estimated turnover of the web consultant's company?
c How long ago did the quantity surveyor leave school?
d What is the name of Joanne McKinley's business?
e What does the company, Creature Feature specialise in?
f How much experience did the Indian takeaway owner have before he started?
g What was the Internet entrepreneur's motivation for starting his own company?

After watching

5 You have already thought about a business you would like to set up in the Students' Book. Now develop that idea with a plan of action! What are you going to do to get this business off the ground? Write eight action points. Think about the things in the box.

> advertising   market research   funding   your partner(s)   your product

© Pearson Education Limited 2006 – Photocopiable

Before watching

1 Read the following sentences and then fill each gap with one of the words below. One of the words is used twice. (You may have to change the tense of some of the verbs.)

> fraud   convict   sentence   sue   arson   appeal

a   The gang who stole the gold bullion _____ against their prison _____ .

b   The gang claimed they had been wrongly _____ .

c   The trial of the gold bullion gang was very dramatic with one of the defending lawyers threatening to _____ the newspapers for what they were saying about the suspected criminals.

d   The drama intensified when the gold bullion office was burnt down suspiciously in the middle of the night before the _____ was passed. Despite the suspicious circumstances it turned out to be a case of _____ - someone wanted to watch the office burn.

e   It also turned out that one of the suspects had previously been arrested for suspicious dealings with money - he had been accused of _____ .

While watching

2 Watch the film and underline the correct word in each of the following sentences.

a   The order for tomorrow is for *£212/£222*.

b   Mr. Holland's boss says that Mr. Holland is *dependable/independent* to the last.

c   Mr. Holland believes that he will always have *happy/sad* memories of the gold bullion office.

d   A little extra money will make a *big/not much* difference to Mr. Holland.

e   Mr. Richards will get his deposit back when the gold *enters/leaves* the bank.

f   The driver of the bullion van is sure that the suspicious vehicle was a *police car/taxi*.

g   The man on the bicycle tells the van driver he has *one/two* flat tyre(s).

h   The Police Inspector reports that it's a *mauve/maroon*-coloured van.

i   The Police Inspector reports the bullion value to be *one/two million*.

After watching

3 Imagine a friend is telling you all about the gold bullion robbery. Work with your partner to write a dialogue between you and your friend. Use as many of the conversational expressions below as you can.

> Go on …   Fancy that …   Pull the other one!   You're kidding!
> The way it goes is that … Cross my heart …

4 Now role play the dialogue with your partner. Swap roles when you've finished.

© Pearson Education Limited 2006 – Photocopiable

Before watching

1   In the film extract you are going to watch, the Prime Minister is asked the question: *Could we just talk about your appearance for a moment?* Discuss the questions below.

   a   Do you think that a politician's physical appearance is important? Why/Why not?

   b   What is the typical appearance of a politician in your country?

   c   In the film extract it is suggested that the Prime Minister's grey hair is darkened? Why might this be?

While watching

2a   Listen to the Prime Minister's opening speech and fill in the gaps below.

   Prime Minister: 'Let us be a) _____ clear about this. We cannot go on b)_____ ourselves more than we c) _____ . The rest of the world does not d) _____ us a living. We must be e)_____ to make sacrifices ... . Who f)_____ this rubbish?'

   Advisor: 'You g)_____ Prime Minister. It's one of your h)_____ speeches.'

   Prime Minister: 'How I)_____ that Godfrey?'

   Godfrey: 'Um ... excellent Prime Minister. Just one thing ...J)_____ you be k)_____ those glasses?'

  b   The Prime Minister in the film extract dismisses a sincere speech as 'rubbish'. Why do you think he says this?

3   Now watch the rest of the film and answer the following questions.

   a   At the end of the exchange about the pair of glasses how does the Prime Minister confess he would like to look?

   b   What does Godfrey think about the Prime Minister's idea of starting with his glasses on and then taking them off?

   c   When Godfrey comments that the Prime Minister's face looks a bit wooden, what does he suggest the tele prompter could turn the PM into? What does he mean by this?

   d   What is so funny about the way the PM then delivers his speech beginning 'Defence expenditure '?

   e   If the PM were to combine a lightish jacket with a darkish waist coat, what effect would this have according to Godfrey?

   f   The PM is described to have a receding hairline. What do you think this means?

   g   How is the PM's forehead described?

   h   What is the PM finally asked to do?

After watching

4   Imagine you are interviewing the Prime Minister, Jim Hacker. Ask him questions on the following variety of topics:

   1   politician's wages

   2   his favourite holiday destination

   3   his relationship with his cabinet colleagues

   4   how he finds his role as Prime Minister

   5   what he does to relax

   6   how important he thinks image is in today's political world.

You can interpret Jim Hacker's character how you like from the film extract. Write your questions and then roleplay the scene with your partner.

© Pearson Education Limited 2006 – Photocopiable

Teaching notes

Unit 1 Good relations

OPTIONAL WARMER

Write *Charles Dickens* on the board. Ask Ss to write down as many books or characters as they can. (*Oliver Twist*, *Bleak House*, *Great Expectations*, *A Tale of Two Cities*, *Barnaby Rudge*, *A Christmas Carol*.) Or, ask Ss to name some classics of English literature.

Before watching

1 ▶ Ss match the sentence halves in each column to form complete sentences. Elicit answers from Ss.

> **Answers:** 1b 2 c 3 a 4 f 5 d 6 e

2 ▶ Elicit a number of problems Ss might have and write these on the board. Ask Ss to discuss who they would go to for help. (Certain people might be better suited for helping with particular problems.) Encourage Ss to use phrasal verbs from Ex. 1

While watching

3 ▶ Ask Ss to read through the sentences. Then, play the film allowing Ss to put them in the correct order.

▶ Play the film again for Ss to check answers. Get feedback.

> **Answers:** a 4 b 5 c 8 d 1 e 3 f 7 g 2 h 6

4 ▶ Get Ss to work in pairs to predict which words may fill the gaps. Play the film allowing Ss to make notes. Play the film again for Ss to check answers. Get Ss to compare their answers with a partner. Elicit answers.

> **Answers:** 1 bear, sorrow, common, uncommon
> 2 many, learned, calamity, Doubtless 3 property,
> right, dispose 4 lucky, able

After watching

5 ▶ Ask Ss to think about Uncle Ralph's personality and to write a short description of him.

> **Possible answer:** He is stern and unsympathetic to his family. He doesn't appear to be sad at the loss of his brother. He displays some anger that Mrs Nickleby is seeking help from him. He is authoritative and bossy.

6a ▶ Ask Ss to think about what sort of person Nicholas is and to write a short description of him.

> **Possible answer:** He seems a very caring man, who is concerned for the welfare of his mother and sister. Nicholas is very polite and seems eager to please too.

b ▶ Ask Ss to compare their impressions in pairs.

OPTIONAL EXTENSION

Ask Ss to write the next scene of the book.

Unit 2 Dream career

OPTIONAL WARMER

Write *fashion designer* on the board. Get Ss to think of as many fashion designers as they can and to write a word or two for each one to summarise their style.

Before watching

1 ▶ Ss work in pairs to decide on some dream careers. Ss then identify qualities needed to fulfil each of these dream careers. Then allow pairs to swap so Ss can read other pair's choices. Refer Ss to the key vocabulary box on page 31 of the Students' Book to help them.

2 ▶ Ss think about and write down the qualities needed to be a fashion designer.

> **Possible answers:** creative flair, a good eye for detail, sociable personality - dealing with variety of fashion world characters, endurance/mental strength - long hours of work to get things absolutely right

While watching

3 ▶ Get Ss to read through the sentences before playing the film. Play the film through allowing Ss to make notes.

▶ Play the film through once again for Ss to check answers. Elicit answers from Ss.

> **Answers:** 1 urban   2 twenty-four   3 Oxford Circus
> 4 large department stores   5 Sindy   6 hard
> 7 energy   8 four   9 self-motivation   10 privileged
> 11 more   12 potential

After watching

4a ▶ Ss write a short description of a typical working day of their dream career using the words in the box.

> **Possible answer:** Ballet Dancer: Every day I get up early to prepare mentally for the busy day ahead. I work with other dancers and the choreography team to come up with new ideas for routines. Qualities such as physical fitness and mental strength are necessary to cope with long practice hours and daily performances. I don't earn a lot of money but I feel very creatively fulfilled. My ambition is to dance the lead in Swan Lake.

b ▶ Ss read out their typical working day one line at a time. At the end of each line their partner has to guess what they think the dream career is. At the end of the activity ask Ss to volunteer to read their descriptions out to the class for other Ss to try and guess. You can also read out the ballet dancer description.

OPTIONAL EXTENSION

Ss write a glowing review for Lindsay's sportsware.

Unit 3   Film Heroes

OPTIONAL WARMER

Write on the board: 'What makes a film hero?' Ask: Ss to discuss this question in pairs. Elicit feedback.

Before watching

1 ▶ Ss discuss the questions in pairs. Ask them to make some notes of each other's responses. Get class feedback.

While watching

2 ▶ Tell Ss they are going to watch a trailer for the adventure film 'Sinbad'. Get the Ss to predict the vocabulary that could fill the gaps.

▶ Play the film trailer through allowing Ss to make notes as they watch.

▶ Play the film through up until the same point again so that Ss can check their answers. Ss can compare in pairs. Elicit answers from the class.

> **Answers:** a heros b forgotten c super d powerful
> e greatest f spectacular g incredible h enchanting

3 ▶ Get Ss to discuss the questions in pairs. Get whole class feedback.

> **Possible answer:** The nouns and adjectives used together are very dramatic and create a very theatrical sense of drama. There are *heros*, *demons*, *sorcerers*, *adventures* and *battles* all described using equally powerful adjectives such as *super*, *powerful*, *greatest*, *spectacular*, *incredible* and *enchanting*. This, together with the music create a very strong impression of the film.

4 ▶ Tell Ss that they are going to watch a trailer for the adventure film 'Ben-Hur'. Get Ss to read through the statements.

▶ Play the film allowing Ss to mark true and false and make notes.

▶ Play the film through again for Ss to check their answers. Elicit answers from the class.

> **Answers:** a F - he was a Prince who became a slave
> b T   c T   d F - they became good friends   e F - he used to be his best friend and now is his enemy   f T

After watching

5 ▶ Get Ss to think why this character is heroic - what is it about their personality or their actions that make them a hero? Ss could use some of the words from Ex.2. Ss swap with their partners at the end to read each others film hero description. Ask Ss to underline any mistakes.

OPTIONAL EXTENSION

Ss find three other students to describe their film hero to. Encourage Ss to listen to each other's descriptions and then ask each other questions about the film hero/heroine and their reasons for choosing them.

Unit 4   Ellen MacArthur

OPTIONAL WARMER

Ask Ss to work in pairs and think of two ways of travelling round the world. They can think of the means of transport as well as good routes to take. E.g. cycling across continents and taking a boat or a plane across oceans. Ask for class feedback.

Before watching

1 ▶ Ss revise grammar from unit 4 expressing obligation. Ask Ss to write sentences describing how they would prepare for a sailing trip round the world. Get Ss to think about diet, fitness, clothing and equipment. Get whole class feedback, writing example sentences on the board.

2 ▶ Ask Ss to work in pairs to decide the meanings of the words in the box. Give out dictionaries, if necessary. Then, ask Ss to work together and write sentences using each of the words to describe the trip.   Ex. 1 will help Ss with possible content. Get class feedback by asking Ss to share one or two sentences with the class. Write them on the board.

While watching

3 ▶ Tell Ss they are going to watch a film about Ellen MacArthur's solo sailing trip around the world. Get Ss to read through the questions.

▶ Play the film through allowing Ss to make notes.

▶ Give Ss time to complete any notes, then play the film again for Ss to check answers. Elicit answers.

> **Answers:** a 33   b space-age - very advanced and state of the art equipment   c The Bombay Globe
> d Navigator, Captain and Crew   e she had to repair a broken mast during a storm   f absolute fitness
> g luxury   h two hours

4 ▶ Get Ss to read through the phrases/sentences. Explain to Ss that they must watch carefully and replace the underlined words with the actual words used in the film. Play the film once allowing Ss to make notes.

▶ Play the film again for Ss to check their answers. Elicit answers from Ss.

> **Answers:** a full of b built   c mentally   d repair
> e exhausted f massive g enough h courage

After watching

5 ▶ Ask Ss to work in pairs and make up interview questions using the content of the film. They can add their own details to substantiate any questions or answers. Ensure Ss do not write down their answers before the interview but answer spontaneously. Ss role play the interview in pairs and then swap roles. Ask any confident Ss to role play to the class.

OPTIONAL EXTENSION

Ss write a summary of their interview with Ellen MacArthur using vocabulary from the film.

Unit 5 Home Road Movie

OPTIONAL WARMER

Ask Ss to recollect a memory from their childhood - it can be connected with school, a holiday, riding a bike, friends, the park, food, a party, etc. Ask Ss to relate the memory to their partner, and ask Ss to notice whether or not remembering it as an adult makes them perceive it differently at all.

Before watching

1 ▶ Ask Ss to read the sentences and the words, and then fill in the gaps. Get Ss to compare answers with their partner before you get whole class feedback.

> **Answers:** a reminiscing b remember c souvenir, reminds d nostalgic e memorable f memory, forgetful

While watching

2 ▶ Tell Ss that they are going to watch a film which involves someone reminiscing about past family holidays. Ask Ss to read 1-8 and also the phrases a-h. Get Ss to predict which sentences might match which phrases. Play the first half of the film up until ...'*We had reached the top. He didn't know it couldn't last,...*' allowing Ss to make notes. Play again for Ss to check their answers.

> **Answers:** 1 c 2 a 3 b 4 d 5 h 6 g 7 e 8 f

3 ▶ Play the second half of the film allowing Ss to make notes. Ss fill in the gaps. Play the second half of film again for Ss to check their answers.

> **Answers:** a dawned b realise c found, stressful d continued, courage e would have f moved, taxed

4 ▶ Ask Ss to individually write down their answers to the questions before they discuss them with a partner.

> **Suggested answers:** 1 there's an excitement and optimism about these fantastic summer holidays in the first half which changes to a rather sad realisation that perhaps everything wasn't as wonderful as they thought when they reflect back as adults. 2 They thought their Dad was invincible, the power behind the fantastic car! 3 They realised that perhaps Dad wasn't quite as invincible as they thought and like anyone he has flaws. 4 Their Dad liked to play things safe as well as part of him perhaps thinking the car would regain its former glory. 5 Ss own answers.

OPTIONAL EXTENSION

Ask Ss to work in pairs to write a short review of the Home Road Movie. Ask them to write three or four facts and three or four sentences expressing their own view.

Unit 6 Bhutan

OPTIONAL WARMER

Write *exploration* on the board and ask Ss to brainstorm as many words connected with exploration as possible. Encourage Ss to remember key vocabulary from unit 6. Ask for class feedback, and get Ss to write down any new words in their vocabulary notebooks.

Before watching

1 ▶ Ask Ss to work together in pairs or small groups to discuss the questions. Monitor the discussions and make notes of interesting answers. Ask one person of each pair or small group to feedback to the class briefly. Encourage other Ss to ask speakers questions.

While watching

2 ▶ Tell Ss that they are going to watch a film about an independent traveller, Michael Palin, travelling in Bhutan. Ask Ss to read the sentences about Bhutan. Play the film through allowing Ss to mark the statements true (T) or false (F) and to make notes.

▶ Play the film through once more for Ss to check their answers. Elicit answers from Ss encouraging them to supply as much vocabulary as possible where the statements are false.

> **Answers:** a T b F - Bhutan is mostly mountain and forest c T d F - he favours the international dishevelled look e T f F - it is one of the strictest in the world g F - in at least 25% of the country's national parks ... h F - the king is much loved i F - Bhutan has taken deliberate steps to make tourism manageable. j T

After watching

3 ▶ Ss match the words on the left with their synonyms on the right. Ss can compare answers with their partner. Elicit answers from Ss.

> **Answers:** 1 very small 2 is on the edge of 3 like 4 space to 5 sternest 6 collected 7 announced 8 ran away 9 able to cope 10 governed

4 ▶ Ask Ss to choose six of the words from Ex. 3 to write a summary summarising the film of Bhutan. Ss swap with each other and underline any mistakes. Ask some Ss to read theirs out to the class for a class feedback session.

OPTIONAL EXTENSION

If Ss have access to the Internet, ask them to choose another small country in the world and use the Internet to find out 8-10 facts about it. They note these down and bring their summary into class to share their findings with Ss.

Unit 7 Vikings

OPTIONAL WARMER

Ask Ss to think of as many unusual ways to spend weekends as they can. Use the example of the Re-enactors to start them off.

Before watching

1 ▶ Ask Ss to read the diary extract and then the sentences which follow. Ask Ss to decide whether each of the sentences is true or false. Elicit answers from the class.

> **Answers:** a false b true c false d true e false

While watching

2 ▶ Tell Ss they are going to watch a film about a group of Viking re-enactors. Ask Ss to read the questions and predict what the answers may be.

▶ Play the film to the end allowing Ss to make notes.

▶ Play the film again for Ss to check their answers. Elicit answers from the class.

> **Answers:** a an ancient fort in England b armour c history, war gaming and warfare d controlled e compartmentalise his life f as authentic as possible g it's fun! h making his own tools and pretty much everybody else's tools i they're not as dark as often perceived j fierce warriors

After watching

3 ▶ Ss review the words and phrases from the film and use these to write both questions and answers for an interview with one of the re-enactors. Ss work in pairs to write the dialogue. Ss then roleplay their dialogues with a partner. When they swap dialogues to role play again, they should swap roles.

OPTIONAL EXTENSION

Ss work in pairs to create a mini advertisement for a special interests magazine promoting re-enactment weekends. Ask them to use at least two passive constructions in their advert. Encourage them to use the information from the exercises they have done in the DVD worksheet for content. Monitor Ss to make sure that they are succinct with language and not over wordy. At the end of the activity ask pairs to swap with each other to read each other's adverts. Then ask Ss to read their adverts out to the class as feedback.

Unit 8 The secrets of success

OPTIONAL WARMER

Ask Ss to list as many well-known successful business entrepreneurs as they can. Ask for class feedback and write entrepreneurs and their trade on the board.

Before watching

1 ▶ Ss brainstorm five key business success factors in pairs. They can draw upon examples set by the entrepreneurs listed in the warmer. Elicit class feedback.

2 ▶ Ss fine tune their sentences from Ex. 1 or add more sentences and try to include relevant key vocabulary from unit 8. Eg: *It's important to review the business regularly and come up with new ideas for generating business.*

While watching

3 ▶ Ss read through the statements before watching. Play the film through allowing Ss to write the person who said each statement next to each one.

▶ Play the film once more to give Ss chance to check their answers. Elicit answers from Ss.

> **Answers:** a Internet entrepreneur b Indian takeaway owner c street performers d card maker e quantity surveyor f web consultant g milliner

4 ▶ Get the Ss to read the comprehension questions and in pairs, predict what the answers might be. Play the film through again allowing Ss to make notes.

▶ Play the film once more to give Ss a chance to check their answers. Elicit answers from Ss.

> **Answers:** a Despite being financially successful, he is not in it for the money. b £200,000 c eight years ago d The Giant Card Company e street theatre, masks and stilts f a little bit g He was dyslexic and told he couldn't do anything with his life.

After watching

5 ▶ Get Ss to refer back to their notes from unit 8, SB DVD page 159, Ex.2: '*If you had the chance to set up your own business, what would it be?*' Ss build on this idea, and develop a plan of action to get this business going. Encourage Ss to draw upon the advice given in the film in Ex. 3, and the vocabulary from unit 8. Ss swap with their partners to compare each other's plans.

OPTIONAL EXTENSION

Divide class into groups of four. Two Ss in the group present their action plans to the other two Ss who must decide whether to give them financial support. To decide this, they must ask the Ss questions to check that the business is viable. When both Ss' plans have been approved, Ss swap roles.

Unit 9   The Bullion Robbery

OPTIONAL WARMER

Ask Ss to discuss with their partner their favourite crime/robbery film. What was good about it? Plot? Characters? Ending? Cinematic effects? Actors/ actresses?

Before watching

1 ▶ Ask Ss to read the key vocabulary words in the box from unit 9. Get Ss to work with their partner to fill in the gaps of the 'mini gold bullion trial' gap fill. Elicit answers from Ss.

> **Answers:** a appealed, sentence   b convicted   c sue
> d sentence, arson   e fraud

While watching

2 ▶ Tell Ss that they are going to watch an extract from a film about a gold bullion robbery. Get Ss to read the sentences before watching the film.

▶ Play the film allowing Ss to underline the correct words.

▶ Play the film again for Ss to check answers. Get Ss to compare their answers with their partner, and then elicit answers from Ss.

> **Answers:** a £212   b dependable   c happy   d big
> e enters   f police car   g one   h maroon   I one

After watching

3 ▶ Ss work in pairs to quickly review the key points of the film plot focussing on the robbery: a) why did the van stop? b) why were there no drivers in the van to allow the robbery to take place? c) were there any other people around? d how scared did Mr Holland look?

▶ Ask Ss to then write a dialogue between a person who has heard/read about the robbery and is telling the story and a person who is listening and exclaiming at the story. Encourage Ss to use as many of the conversational expressions listed as they can.

4 ▶ Ask Ss to roleplay their dialogues with a partner. Get Ss to swap roles so that they have a turn at each character. Choose some pairs to act out their dialogues to the class.

OPTIONAL EXTENSION

Ss write a news report about the bullion robbery. Dictate the following commonly misspelt words. Tell Ss to try to include at least four of the words in their report. Monitor as Ss work to check that they are using the words naturally and in the right context.

robbery, thief, witness, drama, last-minute, speeding, middle-aged

Ss could then swap reports with each other and try to add additional sentences in each other's reports using an extra one or two of the words.

Unit 10   Yes, Prime Minister

OPTIONAL WARMER

Ask Ss to name as many world leaders together with their particular notable achievement as they can. Ask for class feedback.

Before watching

1 ▶ Ss make notes of their answers to the questions individually, then discuss their answers with a partner.

> **Answer** (Ex.1c): The hair could be darkened to make him look younger.

While Watching

2a ▶ Ask Ss to read the passage and predict what the words could be. Play the film up until the line ...'*will you be wearing those glasses?*' Allow Ss to make notes.

▶ Play the extract once more for Ss to check answers. Elicit answers from Ss.

> **Answers:** a abundantly   b paying   c earn   d owe
> e prepared   f wrote   g did   h old   i was   j will
> k wearing

b ▶ Ss discuss this question in pairs. Get feedback.

> **Answer:** Because what he can actually do in reality may be different to the sincerity of the speech!

3 ▶ Get Ss to read through the questions. Play the rest of the film, allowing Ss to make notes.

▶ Play the film once again for Ss to check their answers. Elicit answers from Ss.

> **Answers:** a authoritative and honest   b He
> thinks that would look indecisive.   c a zombie - an
> expressionless character with no communication skills
> d He over exaggerates his movements in an attempt
> not to look like a zombie!   e It would look like the PM
> has an identity problem!   f His hairline is moving back
> – i.e. he is getting balder.   g a high forehead   h to
> smile (to show his teeth)!

After watching

4 ▶ Ask Ss to imagine they are interviewing Jim Hacker for a popular magazine and write out questions from the prompts (topics 1-6) to ask him. Elicit/explain the meaning of 'cabinet colleagues'. Tell Ss to role play the dialogue each taking turns to play the role of Jim Hacker. Monitor the activity and ask some pairs to role play to the class. Ss only write down the questions but produce spontaneous answers without writing them down first.

OPTIONAL EXTENSION

Ss write up their interview for the magazine. Ss do not rewrite the questions, only the spontaneous answers they received. Refer Ss to the useful vocabulary in the Key Vocabulary box (Belief and Opinion) of SB p.143.

Tests

Test A Units 1-5

Grammar

question tags

1 Complete the following sentences with a suitable question tag.

You have worked here for a long time, <u>haven't you?</u>

1 Nothing will happen, _____?

2 Take a sandwich, _____?

3 Let's go out for dinner tonight, _____?

4 I'm taller than David, _____?

5 Somebody was in this room earlier, _____?

6 She hardly ever goes out, _____?

(**3 points**)

present/future modals of possibility

2 Select the correct option.

I haven't seen Bill since lunchtime but he can/<u>could</u>/can't be back in his office so why not have a look there?

1 Linda got the pay rise that she was looking for so she must/may/might be very happy.

2 Why don't you go to that meeting? You never know, it can't/might/should be very interesting.

3 I'm not sure where the kids are right now but they could/can/must be playing in the back garden. I'll go and check.

4 I have just seen John walking about and singing so he mustn't/may/can't be very ill.

(**2 points**)

futures overview

3 Put the verbs in brackets into the correct future form using *will, going to, be bound to* or *the present continuous.*

Jane has eaten far too much chocolate. She <u>is going to feel</u> (feel) sick.

1 I _____ (meet) some of my university friends for a drink around eight this evening. Would you like to come?

2 Karen and Ted _____ (buy) a new house some time next year.

3 I don't know for sure but I think next week's dinner _____ (be) in an Italian restaurant.

4 Ah! So you're going there now. Hold on, I _____ (come) with you.

5 No doubt about it. Ray's team _____ (win) this match because they have much better players.

6 Louise doesn't like the tight deadline she has been given. She _____ (speak) to her boss about it.

(**3 points**)

in case

4 Fill the gaps with either a verb in the correct tense or another suitable word.

I took my mobile phone with me in case someone <u>wanted</u> to contact me urgently.

1 I think I'll take a good book with me tomorrow in case I _____ bored.

2 It might be cold when we go there so take some winter clothes_____ in case.

3 I sent her another email just in case she _____ the first one.

4 We took some sandwiches in case we _____ hungry during the trip.

(**2 points**)

© Pearson Education Limited 2006 – Photocopiable

narrative tenses

5 Fill the gaps in this text by putting the verbs in brackets into an appropriate tense.

I remember when we _went_ (go) to Germany last year for an important meeting with a company called Köln electronics. They (1) _____ (invent) a new type of cable and we (2) _____ (want) to find out more about it. We could see that the Germans (3) _____ (prepare) this meeting for quite some time because their efficiency and professionalism when demonstrating the new product was impressive. While their production manager (4) _____ (show) us some important details on the performance of the new cable, however, I unfortunately (5) _____ (have) to leave the showroom prematurely because I (6)_____ (receive) an urgent message from my wife.

(**3 points**)

articles

6 Complete this text by inserting _the, a/an_ or no article (-).

During _the_ early years of (1) ___ Industrial Revolution, (2) ___ children who were as young as five years of age were required to do (3) ___rather heavy work such as helping to mine coal. (4) ___ adult's life, however, was also far from easy and throughout this Victorian period the average life expectancy for working class men and women was less than forty.

(**2 points**)

expressing obligation

7 Transform these sentences without changing their meaning using the word in brackets.

It was an obligation for us to wear a tie to work every day. (had)
We had to wear a tie to work every day.

1 Your job is to find out as much information about this as possible. (supposed)

2 He made a bad mistake in falling out with his boss. (shouldn't)

3 You are not obliged to speak in public if you don't want to. (have)

4 Before getting my present job, it was necessary for me to pass a series of difficult tests. (had)

5 There were no company laws that told us to lock all office doors after work. (have)

6 It would be an excellent idea to sort out this problem before continuing. (should)

(**3 points**)

emphasis

8 Fill the gaps in these sentences with a suitable word to create an emphatic effect.

_This place is _so_ beautiful that I will have to visit it again in the future._

1 This is _____ a big risk that I would prefer not to take it.

2 I don't particularly like her as a person but she _____ know how to act.

3 This is a very, _____ interesting story indeed!

4 We _____ don't want to cause you any further inconvenience.

(**2 points**)

© Pearson Education Limited 2006 – Photocopiable

used to/get used to/would

9 Select the correct option.

My grandfather used to be a very hard worker and he got used to/would/was used to sometimes work 14 hours a day.

1 This *used to/would/was used to* be a very quiet little town but it has changed a lot in recent years.

2 Gareth can be quite an awkward customer sometimes but now we are used *dealing/to dealing /to deal* with him.

3 It takes a while before many people *are used to/ used to/get used to* changes in their job.

4 I *was used to/got used to/would* often read adventure novels when I was a boy.

(2 points)

expressing ability

10 Fill the gaps in the text with ONE word only.

I *can* remember a great fishing adventure that I had on the South-west coast of Scotland when I was a young boy. My brother and I had to go down some potentially dangerous rocks in order to get near to the water. We (1) _____ both climb very well but on this occasion I slipped and fell onto a flat piece of rock about two metres below me. I got a terrible fright and at first I wasn't (2) _____ to move my right leg. After a few minutes, however, I (3) _____ to get up, although I was still in pain. In the end, I had a twisted ankle and some nasty bruises and I (4) _____ walk properly for quite some time. To cut a long story short, we succeeded (5) _____ catching an impressive number of very good fish despite this accident and the bad Scottish weather! Looking back, I'm afraid I really (6) _____ believe that we were mad enough to do these things!

(3 points)

(Total: 25 points)

Pronunciation

1 Put these words into the correct column according to the vowel sound of the underlined syllable.

/iː/	/eɪ/
colleague	wavelength

acquaintance labour loneliness previous

straight detail ancient afraid

antique lean shaven relieved

(4 points)

2 Underline the words that are stressed in these sentences.

We've got so many problems at work now.

1 I do believe that we still have an opportunity.

2 We talked about travelling, music and many, many more things.

3 It was definitely the job I liked doing most.

(3 points)

3 Mark the stressed syllable in these words.

lonely frustrated success

intellectual intellect responsibility

engineer satisfaction detail

apply resign redecorate

(3 points)

(Total: 10 points)

© Pearson Education Limited 2006 – Photocopiable

Vocabulary

1 Fill the gaps with the right word(s) to complete the phrasal verbs in each sentence.

I was surprised when I heard that Helen had split up with Roy because they always seemed so happy together.

1 I get ____ ____ Albert really well and it's quite frankly a pleasure to work with him.

2 I don't like the way Gerard tries to show ____ all the time. He really has nothing to prove.

3 After this incident I fell ____ ____ my sister and she didn't speak to me again for weeks.

4 I was brought ____ in quite a rough neighbourhood but when I was around twelve, we moved to a nicer area.

5 I really look ____ ____ Clare because she has so many good personal qualities.

6 Frank definitely takes ____ his father. They are very alike in many ways.

(**3 points**)

2 Choose the correct alternative for these sentences.

I have been selling gold and silver jewellery during/ since/for about two years now.

1 Raymond bought his new computer a week ago. *From that point on/Since then/Up until that point* he had been borrowing mine.

2 *Since/While/During* I was looking at some trendy leather jackets in the shop, I bumped into an old friend of mine.

3 My boss was complaining *in/throughout/up until* the whole meeting.

4 I will always remember my early days in London. *Since then/From that point on/At that time* I was doing at least two different jobs.

5 I graduated as a chartered accountant in 1998 and *since then/after that/at that time* I have been working for a large, multinational company.

6 Pauline is going to continue living in that flat *for/ from/until* early next year.

(**3 points**)

3 Unjumble the words about appearance in brackets to fill the gaps.

She had long straight, (thstriga) dark hair and green eyes.

1 I think you should buy that dress because it makes you look really _____. (aegnetll)

2 He had a rather _____ (fysurcf) appearance and looked as if he needed a shower, a good shave and a change of clothes.

3 She used to go to the beach a lot. I think that's why she always had such a _____ (ntndea) complexion.

4 The lead singer of Green Day often has _____ (yded), spiky hair.

5 Sheila told me she wants to go on a strict diet. She certainly isn't fat but perhaps she is a little on the _____ (bcyhbu) side.

6 Many middle-aged people are keen to hide their _____ (selrkiwn) by using face creams or getting plastic surgery.

7 He goes to the gym nearly every day. That's why he looks so _____ . (ruusmcla)

8 I am definitely a bit _____ (twoehigevr) at the moment so I think I'm going to have to lose a few kilos one way or another.

(**4 points**)

Total: 10 points

© Pearson Education Limited 2006 – Photocopiable

Test A Units 1-5

Reading

1 Read this text about inventors from India and answer the questions.

It is a motorcycle with a difference. By removing the back wheel and replacing it with a spiked cylinder, it doubles as a tractor. It was devised and built by Mansukhbhai, who could not afford to buy a tractor. This is just one example of the ideas that are <u>flooding</u> into the National Innovation Foundation, or NIF, in India. Its aim is to collect good ideas from ordinary people and develop them. The NIF has set up a special fund for individuals who have no bank account and yet have ideas for innovations that <u>warrant</u> investment of risk capital.

The foundation was established three years ago with a single <u>grant</u> of 200 million rupees ($4m). The members believe that these small-scale innovations are as important as those that are developed in big laboratories. 'There are innovators who innovate in the 'laboratories of life' and yet they never get recognised", they say. "Their innovations are as good or even more important. As far as India is concerned, when we say someone is <u>illiterate</u>, we tend to ignore them. We cannot really appreciate that they can be a genius.'

In a country with 600,000 villages where electricity and water still remain big problems, people continuously find alternative ways of meeting their needs. Like Sunda Ram Verma, who devised a technique of keeping plants alive in the desert without watering them more than once a year. He conserves the water under the ground that is normally lost to unwanted <u>weeds</u> and by water naturally rising up through the top soil. He does this by frequently breaking up the top layer of the soil after the first monsoon rains. Crops can be planted half a metre down to obtain the full benefit. One of the NIF's aims is to <u>patent</u> such ideas so that, if they are developed, the inventor gains, and no one else can come along and "borrow" the idea. Some of the NIF's innovators, however, are not waiting for patents – they are already marketing their inventions.

Another excellent invention comes from Balubhai Vasoya, who developed a <u>stove</u> that uses both kerosene and electricity. Running the stove for an hour costs one and a half rupees in total. No smell in the kitchen, no smoke, it burns just like natural gas.

From machines that wash cows to ones that remove cotton or make mats from palm leaves, the innovations keep pouring in. 16,000 people have sent in their ideas so far; and as word of the foundation's existence spreads, they are coming in faster and faster.

2 Look at the <u>underlined</u> words carefully in their context and select the correct definition.

flooding means *a) arriving in huge numbers* b) generating great interest c) arriving from time to time

1 to <u>warrant</u> means a) to guarantee b) to deserve c) to cause

2 <u>a grant</u> is a) economic aid for a project b) an investment c) a loan

3 <u>illiterate</u> refers to someone who a) doesn't have money to invest b) doesn't have academic qualifications c) can't read or write

4 <u>weeds</u> are a) insects that eat crops b) unproductive plants c) bad fertilizers

5 a <u>stove</u> is mainly for a) burning things b) cooking c) heating the house

6 to get a <u>patent</u> on an invention means the inventor a) can't sell his idea b) has the right to make and sell his invention and no one else has that right c) can 'borrow' other people's ideas

(6 points)

3 Answer the following questions in your own words as far as possible.

Why did Mansukhbhai invent his motorbike-tractor? He didn't have enough money to buy a tractor.

1 What does the author of the text mean exactly by the 'laboratories of life'?

2 Why are some people's inventions not considered in India and why is this a mistake?

3 Why do people in India constantly find alternative ways to meet their needs?

4 How does Sunda Ram Verma manage to save the underground water for plants in the desert?

5 Who benefits from the NIF's patents and why?

6 Are everyone's inventions protected? Why/Why not?

7 What are the advantages of Balubhai Vasoya's invention?

(14 points)

Total: 20 points

200

© Pearson Education Limited 2006 – Photocopiable

Listening

1 Select the correct alternative.

Carol had a) clear ideas b) some general ideas c) <u>no idea at all</u> about what career path to take when she was very young.

1 When things turn nasty, Carol believes that it is necessary to a) keep calm. b) intervene. c) give advice.

2 In the future she wants to a) go back to university. b) keep the same job. c) do evening classes.

3 Pete is a/an a) quality control manager. b) engineer. c) quantity surveyor.

4 In the long-term future, Pete a) wants to do the same job. b) isn't sure. c) wants to change his profession.

5 He is good at meeting deadlines thanks to a) his technology. b) his experience. c) his team of workers.

6 The thing he likes most about his work is a) the remuneration. b) job satisfaction. c) the flexibility it offers.

(**6 points**)

2 Answer the following questions.

Who convinced Carol to start a career as a social worker?
<u>A social worker she met at a party.</u>

1 Why was Carol interested in doing this type of work?

2 What can be unpleasant or stressful about her job?

3 What necessary qualities does she think she possesses for the job?

4 Why does Carol want to do something different?

5 What university qualification did Pete get?

6 Why does Carol think that Pete's job is challenging?

7 According to Pete, what two things must you have to be good at his job?

(**14 points**)

Total: 20 points

Writing

Choose ONE of the following topics and write a composition of about 250-300 words.

1 Describe the member of your family who you feel is most similar to you. In what ways has he/she influenced you during your life?

2 Describe your current job and state whether you like it or not and why. What things would you like to change in your workplace and/or about the job itself?
If you are not working at the moment, what type of job would you like to do in the future and why?

3 Describe a famous hero or heroine from your country and write about his/her most heroic actions.

4 In order to be successful in life, is it necessary to sometimes take risks? Give examples to support your opinion.

5 Tell the story of one of your most memorable experiences from the past.

(**15 points**)

100
points

© Pearson Education Limited 2006 – Photocopiable

Test B Units 1-5

Grammar

any/every/no/some

1 Fill the gaps in these sentences with the right word.

I think there is somebody in that room because I can hear chairs being moved.

1 George will get the promotion. At least that's what _____ in the office thinks.

2 I've looked _____ but I can't find my mobile phone.

3 She didn't have _____ to read, so I lent her a book.

4 I can't seem to be able to go _____ without getting lost.

5 You look thirsty. Would you like _____ to drink?

6 We would like to go _____ hot on holiday this year.

3 points

present/future modals of possibility

2 Choose the correct option to complete this dialogue.

Theresa: 'What's that noise?'

Jack: 'I'm not sure but it *must/can't/might* be some windows getting broken.'

Theresa: 'Don't be daft, Jack. It (1) *can't/could/ mustn't* be that. It sounds more like a thudding noise than a crash. Ah! That's right. Our neighbours are moving out today. Someone (2) *must/should/can* be dropping heavy boxes.'

Jack: 'You (3) *can/have to/may* be right but I really think it does sound like something being broken. Listen! That's our dog barking. Someone (4) *would/must/ couldn't* be in our garden.'

2 points

futures overview

3 Fill the gaps in this short text with a suitable verb of your choice using *will, going to, be bound to* or *the present continuous*.

Tonight we *are having* dinner in a very good restaurant. We (1)_____ a really good time as a well-known comedian (2)_____ some jokes and sing a few songs. I think this (3)_____ a night to remember for quite some time to come and to make the weekend complete, we (4)_____ to a jazz concert tomorrow night at The Royal Albert Hall. I have already bought the tickets.

2 points

Future Perfect and Continuous

4 Using either the Future Perfect or Continuous, complete these sentences with the verb in brackets.

At 8pm tomorrow evening I'll be studying for my English exam.

1 When you arrive, I _____ (finish) my work for the day so we'll be able to go out for a drink immediately.

2 By the time I phone her this afternoon, she _____ (receive) my email.

3 At this time on Tuesday I _____ (lie) on a beach in Greece. I can't wait.

4 Before the end of the day I _____ (send) my report to Paris because it's urgent.

5 Just after Christmas Nicola _____ (work) in a different company.

6 Please don't phone between one and four o'clock because I _____ (drive) to Birmingham then.

3 points

© Pearson Education Limited 2006 – Photocopiable

narrative tenses

5 Put the verb in brackets into the correct tense.

As soon as he <u>arrived</u> (arrive) home he switched on the TV.

1 He_____ (work) on his last project for quite some time before his tragic death.

2 We_____ (stand) in a long queue when the ticket office closed.

3 I grabbed my jacket from the wardrobe and literally _____ (run) down the stairs.

4 She made herself a nice cup of tea after she _____ (put) the kids to bed.

(**2 points**)

adjectives and adverbs

6 Use adverbs derived from the underlined words and rewrite the sentences.

It is <u>usual</u> for us to buy trendy clothes.
We usually buy trendy clothes.

1 Samantha is very <u>good</u> at playing tennis.

2 It was a <u>surprise</u> that they lost the match.

3 It is <u>probable</u> that they will come back to visit us again in the future.

4 It was me who made that mistake but it was <u>unintentional</u>.

5 I will fly to Rome on business next week and this is <u>definite</u>.

6 This computer has been programmed by <u>experts.</u>

(**3 points**)

if structures (1)

7 Put the verb in brackets into the correct tense or form.

If they <u>had obeyed</u> (obey) the safety regulations, they wouldn't have had the accident.

1 If you finish work early, _____ (give) me a call and we can go to the cinema.

2 If we had been better prepared, we_____

(not lose) the contract.

3 If I get paid today, I_____ (buy) a new woollen sweater this evening.

4 If we_____ (be given) an opportunity like this, we would take it without even thinking.

5 I would have saved a lot of time if I_____ (think) of that earlier.

6 If I had longer holidays in the summer, I_____ (travel) to Asia.

(**3 points**)

expressing obligation

8 Fill the gaps in this text with an appropriate word.

> Here are some rules and advice about playing golf. If you are not a member of a club, you <u>should</u> reserve a day and a time because sometimes there are competitions. You are
> (1) _____ to wear the right type of clothes, otherwise they might not let you go out onto the golf course but these clothes don't
> (2) _____ to be very expensive. You
> (3) _____ keep quiet when someone is about to play a shot, and finally, you
> (4) _____ always take an umbrella with you in case it rains.

(**2 points**)

© Pearson Education Limited 2006 – Photocopiable

used to/get used to/would

9 Rewrite the <u>underlined</u> words without changing the meaning of these sentences.

We <u>are familiar with</u> working long hours.
We are used to working long hours.

1 When I went to discos I <u>used to</u> dance a lot.

2 Little by little I am <u>becoming more comfortable with</u> telephoning clients.

3 Now she is <u>accustomed</u> to the situation.

4 My friends and I <u>had the habit of riding</u> motorbikes when we were younger.

[**2 points**]

although, but, however, nevertheless

10 Insert the word in **bold** and use commas if necessary to rewrite these sentences.

Paul ate a lot of food. He was hungry again only two hours later. **however**

Paul ate a lot of food. However, he was hungry again only two hours later.

1 We stayed up very late to watch the film. We were feeling very tired. **although**

2 I think I should think more about my future than reminisce about my past. I think it can sometimes be useful to remind ourselves of the mistakes we made. **nevertheless**

3 He is scruffy. He is quite attractive. **although**

4 I know that Freda can be a pain in the neck sometimes. I need to work with her on this project. **but**

5 He looked a bit suspicious at first. We soon got used to him. **however**

6 My sister likes to have curly hair. I prefer mine straight. **but**

[**3 points**]

[**Total: 25 points**]

Pronunciation

1 Underline the stressed words in these sentences.

Tarek <u>might</u> change his <u>mind</u> about <u>lending</u> you his <u>car</u>.

1 Terry must be stuck in traffic. He's never normally late.

2 We could go and visit my brother in Manchester at the weekend.

3 Jane can't want to go to Morocco this summer. She hates hot weather.

[**3 points**]

2 Put these words into the correct column of the table according to their vowel sound.

/aʊ/	/əʊ/
power	*snow*

shown   crow   <u>tower</u>   <u>lower</u>

howl   crown   bowl   thrown

clown   grown   vow   frown

[**4 points**]

3 Mark the stressed syllable in these words.

<u>ancient</u> <u>antique</u> <u>traditional</u>

second-hand   elderly   old-fashioned

until   porcelain   endurance   substantial

throughout   memorable   overweight

reminisce   souvenir

[**3 points**]

[**Total: 10 points**]

© Pearson Education Limited 2006 – Photocopiable

Vocabulary

1 a Make nouns from the following adjectives.

responsible ► responsibility

jealous ►

important ►

intellectual ►

successful ►

b Make adjectives from the following nouns.

fanaticism ► fanatical

art ►

loner ►

frustration ►

skill ►

⟨ **4 points** ⟩

2 Fill the gaps with the correct preposition.

This story is very different from the one you told me yesterday.

1 My father is quite keen ____ taking early retirement as he wants to travel a lot.

2 Your new furniture is very similar ____ some of mine.

3 My uncle and aunt are very good ____ gardening.

4 Francesca insisted ____ going to the party so we all went in the end.

5 My job consists ____ preparing invoice documents and negotiating payment conditions with new clients.

6 The success of our new project largely depends ____ the economic climate and market forces.

⟨ **3 points** ⟩

3 Insert a verb in the correct form to complete these phrasal verbs with *out*.

After about twenty minutes, the firemen managed to put out the fire.

1 I'll meet you in the pub later on but first I have to _____ out a few problems at home.

2 He seemed to be such a nice person in the beginning but then he _____ out to be the devil in disguise.

3 It looks like we have _____ out of bread so I'll just pop round to the bakery.

4 It looks like Sonya and Kevin have _____ out with each other because they aren't on speaking terms at the moment.

5 It took Trish three minutes to_____ out the solution to the problem.

6 I don't know much about this particular market at the moment but I plan to _____ out more information this week.

⟨ **3 points** ⟩

Total: 10 points

205

© Pearson Education Limited 2006 – Photocopiable

Test B Units 1-5

Reading

1 Read this text about space exploration and answer the questions.

Chris Hadfield has a pastime that few of us will ever have – taking photos of Canada from space. Despite the enormous risk involved, astronaut Chris believes that it is important to the world that manned space flight should be continued. 'Humankind will never stop exploring …', he said, 'If we give up space exploration, we shall be denying ourselves the opportunity to participate in the exploration of the universe and, by so doing, to contribute to the improvement of life here on earth. Exploration has never been a risk-free enterprise, but risk has always been part of the price that mankind has paid for progress.'

Chris Hadfield is a different type of traveller from most of us – and has the pictures to prove it. He was the first Canadian to leave a spacecraft and float in space. <u>During the course of this</u> and other adventures, Hadfield took hundreds of pictures, many of which showed technical aspects of the missions and the condition of the shuttle but others are beautiful pictures of some of the wonders of the world from space.

One thing he's learned is that taking pictures is <u>far from being a snap</u>. 'In the first place', Hadfield explains, 'there are <u>all the problems weightlessness entails</u>. Then there is the speed at which the spacecraft is travelling, which means that what you want to photograph is only in your viewfinder <u>for the briefest of intervals</u>. <u>What it boils down to</u> is that you have to prepare for a photograph well in advance. The speed of the spacecraft, of course, means that many pictures <u>end up in a blur</u> but when you get the occasional great picture, you realise it is worth all the trouble. After all, a picture is often worth a thousand words. Space photography allows us to see Earth from a unique perspective and to observe significant changes in the environment.'

When Hadfield visited a space station recently, he was fascinated by the change in the minds of the permanent crew – '<u>they had come to regard Earth as a separate and distant entity</u>'. Hadfield believes that this is the kind of mental adjustment that is needed in order to live in space and before we go to Mars. Hadfield seems to have little doubt that there will be manned flights to Mars – and perhaps <u>permanent settlement</u> here or on other planets. <u>He draws an interesting historical parallel</u>: 'When the early navigators first developed the confidence to sail out of sight of land and visit the then unexplored areas of the globe, there was no idea of settlement but, of course, that came later.'

2 Look at the underlined expressions carefully in their context and explain their meanings.

During the course of this: while this was happening

1 far from being a snap:
2 all the problems weightlessness entails:
3 for the briefest of intervals:
4 What it boils down to:
5 end up in a blur:
6 they had come to regard Earth as a separate and distant entity:
7 permanent settlement:
8 He draws an interesting historical parallel:

8 points

3 Answer the following questions in your own words as far as possible.

What could potentially discourage someone like Chris Hadfield from wanting to continue exploring in space? The great danger that comes with it.

1 How does Hadfield justify the risk factor in exploration?
2 Are all of his photographs of beautiful and spectacular things? Explain your answer.
3 If you want to increase your possibilities of taking a good quality photo, what must you do?
4 What things are extremely important about space photography?
5 Why does Chris have a lasting impression about the people who worked on a space station?
6 What is his opinion about the possibility of people travelling to Mars one day?

12 points

Total: 20 points

© Pearson Education Limited 2006 – Photocopiable

Listening

1 Choose the correct option.

Charlie makes a joke about a) becoming overweight.
b) going bald. c) his emotional feelings.

1 When she was young, Doris a) went out with a lot
of young men. b) had a serious boyfriend. c) met a
couple of men she liked.

2 She got on with a) everybody. b) not very many
people. c) nearly everybody at work.

3 Charlie thinks that the feeling of pressure is worst
a) from adolescence to adulthood.
b) during adolescence. c) during adulthood.

4 At the seaside, Charlie's family used to stay in a) a
guest house. b) a hotel. c) a rented cottage.

5 Charlie's parents were quite a) strict. b) laid- back.
c) hard-working.

6 He used to a) ignore b) admire c) copy his brother.

(**6 points**)

2 Answer the following questions.

What does Doris think could be the reason for her
thinking that she was happier in the past?
Her mind could be playing tricks on her.

1 Social life apart, what gave Doris a good feeling
when she started work?

2 What did she dislike about her boss?

3 When did this problem disappear?

4 What expression does Charlie use to describe his
childhood?

5 How does Charlie describe children's freedom from
responsibility?

6 Apart from going to the seaside, what else did
Charlie's family use to do during the holidays?

7 Why did Charlie feel so grateful towards his parents?

(**14 points**)

Total: 20 points

Writing

Choose ONE of the following topics and write a
composition of about 250-300 words.

1 Describe the member of your family who you feel
is most similar to you. In what ways has he/she
influenced you during your life?

2 Describe your current job and state whether you
like it or not and why. What things would you like
to change in your workplace and/or about the job
itself?
If you are not working at the moment, what type of
job would you like to do in the future and why?

3 Describe a famous hero or heroine from your
country and write about his/her most heroic actions.

4 In order to be successful in life, is it necessary to
sometimes take risks? Give examples to support
your opinion.

5 Tell the story of one of your most memorable
experiences from the past.

(**15 points**)

100
points

© Pearson Education Limited 2006 – Photocopiable

Test A Units 6-10

Grammar

Present Perfect Simple and Continuous

1 Fill the gaps in these sentences by putting the verbs in brackets into the correct tense.

I have been going (go) to the gym for about three months now and I really love it.

1 I'm definitely not going out because it _____ (rain) all day.

2 Sandra _____ (experience) all kinds of interesting things in her life.

3 Rashid _____ (call) four clients so far this morning.

4 I have a good friend in China. We _____ (send) emails to each other for well over a year.

5 I think I _____ (see) this film at least twice.

6 My girlfriend and I are getting married next year. We _____ (go) out together for over five years.

3 points

making comparisons

2 Transform these sentences using the word given in **bold** to keep the same meaning.

My maths exam was far easier than my philosophy one. **much**

My philosophy exam was much more difficult than my maths one.

1 Sergio and I have the same level of English. **well**
Sergio speaks English _____ me.

2 The Renault was a bit more expensive than the Peugeot. **slightly**
The Peugeot was _____ the Renault.

3 I think history is a lot more interesting than science. **far**
I think science is _____ than history.

4 Ankara is nearer to my town than Istanbul. **from**
Istanbul is _____ my town than Ankara.

2 points

countable and uncountable nouns

3 Select the correct option to fill the gaps

As usual, I got up early and had a *few/lot/little* coffee with a (1) *deal/little/slice* of buttered toast. I had a difficult day to face because I knew that (2) *lots/much/many* mistakes had been made the day before. A great (3) *piece/deal/part* of time and energy had been spent on getting (4) *some/an/a few* information that turned out to be useless. We heard (5) *a/much/some* news that a large competitor was going to sell products similar to ours, so I urgently wanted to give an important (6) *deal of/piece of/lot of* advice to our production manager.

3 points

passives

4 Using the passive, fill the gaps with the correct tense of the verbs in brackets.

I think I *was spoilt* (spoil) by my mum and right up to the age of about 14. I (1) _____ (give) any type of food I wanted, which usually wasn't the healthiest in the world. Since then, I (2) _____ (influence) a lot by my older sister, who takes the issue of healthy diets very seriously indeed. I have picked up a lot of important ideas from her, for example, eggs (3) _____ (should boil) rather than fried and I know that I (4) _____ (will persuade) to continue improving my eating habits in the future.

2 points

© Pearson Education Limited 2006 – Photocopiable

it's time/I'd rather/I'd better

5 Complete the sentences with ONE word.

I'd rather you didn't phone me tonight because I'm going to be very busy.

1 That chair is still broken. It's time you _____ it.

2 I've run out of sugar. I think I'd _____ go and buy some more.

3 I'd rather _____ at home and listen to music than go out tonight.

4 If you're feeling as bad as that you'd _____ call the doctor.

5 This floor is absolutely filthy! It's high _____ we cleaned it.

6 He'd _____ we didn't bother him right now because he's feeling a bit depressed.

(**3 points**)

reported speech

6 Convert the following sentences from direct to reported speech.

'The right preparation before each match is extremely important.'
He explained that the right preparation before each match is very important.

1 'Let's visit some friends of mine.'

She suggested _____.

2 'I will definitely study harder.'

He promised _____.

3 'It was me who used the computer.'

She admitted _____.

4 'Don't forget to switch off the light, John.'

He reminded_____.

(**2 points**)

must, might, can't have

7 Fill the gaps in this dialogue with ONE suitable word using *must*, *might* or *can' t have*.

Tina:	'Blast! I can't believe that we've just been burgled. It *must* have been because I hadn't closed one of the windows properly.'
Rosemary:	'Don't blame yourself like that. It (1) _____ have occurred for a completely different reason. Anyway, they (2) _____ have come through the window anyway. Look how high up we are.'
Tina:	'Don't be so sure. Nothing like that would put real professional burglars off. Of one thing I'm certain. They (3) _____ have been watching the house, otherwise they wouldn't have known we were out.'
Rosemary:	'Perhaps. I think it would be a good idea to talk to the neighbours as they (4)_____ have seen or heard something.'

(**2 points**)

relative clauses

8 Correct the mistakes in these sentences.

He is the man, who was convicted for armed robbery.
He is the man who was convicted for armed robbery.

1 The museum which is of great historical significance is to be rebuilt next year.

2 He declared himself innocent which was the best thing to do at the time.

3 This area of Northern England, where is considered to be one of the most beautiful parts of the country, has prospered a lot.

4 This is the appeal who was made to the court yesterday.

5 The person, who is suing you, is here now.

6 The university, which it is one of the most prestigious in England, has over five thousand students.

(**3 points**)

© Pearson Education Limited 2006 – Photocopiable

reflexive pronouns

9 Fill the gaps in this text with ONE suitable word.

> The other day, the manager had a word with a couple of my workmates and told _them_ to stop talking to (1)_____ other and get the job done. Apparently he was very rude and I reckon that if I was in the boss's position (2)_____, I would have asked for (3) _____ cooperation in a more civilised way. I would have been firm but polite and I'd have reminded them that they should consider (4) _____ privileged to have such a well-paid job in these hard times.

(**2 points**)

gerunds and infinitives

10 Fill the gaps in these sentences using the correct form of the verb in brackets.

They encouraged me to continue (continue) playing despite the fact I was very tired.

1 I regretted _____ (break) that vase into small pieces because it cost a lot of money.

2 We will arrange _____ (have) the party some time next month.

3 They agreed _____ (buy) our products on condition that we gave them a discount.

4 She walked along the corridor and then stopped _____ (make) a telephone call.

5 I can remember _____ (shake) hands with him but I don't remember what we said.

6 He avoided _____ (get) into even more trouble by leaving early.

(**3 points**)

(**Total: 25 points**)

Pronunciation

1 Mark the main stress for these adjectives.

fascinated   annoying

annoyed inspiring daunting worried
petrifying worrying disgusted challenged
fascinating disgusting petrified inspired

(**3 points**)

2 <u>Underline</u> the stressed words in these sentences.

I think that something may not be true or is unlikely to happen.

1 I feel almost certain that something is true.

2 I agree with and support a plan, idea or system.

3 I think something is true or is likely to happen.

(**3 points**)

3 Put these words into the correct column according to the pronunciation of the <u>underlined</u> vowel sound.

/uː/	/juː/	/ʌ/
true	*ass<u>u</u>me*	*b<u>u</u>mpy*

<u>mu</u>mble so<u>u</u>venir thr<u>ou</u>gh interr<u>u</u>ption
t<u>u</u>ne ind<u>u</u>lge <u>u</u>niform scr<u>e</u>w
h<u>u</u>ge s<u>u</u>e p<u>u</u>blicity cons<u>u</u>me

(**4 points**)

(**Total: 10 points**)

© Pearson Education Limited 2006 – Photocopiable

Vocabulary

1 Complete these money related sentences with ONE word only.

I got a 20% discount on this jacket because it was part of last year's stock.

1 You only paid £6,500 for that car! That's fantastic. You got a real _____ there.

2 I think you'd get more money for your antique collection if you put it up for _____ .

3 It's always very important to keep your _____ every time you buy a product just in case you need to take it back.

4 These shoes have really gone up in price a lot. Now I can't _____ them.

5 If your product is faulty, within 14 days of the purchase you can claim a _____ in this store.

6 My bank manager wants to speak to me urgently because my account is _____ .

7 After _____ for over ten minutes I managed to buy the carpet at a very good price at the market.

8 Our company made an annual _____ of $3.2 million last year, so the boss is very happy.

⟨ **4 points** ⟩

2 Underline the option which is NOT possible in these sentences.

I thought that Elaine's gesture was completely/ extremely/very nice

1 We had a (an) *extremely/very/really* huge celebration after our team had won the championship.

2 The chairman's speech was *very/absolutely/ extremely* interesting.

3 We are going to have to clean the bathroom because it is *very/really/absolutely* filthy.

4 Helen thought that the first act of the play was *absolutely/extremely/completely* awful.

5 The reports we have heard on our project so far have been *absolutely/extremely/very* good.

6 These tomatoes are *really/absolutely/very* delicious.

⟨ **3 points** ⟩

3 Fill the gaps in the following sentences with a suitable word.

When a film receives enough hype, it is almost guaranteed to do well.

1 A lot of curious and unknown things may be stored in our _____ mind.

2 'Connecting people' has been a very successful international _____ for Nokia.

3 He tried hard to convince me but I still have my _____ about whether his scheme would actually work.

4 It can be quite irritating when you are watching a good film on TV and every twenty minutes or so they have a commercial _____.

5 I wish Anna would speak a bit more clearly. She seems to _____ all the time.

6 When Patrick received the bad news, he looked as if he was _____ for words.

⟨ **3 points** ⟩

Total: 10 points

© Pearson Education Limited 2006 – Photocopiable

Reading

1 Read the text about obesity problems in young people and answer the questions.

Determining if a child has a weight problem can be <u>challenging</u>. How do you know whether your child's weight is part of the natural growth process and will just grow out of it or if it is negatively affecting his or her health?

Along with the <u>rise</u> in childhood obesity, there has been an increase in the medical conditions in children and adolescents that were considered rare in the past. More frequent cases are occurring of obesity-related diseases such as diabetes, asthma and hypertension that once were considered adult conditions. There are some <u>telltale</u> signs that may help you determine if your child has or risks having childhood obesity, such as family history of obesity and obesity-related health risks, patterns of behaviour where too much time is spent sitting around, and low physical activity levels.

It is important for parents and healthcare professionals to be sensitive to the youngsters and focus on the positive. Small and <u>achievable</u> weight loss goals should be set to avoid discouragement and to allow for the normal growth process. Also, weight control programmes that involve both parents and the child have shown improvement in long-term effectiveness compared to directing the programme only to the child.

There is clearly a <u>steady decline</u> in the diet quality of children and adolescents as they get older. Consultation with a dietician that specialises in children's needs is often a valuable part of obesity treatment. Nutrition consultants can <u>outline</u> specific and appropriate nutritional needs for healthy growth. Eating behaviour that consultants typically encourage includes taking smaller bites, chewing food longer and avoiding eating too quickly by putting the fork down between bites.

Moderate physical activity is recommended for children every day for at least 60 minutes. Or if a child cannot meet this goal, an individualised programme should be designed according to fitness level. It is also useful to record diet and exercise patterns in a diary <u>to keep track of</u> types and amount of foods eaten and exercises performed. Identify and avoid high-risk situations such as having too many high-calorie foods in the house and watching TV during meal times (this encourages eating every time the TV is on). Reward positive actions such as meeting an exercise goal or eating less of a certain type of food by giving something very positive such as verbal praise or sports equipment rather than food, especially high-calorie foods, as this only makes them more desirable. The family should work as a unit in setting weekly activity goals.

2 Look at the <u>underlined </u>words and expressions carefully in their context and choose the right option.

challenging means a) nearly impossible b) uncomplicated c) difficult but stimulating

1 <u>rise</u> means a) increase b) extra attention c) reduction

2 <u>telltale</u> means a) very evident b) interesting c) uncertain

3 <u>achievable</u> means a) easy b) possible c) extremely difficult to get or accomplish

4 <u>steady decline</u> means a) fast deterioration b) slow deterioration c) constant deterioration

5 <u>outline</u> means a) give general information about b) write about c) represent on a graph

6 <u>to keep track of</u> means a) to analyse b) to discuss c) to stay up to date with something so you know what is happening

(**6 points**)

3 Answer these questions in your own words as far as possible.

What specific type of health problems has obesity in children led to?
More common occurrences of connected illnesses.

1 What is curious about children having diseases of this type?

2 How should parents and health workers treat children suffering from obesity?

3 Why should weight loss goals not be set too high?

4 Why is it important to consult a dietician who specialises in children's needs?

5 What type of eating behaviour do consultants particularly recommend?

6 What happens if a child cannot achieve a physical activity objective?

7 Why is eating while watching TV considered to be potentially dangerous for the health?

(**14 points**)

Total: 20 points

© Pearson Education Limited 2006 – Photocopiable

Listening

1 Choose the correct option.

On his first visit to Australia, Ian wants to a) try to become nationalised. b) experiment to see if he likes it. c) only have a short holiday.

1 Ian thinks he has a) excellent. b) fairly good. c) very few possibilities of getting a permanent work visa on the points system.

2 The easiest way to get Australian nationality is to a) excel on the points system. b) have a specialised job. c) marry an Australian.

3 Ian wants to scuba dive, windsurf and a) hang-glide. b) sky dive. c) go rafting.

4 The hot temperatures will be a) a terrible problem. b) a bit of a problem. c) unimportant.

5 Sharon has good possibilities to work abroad because of her a) profession. b) experience. c) language qualifications.

6 The Mediterranean weather is a) what attracts Sharon most. b) important but not necessarily the most important aspect. c) not very important for Sharon.

(**6 points**)

2 Answer the following questions.

What type of visa will Ian have when he goes to Australia next year?
A holiday visa.

1 What nickname does Sharon give to Australian people?

2 Why does Ian think that the world has become smaller?

3 What do the Australian and Mediterranean lifestyles have in common?

4 What experience does Sharon have of working abroad?

5 What incentives are there for her to live and work in America?

6 What two difficulties does Sharon expect to find when moving to a Mediterranean country?

7 What has she always loved doing when she is abroad?

(**14 points**)

`Total: 20 points`

Writing

Choose ONE of the following topics and write a composition of about 250-300 words.

1 Have you ever lived and worked or studied abroad before? What was it like? If you have never lived in a foreign country, would you like to? Why / Why not?

2 Do you like cooking? Describe in detail how you would prepare a typical dish from your country.

3 What professional and personal qualities are necessary to be successful in the job that you currently do or would like to do in the future?

4 Is crime a major problem in your area or town? What do you think would be the best strategy to reduce the level of crime in society?

5 Tell the story of an experience you had in the past when you used your willpower, power of persuasion or sixth sense to solve a problem or to gain something important.

(**15 points**)

100 points

© Pearson Education Limited 2006 – Photocopiable

Test B Units 6-10

Grammar

Present Perfect Simple and Continuous

1 Put the verbs into the Present Perfect Simple or Continuous or the Past Simple.

> Last week Sean, a friend of mine, _told_ me about his plans to go mountaineering in the Andes next year. He (1) _____ (climb) high mountains since he was a child, but even to him these South American mountains are a daunting challenge. He (2) _____ (visit) this part of the world only twice in his life and still (3) _____ (not conquer) Aconcagua, the highest mountain in Argentina and the whole continent. However, three years ago he (4) _____ (manage) to reach the summit of Cotapaxi in Ecuador, which is just less than 6,000 metres high.

(**2 points**)

questions

2 Change the following direct questions into indirect ones.

Why didn't you ask her to help you?
Could I ask you why you didn't ask her to help you?

1 How long have you been travelling abroad on business?
   May

2 When was the last time you experienced culture shock?
   Can you

3 Are you going there as an independent traveller?
   Can I

4 Do you ever have itchy feet?
   Could you

5 Will you ever learn another language?
   May

6 Have you finished preparing the report yet?
   Could I

(**3 points**)

passives

3 Convert the following active sentences into the passive form.

Diana scrambled a couple of eggs for breakfast this morning.
A couple of eggs were scrambled by Diana for breakfast this morning.

1 They haven't informed us yet.

2 You must cut the meat like this.

3 This company is going to make a heavy loss next year.

4 They were rebuilding the train station at that time.

(**2 points**)

have/get something done

4 Rewrite the sentences without changing their meaning.

I need someone to check my engine.
I need to have my engine checked.

1 I'm going to find a person to look after my dog.

2 Someone is going to fix my computer.

3 I want a person to paint my flat.

4 Somebody has just cut my grass for me.

5 She will cut my hair tomorrow morning.

6 They inspect our accounts once a year.

(**3 points**)

© Pearson Education Limited 2006 – Photocopiable

reported speech

5 Transform these sentences into reported speech using the verbs in brackets.

Leroy: 'I had trouble finding work abroad.' (say)
<u>*Leroy said that he had trouble finding work abroad.*</u>

1 Veronica: 'Yes, I think I'll go to this party.' (reply)

2 Vincent: 'I must attend this meeting.' (tell)

3 Mum: 'Remember to clean your teeth!' (remind)

4 Gabriel: 'Should we continue working on this case?' (ask)

5 Hilda: 'It's about time you came to visit me.' (say)

6 Omar: 'Right! I'll definitely watch this play at the theatre.' (decide)

(**3 points**)

hard and hardly

6 Fill the gaps with either *hard* or *hardly*.

> I sometimes think that life is pretty <u>*hard*</u> because sometimes I get the impression that no matter how (1) _____ we work, we (2) _____ receive any gratitude at all in this company. My boss has a remarkably (3) _____ character and the low salary he pays me (4) _____ makes up for all the pain and trouble that he has caused me.

(**2 points**)

sequencing devices

7 Complete these sentences with a verb of your choice in the correct form.

After <u>washing</u> my hands, I sat down at the dinner table.

1 Having _____ found guilty, the robber was led out of the court by two policemen.

2 After _____ the brand-new car, he showed it off to all his friends.

3 Having _____ a vital clue, the detective closed in on the criminal.

4 After _____ some delicious home-made cakes, I was no longer hungry and decided to have dinner later than usual.

5 Having _____ a last-minute decision to go with us to the cinema, she put on her coat and quickly left the office.

6 After _____ the man to ten years in prison, the judge described him as a very dangerous person.

(**3 points**)

must, might, can't have

8 Fill the gaps using *must have, might have* or *can't have* with a verb of your choice in the correct form.

Eve doesn't look at all happy. She <u>can't have passed</u> the exam.

1 Barry is a bit late today. I wonder why. He _____ the bus.

2 Brenda is in bed with a terrible hangover. She _____ too much wine last night at dinner.

3 Lee Du Wei _____ me before because I would have remembered.

4 She _____ back into her office as I've just called there and no-one answered the phone.

(**2 points**)

© Pearson Education Limited 2006 – Photocopiable

gerunds and infinitives

9 Complete this short text by using an appropriate verb in the correct form.

> I'm going to participate in an important tennis tournament next week and I hope *to reach* the semi-finals at least. I have always believed that I need to practise at least five or six hours a day (1) _____ this type of goal. By way of preparation, I have already stopped (2) _____ large meals in the evening and my trainer has even suggested (3) _____ to bed before 10pm over the next couple of weeks or so. I must remember (4) _____ lots of vitamins as well.

(**2 points**)

if Structures (2)

10 Fill the gaps with the correct form of the verbs in brackets.

If this film hadn't received (receive) so much hype, it would never have been so successful.

1 If I had done better at school when I was a kid, now I _____ (have) a more interesting job.

2 If you trust your intuition, you normally _____ (make) a wise decision.

3 If Frank _____ (not eat) so many fatty foods, I'm sure he would be a lot slimmer.

4 If I had gone to the trouble of preparing a better CV, I _____ (can get) that job.

5 If Vanessa wasn't such a nice person, she _____ (shout) at us for what we did last night.

6 You _____ (might win) that match if you had concentrated harder.

(**3 points**)

Total: 25 points

Pronunciation

1 Put three more words in each column according to the vowel sound.

/iː/	/eə/	/e/
eat	pear	bread

beak feathers tear (v) tear (n) heart
swear ecstatic suspended plea bear

(**3 points**)

Which word rhymes with *far* (ɑː) and does not belong in the table? _____

(**1 point**)

2 Mark the stressed syllable in these words.

independent experience showery

drizzle vegetarian overdrawn arson

advertise manipulative selfish

advertisement advert recipe

appeal misunderstand

(**3 points**)

3 Mark the stressed words in these sentences.

He is the person who directed this film.

1 The detective, whose car was parked just outside, spoke to us for half an hour.

2 This is the book that I feel sceptical about.

3 The woman, who was convicted of arson, is serving time in prison.

(**3 points**)

Total: 10 points

© Pearson Education Limited 2006 – Photocopiable

Vocabulary

1 Fill the gaps with ONE word only.

Kate: 'Which dessert would you like?'
Gordon: 'I think I'll go <u>for</u> the banana split.'

1 I'm sorry I couldn't come to see you but I went _____ with a heavy cold and had to stay in bed.

2 The great thing with Don is that whenever he makes a promise, he doesn't go _____ on his word.

3 We've been _____ the go all week so that's why I haven't replied to your email.

4 It goes without _____ that she has all the necessary qualities to become a great writer.

5 I am truly grateful to Mr. Brown because he went to great _____ to help me.

6 We're going _____ on holiday next week so I'll see you when I get back.

⬭ 3 points ⬭

2 Write the things or actions that correspond to these definitions.

This is the metal object that we normally use when we cook things in with oil.
A frying pan.

1 The verb that means to cook meat in the oven. _____

2 Someone who doesn't eat meat. _____

3 The adjective that we use when a steak has only been cooked for a short time. _____

4 A set of written instructions and ingredients to help us prepare a particular dish. _____

5 A verb that means to rub carrots or cheese against a rough metal object in order to break it into very small pieces. _____

6 This is the adjective that we use to refer to food that is totally uncooked. _____

⬭ 3 points ⬭

3 Complete these phrasal verbs by filling in the two particles that go with the verb.

My friend was walking about 100 yards ahead of me so I ran to catch <u>up</u> <u>with</u> him.

1 I'm really looking _____ that dinner party next week. It'll be great!

2 I think I'd better cut _____ all the sweet things I eat because I'm starting to get fat.

3 I look _____ Mary a lot because she is a wonderful person.

4 If you let those kids get _____ speaking to you like that, they'll do it again.

5 My colleague came _____ a brilliant idea that will reduce our workload.

6 I simply can't put _____ lazy flatmates who never bother to clean anything.

7 We can make _____ the time that we lost yesterday by working until late than this evening.

8 He's new at this and he finds it hard to keep _____ the rest of us but I'm sure he'll learn to work faster with time.

⬭ 4 points ⬭

⬛ Total: 10 points ⬛

© Pearson Education Limited 2006 – Photocopiable

Reading

1 Read this text about dealing with crime in New York and answer the questions.

> William J. Bratton is one of the most effective law enforcement leaders in the United States today. Thanks to his hard work and successful strategies, New York city achieved an amazing 36% decrease in serious crime, including <u>a 45% drop</u> in murder. Before he took up his position in 1994, the New York subway was considered to be one of the most dangerous places in the world. There are 700 entranceways into the city's 450 or so subway stations and every one of them seemed like a walk down into hell. They were dirty and the <u>stench</u> was sometimes so bad you had to hold your breath. It was very common <u>to bump into</u> petty thieves, graffiti artists and aggressive beggars as well as more <u>deadly</u> types of criminals.
>
> Bratton explains: 'To deal with the problem, we began by aggressively arresting the <u>fare evaders</u> and throwing out disorderly people from the subway. The truth is that the chances of being a victim of a crime in the subway around this time were statistically like the chances of winning the lottery. But what people saw every day – the disorder, the fare evaders, and police not doing anything about it – reinforced their fears and people were beginning to stay away.
>
> We began to turn this around by having our officers enforce quality-of-life rules in the subway system. We found that one out of every seven people arrested for fare evasion was wanted by the police and one out of every twenty-one was carrying a weapon. In all probability they were not coming into the subway just to travel to work: they were at work, and you and I were the people they were looking to work on. By arresting them on a large scale and putting police out in so many different ways, we began to change and control behaviour and the reduction in crime has been <u>astounding</u>.
>
> Mayor Giuliani asked me if I could do the same thing in the streets. I told him we could but this was going to require his political will, as mayor, to focus on the issues of primary concern – the economy, crime and the schools. Secondly, all the activities of government agencies would have to be coordinated.'
>
> Bratton explains that a key priority was to penalise public drinking and other things that caused fear while the rest of city government was involved in solving and removing the visible signs, such as graffiti. In this way, the government and police, by working together, were able <u>to address</u> the signs of crime as well as the crime itself, and so begin to reduce the fear.'

2 Look at the <u>underlined</u> vocabulary carefully in context and then give a short definition for each term.

a 45% drop: a reduction of 45%

1 <u>stench</u>:

2 <u>to bump into</u>:

3 <u>deadly</u>:

4 <u>fare evaders</u>:

5 <u>astounding</u>

6 <u>to address</u>

(**6 points**)

3 Answer the following questions in your own words as far as possible.

Why did entranceways to the New York Subway 'seem like a walk down into hell?'
<u>They weren't clean, you could hardly breathe and you could have encounters with some undesirable people.</u>

1 Did the New York subway deserve its reputation as being one of the most dangerous places in the world? Explain your answer.

2 What effect did the police's initial lack of positive action have on passengers?

3 What did passengers start to do because of this?

4 What does Bratton mean when he says '…and you and I were the people they were looking to work on.'?

5 What effect did the enormous police effort have on life in the subway?

6 For what two purposes was the mayor's political influence needed to reduce crime in the streets?

7 In what ways did both the police and government agencies aim to clean up street crime?

(**14 points**)

Total: 20 points

© Pearson Education Limited 2006 – Photocopiable

Listening

1 Choose the best option.

*The interviewer describes the déjà vu feeling as
a) exciting. b) interesting. c) very strange.*

1 Dr. Milos believes most people experience déjà vu
a) very frequently. b) quite often. c) rarely.

2 The interviewer thought that déjà vu could be
caused by a) a coincidence. b) the mind's hidden
powers. c) reincarnation

3 How does the doctor generally feel about existing
theories related to déjà vu?
a) sceptical b) indifferent c) fascinated

4 Both speakers feel a) doubtful. b) uninterested.
c) frightened with regard to the full potential of the
human mind.

5 The interviewer thinks that telepathic
communication can be explained mostly by a) the
subconscious. b) a special power possessed by only
a few people. c) coincidence.

6 Dr. Milos's latest book is about a) the sixth sense. b)
dream analysis. c) hypnosis.

(**6 points**)

2 Answer the following questions.

*What are Dr. Milos's two professions?
He is a psychologist and an author.*

1 What does he think could be the cause of the brain
receiving a late or distorted message?

2 How does the doctor react to the possible cause of
déjà vu suggested by the interviewer?

3 What other two possible causes of déjà vu does he
mention?

4 What do some people believe we can train our
minds to do?

5 What is telekinesis?

6 How does Dr. Milos define our 'sixth sense'?

7 How does he explain the reason for us having 'a
sixth sense'?

(**14 points**)

Total: 20 points

Writing

Choose ONE of the following topics and write a
composition of about 250-300 words.

1 Have you ever lived and worked or studied abroad
before? What was it like? If you have never lived
in a foreign country, would you like to? Why / Why
not?

2 Do you like cooking? Describe in detail how you
would prepare a typical dish from your country.

3 What professional and personal qualities are
necessary to be successful in the job that you
currently do or would like to do in the future?

4 Is crime a major problem in your area or town?
What do you think would be the best strategy to
reduce the level of crime in society?

5 Tell the story of an experience you had in the past
when you used your willpower, power of persuasion
or sixth sense to solve a problem or to gain
something important.

(**15 points**)

100
points

© Pearson Education Limited 2006 – Photocopiable

Answer key

Test A Units 1-5

Grammar

1 question tags
1 will it? 2 will you? 3 shall we? 4 aren't I? 5 weren't they?
6 does she?

2 present/future modals of possibility
1 must 2 might 3 could 4 can't

3 futures overview
1 am ('m) meeting 2 are going to buy 3 will be 4 will ('ll) come 5 is bound to win 6 is ('s) going to speak

4 *in case*
1 get/feel 2 just 3 hadn't received 4 felt

5 narrative tenses
1 had invented 2 wanted 3 had been preparing 4 was showing 5 had 6 had received

6. articles
1 the 2 (-) 3 (-) 4 An

7 expressing obligation
1 You are supposed to find out as much information about this as possible.
2 He shouldn't have fallen out with his boss.
3 You don't have to speak in public if you don't want to.
4 Before getting my present job, I had to pass a series of difficult tests.
5 We didn't have to lock all office doors after work.
6 We/You should sort out this problem before continuing.

8 emphasis
1 such 2 does 3 very 4 really

9 *used to/get used to/would*
1 used to 2 to dealing 3 get used to 4 would

10 expressing ability
1 could 2 able 3 managed 4 couldn't/wasn't able to
5 in 6 can't

Pronunciation

1

/iː/	/eɪ/
colleague	wavelength
loneliness	acquaintance
previous	labour
detail	straight
antique	ancient
lean	afraid
relieved	shaven

2
1 I do believe that we still have an opportunity.
2 We talked about travelling, music and many, many more things.
3 It was definitely the job I liked doing most.

3
intellectual intellect responsibility
engineer satisfaction detail
apply resign redecorate

Vocabulary

1
1 on with 2 off 3 out with 4 up 5 up to 6 after

2
1 Up until that point 2 While 3 throughout 4 At that time
5 since then 6 until

3
1 elegant 2 scruffy 3 tanned 4 dyed 5 chubby
6 wrinkles 7 muscular 8 overweight

Reading

2
1 b) 2 a) 3 c) 4 b) 5 b) 6 b)

3
1 Situations of real-life necessity (rather than traditional scientific laboratories).
2 Certain inventors can't read or write but this doesn't mean that they can't be extremely clever.
3 Because of the lack of electricity and water.
4 He removes weeds and breaks up the top part of the earth in order to reduce the natural flow of water to the surface.
5 The inventors benefit because it stops other people copying their ideas.
6 No, because some inventers already have their inventions in the market.
7 It is cheap to run and there is no smell or smoke.

Listening
Tapescript
P=Pete C=Carol

P: Did you always plan to be a social worker, Carol?
C: No, not at all. I didn't have a clue what to do with myself when I was younger but one night I met someone at a party who just happened to be a social worker. Well, we got talking and he convinced me ... you know ...
P: ... convinced you to give it a go?
C: Yeah ... I suppose he did. ... He was really enthusiastic about it ... really passionate about helping people ... and I've always wanted to do something worthwhile ... you know ... something really useful with my life ...
P: It's not an easy job though, is it?
C: No. But it does bring out the best in you. Obviously you sometimes find yourself in very unpleasant situations ... you know ... dealing with people's problems can be very stressful ... but you just have to keep calm under pressure.
P: So, would you say you're a natural?
C: I don't know about that! But I've always been a good listener ..that helps ... and I'm definitely a people person.
P: Oh yes, absolutely. I can see that ... So do you see yourself being a social worker for ever?
C: Hmmm. I'm not sure. It's hard work you know .. .there's a lot of pressure ... and I do get quite tired and stressed sometimes. I'd quite like to get into something different when I'm a bit older.
P: Really?
C: Yes, it would be good to have a change. A long time ago - before I went to university in fact- I took a year out to teach English in Italy. It was such fun - a really fantastic experience - and I'd love to do something like that again. I'd need a qualification though so I'll have to sort out some evening classes ...
P: So you might be applying for teaching posts one day?
C: Well, you never know ... . Anyway, what about you Pete? Did you plan your career path very carefully?
P: Yes, I suppose you could say that. I take after my father you see ... I even studied for the same degree in engineering. When I finished university, I had a very clear idea in my head about what I wanted to do ... where I wanted to go in life ...
C: So you've always wanted to be an engineer?
P: That's right ... I've never wanted to do anything else and I'll probably be doing the same thing in twenty years time!
C: It must be challenging though ... you know ... when you think about all the responsibility it involves.
P: Yes, I suppose so. But like everything else, it's a question of training and experience ...
C: ... and you've had plenty of both...
P: Yes, I suppose I have. We sometimes have to meet some pretty tight deadlines but I'm good at that because I've been through it all so many times.
C: So there's a lot of job satisfaction?
P: Oh, definitely ... that's the best thing about it ...

1
1 a) 2 c) 3 b) 4 a) 5 b) 6 b)

2
1 She had always wanted to do something useful with her life.
2 Having to deal with people's problems.
3 She is a good listener and a people person.
4 Because social work is hard and there is a lot of pressure.
5 A degree in engineering.
6 Because it involves a lot of responsibility.
7 Training and experience

Test B Units 1-5

Grammar

1 any/every/no/some
1 everyone/everybody 2 everywhere 3 anything
4 anywhere 5 something 6 somewhere

2 present/future modals of possibility
(1) can't (2) must (3) may (4) must

3 futures overview
(1) are bound to have (2) is going to tell
(3) will be (4) are going

4 Future Perfect and Continuous
1 will ('ll) have finished 2 will ('ll) have received 3 will ('ll) be
lying 4 will ('ll) have sent 5 will be working 6 will ('ll) be driving

5 narrative tenses
1 had been working 2 were standing 3 ran 4 had put

6 adjectives and adverbs
1 Samantha plays tennis very well.
2 They surprisingly lost the match.
3 They will probably come back to visit us again in the future.
4 It was me who unintentionally made that mistake.
5 I will definitely fly to Rome on business next week.
6 This computer has been expertly programmed.

7 if structures (1)
1 give 2 wouldn't have lost 3 will ('ll) buy 4 were
given 5 had thought 6 would ('d) travel

8 expressing obligation
(1) supposed (2) have (3) must (4) should

9 used to/get used to/would
1 When I went to discos I would dance a lot.
2 Little by little I am getting used to telephoning clients.
3 Now she is used to the situation.
4 My friends and I used to ride motorbikes when we were younger.

10 although, but, however, nevertheless
1 We stayed up very late to watch the film, although we were feeling very tired.
2 I think I should think more about my future than reminisce about my past. Nevertheless, I think it can sometimes be useful to remind ourselves of the mistakes we made.
3 Although he is scruffy, he is quite attractive.
4 I know that Freda can be a pain in the neck sometimes but I need to work with her on this project.
5 He looked a bit suspicious at first. However, we soon got used to him.
6 My sister likes to have curly hair but I prefer mine straight.

Pronunciation

1
1 Terry <u>must</u> be stuck in <u>traffic</u>. He's never <u>normally</u> late.
2 We <u>could</u> go and visit my <u>brother</u> in <u>Manchester</u> at the <u>weekend</u>.
3 Jane <u>can't</u> want to go to <u>Morocco</u> this <u>summer</u>. She <u>hates</u> hot weather.

2
/aʊ/: <u>power</u>, <u>tower</u>, howl, crown, clown, vow, frown
/əʊ/: snow, shown, crow, <u>lower</u>, bowl, thrown, grown

3
second-<u>hand</u> <u>elderly</u> old-<u>fashioned</u> <u>until</u> <u>por</u>celain
<u>en</u>durance sub<u>stan</u>tial through<u>out</u> <u>mem</u>orable over<u>weight</u>
<u>rem</u>inisce <u>sou</u>venir

Vocabulary

1
a jealousy importance intellect success
b artistic lonely frustrating skilful

2
1 on 2 to 3 at 4 on 5 of 6 on

3
1 sort 2 turned 3 run 4 fallen 5 work 6 find

Reading

2
1 very different from a normal photo (which is easy to take) 2 all the difficulties related to our bodies floating because of gravity
3 for a very short time 4 the most important thing 5 finally have poor quality with little or no clarity 6 They considered our planet as something far away that they didn't form part of. 7 staying to live forever 8 He presents an interesting similarity from history.

3
1 In order to advance and evolve, the human race has always had to do dangerous things. 2 No, some pictures were of a purely technical nature. 3 Prepare for the photo a long time before you take it. 4 It permits us to see our planet in a different way as well as view important environmental changes. 5 They had changed their way of thinking and saw Earth in a completely different way.
6 He is practically sure this will happen.

Listening

Tapescript
D=Doris C=Charlie
D: It's a funny old world, Charlie. Whenever we reminisce about the past, I start thinking that those really were the good old days...that we were happier then ... but maybe it's not true. It could just be my memory playing tricks on me ...
C: Yes, I know what you mean. I sometimes think it's not just my hair I'm losing ... So what was the best time for you then, Doris? What age did you enjoy the most?
D: Oh, I don't know really ... There've been lots of good times ...
C: But what was the best ...?
D: Well, I really enjoyed my late teens and early twenties. That was a wonderful time...I'd just started work and I really enjoyed the feeling of independence... being treated as an adult ... and meeting all those new people of course...
C: ... all those young men, you mean?
D: ... well, there were one or two ... nothing serious though ...we all had such fun in those days...
C: I can imagine. It must have been nice having a bit of freedom for a change... So how did you get on at work? What were the people like?
D: ...the girls in the office? Oh they were wonderful ...we all clicked right from the start and we used to go out dancing practically every night. But ...you know what life's like. You don't always see eye to eye with everyone. My first boss for example ...
C: A bit strict, was he?
D: I'll say! He was a real pain in the neck ... he used to get annoyed over the slightest thing and was constantly reminding me to do things ...
C: Oh dear, how irritating! So you were always in trouble then ...?
D: No, not really... I got a new boss after a while and everything was fine after that. So what about you, Charlie? Do you ever feel nostalgic?
C: Well, we all feel a bit nostalgic for our childhood, don't we? It was such an age of innocence ... you know ... nothing seemed to matter too much and you never had that feeling of pressure you get when you're an adult. You can just do your own thing when you're a kid, can't you?
D: Yes, it was lovely then, wasn't it? Do you have any special memories?
C: Oh yes ... I have some wonderful memories of family holidays ... you know ...with my parents and brother ... we didn't have much money but we always managed to go away somewhere ...
D: ... to the seaside?
C: Yes, we sometimes used to stay in a guest house at the seaside. We used to go camping too ...and walking in the mountains ...we used to go somewhere different every year even when we were very young ...
D: It sounds marvellous
C: Yes, it was. Those holidays were fantastic ... quite unforgettable really ...
D: I bet you were fond of your parents, weren't you?
C: Oh yes. They were quite strict but they brought us up very well. I was really fond of my brother too...
D: Your older brother?
C: Yes, that's right. He was my hero when I was younger ... I really used to look up to him ...

1
1 c) 2 c) 3 c) 4 a) 5 a) 6 b)

2
1 Her new independence and being treated as an adult. 2 He got annoyed very easily and was constantly reminding her to do things.
3 When she got a new boss. 4 'An age of innocence.' 5 You can 'just do your own thing when you're a kid.' 6 They used to go camping and walking in the mountains. 7 They brought him and his brother up very well.

Test A Units 6-10

Grammar

1 Present Perfect Simple and Continuous
1 has been raining **2** has experienced **3** has called **4** have been sending **5** have seen **6** have been going

2 making comparisons
1 as well as **2** slightly cheaper than **3** far less interesting/far more boring **4** farther/further from

3 countable and uncountable nouns
(1) slice (2) many (3) deal (4) some
(5) some (6) piece of

4 passives
(1) was given (2) have been influenced (3) should be boiled (4) will be persuaded

5 *it's time/I'd rather/I'd better*
1 repaired/fixed **2** better **3** stay
4 better **5** time **6** rather

6 reported speech
1 She suggested visiting some friends of hers.
2 He promised to study harder.
3 She admitted using the computer.
4 He reminded John to switch off the light.

7 *must, might, can't have*
(1) might (2) can't (3) must (4) might

8 relative clauses
1 The museum, which is of great historical significance, is to be rebuilt next year.
2 He declared himself innocent, which was the best thing to do at the time.
3 This area of Northern England, which is considered to be one of the most beautiful parts of the country, has prospered a lot.
4 This is the appeal which (that) was made to the court yesterday.
5 The person who is suing you is here now.
6 The university, which is one of the most prestigious in England, has over five thousand students.

9 reflexive pronouns
(1) each (2) myself (3) their (4) themselves

10 gerunds and infinitives
1 breaking **2** to have **3** to buy
4 to make **5** shaking **6** getting

Pronunciation

1
ann<u>oy</u>ed insp<u>i</u>ring d<u>au</u>nting w<u>o</u>rried
p<u>e</u>trifying w<u>o</u>rrying disg<u>u</u>sted ch<u>a</u>llenged
f<u>a</u>scinating disg<u>u</u>sting p<u>e</u>trified insp<u>i</u>red

2
1 I <u>feel</u> almost <u>certain</u> that <u>something</u> is <u>true</u>.
2 I <u>agree</u> with and <u>support</u> a <u>plan</u>, <u>idea</u> or <u>system</u>.
3 I <u>think</u> something is <u>true</u> or is <u>likely</u> to <u>happen</u>.

3

/uː/	/juː/	/ʌ/
true	assume	bumpy
souvenir	tune	mumble
through	uniform	interruption
screw	huge	indulge
sue	consume	publicity

Vocabulary

1
1 bargain **2** auction **3** receipt **4** afford **5** refund
6 overdrawn **7** haggling **8** profit

2
1 very **2** absolutely **3** very **4** extremely **5** absolutely **6** very

3
1 subconscious **2** slogan **3** doubts **4** break
5 mumble **6** lost

Reading

2
1 a) **2** a) **3** b) **4** c) **5** a) **6** c)

3
1 They were previously uncommon among very young people and more associated with adults.
2 They should be sensitive and concentrate on positive things.
3 Goals which are too difficult may reduce motivation and discourage children.
4 They can provide information on the right kind of foods needed for children to grow healthily.
5 Having less food in the mouth, chewing it longer and eating more slowly by putting the fork on the table after each mouthful.
6 A personalised programme should be prepared that suits their physical condition.
7 The desire to eat something is increased whenever the TV is on.

Listening

Tapescript
S=Sharon I=Ian
S: I hear you're off to work in Australia next year Ian. How exciting!
I: Yeah, that's right. I've got a holiday visa but I'll try and find work while I'm there …
S: So how long are you going for then?
I: Just for three months or so … but it'll be long enough to test the water … I'm thinking about emigrating you see …
S: Isn't it really difficult to get a permanent visa?
I: Yes, it is. Apparently, it's done on a type of points system … they give priority to certain professions … but as a mechanical engineer, I should stand a reasonable chance.
S: I guess the other option would be to fall in love with a nice Australian girl …
I: Well, you never know …
S: Won't you miss England though?
I: Well, I'll miss my family and friends of course … but the world's become a much smaller place with the internet and cheap international flights … The truth is I've got itchy feet …
S: So you've been bitten by the travel bug, have you?
I: Yes, I guess so … it's a spectacular country and life in Australia's supposed to be really laid-back …
S: So do you think you'll get on well with the Aussies?
I: Yeah … they're really easy-going … and they love the outdoor life. The thought of doing adventure sports like scuba diving, hang-gliding and windsurfing really appeals to me …
S: The weather'll be nice too, wont' it?
I: Yeah. Apparently it can get really hot … really scorching in the summer but I'm sure I'll get used to that. Wouldn't you like to work abroad, Sharon?
S: Oh yeah, definitely. I went grape-picking in the South of France a couple of years back and absolutely loved it. … and of course, now that I'm a qualified nurse, I've got a lot more options.
I: So where would you like to go?
S: Well one option would be The States … I'd certainly earn a lot more money there …
I: Yeah, that would be good and the cost of living isn't as high either.
S: That's true … but money isn't everything. What I really fancy is living in a Mediterranean country..you know … Greece … Southern Spain … somewhere like that …
I: Yeah, you'd get good weather there.
S: … and I think the lifestyle's more easy-going … although it might be a bit of a bumpy ride at first with culture shock ..a new language and so on …
I: … but it'd be fun getting to know a new culture … and you've always loved wandering around exploring new places …
S: Yeah … I think I'd find it really interesting …

1
1 b) **2** c) **3** a) **4** b) **5** a) **6** b)

2
1 Aussies.
2 Because of the Internet and cheap international flights.
3 They are both laid-back / easy-going countries.
4 She has been grape-picking in the south of France.
5 A better salary and a lower cost of living.
6 The culture shock and a new language.
7 Wandering around and exploring new places.

Test B Units 6-10

Grammar

1 Present Perfect Simple and Continuous
(1) has been climbing   (2) has visited   (3) hasn't conquered
(4) managed

2 questions
1 May I ask you how long you have been travelling abroad on business?   2 Can you tell me when the last time you experienced culture shock was?   3 Can I ask you if (whether) you are going there as an independent traveller?   4 Could you tell me if you ever have itchy feet?   5 May I ask you if you will ever learn another language.
6 Could I ask you if you have finished preparing the report yet.

3 passives
1 We haven't been informed yet.
2 The meat must be cut like this.
3 A heavy loss is going to be made by this company next year.
4 The train station was being rebuilt at that time.

4 have/get something done
1 I'm going to have (get) my dog looked after.
2 I'm going to have (get) my computer fixed.
3 I want to have (get) my flat painted.
4 I have just had (got) my grass cut.
5 I will have (get) my hair cut tomorrow morning.
6 We have (get) our accounts inspected once a year.

5 reported speech
1 Veronica replied (that) she thought she would go to that party.
2 Vincent told me (that) he had to attend that meeting.
3 Mum reminded me to clean my teeth.
4 Gabriel asked if (whether) we should continue working on that case.
5 Hilda said that it was about time we (I) went to visit her.
6 Omar decided he would definitely watch that play at the theatre.

6 hard and hardly
(1) hard   (2) hardly   (3) hard   (4) hardly

7 sequencing devices
1 been   2 buying   3 found/discovered   4 eating   5 made
6 sentencing

8 must, might, can't have
1 might have missed   2 must have had (drunk)   3 can't have met
4 can't have gone

9 gerunds and infinitives
(1) to achieve   (2) having (eating)   (3) going   (4) to take

10 if structures (2)
1 would have   2 make   3 didn't eat   4 could have got   5 would have shouted   6 might have won

Pronunciation

1

/iː/	/eə/	/e/
eat	pear	bread
beak	tear (v)	feathers
tear (n)	swear	ecstatic
plea	bear	suspended

heart rhymes with *far*

2
drizzle vegetarian over<u>draw</u>n <u>ars</u>on <u>advertise</u> manipulative
<u>selfish</u> ad<u>vertisement</u> <u>advert</u> <u>recipe</u> <u>appeal</u> mi<u>sunderstand</u>

3
1 The <u>detective</u>, whose <u>car</u> was parked just <u>outside</u>, <u>spoke</u> to us for half an <u>hour</u>.
2 <u>This</u> is the <u>book</u> that I feel <u>sceptical</u> about.
3 The <u>woman</u>, who was <u>convicted</u> of <u>arson</u>, is <u>serving</u> time in <u>prison</u>.

Vocabulary

1
1 down   2 back   3 on   4 saying   5 lengths   6 away/off

2
1 to roast   2 a vegetarian   3 rare   4 recipe   5 to grate   6 raw

3
1 forward to   2 down on   3 up to   4 away with   5 up with   6 up with   7 up for   8 up with

Reading

2
1 a horrible smell or stink   2 to meet by chance or accident
3 extremely dangerous   4 people who try to avoid paying for their ticket   5 amazing, astonishing   6 to face, confront, deal with

3
1 No. The statistical possibility of suffering any criminal action was extremely low.   2 It made them feel afraid.   3 They began to stop using the subway service.   4 They saw people like us as possible victims of their next crime.   5 People, especially criminals, began to act in a different way and the crime rate was greatly decreased.   6 to concentrate on the most important matters (economy, crime and schools) and to make government agencies work together.   7 The police acted against the type of activities that made people afraid. The other agencies tried to remove visible signs of crime.

Listening
Tapescript
I=Interviewer   D=Dr Milos
I: Good evening and welcome to *'Focus'*. Tonight's programme explores the subject of strange mental phenomena and we're very pleased to welcome an expert in this area ... psychologist and best-selling author ... Dr Frederick Milos.
D: Good evening. It's very nice to be here.
I: Now we've all experienced that strange feeling of déjà vu ...when you go somewhere for the first time ... some place you've never seen or visited before ... and then suddenly you get this weird ... almost unearthly ... feeling that you *have* been there before ... what do you make of these strange feelings of déjà vu, Dr Milos? Can you give us any explanation for them?
D: Well, I think most people go through this type of experience now and again and there are several possible explanations for it. One theory is that its due to a delayed message to the brain ...our eyes perceive an object, or a situation, but the message gets to the brain late - and possibly in a distorted form - due to lack of blood or oxygen or whatever ... and this is what causes the déjà vu effect.
I: So it's not a manifestation of the mind's hidden powers then ...?
D: I'm not really sure I know what you mean but ... you know, anything's possible. Scientists have been doing research on this for many years and there are many other theories: the feeling of déjà vu could be a memory of something we've dreamt about ... and there are those who believe it's connected to reincarnation ... you know ... something which happened to us in a former life. But at the end of the day, theories are all we've got and no-one has come up with any conclusive evidence.
I: But going back to the subject of the mind's unexplored potential ... is it true that we only use about 10% of our brain capacity? If we learnt how to expand on this, the potential power of our minds would be scary, don't you think?
D: For sure. People have come up with all kinds of theories about what our minds could do if we only knew how to use them properly. For example, there are those who believe we can train our minds to see into the future ...there are those who believe in telekinesis ... you know ... the ability to move objects with our minds and then of course, there's hypnosis and telepathy ...
I: That's easy to explain though. Isn't it just coincidence? It seems logical enough that two good friends could be thinking about exactly the same thing at the same time.
D: Yes, that's very true ... and I think we all have a sort of sixth sense ... a special type of intuition that tells us if we're in danger...but I put this down to nature ... it's a basic animal instinct that we've developed in order to increase our chances of survival.
I: So are there any other strange mental phenomena you'd like to tell us about?
D: Well, the subject of dream analysis is a very interesting area ... in fact it's the subject of my latest book ...

1
1 c)   2 b)   3 a)   4 c)   5 c)   6 b)

2
1 Lack of blood or oxygen.
2 He laughs because he doesn't fully understand the question but agrees that anything is possible.
3 A memory of something we have dreamt about and reincarnation.
4 To see into the future.
5 The ability to move objects with our minds.
6 A special type of intuition that tells if we're in danger.
7 It's a basic animal instinct that increases our survival possibilities.

Pearson Education Limited,
Edinburgh Gate, Harlow
Essex, CM20 2JE, England
and Associated Companies throughout the world

www.longman.com

© Pearson Education 2006

All rights reserved: no part of this publication may be reproduced, stored in a retrieval system, or transmitted in any form or by any means, electronic, mechanical, photocopying, recording or otherwise without the prior permission of the copyright holders.

The right of Araminta Crace, Rawdon Wyatt, Alison Bewsher and John Peebles to be identified as authors of this work has been asserted by them in accordance with the Copyright, Designs and Patents Act 1988.

First published 2006

Designed by Richard Jervis Design

Illustrated by Andy Robb and Peter Richardson (Beehive Illustration)

Set in Meta Plus Book 9.5pt
Printed in UK
by Anthony Rowe Ltd.

ISBN-13: 978-0-582-846340 (Teacher's Resource Book for pack)
ISBN-10: 0-582-84634-X

ISBN-13: 978-1-405-843072 (Test Master CD-ROM for pack)
ISBN-10: 1-405-84307-1

ISBN-13: 978-1-405-843225 (Teacher's Resource Book and Test Master CD-ROM pack)
ISBN-10: 1-405-84322-5

We are grateful to the following for permission to reproduce copyright material:
Imperial Oil Limited for an extract from the article 'Travels in Space' by Wynne Thomas taken from the Imperial Oil Limited website www.imperialoil.ca; and The Heritage Foundation for an extract from the article 'Cutting Crime and Restoring Order: What America can learn from New York's Finest' by William J. Bratton taken from The Heritage Foundation website www.heritage.org.

In some instances we have been unable to trace the owners of copyright material and we would appreciate any information that would enable us to do so.